Optimizing Network Traffic

Microsoft Press

PUBLISHED BY
Microsoft Press
A Division of Microsoft Corporation
One Microsoft Way
Redmond, Washington 98052-6399

Library of Congress Cataloging-in-Publication Data
Microsoft Corporation
Optimizing Network Traffic / Microsoft Corporation.
p. cm.
Includes bibliographical references (p.).
ISBN 0-7356-0648-X
1. Computer networks. I. Title.
TK5105.5.M5474 1999
004.6--dc21 98-52138
CIP

Printed and bound in the United States of America.

1 2 3 4 5 6 7 8 9 QMQM 4 3 2 1 0 9

Distributed in Canada by ITP Nelson, a division of Thomson Canada Limited.

A CIP catalogue record for this book is available from the British Library.

Microsoft Press books are available through booksellers and distributors worldwide. For further information about international editions, contact your local Microsoft Corporation office or contact Microsoft Press International directly at fax (425) 936-7329. Visit our Web site at mspress.microsoft.com.

Acquisitions Editor: Anne Hamilton
Project Editor: Thom Votteler

Contributors

We dedicate this volume to the authors, contributors, and reviewers who generously gave their time, experience, and vast knowledge to make this title a reality.

Program Manager

Michael Ohata

Senior Technical Editor

Bob Haynie

Chapter Contributors

Anthony Baron, Nigel Cain, Jim Gowler, Alexander Levin, Andreas Luther, Wally Mead, Gary Milne, Thomas Schenkman, Janet Sheperdigian, Michael Shinozaki, and Matthew Storer

Additional Contributors

Michael Andrade, Jason Bakke, Kevin Cassady, Theresa Doyle, Margaret Johnson, Bruce Jones, Mark Lawrence, Bruce McNaughton, Dean Murray, Jim Pierson, Bob Tedesco, and Diana Trickey

Technical Review

Jay Alecea, Hilal Al-Hilali, Mark Brown, Behrooz Chitsaz, Don Hacherl, Michael Laviano, Mark Lawrence, Anthony Milano, Jeff Parham, Matthew Peart, and Michael Primeaux

Technical Writer

Kelly Chalfant

Production Specialist

Heidi Wrightsman

Indexer

Richard S. Shrout

Project Editor

Thom Votteler

Welcome

In this day of rapidly evolving technology and growing complexity in network computing, Information Technology professionals can find it tough to keep up with daily troubleshooting, long-range planning, and frequent systems integration projects—let alone ride the leading edge of the technological wave. At Microsoft, we know about your problems: every day, Microsoft Consulting Services works in the field with IT professionals like you to build network infrastructures that allow organizations to keep up *and* stay ahead. The *Notes from the Field* series captures this experience, tried-and-tested best practices, and wealth of knowledge.

There is no shortage of references and resources for the IT pro, and for that we can all be thankful. Our copies of the compendiums and encyclopedias are usually well-thumbed, because we often need to find accurate information quickly. But we also need help when it comes to *doing* things, and this is information of a different kind.

The *Notes from the Field* series offers practical information derived from real-world experience—and you know there is no substitute for experience—all of which has been worked out and tested in the field. The complexity of network management arises from the interconnectedness of planning, testing, management, and troubleshooting—all those currents that keep you in constant motion. This series provides you with a tactical tool to sort through the issues and keep moving ahead.

Optimizing Network Traffic discusses the many facets of this complex topic from the ground up. It begins with a discussion of what makes up the flow over your network, and concludes by investigating how the new Windows 2000 Active Directory affects traffic patterns associated with basic system administration. It presents information to help you understand, predict, and manage traffic today so that you can effectively plan for it tomorrow, through the extension of your Windows NT 4.0 network, to your implementation of Windows 2000.

Sincerely,

Frank Artale

Frank Artale
General Manager,
Windows NT Server and Enterprise

Contents

Part 2 Real-World Network Infrastructure Scenarios

Introduction

Welcome to *Optimizing Network Traffic,* third in the *Notes from the Field* series, featuring best practices from Microsoft Consulting Services. Designed for information technology (IT) and information systems (IS) professionals, this book condenses and organizes the broad expertise of field consultants and support engineers, and offers you the benefit of their real-world experiences. Most of the chapters use fictitious customer names, but all of the case studies derive from customer scenarios or an amalgamation of several technical implementations where consultants tested and proved their approaches and techniques.

You should use this book as a supplement to the Microsoft Windows NT Server and Workstation 4.0 product documentation and the *Microsoft Windows NT Server 4.0 Resource Kit.* The resource kit contains a wealth of information, ranging from high level (Windows NT architecture) to fine detail (installing, configuring, and using point-to-point tunneling protocol—PPTP), and a collection of tools essential to optimizing and managing Windows NT networks. The book you are reading now often refers you to it for general and background information.

No single book can cover every implementation and maintenance topic for a product as complex as Windows NT Server, and this book doesn't try to. Instead, it focuses tightly on building the framework for analyzing, optimizing, and troubleshooting Windows NT-based traffic, dealing with slow links over wide area networks, and setting the foundation for planning for Windows 2000 Active Directory traffic. It is not a primer on setting up a Transmission Control Protocol/Internet Protocol (TCP/IP)–based network. Nor does it cover client-server traffic related to Microsoft Exchange Server—see *Deploying Microsoft Exchange Server 5.5,* the first *Notes from the Field* title, for that. The fourth *Notes* title, *Managing a Microsoft Windows NT Network,* deals with administering and supporting the network system.

What's In This Book

There are three parts, each with several chapters.

Part 1: What We're Talking about When We Talk about Network Traffic

This section builds a framework for analyzing *and* optimizing traffic generated on a Windows NT network. Chapter 1 reviews the essentials, looking at traffic created by Windows NT services such as NetLogon, browsing, DHCP, WINS, Domain Name System, and directory replication. Chapter 2 takes a peek into Microsoft's immense information infrastructure, examines what flavors and levels of traffic cross it during a normal day, and demonstrates ways to identify and isolate anomalous patterns so you can troubleshoot them. Chapter 3 examines ways of understanding and calculating network capacity, showing you how to determine what sorts of traffic are moving through the network and how to gauge their relative predictability.

Part 2: Real-World Network Infrastructure Scenarios

These chapters draw on the experience MCS has built up through extensive collaboration with enterprise customers. Each chapter begins with a synopsis of the facts of the case study and its challenges, and follows with details on the technical design and implementation that were developed to optimize network infrastructure. Chapters 4, 5, and 6 explore tuning Windows NT Server for branch offices, dial-on-demand configurations, and satellite networking. Chapter 7 steps back and looks at the broader perspective—how to plan for traffic in a wide area network design. Chapter 8 explains how to structure Systems Management Server installation jobs over slow links. Chapter 9 taps into the expertise of Microsoft's Information Technology Group to show how application design can affect network performance and traffic.

Part 3: The *Future* Scenario—Windows 2000 Networking Traffic

Part 3 examines Windows 2000 Active Directory architecture and database replication to help you plan your future implementation of Windows 2000 *with traffic in mind.* Because database size is a crucial element in directory replication, Chapter 10 uses tests based on real-world samples to show you how to size the Active Directory database. Chapter 11 then introduces the replication architecture and presents network traffic statistics and test results that can help you build an effective replication topology.

Additional Information

The Appendix lists references and resources, including support offerings, Web sites, white papers, and Microsoft Technical Support Knowledge Base articles on Windows NT Server, including a complete list of the fixes in Service Pack 4 (SP4).

The last thing in the book may be the first thing you'll want to take advantage of: a Microsoft TechNet sample CD that includes a representative selection of one issue's contents *and* the sample code files and tools mentioned in Chapters 5 and 8. For a book such as this one, drawn from first-hand accounts and experience, TechNet is the obvious companion piece: it is *the* support resource for professionals in the trenches. Each month, it provides subscribing IT professionals with in-depth information on evaluating, deploying, managing, and supporting Microsoft products and technologies.

Conventions Used

Convention	Description
ALL CAPITALS	Acronyms, filenames, and names of commands.
bold	Menus and menu commands, command buttons, property page and dialog box titles and options, command-line commands, options, and portions of syntax that must be typed exactly as shown. First occurrences of special terms, and book titles.
Initial Capitals	Names of applications, programs, servers, windows, directories, and paths.
Italic	Information you have to enter. Used also for emphasis as dictated by context.
`monospace type`	Sample command lines, program code, and program output.
Q123456, Title: How to Optimize Network Traffic over Windows NT	Knowledge Base article titles. Search for them on Microsoft TechNet or at http://support.microsoft.com/support/a.asp?M=F using the “Q” number (no spaces).

Icons that Highlight Text

These sidebar icons provide you with simple signposts:

Icon	Description
	**Caution** or **Warning**. Advises you to take or avoid specific action to avoid potential damage.
	**Note**. Emphasizes, supplements, or qualifies points in the text.
	**Best Practices** or **Guidelines**. Highlights proven practices, techniques, or procedures from MCS real-world experiences.
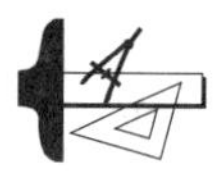	**Tools**. Indicates sample code, Windows NT utilities, or tools provided on the companion CD.

Some Important Business

The example companies, organizations, products, people and events depicted in this book are fictitious. No association with any real company, organization, product, person or event is intended or should be inferred.

Warning Throughout this book you'll find recommendations for optimizing or tuning the Windows NT registry using the Registry Editor. Using the Registry Editor incorrectly can cause serious, system-wide problems that require you to reinstall Windows NT. Microsoft cannot guarantee that any problems resulting from the use of Registry Editor can be solved. Use this tool at your own risk.

PART 1

What We're Talking about When We Talk about Network Traffic

This section builds a framework for analyzing *and* optimizing traffic generated on a Microsoft Windows NT network. Chapter 1 reviews the essentials, looking at traffic created by Windows NT services such as NetLogon, browsing, DHCP, WINS, Domain Name System, and directory replication. It concludes with some basic information on Network Monitor. Chapter 2 takes a peek into Microsoft's immense information infrastructure, examines what flavors and levels of traffic cross it during a normal day, and demonstrates ways to identify and isolate anomalous patterns so you can troubleshoot them. Chapter 3 examines ways of understanding and calculating network capacity, showing you how to determine what sorts of traffic are moving through the network and how to gauge their relative predictability. It picks up the discussion of Network Monitor and explains how to use this tool to study local and remote network elements.

CHAPTER 1

Reviewing Basic Concepts

By Wally Mead and Janet Sheperdigian—PBS Courseware

This chapter explains some basic, but essential concepts of network traffic generated by Microsoft Windows NT Server networking services, providing a framework for analyzing, optimizing, and predicting traffic. It defines amounts of traffic created by these services and their frequency, and organizes them by function: client initialization, and client-to-server and server-to-server communication.

The discussion describes each network service's impact on the network and how effectively its traffic can be optimized, and it provides baseline numbers for specific types of traffic (based on a small local area network—LAN). These are general figures, so actual traffic in your organization may vary. The final sections of this chapter include test results based on the sample LAN to help you assess potential traffic as your organization grows, and information on Network Monitor to help you examine actual traffic. NetMon is included with Windows NT Server and Systems Management Server.

Use the information in this chapter as a foundation on which to build a more efficient network for your organization. Systems administrators familiar with these concepts, or who have taken training on *Microsoft Windows NT Server 4.0 Network Analysis and Optimization,* may want to go right to Chapter 2 and read about everyday traffic on Microsoft's network.

What You'll Find In This Chapter

- **Description of Microsoft Windows NT Server networking services.**
- **Explanations of how services impact network traffic.**
- **Walkthrough of client initialization traffic.**
- **Review of client-to-server network traffic.**
- **Detailed look at server-to-server traffic.**
- **Tips for optimizing service-based network communications.**

Warning This chapter makes recommendations for tuning the Windows NT registry using the Registry Editor. Using the Registry Editor incorrectly can cause serious, system-wide problems that require you to reinstall Windows NT. Microsoft cannot guarantee that any problems resulting from the use of Registry Editor can be solved. Use this tool at your own risk.

Windows NT Server and Networking Services

Windows NT automatically installs various network services, some providing essential network communication and others providing optional functionality. You must configure them correctly or they can bog down the network.

This section describes the Windows NT services covered in this chapter, lists different ways of characterizing them, and describes how the traffic generated by these services varies according to protocol.

Windows NT networking services.

Service	Description
NetLogon	Validates user account logon and synchronizes domain accounts. Also supports the establishment and maintenance of trust relationships.
Computer Browser	Provides browsing capabilities that allow users to find resources on the network without having to remember connection syntax and locations.
DHCP	Provides automated administration of TCP/IP addresses and other configuration parameters for DHCP clients.
WINS	Provides a centralized location to resolve computer names for browsing and resource access.
Directory Replicator	Provides automated duplication of directories among multiple Windows NT-based computers.
Domain Name System (DNS)	Provides for name resolution of TCP/IP host names into IP addresses.
Microsoft Internet Explorer	Provides access to World Wide Web (WWW) locations for viewing and downloading files.

Characterizing Services

You can characterize Windows NT Server services by:

- The type of traffic they generate.
- How often they generate it.
- The traffic's relative impact on the network.

To analyze the functionality of a specific service:

1. Use an isolated network.
2. Use a network capturing and analysis tool, such as Network Monitor.
3. Initiate network traffic relative to the service you want to characterize.
4. Identify each frame in the capture.

Comparing Network Protocols

The type of traffic a network service generates depends somewhat on the protocol it uses. Traffic consists of frames, which contain address and protocol information, and the data being transferred. There are three types:

- **Broadcast frames**. Delivered to *all network hosts*. These can have a specific host as their destination, but because of protocol or addressing reasons, they go to all hosts, creating more network traffic than is probably necessary.
- **Multicast frames**. Delivered to a *subset of network hosts*. Although they do not generate as much traffic as broadcasts, they create more traffic than frames sent to a specific destination media access control (MAC) address.
- **Directed frames**. Delivered to a *specific network host*. Hosts that receive directed frames and do not find their own MAC address can discard them. Protocols that use directed frames generate the least amount of network traffic.

Protocols supported by Windows NT differ in their implementation of *frames* (units of communication) and this often influences the amount of traffic placed on the network. For instance, NWLink initiates broadcast frames, putting a lot of traffic on the network, while Transmission Control Protocol/Internet Protocol (TCP/IP) initiates directed frames, which creates less traffic and makes it a more popular choice.

Broadcast traffic has a large effect on a network's ability to operate efficiently. It tends to go unnoticed on LANs, which usually have plenty of available bandwidth, but it is still a good idea to minimize it. On the WAN, where there are more contenders for available bandwidth, broadcast traffic is more troublesome. You can reduce it on the WAN by configuring routers so that they do not forward broadcasts. This reduces overall traffic, but it has a downside in that applications using broadcasts will not have full functionality throughout the entire enterprise even though they will on the LAN, where they do not have to cross routers. This may be an acceptable solution, in which case you are home free, but there obviously are several sides to consider when approaching this issue.

TCP/IP was designed to avoid the disadvantages of other protocols (such as NetBEUI—the NetBIOS Enhanced User Interface) that broadcast a high percentage of frames. TCP/IP delivers directed frames over a routed network environment while using minimum bandwidth. For this reason, TCP/IP is a good choice as a network protocol, and this chapter uses it exclusively when examining network traffic.

Client Initialization Traffic

Network services generate varying amounts of traffic. To understand their impact during a normal workday, it helps to look at them to see what types of traffic they generate and when they generate it. The first type of network traffic occurs when a client computer initializes.

Network services that generate client initialization traffic.

Traffic type	When generated
DHCP	During IP address acquisition, renewal, and release.
WINS	During NetBIOS name registration, resolution, renewal, and release.
File session	When two computers set up a session.
Logon validation	When a user logs on to the network and is validated by a domain controller (DC).

Capture and analysis of these network tasks provides information you can use to control or reduce client initialization traffic, which normally represents 20 percent of the traffic clients generate.

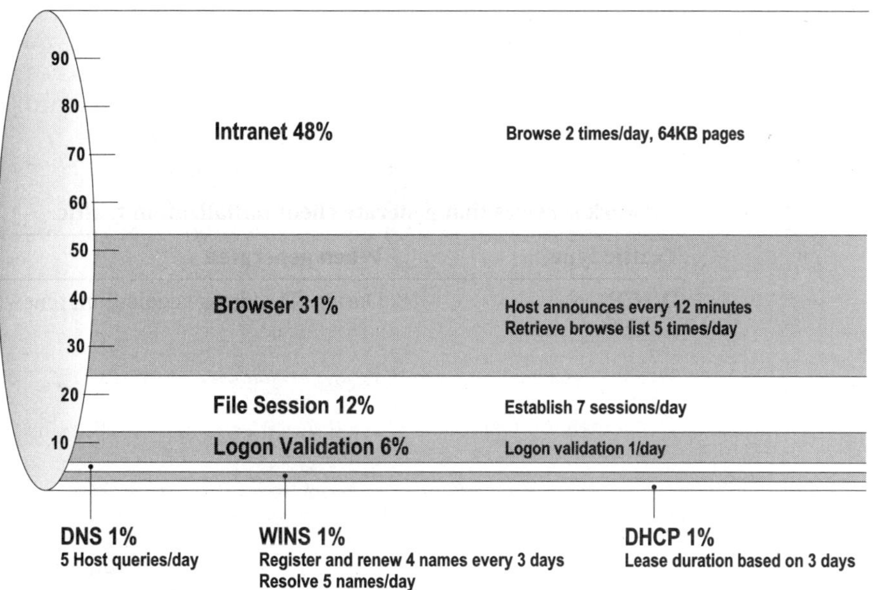

Figure 1.1 Approximate percentage of client traffic in an eight-hour day.

Note This illustration reflects the percentage of each task's traffic based on an eight-hour day, assuming the levels of use as noted in the figure. If users log on five times each day, or only once every two weeks, then the percentages of other traffic adjust accordingly.

DHCP Traffic

In an Internet Protocol (IP) network environment, before a host (computer, router, printer, and so on) can access the network and communicate with other hosts, it must have a properly configured IP address and subnet mask (which blocks the shared address information and reads only the significant information). You can configure these values manually or use dynamic host configuration protocol (DHCP), which assigns them automatically. The process of acquiring an address occurs one time for each client on the network and generates four frames:

Requesting an IP address with DHCP.

Frames	Description
DHCP Discover	Client's broadcast to locate a DHCP server.
DHCP Offer	DHCP server's response identifying the IP address the client can lease.
DHCP Request	Client's response indicating it accepts the server's offer.
DHCP ACK	Server's response acknowledging (ACK) the lease by providing the lease life and any TCP/IP parameters.

If you use DHCP, communications generally occur when:

- A DHCP client initializes for the first time (requires all four frames).
- During an automatic renewal at one-half lease life, requiring two frames (DHCP Request and DHCP ACK), and approximately 200 milliseconds.
- Client moves to a new subnet (requires DHCP Request, DHCP NACK, and then four frames as if it were a new client).
- DHCP client replaces its network adapter card (requires all four frames).
- Client manually refreshes or releases its address with IPCONFIG.
- Client restarts (DHCP Request and DHCP ACK as broadcast traffic, similar to the automatic renewal).

Note The default lease life is 3 days (72 hours). Using this default, automatic renewal will occur at one-half lease life (36 hours).

Relative Network Impact

DHCP does not significantly increase network traffic: acquiring an IP address lease through DHCP takes less than one second (approximately 300 milliseconds). If DHCP is generating an excess amount of network bandwidth, it can be due to an extremely small lease duration, or to a router forwarding DHCP messages from other subnets. DHCP leasing traffic includes two phases.

DHCP lease phases.

DHCP Traffic	Frames	Bytes	Frequency
Acquire IP Address Lease	4	1,368	Once per client
Renew IP Address Lease	2	684	Every startup and at one-half lease life

IP Address Lease Acquisition

When a new DHCP client initializes, it first uses DHCP to acquire an IP address by sending four frames to the server (see the table "Requesting an IP address with DHCP" above).

IP Address Lease Renewal

To renew its lease before expiration, a client uses the last two DHCP frames of the IP address. There are two methods of DHCP lease renewal:

- At startup, the client computer requests a renewal of its current IP address with a DHCP request frame. If successful, the DHCP server responds with a DHCP ACK (acknowledgement) frame. This process uses broadcast frames.
- At one-half of the lease duration period a client issues a DHCP request frame directly to its DHCP server. If the client's address is valid, the server responds with a DHCP ACK frame. The request and ACK use directed frames because the client has already renewed the address from its server at startup.

If a DHCP client cannot complete its renewal at 50% of lease duration, it tries to renew at 87.5% and at 100% before it returns to the four-frame initialization mode.

Optimizing

To reduce the amount of traffic generated by DHCP you can:

- **Adjust the duration of the IP address lease** in the **Scope Properties** dialog box of DHCP Manager. For instance, if you increase the default lease life of three days to 30 days you reduce the frequency of client renewals. If the number of clients using DHCP equals the number of available DHCP IP addresses on your network, use a short lease life. If the number of DHCP clients is less than the number of available DHCP IP addresses on your network, use a longer lease.
- **Configure a relay agent to forward DHCP broadcasts to other subnets**. You can configure IP addresses for DHCP servers using most DHCP relay agent software. The relay agent eliminates traffic by forwarding DHCP requests to only the subnets containing DHCP servers.

Note For more information on IP address lease frames, see "Configuring DHCP" in *Windows NT Sever 4.0 Resource Kit: Networking Guide*.

WINS Client Traffic

After a Microsoft TCP/IP client initializes its IP address it registers NetBIOS names (its computername, which is also the TCP/IP host name). When using these "friendly" names to access other systems, the NetBIOS names must be resolved to IP addresses. NetBIOS names are registered, resolved, renewed, and released using either b-node broadcasts or a NetBIOS Name Server, such as Windows Internet Naming Service (WINS). (For information on NetBIOS node types, sees p. 130.)

Relative Network Impact

WINS client-related traffic affects available network bandwidth, but not significantly. Even so, if you understand the traffic, you can plan for it. If the network is saturated, you can reduce WINS traffic frequency to free up bandwidth for other services.

Types of WINS traffic.

WINS traffic	Frames	Bytes	Frequency
Registration	2	214	Once per service or application at startup
Renewal	2	214	Once per service or application every one-half time to live (TTL—the period after which the client must renew its name)
Resolution	2	196	Varying frequencies
Release	2	214	Every service shutdown

Name Registration

NetBIOS names are registered for every service or application that supports NetBIOS. Examples include Windows NT Workstation and Server services, Network Monitor, and special names to indicate roles on the network, such as primary domain controller (PDC) or backup domain controller (BDC). The number of names registered depends on the number of network services and applications the client computer initializes, typically three or four.

Name Renewal

A name is successfully registered when the WINS server responds with a message that includes a time-to-live (TTL) after which the client must renew the name. The TTL determines the amount of traffic that WINS renewals generate. The WINS server default configuration for a renewal interval is 144 hours, or six days—the server assigns a TTL of 518,400 seconds. This pattern repeats every three days because WINS clients renew their names every one-half TTL.

Common names registered by a Microsoft client computer.

Name registered	Description
Computername <00>	Registered by the client's Workstation service.
Computername <03>	Registered by the Messenger service, allowing the host to receive messages, such as *net send computername*.
Username <03>	Registered by the Messenger service, allowing the user to receive messages, such as *net send username*.
Computername	Registered by the Server service. It appears as *computername <20>,* depending on the utility used to view the names registered, allowing the host to receive connection requests from other hosts.
Workgroup or domainname <00>	Registered as a group NetBIOS name, as opposed to a unique NetBIOS name, similar to the computername. This registers the computer as a member of the domain or workgroup.
Workgroup or domainname <1E>	Registered as a Group NetBIOS Name and used for browser elections.
Domainname <1B>	Registers the local computer as the Domain Master Browser for the domain. Registered as a unique NetBIOS name.
Domainname <1C>	Registers the local computer as a DC for the domain. Registered as a group NetBIOS name.
Workgroup or domainname <1D>	Registers the local client as the local subnet's Master Browser for the workgroup or domain. Registered as a unique NetBIOS name.

Name Resolution

For TCP/IP networks, WINS acts as a NetBIOS name server to resolve registered names into IP addresses. Name resolution traffic occurs very frequently on the network: during logon validation, resource browsing, server connections, and print job notifications.

Name Release

The client (host) owns the registered name until it releases it by stopping a service or shutting down making it available for another computer to register.

Optimizing

You can use several techniques to reduce WINS registration and renewal traffic.

- **Disable unnecessary services**. For instance, if the client does not provide any network resources, you can disable the server service.
- **Increase the NetBIOS name cache**. After a NetBIOS name is resolved, it is placed into the client's internal NetBIOS name cache. Whenever name resolution occurs the cache is checked before initiating a request to the WINS server. By default, entries stay in the cache for 10 minutes (600,000 milliseconds). You can reduce WINS queries for frequently used servers by increasing the value of the registry subkey:

  HKEY_LOCAL_MACHINE\SYSTEM\CurrentControlSet\Services\NetBT\Parameters\CacheTimeout

- **Implement the LMHOSTS file**. This file resolves NetBIOS names to IP addresses using a static ASCII text file. A disadvantage is that the LMHOSTS is not dynamic like the WINS server: when you bring new servers online you need to add them manually to the LMHOSTS file.

  The LMHOSTS file is scanned when the client starts (or restarts). You can pre-load specific entries into the NetBIOS name cache to prevent any network traffic from occurring during resolution (because the name is already in the NetBIOS name cache). This is helpful if a server or set of servers is frequently accessed.

Note You can further reduce traffic by sharing the contents of a *centralized* LMHOSTS file. This produces network traffic only at startup to find the file, when searching for pre-loaded entries, and during name query attempts.

- **Adjust the name resolution TTL in WINS Manager**. The default is six days. Increasing the TTL decreases network traffic.

File Session Traffic

Unless you are using DHCP, WINS, or DNS, all computers generate network traffic when they establish a file session with a server.

Relative Network Impact

The amount of traffic is not large, only about 11 frames totaling 1,300 bytes. If a user connects to multiple resources on a single server, only one session is established. Each connection generates the traffic necessary to establish the connection, but not the session. Traffic can increase if each user establishes multiple sessions per day. However, most file session traffic occurs after session establishment, when the files are accessed on the server.

Types of file session traffic.

File session traffic	Frames	Bytes	Frequency
Address Resolution	2	120	Every connection
TCP Session	3	180	Every initial connection to server
Establish NetBIOS Session	2	186	Every initial connection to server
SMB Protocol Negotiation	2	~365	Every initial connection to server
Connection Sequence	2	~360	Every connection attempt
Session Termination	5	360	Final disconnect from each server

Optimizing

File session traffic is relatively light (compared to the traffic typically generated after a connection is made), and there is little you can do to optimize it. However, the same set of frames is used during several types of communications, which is helpful in analyzing other types of traffic.

To limit the amount of file session traffic.

- Remove any excess protocols (connection requests are sent over all protocols simultaneously).
- Place commonly accessed clients and servers close together. For instance, if a single group of clients on one subnet generates the most activity to a specific server, move that server to that client's subnet, to eliminate adding traffic to other subnets during file session activity.

Logon Validation Traffic

One of the first functions a network provides to a user is logon validation. The user requests validation by entering a user name and password in a logon dialog box. Once the logon server is located, communication to validate the logon request, check the system time, and possibly run logon scripts, user profiles, and so on occurs.

Relative Network Impact

To determine the network impact of logon validation, you must assess the number of logon servers, when logon traffic occurs, and if remote clients are logging on to the domain. The minimum amount of client logon traffic is 3105 bytes, in 24 frames.

Types of logon traffic.

Logon traffic	Frames	Bytes	Frequency
Session Establishment	15	2,000	Once per logon session
Validation (Windows 95)	4	760	Once per logon session
Validation (Windows NT)	20	2,700	Once per logon session
Session Termination	5	360	Once per logon session

Finding a Logon Server

Finding a DC to validate the user account is accomplished in two ways:

- For Windows *9x*- and Windows NT–based client computers, a request is broadcast to the NETLOGON mailslot, requiring at least two frames.
- For clients configured as h-node WINS clients, WINS is queried for all registered DCs in the domain and then validation is requested using directed frames.

Validating the Logon Request

Next, the client takes the first server response to its request, and initiates this traffic.

- The client resolves the NetBIOS name of the selected logon server, either by querying WINS, or by broadcast.
- A TCP session is established with the logon server using the TCP three-way handshake process.
- A NetBIOS session is established with the logon server.
- Server Message Block (SMB) protocol negotiation occurs.
- SMB tree connection to *logonserver*\IPC$ is established.

For Windows 9*x* clients, after the logon request process is complete, the client validates the logon by communicating with the logon server using remote API calls.

Windows NT–based computers use three unique steps to validate a logon request:

- A list of trusted domains is accessed through the Logon Information dialog box.
- A secure channel between the Windows NT–based computer and the validating DC is established generating eight frames (approximately 1,400 bytes) of traffic.
- Logon is validated using remote API calls generating around 900 bytes of traffic depending upon name lengths (user, computer, and domain).

After the client account is validated, logon scripts, user profiles, or system policies can begin, resulting in additional network traffic.

Session Termination

The session ends when the connection to interprocess communication (IPC$) is closed, and the NetBIOS and TCP sessions are terminated.

Optimizing

You can optimize logon validation services by:

- **Scaling your DCs sensibly**. A conservative recommendation is that one DC can handle normal logon validation requests for about 2,000 user accounts. To make sure you have enough DCs use these Performance Monitor counters to monitor logon requests:

  Performance Monitor counters.

Object/counter	Description
Server: Logon/sec	Monitors the number of logon requests per second. These include both successful and unsuccessful attempts for interactive, network, and service account logon requests.
Server: Logon Total	Monitors the total number of interactive, network, and service account logon requests, both successful and unsuccessful attempts, since the server was last started.

- **Increasing simultaneous logon validations**. By default, DCs have their Server service configured for **Maximize Throughput for File Sharing**. While this is the proper setting for a file and print server, it does not provide the best performance for a DC that needs to validate logon requests. Instead, configure the Server service of all DCs for **Maximize Throughput for Network Applications**. If you properly configure this option, most DCs can triple their number of simultaneous logons, from about 6 or 7 per second, to around 20.
- **Placing the DC in an appropriate location**. Generally, the closer the DC is to the client, the quicker validation can be processed.

  For a remote site, you must balance the cost of logging on over the WAN to a central DC against the cost of placing a BDC at the remote site. Even if you can afford to put a DC at each remote site, it increases WAN traffic during directory services synchronization (replication) and increases the possibility of a directory services database getting out-of-date if the WAN goes down.
- **Determining hardware requirements for DCs**. Use the number of accounts in the directory services database to see if you need to upgrade hardware.

Client-to-Server Traffic

When a client computer communicates with a server computer these types of traffic are generated:

Network services that generate client-to-server traffic.

Traffic type	Description
Browser	Traffic generated when clients register as possible providers of network resources, retrieving a list of backup browsers, a list of servers on the network, and a list of resources on a server.
Domain Name System (DNS)	Traffic generated by TCP/IP hosts during TCP/IP host name resolution. Usually generated by TCP/IP utilities such as Ping and Telnet, or applications such as Internet Explorer.
Web-based browsing	Traffic generated by the Internet Explorer browser application to download pages from a Web site.

Note Client-to-server traffic represents 80 percent of total client-generated traffic.

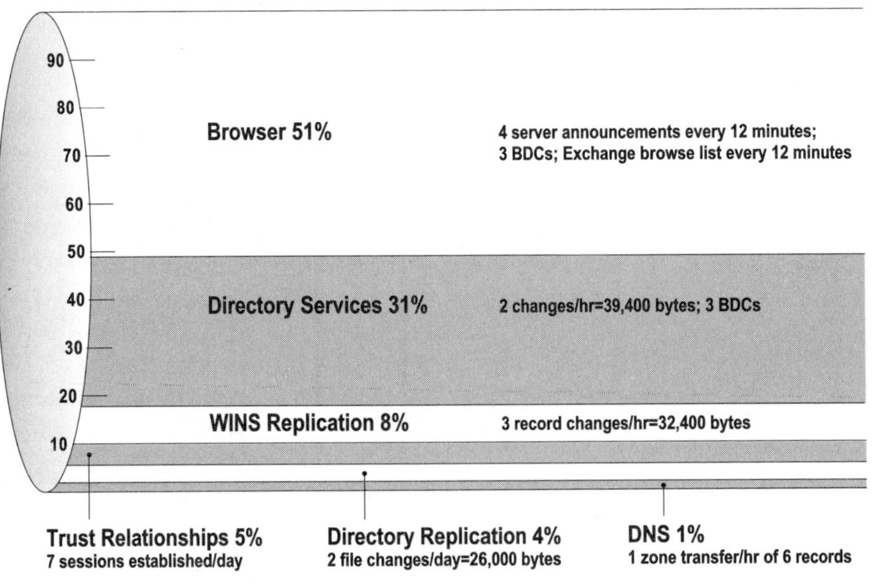

Figure 1.2 Approximate percentage of client traffic in an eight-hour day.

Browser Service (Browsing) Traffic

The browser process helps users locate network resources:

1. Servers are added to the browse list by issuing announcements to the master browser.
2. The master browser shares the list of servers (as well as domains) with the backup browsers.
3. A client computer retrieves a list of backup browser computers from the master browser.
4. The client computer contacts a backup browser to retrieve a list of servers.
5. The client contacts the server to retrieve a list of shared resources on the server.

Each of these steps produces network traffic.

Relative Network Impact

The basic types of traffic are shown in the table below. Remember that browsing differs from protocol to protocol, significantly affecting network impact.

Types of client browser traffic.

Client browser traffic	Frames	Bytes	Frequency
Host Announcement	1	243	Once per server every 12 minutes (at a steady state)
Find Backup Browser	2	450	Once per browsing computer at initial browse attempt
Election	Many	225	After each computer capable of becoming the master browser initializes
Retrieve Browse List	20	2,150	Every browse attempt by client and every 12 minutes for each backup browser
Retrieve Shared List (Windows 9*x*)	16	1,900	Every browse list by client
Retrieve Shared List (Windows NT)	19	3,300	Every browse list by client

Host Announcements

Computers that can provide network resources announce themselves every 12 minutes, and more frequently during initialization to ensure the server's addition to the browse list. These announcements occur automatically, regardless of whether the computer has any shared resources.

Retrieving a Browse List

To access shared resources, the client retrieves a list of available resources by first finding the local master browser and retrieving a list of backup browsers. It then contacts a backup browser, and connects to it, retrieving the browse list. The amount of traffic generated varies depending on which domain is being browsed, how many entries are in the browse list, and how many shared resources are available on the target server.

Note Most routers on remote subnets are not configured to forward browser broadcasts. WINS makes it possible to browse network resources throughout the enterprise without forwarding broadcasts.

Optimizing

You can optimize client browser traffic by:

- **Disabling unnecessary server components**. If a computer rarely shares network resources, consider disabling its server component. This removes the announcements, and reduces the size of the browse list that must be maintained and transferred.

  Every server requires 27 bytes in the browse list, plus additional space for the comment, if assigned. Consider limiting or reducing the size of computer comments.

- **Controlling the number of potential browsers**. Reduce the registration, renewal, and release of the NetBIOS names with WINS or b-node broadcasts. For Windows NT, set this registry subkey value to **No**:

  HKEY_LOCAL_MACHINE\SYSTEM\CurrentControlSet\Services\Browser\Parameters\MaintainServerList.

  For Windows 95, use the Network icon in Control Panel to configure the **File and Printer Sharing Properties** Browse Master parameter to **Disabled**.

  For Microsoft Windows for Workgroups, add **MaintainServerList** to the [network] section of SYSTEM.INI, and set it to **No**.

- **Eliminating unnecessary network protocols**. The browsing system is protocol dependent, meaning that browsing occurs on a protocol-by-protocol basis on each network segment (there is a master browser and backup browsers for each protocol *on each* network segment). If a network uses three protocols, all browser announcements and elections are repeated three times, one for each protocol. Reducing the number of protocols has a large impact on reducing browser-related network traffic.

DNS Traffic

When users access a computer using standard Windows networking commands and utilities, such as Network Neighborhood or the *net* command, the NetBIOS name of the target computer must be resolved (often by WINS) into an IP address. When users access a computer using TCP/IP utilities, such as Internet Explorer or the PING command, the IP host name of the target computer must be resolved into an IP address. This process, called host name resolution, can be accomplished using the Domain Name System (DNS).

Relative Network Impact

DNS traffic affects the network in two ways: the number of requests generated by clients and the number of recursive lookups generated by servers.

Types of DNS traffic.

DNS traffic	Frames	Bytes	Frequency
Name Lookups	2	~180	Every name resolution
Zone Replication—A zone is a database file that contains records for a particular domain.	4	~200	At addition of secondary server to the zone, and periodically (every 60 minutes by default)
Integration with WINS	4	240	Every non-local name lookup

DNS Lookups

DNS lookups are the client request and server response communications. When an IP client needs to resolve a TCP/IP host name into an IP address, it sends a DNS query to its DNS server. This request is a frame of varying size, depending upon the length of the host name to be resolved. Host names can be up to 256 characters.

DNS Recursive Lookups

When the DNS server receives the client's request, the server determines if it has an entry and, if it does, issues a directed response that includes the IP address of the host name in question.

If the client's configured DNS server does not contain a listing for the requested name, it forwards the request to another DNS server for resolution. The process of forwarding requests is called recursion or zone transfer, and must be configured by the administrator.

Optimizing

Reduce recursion traffic by:

- **Not configuring recursion**. Of course, this limits the number of requested names DNS can supply, and it requires that all host names be added to each DNS server, which is an administrative burden.
- **Designating DNS server**. Ensuring that the DNS server that will most likely resolve most of the names for a particular client is designated as its DNS server. This reduces the chance of a recursive lookup and its associated traffic.
- **Increasing the TTL of cached entries using DNS Manager**. DNS Manager Help explains how to configure for all records in a zone, for an individual record, or for WINS records.

Intranet Browsing Traffic

Relative Network Impact

As intranet browsing becomes more popular as a means of accessing files, it contributes larger amounts of client-based network traffic as a result of large file downloads.

Types of intranet traffic.

Intranet traffic	Frames	Bytes	Frequency
Connecting to a Web site	2	180	Each connection to server
Requesting a Web page	2	360+	Multiple per page
Browsing Security	varies	varies	Multiple per page

Connecting to a Web Site

To connect to a Web site, the Web server's name is resolved using a method of name resolution, such as DNS lookup. Once the client is connected, it requests pages (files) from the Web server using the Hypertext Transfer Protocol (HTTP) command GET. The requested file is specified in the HTTP section of the frame. Additional HTTP GET messages are sent if there are images or graphics that need to be downloaded. Each requested file transfer requires a new TCP session (and TCP Port).

When the Web server receives the request and determines that the requested file is available, it sends HTTP response frames. If the response is larger than 1,238 bytes it takes at least two response frames to transfer the file. Subsequent frames carry 1,450 bytes of file data because most of the HTTP header information is not included.

For example, downloading the /samples/default.htm (from a Microsoft Internet Information Server—IIS—2.0 installation) generated 76 frames (including the DNS lookup and response) and 48,539 bytes of traffic. Ten files totaled 38,343 bytes. The other 10,200 bytes were used by the DNS lookup and response, the 10 HTTP GET commands, the required TCP session, and the TCP acknowledgements.

Intranet Browsing Security

The default configuration for IIS 3.0 enables anonymous connections. User accounts and passwords are not needed to access sites. If Windows NT challenge-response security is enabled on the server, it responds to a client request with an *access denied* HTTP frame and terminates the session. The client establishes a new TCP session with the server, and sends its un-encoded information to the server. The server responds with the appropriate encryption key to use.

Without security, downloading the /samples/default.htm page took 74 frames and 48,375 bytes (excluding the two DNS frames). With Windows NT challenge-response security enabled, the same page took 115 frames and downloaded 56,145 bytes.

Optimizing

Because intranet browsing can generate significant amounts of network traffic, any measure to optimize this traffic is beneficial.

- **Keep Web site pages small**. As a general rule, a good HTML design limits page scrolling.
- **Limit the size of graphics or .AVI files used**. Reuse common graphics throughout the intranet.
- **Consider level of security needed with your site**. Security requires additional authentication traffic for each session that is established. Allowing anonymous connections prevents the authentication traffic from occurring on the network.
- **Instruct users to increase the client's local cache**. Previously downloaded files do not have to be downloaded again.

Server-to-Server Traffic

Server-to-server traffic, generated between server computers carrying out network maintenance tasks, includes:

Network services that generate server-to-server traffic.

Traffic type	Description
Account synchronization	Synchronization of the user accounts databases between the PDC and BDCs.
Trust relationships	Establishment of a trust relationship, as well as the importing of trusted accounts. Also includes traffic generated by pass-through authentication.
Server browser traffic	Server announcements, master browser elections, and browse list exchanges between browser servers.
WINS replication	Replication of WINS server database records to another WINS server.
Directory replication	The automatic duplication of a directory structure among computers.
DNS server	DNS server zone transfers.

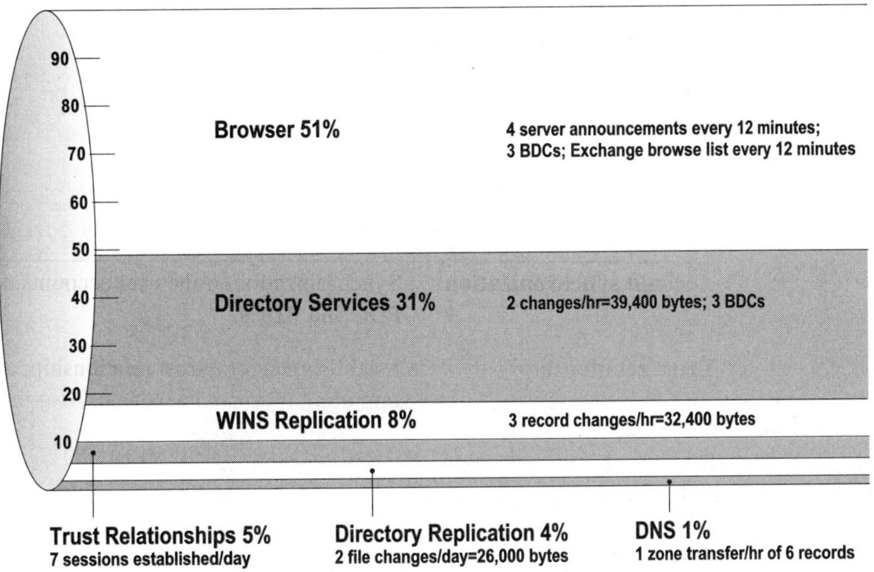

Figure 1.3 Approximate percentage of server-to-server traffic in an eight-hour day.

Account Synchronization Traffic

In a Windows NT Server network, user logon validation requests are processed by either the PDC or a BDC. Changes to the user accounts database are made only on the PDC so for logon requests to be properly validated, each BDC must have an updated copy of these databases.

User accounts that are synchronized.

Database	Contents
SAM Accounts	User and group accounts, all built-in global groups, and computer accounts added to the domain such as DCs and Windows NT Workstation-based computers.
SAM Built-in	Built-in local group accounts such as Administrators, Users, and Guests.
LSA	LSA Secrets that are used for trust relationships, DC computer account passwords, and account policy settings.

Relative Network Impact

Multiple updates to the accounts database generate a large amount of network traffic. The configuration of the NetLogon service, which performs synchronization, determines the frequency and amount of traffic.

Types of account synchronization traffic.

Account synchronization traffic	Frames	Bytes	Frequency
Finding the PDC	4	745	Once per BDC startup
Establishing a Session	11	1,280	Every synchronization event
Establishing a Secure Channel	8	1,550	Once per BDC startup
Verifying Database	6	1,350	Once per BDC startup
PDC Update Notice	1	400	Every synchronization event
Synchronizing Database	7	2,000 +	Every synchronization event

Complete Database Updates

Beginning with Windows NT 3.5*x*, most synchronization events are partial—only updated records are transferred to the BDC—but full synchronization is used to ensure database integrity when:

- A new backup DC is installed.
- The change log file fills, and starts wrapping (over-writing changes).
- An error occurs during a partial synchronization.
- The administrator at the BDC issues a net accounts/sync command.

Finding the Primary Domain Controller

When a BDC initializes it must verify and possibly update its user accounts database by locating the PDC. The BDC caches the entry for later use.

Establishing a Session

The session between the BDC and the PDC involves: name resolution, address resolution, a TCP session, a NetBIOS session, server message block (SMB) protocol negotiation, and a connection to IPC$.

Establishing a Secure Channel

After a session is established, the BDC establishes a secure channel with the PDC. The secure channel is not broken until one of the two DCs is shut down, allowing new sessions, verification, and updates to occur (because they can time-out) without requiring re-establishment of the secure channel.

Verifying the Database

Once the required sessions and secure channel are established, database verification can proceed. This takes about 1,344 bytes (six frames—more are used if updates are included) depending on the computer names.

Partial Database Updates

By default, the PDC verifies its databases every five minutes, looking for changes to any of the three databases. When the PDC finds a change it sends an update message to any BDC without an up-to-date database. To determine which BDCs require the update, the PDC consults a table it maintains of BDCs and their database version IDs.

Note By default Windows NT Server 4.0 sends update announcements to ten BDCs at a time. If there are more than ten, the PDC sends a second round of announcements when synchronization is complete for one BDC and continues in this fashion until all BDCs have synchronized.

When the BDC receives the update announcement, it compares version IDs and requests updated data if they are different. If the BDC and PDC session is still viable, the BDC generates four frames to verify the account database using NetLogon Service. The PDC sends the updated data using SMB or RPC calls (depending on the size of the update), generating multiple frames. This entire process can take as few as ten frames to complete.

Optimizing

You can control user account synchronization traffic by configuring registry parameters for the NetLogon service in this subkey:

HKEY_LOCAL_MACHINE\SYSTEM\CurrentControlSet\Services\Netlogon\Parameters

ReplicationGovernor

This is the most commonly modified NetLogon parameter. It controls the percentage of network bandwidth the NetLogon service can use while synchronizing user accounts. Its default value is 100, meaning NetLogon can use 100 percent of the network bandwidth while the PDC buffers 128 KB of data, which of course is disastrous in a WAN environment where users need bandwidth.

If you add the ReplicationGovernor to the NetLogon key and set it to 50, NetLogon buffers only 50 percent as much data (64 KB) for transmission, and has synchronization messages on the network only 50 percent of the time. Do not set it too low (never lower than 25), or synchronization may never complete.

Other NetLogon Parameters

These parameters can help control the amount of network traffic generated during synchronization:

NetLogon parameters.

Parameter	Controls
Pulse	How often the PDC looks for changes to its directory services database. The default is five minutes; the maximum is 48 hours. Don't set this too high: if BDCs are not synchronized with the PDC for a long period of time, a full synchronization occurs.
PulseMaximum	How often the PDC sends a pulse message to each BDC even if its user accounts database is up-to-date. The default is every two hours; the maximum is 48 hours. Increasing it reduces the number of pulse messages.
ChangeLogSize	How many changes are made to the user accounts database. The default value is 64 KB (about 2,000 32-byte changes). When this limit is hit (for example, if lots of users change passwords), log entries are overwritten, forcing a full synchronization. The result is that more traffic is sent to the BDC than is really necessary.
PulseConcurrency	How many announcements the PDC sends to BDCs during synchronization. The default is 10 for Windows NT Server 4.0. Increasing this uses more network bandwidth for synchronization; decreasing it uses more time.

Trust Relationships

A master accounts domain with multiple resource domains is a good solution for environments that have centralized administration and individual control of distributed resources. Trust relationships allow user accounts from the accounts domain to access resources in the resource domains.

Relative Network Impact

Three areas generate network traffic:

- Establishing a trust relationship takes approximately 110 frames (16,000 bytes).
- Using trusted accounts when permissions are granted to trusted domain users so they can access a local resource, and when a trusted account is added to a local group.
- Pass-through authentication (the most frequent generator of trust traffic) is of two types: when a user in a trusted domain requests access to a resource in a trusting domain, and when a user at a Windows NT Workstation computer attempts to log on using a trusted account and the computer it is attempting to log on is a member of a trusting domain.

Types of trust relationship traffic.

Trust relationship traffic	Frames	Bytes	Frequency
Establish trusts	110	16,000	One time
Import accounts	110	16,000	Every import attempt
Pass-through authentication	20	3,200	Every access of new server in trusting domain

Optimizing

Trust relationships do not produce much network traffic, but you can reduce it by:

- **Reducing the number of trusts**. Review existing or planned resource domains to ensure that each one is appropriate and necessary. Break non-essential trusts.
- **Reducing verifications**. Reduce traffic associated with the verification of trusted accounts by adding the appropriate users to a global group or adding the trusted global group to a local group or local resource.

  Example: In a simple test, looking up a single security ID (SID) for a global group took 552 bytes, but the same lookup for SIDs for two trusted user accounts took 636 bytes. That is not much difference, but this tested only two users. When many users are allowed access to a resource in a trusting domain, you can reduce traffic substantially by using a global group.

Server Browser Traffic

Servers generate several types of browsing traffic. All computers with server components (that is, the ability to share network resources) announce themselves to the master browser in their local domain. Servers that operate as a potential browser, backup browser, or master browser are involved in several other communications:

- Browser elections occur whenever the master browser cannot be located on the local subnet and whenever a DC initializes.
- Master browsers in different domains communicate with each other so that servers and resources can be accessed throughout the network.
- Backup browsers receive updated browse lists from the local master browser.

Relative Network Impact

Server browsing produces a large share of network traffic.

Types of server browser traffic.

Server browser traffic	Frames	Bytes	Frequency
Host Announcement	1	243	Once per server every announcement period (12 minutes at a steady state)
Local Master Announcement	1	250	After each announcement request or election and every 12 minutes
Workgroup Announcement	1	250	Once per master browser every announcement period (15 minutes at a steady state)
Elections	20	5,300	Every restart of a DC
Browse List Exchange	36	3,900	Every browse attempt by client, and every 12 minutes for each backup browser

The basics of the server browsing process are:

- At startup, the domain's PDC assumes the role of domain master browser and the BDCs become backup browsers; if there is no master browser, BDCs become local masters.
- Every 15 minutes, each master browser (on each subnet) announces itself to the master browsers of other domains on the local subnet.
- Every 12 minutes, each domain master browser contacts WINS for a listing of all domains.
- Every 12 minutes, each master browser contacts the domain master browser to update the browse lists.
- Every 12 minutes, each backup browser contacts its local master browser to retrieve an updated browse list.

Optimizing

You can reduce browsing traffic by:

- **Reducing network protocols**. The browsing process runs separately on each installed and bound protocol. If TCP/IP, NWLink IPX/SPX, and NetBEUI are all active on the network, each set of browser traffic, elections, host announcements, workgroup announcements, and so on, occur on each protocol independently. This can triple network traffic. Eliminate unneeded protocols.
- **Reducing browser entries**. If computers do not require resource sharing, disable their server components to reduce browse lists and, therefore, the traffic passing between browser servers. Each client type (Windows for Workgroups, Windows 95, or Windows NT) has a different method for disabling the server service. Besides the basic 27 bytes, each browse list entry can include server comments. Reduce server comments to save space.
- **Tuning optimization parameters**. Browsing registry parameters are under

  HKEY_LOCAL_MACHINE\SYSTEM\CurrentControlSet\Services\Browser\Parameters.

  Configure these parameters to control the amount of network traffic generated by the browser:

  - **MasterPeriodicity**

    Specifies how frequently a master browser contacts the domain master browser. The default is 720 seconds; the minimum is 300 seconds; the maximum is 4,294,967 seconds. This parameter is added as a registry entry (REG_DWORD) and can be changed dynamically without restarting the computer. It affects WAN traffic because subnet master browsers must communicate with the domain master browser.
  - **BackupPeriodicity**

    Specifies how frequently a backup browser contacts the master browser. The default is 720 seconds. Setting it to 1800 (30 minutes) reduces the frequency of browse list updates. Adding it as a REG_DWORD requires restarting the computer. This parameter does not effect the WAN because backup browsers always communicate with a local master browser, never with a remote one.

WINS Replication Traffic

A single WINS server can support 10,000 WINS clients, but if it does not provide the required level of fault tolerance and performance a backup server may be advisable. If multiple WINS servers are configured, clients can register and query while servers replicate or share databases *and* they get faster name resolution because each WINS server can identify clients registered with its WINS partners.

WINS Record Sizes

WINS database entries vary in size, depending on type:

- If the client has a single network adapter card, the amount of data stored depends on whether a scope ID is configured (40 bytes without, 280 bytes with).
- If the client has multiple network adapters configured for TCP/IP (is multi-homed), the amount of data stored depends on the number of configured IP addresses (40 to 280 bytes per host).
- If the registered name is an Internet group name, such as *Domainname* <1C>, the amount of data stored depends of the number of registered hosts (maximum is 25 hosts, 480 bytes).

Relative Network Impact

The amount of traffic generated by WINS replication depends on the size of records in the WINS database, the number of updated records, and the frequency of replication.

Types of WINS traffic.

WINS traffic	Frames	Bytes	Frequency
Establishing Relationship	20	2,300	Once per replication relationship
Verifying Databases	12	900	Once per update request to each replication partner
Updating Databases	14	1,200	Once per update request to each replication partner

Three distinct steps are involved in the WINS replication process: establishing the replication relationship, verifying the database version numbers, and replicating records.

Establish Relationship

The first step in the replication process, adding a WINS server as a replication partner, is done by using WINS Manager. This process uses approximately 20 frames (about 2,000 bytes). The first 54 bytes in each frame are normal Ethernet, IP, and TCP packet headers; the remainder contain the appropriate WINS RPC call.

Verify Database

Once the relationship is established replication can occur at predefined intervals or after some number of records are updated. Once the relationship is triggered, it and the databases must be verified. This is a simple process that generates about 12 frames (900 bytes of traffic) using a standard TCP session, two requests and responses, and TCP session termination frames.

Update Database

Once the replication partner relationship is configured and verified, databases are updated by transferring records between the WINS servers. This transfer uses TCP Port 42.

Optimizing

WINS database replication can significantly affect WANs with slow link speeds, but you can optimize WINS traffic by changing the configuration of WINS replication partners. WINS replication partners are configured as *push*, *pull*, or both. *Push* partners send announcements to their configured partners when a specific number of database entries have changed. *Pull* partners request updates at configured intervals or when their push partner notifies them of updates.

- **Push Partners**

  Change the configuration of push notification to occur after a specific number of records are updated: the default is 20. Database changes, not time intervals, are used to initiate push notifications and replications. Increasing this number reduces the frequency of WINS replication, and increases the number of updated records in a batch. It also increases *latency*, so you must tune this carefully.

  For instance, a value can be configured as a percentage of the total names in the database, such as 25 percent. This allows more control over the replication.

- **Pull Partners**

  Change the configuration of pull requests to occur at a specific time interval. For example, you might configure WINS to send pull requests every 30 minutes for local WINS servers, every hour for remote WINS servers connected by high-speed links (T1 or higher), and every six hours for remote WINS server connected by means of slow-links (56 Kbps). This allows you to control data transfer frequency.

Directory Replication Traffic

The Directory Replicator service allows automatic replication of a directory tree between computers. Most commonly, it replicates user logon scripts between PDC and BDCs, ensuring that a client can run its logon script no matter which DC validates it.

Relative Network Impact

Logon scripts are not extremely large and do not change often enough to generate much replication traffic. However, if the Directory Replication service needs to replicate other files it can create significant network traffic.

Types of directory replication traffic.

Directory replication traffic	Frames	Bytes	Frequency
Announcement	1	340	Once per importing domain or server for every update of the export tree
Establish Session	11	1,1280	Once from each import computer every update event
Verify Directory	30	~5,100	Once from each import computer every update event
Update Directory	Various		Once from each import computer every update event

Optimizing

You can optimize directory replication traffic by:

- **Creating a flat, shallow directory structure**. With large, deep, top-level replicated directories, the Directory Replicator service checks and then copies an entire top-level directory if any file in that directory has changed. Because files are always likely to change, the service is constantly rechecking and recopying entire directories. You can decrease network replication traffic by creating multiple, shallower, top-level directories.
- **Using Server Manager to control replication**. Server Manager prevents the Directory Replicator service from exporting specific directories during certain periods of the day. You can add a lock to the export server, for instance, to prevent it from replicating directories during heavy network usage times.
- **Updating registry parameters**. Directory replication entries are found in the Registry under:

  HKEY_LOCAL_MACHINE\SYSTEM\CurrentControlSet\Services\ Replicator\Parameters.

  To control the Directory Replicator service modify:

  - **Interval**. Determines how often the originating (export) server checks for updates to its specified directory structure. It also sends notifications to its target (import) computers to retrieve the new data. Default is five minutes. You can increase it to 60 minutes or more (on the export server) to reduce replication frequency, although this leaves changes unreplicated for longer intervals.
  - **Pulse**. Acts as a counter to control how often an import computer contacts an export server. If an import computer fails to hear from the export server after *Pulse* X *Interval* minutes, it contacts the export server for an update. Default is two minutes. Increasing the Pulse parameter can reduce traffic by giving the export server more time to contact the import computer.

Domain Name System Server Traffic

Larger organizations can implement primary *and* secondary Domain Name System (DNS) name servers for a zone (a database file that contains records for a particular domain) to provide sufficient name resolution services for clients.

Relative Network Impact

The transfer of database files from the primary name server to the secondary name servers (zone transfer) generates network traffic. (See "Client-to-Server Traffic" section above for more information on client-based DNS traffic.) A DNS record averages 26 bytes (compressed). Multiply the number of records in the zone file by 26 to estimate the traffic generated in a zone transfer.

Types of DNS traffic.

DNS traffic	Frames	Bytes	Frequency
Name Lookups	2	~180	Each DNS name lookup request by client.
Zone Replication	3	180	At addition of secondary server to the zone, and periodically (every 60 minutes by default).
Replication Request	2	403	Each DNS name lookup request by client.
Session Termination	2	240	Each DNS name lookup request by client.

Optimizing

You can use DNS Manager to control zone transfers. In the **Zone Properties** dialog select the **SOA Record** tab. You can configure these values:

Zone transfer parameters.

Parameter	Description
Refresh Interval	How long the secondary name server waits before it queries the primary to initiate a zone transfer. Default is 60 minutes.
Retry Interval	How long the secondary name server waits before attempting to initiate a zone transfer upon failure. Default is 10 minutes.
Expire Time	How long the secondary name server continues to respond to name queries even though it cannot connect to the primary name server for an update.

For tuning, Refresh Interval is the most useful parameter: decreasing its frequency increases zone transfers. This means more frequent updating, but more network traffic.

Network Monitor

To analyze the traffic generated by the networking services on your system, you can use the Network Monitor analysis tool. A simple version is included in Windows NT Server 4.0; the full version is included with Microsoft Systems Management Server. Refer to the Windows NT Server *Concepts and Planning Manual,* "Chapter 10: Monitoring Your Network," and the *Microsoft Windows NT Server 4.0 Resource Kit Supplement 1,* "Chapter 7: Monitoring Bandwidth and Network Capacity" for complete information.

The simple version of Network Monitor captures frames only on a local network, whereas the full version captures traffic on both local and remote networks and can automatically filter and edit the traffic.

Versions of Network Monitor.

Function	Network Monitor (simple)	Network Monitor (full)
Local capturing	To and from the computer running Network Monitor only	All devices on the entire subnet
Remote capturing	Not available	Yes
Determining top user of network bandwidth	Not available	Yes
Determining which protocol consumed the most bandwidth	Not available	Yes
Determining which devices are routers	Not available	Yes
Resolving a device name into a media access control address	Not available	Yes
Editing and retransmitting network traffic	Not available	Yes

Network Monitor provides a **Capture** window that displays four areas of information you can use to analyze network performance:

Network Monitor Capture Window.

Pane	Description
Graph	Bar charts of current activity: Percentage of network utilization, frames per second, bytes per second, broadcasts per second, and multicasts per second.
Session Statistics	Summarizes host communication including the initiated frame type.
Total Statistics	Statistics for traffic on the entire network, captured frames, per second utilization, and network adapter card.
Station Statistics	Summarizes frames by host, type, and the total number sent and received.

Network Monitor requires a supported network adapter card. Windows NT 4.0 supports a newer version of the network device interface specification (NDIS) that has a capturing mode called "local only." You install the Network Monitor Agent driver onto a network card in a Windows NT system. This sets the card in promiscuous mode, which allows the monitor to watch all network packets that go through the system—even packets for other destination systems are copied and passed up to the Network Monitor Application.

See the Windows NT 4.0 Hardware Compatibility List (HCL) for a list of Network Monitor tested and supported network adapters.

Predicting Network Traffic

Most networks are in a constant state of flux, growing and changing according to the needs of their users. The better you understand how your network operates, the more effectively you can optimize communication and predict the effect of adding servers, services, or additional clients. Use these guidelines to project the amount of generated traffic:

- Identify the service that will be added to the network.
- Determine variables associated with implementing the added service. For instance, for DHCP, determine how many DHCP servers will be installed, how many DHCP clients will be used, and how long the lease duration is.
- Estimate:
  - Traffic that one client or server would generate.
  - Impact of implementing the service using a given number of clients or servers.
  - Frequency of that traffic.
- Recognize that predicting network traffic is not an exact science, but a process to help understand and plan for network traffic. In most cases, adding a service increases network traffic, but you have to balance the benefit against the cost.

The numbers in the table below are based on a sample test LAN. They do not precisely indicate numbers you can expect on your organization's network (see Chapter 2 for a case study), but they can provide a relative baseline that helps you predict the impact of network services.

Network service traffic for prediction purposes.

Service	Traffic	Frequency
DHCP	Acquire IP address—4 frames (1,368 bytes)	Once per client.
	Renew IP address lease— 2 frames (684 bytes)	Every startup and at one-half lease life.
WINS client-to-server	Registration—2 frames (214 bytes)	Once per service or application at startup.
	Renewal—2 frames (214 bytes)	Once per service or application every one-half time to live (TTL).
	Resolution—2 frames (196 bytes)	Varying frequencies.
File sessions	Address resolution—2 frames (120 bytes)	At each attempt to communicate with another TCP/IP host (when aged from ARP cache).
	TCP session— 3 frames (180 bytes)	Once per first connection to each target TCP host.
	NetBIOS session— 2 frames (186 bytes)	Once per first NetBIOS connection to a target computer.
	SMB protocol negotiation—2 frames (~350 bytes)	Once per first Server Message Block (SMB) connection to a target computer.
	Connection sequence—2 frames (~350 bytes)	Once per network resource access.
	Session disconnection—5 frames (360 bytes)	Once per final connection to TCP host disconnection.

Network service traffic for prediction purposes. *(continued)*

Service	Traffic	Frequency
Logon validation	Session establishment— 15 frames (2,000 bytes)	Once per user logon.
	Validation sequence—4 frames (760 bytes) Windows 95	Once per user logon.
	Validation—20 frames (3,700 bytes) Windows NT	Once per user logon.
	Session breakdown—5 frames (360 bytes)	Once per user logon.
	Scripts, policies, profiles—traffic varies	Optional—once per user logon.
Browser	Host Announcement—1 frame (243 bytes)	Once per "server" computer every announcement period (12 minutes at steady state).
	Local Master Announcement—1 frame (250 bytes)	After each announcement request or election, and every 12 minutes.
	Workgroup Announcement—1 frame (250 bytes)	Once per each master browser every announcement period (15 minutes at steady state).
	Elections—many frames (225 bytes each)	After each computer capable of becoming the master browser initializes.
	Finding a backup browser—2 frames (~450 bytes)	Once per browsing computer at initial browse attempt.
	Retrieving a browse list—20 frames (2,150 bytes)	Every browse attempt by client, and every 12 minutes for each backup browser.
	Retrieving a list of shared resources—16 frames (1,900 bytes for Windows 95) 19 frames (3,300 bytes for Windows NT)	Every browse list by client.
	Retrieve list of domains.	Every 12 minutes by each domain master browser.

Network service traffic for prediction purposes. *(continued)*

Service	Traffic	Frequency
DNS	Name lookups—2 frames (~180 bytes depending upon name length). Traffic is multiplied if recursion is required.	Each DNS name lookup request by client. Recursion traffic may not be required if name is still cached at queried DNS server.
	TCP session—3 frames (180 bytes)	At addition of secondary server to the zone, and periodically (every 60 minutes by default).
	Request transfer (~85 bytes).	
	Transfer zone records—1 frame, depending upon size and number of records.	
	TCP session termination—4 frames (240 bytes)	
Intranet browsing	Downloading a page—3 frames (180 bytes)	Once per file requested (page, graphic, AVI, and so on).
	GET command—1 frame (~350 bytes depending upon host name and file structure)	Required at each load attempt.
	Download file—multiple frames (up to 1514 bytes)	Required if new or updated file.
User accounts database synchronization	Finding the PDC—4 frames (~745 bytes)	Once per BDC startup.
	Establish session—11 frames 1,280 bytes	Every synchronization event.
	Establish secure channel—8 frames (1,550 bytes)	Once per BDC startup.
	Verify the databases—6 frames (1,350 bytes)	Once per BDC startup.
	PDC Update notice—1 frame (~400 bytes)	Every synchronization event.
	Synchronization of the database—2 frames (~1,400 bytes for one user modification)	Every synchronization event.

Network service traffic for prediction purposes. *(continued)*

Service	Traffic	Frequency
Establishing a trust relationship	~110 frames (16,000 bytes)	Once per each trust relationship created.
Importing trusted accounts	~115 frames (18,600 bytes) for 12 trusted accounts.	Each attempt to import a trusted account into a trusting domain.
Verification of trusted account	~45 frames (7,000 bytes) for a single account (Global Group).	Every attempt to view a resource (or group) that contains a trusted account.
Pass-through authentication	20 frames (~3,700 bytes)	Once for the first attempt to access a resource on a trusting computer, or logon to a trusted domain from a trusting computer.
Directory replication	Announcement—1 frame (~340 bytes)	Once per importing domain or server for every update of the export tree.
	Establish session—9 frames (~1,300 bytes)	Once from each import computer every update event.
	Verify directory—30 frames (~5,100 bytes)	Once from each import computer every update event.
	Update directory—various amounts of network traffic.	Once from each import computer every update event.
WINS replication	Establish relationship—20 frames (2,300 bytes)	Once per replication relationship.
	Database verification—12 frames ~ (900 bytes)	Once per update request to each replication partner.
	Database update—approximately 14 frames (~2,100 bytes varies with number of updates)	Once per update request to each replication partner.

CHAPTER 2

One Network Day at Microsoft

By
Alexander Levin, Microsoft Information Technology Group—Network and Systems Analysis

Microsoft has a large internal information infrastructure. This chapter discusses how it works and what flavors and levels of traffic cross it during a normal day. Networks are all the same (in essence) and yet all different (in particular). Looking at a day in the life of one network, however, especially a large and complex one, should show some patterns from which useful observations and inferences can be drawn. Then, too, the previous chapter discusses the various types of network traffic, so this is a good time to show how these types occur and move on a daily basis.

In Focus

Enterprise
An inside view of some network analysis done by Microsoft's Information Technology Group.

Network
This discussion contains a collection of best practices and recommendations derived from looking at a variety of intranet applications put into production on Microsoft's corporate network.

Challenge
Improving the performance of an application, especially over the wide area network.

Solution
Build efficiencies in network communication into your corporate intranet applications, developing them with WAN performance in mind.

What You'll Find In This Chapter

- **A discussion of traffic capturing and analysis techniques, based on analyses conducted on Microsoft's network infrastructure.**

- **A clear analogy to understand the complexity of network traffic, and a review of some basic definitions.**

- **Basic traffic capture and analysis concepts.**

- **A description of a test file-transfer case**

- **A case study of a troubleshooting analysis conducted over the WAN.**

Infrastructure

First things first. It is difficult to discuss this topic (as the paragraph above shows) without resorting to the term *infrastructure*. What *is* an infrastructure?

At the Mall

Suppose you go to the opening of a new mall—one of those state-of-the-mallmaker-art capitalist shrines currently replacing suburban scenery all over America and the world. This one has been super-hyped (now *there's* something new) and promises to have the best stuff to buy (ditto), the cleanest, most convenient setup. The works. On opening day you go to have a look.

But you see problems immediately. For starters, you can't get into the parking lot because it is packed with trucks delivering goods. You park in the next county and hike in: the entranceways are a gauntlet of advertisements and promotion booths. People are stacking up like jets over Newark. And when you finally get inside, you can't even get into the stores along the court because too many people are cleaning floors, stocking shelves, using the doorways, stacking the highly-vaunted first-class merchandise in the aisles.

All of these impediments are *support activities*. They are necessary, but they obviously should not supersede the mall's primary activity, which is to sell things by the ton. These functions and the store buildings and walkways are its infrastructure: an underlying foundation or framework that is (or should be) seamless. These services have to be there but they should be invisible to you when you try to buy something. Internal support should help, not prevent or degrade, the primary activity.

An Information Infrastructure

A business network is a combination of computers (2 or 20,000) and networks (software and hardware connections) linked so that they can share data and peripheral devices for a purpose, usually creating a product or providing a service. The support structure here is the information infrastructure—the computers and connections that acquire, store, and transfer information. As with the stocks at the mall, the information infrastructure should be hidden from the user, who should focus on business, not on the network's foundation or its support and repair. By creating, implementing, and maintaining a seamless infrastructure, information technology specialists add significant value to the company.

This is one of the possible ways to present an information structure of any significant size company (Fig. 2.1).

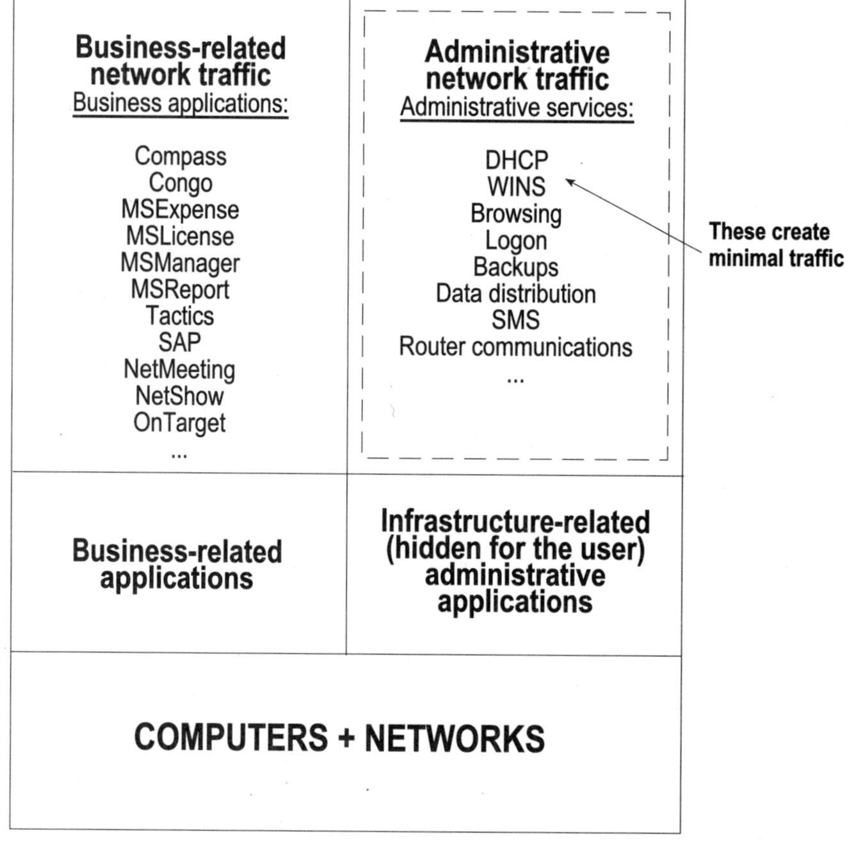

Figure 2.1 Representation of network traffic in relation to network infrastructure.

Three Windows 2000 infrastructure services generate significantly more network traffic than all others: Server Browser (meaning the browsing function in general—there are several flavors of browsing), WINS Replication, and Directory Services. These services are integral to the operating system, running automatically when computers are booted or connected. They can be tuned, but doing so requires testing, study, and in-depth understanding of your network operations.

A fourth service, backup, is different in that network designers and implementers have to plan and configure it, and if they do these things poorly the infrastructure can take a beating from lots of unnecessary traffic, slow communications, impaired business operation, and surly users.

The rest of this chapter shows how these services look at Microsoft. Tests show how Server Browser (the browsing function), WINS Replication, and Directory Services affect the network: the type and amount of traffic they generate, how it accrues and increments, etc.

A section on backup shows how it can create special problems. The demands it places on the network and on technicians at Microsoft are enormous. In one case shown in the tests, a server's backup volume was too high to complete during off hours, and technicians had to resort to completing it during normal business hours, loading the network. The charts presented in the backup section clearly show the high levels of additional traffic that resulted during normal business hours. Short of resorting to partial backups (an unacceptable alternative) this problem requires increasing backup capacity by adding hardware.

Capturing and Analyzing Traffic

Most servers at the Microsoft corporate data center are connected to Cisco Catalyst switches with further ATM uplinks to the corporate network backbone. With a Switched Port Analyzer (SPAN), you can analyze traffic on any of these servers without service interruption, because Catalyst switches allow you to mirror traffic on any port. This means you can create a copy of the traffic as it passes through, divert it, then analyze it by connecting a sniffer or RMON probe to the port. This is a standard capturing technique, and the users on the network are in no way inconvenienced by the en-route capture of a mirrored stream of their traffic.

The analysis that follows was performed with two software tools: Microsoft Network Monitor (version 4.00.352) and a NetXRay (version 3.0.3) from Network General (Network Associates). NetMon was used for detailed packet-by-packet analysis because it can decode MSRPC packets. These packets are used in several types of network traffic (replication, e-mail, etc.) and if you can't decode them they are shown as TCP packets, which makes it almost impossible to understand what higher level protocol is being used. Version 3.0.3 of NetXRay cannot decode MSRPC packets (the SnifferPro product version 2.0.01 can), but it is a good tool for gathering statistics over a period of time.

The difficulty behind this sort of monitoring is to find the correct network point (connector, hub, router, etc.) where the traffic you want to analyze will pass through, then use a tool to capture it (by port mirroring, for example). In the good old days (in terms of networking technology, a few months ago) it was almost always possible to find such a capture point.

Now, however, the proliferation of switches and ATM connections from the WAN to the ATM company backbone is making it harder and harder to capture specific data streams without very expensive equipment and circuit intrusion—sometimes impossible. When data flowed only through routers or shared hubs, it was possible to find a point at which to intercept the traffic you were interested in. Data streams that go into switches over high-speed media, full-duplex transfer modes, and ATM, however, cannot always be parsed and captured, so traffic analysis is developing a new set of challenges.

Browsing and Replication Traffic Between Domain Controllers

To return to the case at hand, the capture was easy enough to effect. A computer running Network Monitor and NetXRay was connected to a port on the Catalyst switch to which a domain controller's to/from traffic was mirrored. An IP filter was configured on both tools to capture traffic between the primary domain controller (PDC) and one of the backup domain controllers (BDCs). Figure 2.2 is a snapshot of that traffic.

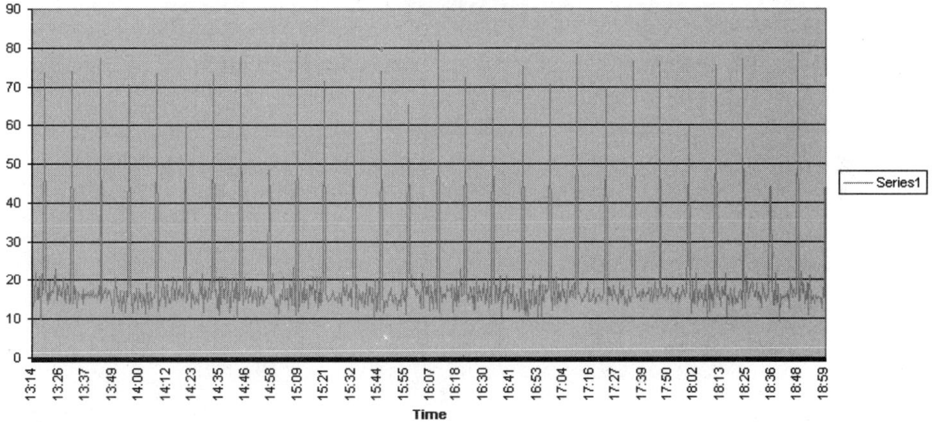

Figure 2.2 Traffic volume between PDC and one BDC.

Spikes on this graph represent results of the browser-type function, which invoked at 12-minute intervals and resulted in delivering a substantial amount of information within a short period of time. The browser is a network resource enumeration tool. It maintains a list, called a browse list, of all available servers, workgroups, and domains. When a user attempts to connect to any network resource using Network Neighborhood, the list of servers that appears is provided by a browser in the local computer's workgroup or domain. This is a Windows service and it can generate substantial traffic. For more information see http://www.microsoft.com/win32dev/netwrk/browse1.htm and http://www.microsoft.com/win32dev/netwrk/browse2.htm.

NetXRay averaged the spike level for the 30-second timeframe, so the actual browser spike level is a little higher than the value shown. Duration of the data transfer on the LAN after the announcement is 7 to 13 seconds and the amount of data transferred is 115 to 135 Kb, which means that peak levels are going as high as 140 Kbits/sec. In a highly utilized 10-Mbps Ethernet, these data transfers can cause traffic slow downs and even some packet discards. They can be even more disruptive on a WAN, especially on slow links. You can tune announcement periodicity in the registry, but that sort of procedural detail is beyond the scope of this chapter.

Directory Services Traffic

Figure 2.3 shows that actual data replication (directory replication) traffic is pretty low (on the LAN). Keep in mind that these levels of traffic were averaged during 30 seconds. It means that actual average traffic levels are around 30 Kbits/sec. (calculated from a data capture). This graph represents traffic levels between 12-minute browser spikes, which are shown on a different scale in the two figures. Note that the graph covers approximately 11 minutes—just a fragment of the larger capture.

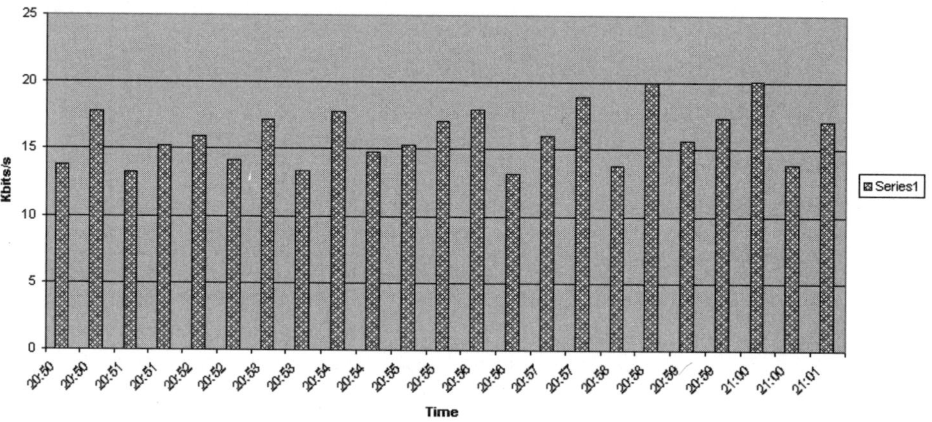

Figure 2.3 Domain replication traffic.

Figure 2.3 shows a normal mode of partial replication, which is accompanied by these messages in the Windows NT EVENT.LOG. Notice that the more recent entry is at the top.

10/5/98 11:59:08 PM NETLOGON Information None 5715 N/A NAME The **partial synchronization replication** of the Security Accounts Manager (SAM) database from the primary domain controller \\Controller_NAME **completed successfully. 7 change(s) is(are) applied to the database.**

10/5/98 11:49:08 PM NETLOGON Information None 5715 N/A NAME The **partial synchronization replication** of the SAM database from the primary domain controller \\Controller_NAME **completed successfully**. **2 change(s) is(are) applied to the database.**

Four types of accounts are stored in the SAM database: user, computer, global group, and local group.

But problems can occur in the replication process, in which case messages such as these (more recent entry first) appear in the EVENT.LOG:

10/6/98 12:44:26 AM NETLOGON Information None 5717 N/A NAME The **full synchronization replication of the SAM database from the primary domain controller** \\Controller_NAME **completed successfully**.

10/6/98 12:37:45 AM NETLOGON Warning None 5716 N/A NAME The partial synchronization replication of the SAM database from the primary domain controller \\Controller_NAME **failed** with the following error: (error in HEX)

In case of the above mentioned failure, a traffic graph of the full synchronization process will look as follows:

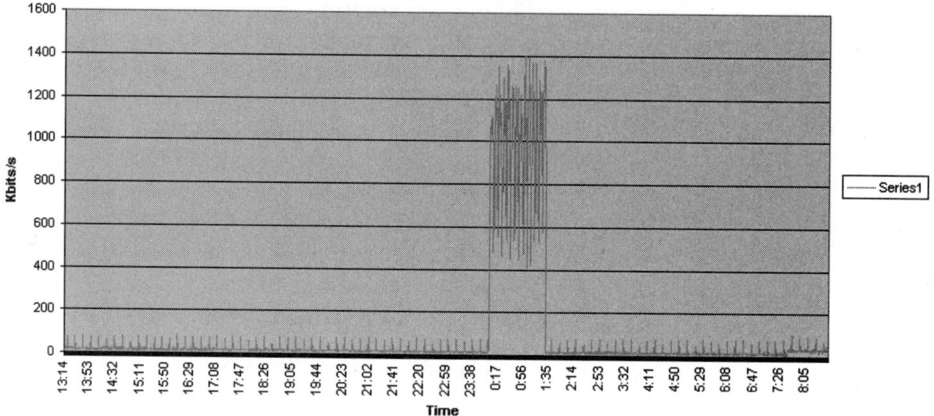

Figure 2.4 Traffic volume spike during full synchronization between PDC and one BDC.

This is a pretty high level (up to 1.4 Mb/sec.) of traffic with a long duration (approximately 1.5 hours).

WINS Replication Traffic

WINS servers are dedicated to name resolution, which is necessary in a network environment. In dynamic environments there is no manual *IP address – server name* administration, and computers' IP addresses can change whenever they boot up or change location. Even in a static environment people cannot be expected to remember IP addresses.

Users *can* remember server names reasonably well, so most network servers are given names. That helps users immeasurably, but it does nothing for traffic in the wire, which can find servers only by address, not by name. So the network uses a mechanism such as WINS to *resolve* names—match them to their assigned IP addresses. Most organizations have more than one WINS server (for fault tolerance as well as performance), and they create network traffic when they update databases among themselves. A capture of the traffic to/from one of the WINS servers on Microsoft's network looks like this (presented in Kbits/sec. and packets/sec.).

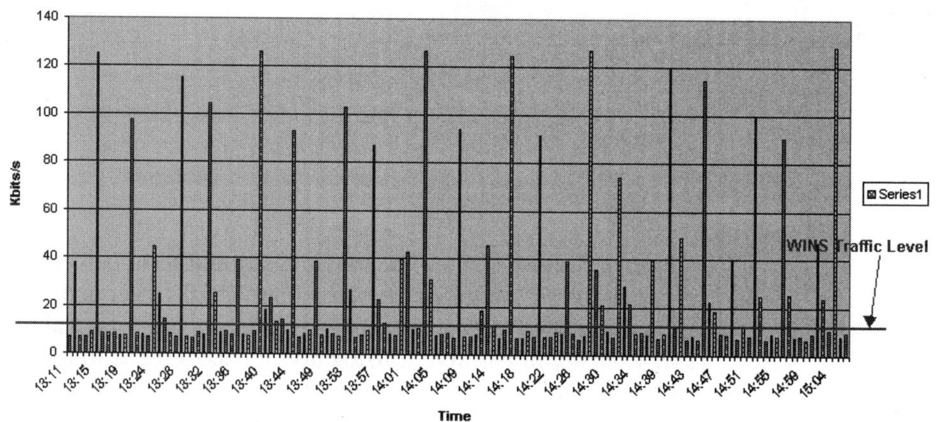

Figure 2.5 Traffic volume to/from one of the WINS servers in Kbits/sec.

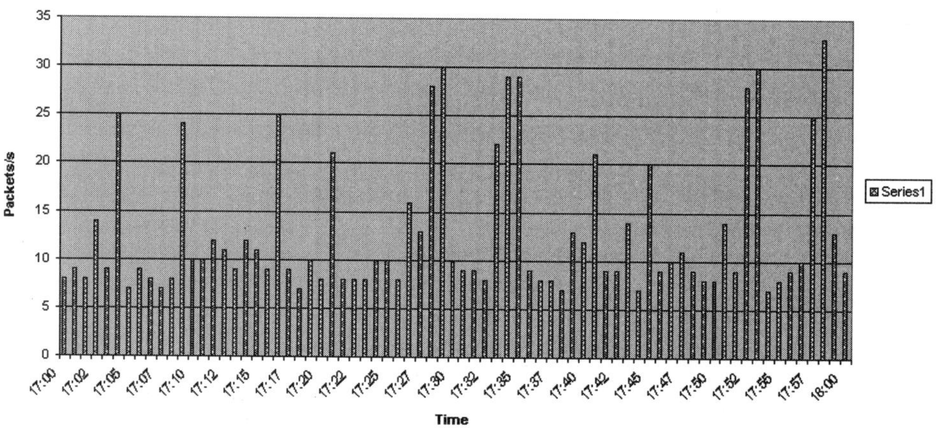

Figure 2.6 Traffic volume to/from one of the WINS servers in packets/sec.

The good news is that WINS resolution traffic is pretty low—no higher than 8-10 Kbits/sec. (7-10 packets/sec.). But there is more to look at. The capture shows that every 12 minutes the WINS server provides browser data for browse masters (browsing is explained in the "Browser Service (Browsing) Traffic" section of Chapter 1). Each request generates a response; the total response volume in the analyzed case was 247 packets of data and acknowledgements. The capture size of the saved response for the browser request consisted of 164 full-size packets (1514 bytes each). It takes 0.34 seconds to complete a transaction, so the spike level calculates out to approximately 5.8 Mbits/sec. (captured on the 100-Mbps Ethernet).

Notice that on the chart (Figure 2.6) it looks much lower; this is because the capturing tool averaged the traffic level for the 30-second period. The WINS server that was observed was in communication with 11 major servers—some were domain controllers, some were WINS servers, but all of them were master-browsers. A spike level such as this can be dangerous on lower-speed networks or highly-utilized Ethernets because longer response transmission times can overlap and create a substantial "noise" level.

Figures 2.7 and 2.8 show the traffic distribution (in percentages and MBs, respectively) of the traffic between one WINS server and the 20 others with which it communicates to exchange lists of domains, servers, and user computers. This represents administrative traffic only. It makes sense to learn traffic patterns on your network and tune this service, because data exchange and traffic volumes correlate to the return on investment of the company network.

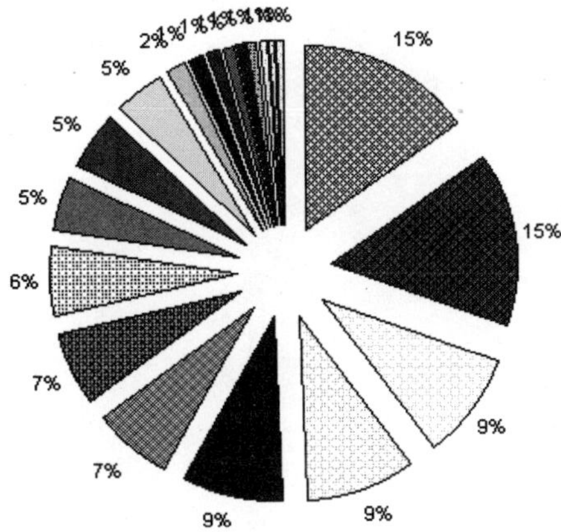

Figure 2.7 Traffic distribution to/from one of the WINS servers over 24 hours in percentages.

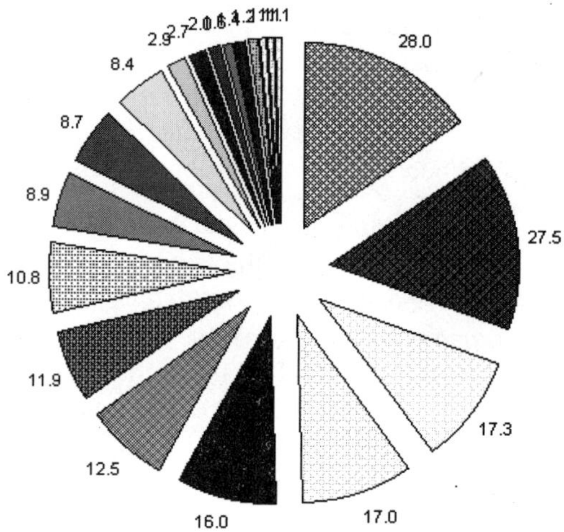

Figure 2.8 Traffic volumes to/from one of the WINS servers over 24 hours in total MBs.

DHCP Traffic

DHCP (Dynamic Host Configuration Protocol) makes it easier to manage large TCP/IP networks by offering automatic TCP/IP configuration. Computers can be configured to obtain IP addresses automatically from the DHCP server, so during initial configuration users need not be concerned with configuring IP manually and registering the static IP address in the database. It helps even more when users travel, making it possible for them to connect a laptop computer in any office of the company all around the world and automatically obtain and register a valid IP address for the network they are connected to.

A capture of the traffic to/from one of the DHCP servers on Microsoft's network looks like this (presented in Kbits/sec. and packets/sec.).

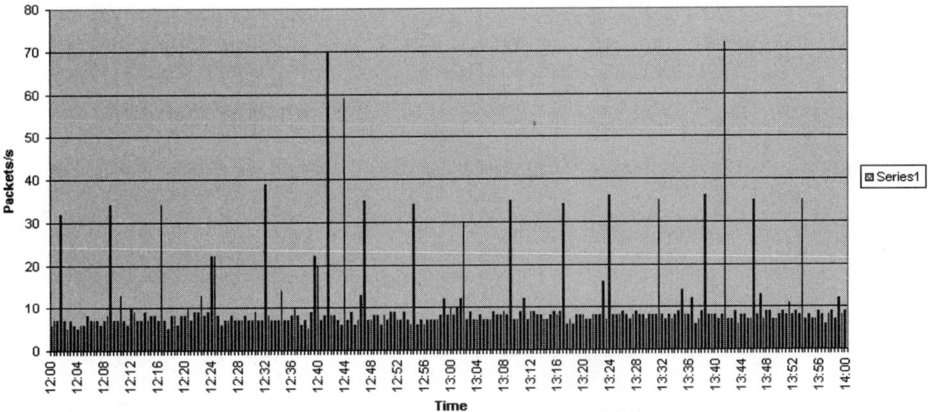

Figure 2.9 Traffic volumes to/from one of the DHCP servers in packets/sec.

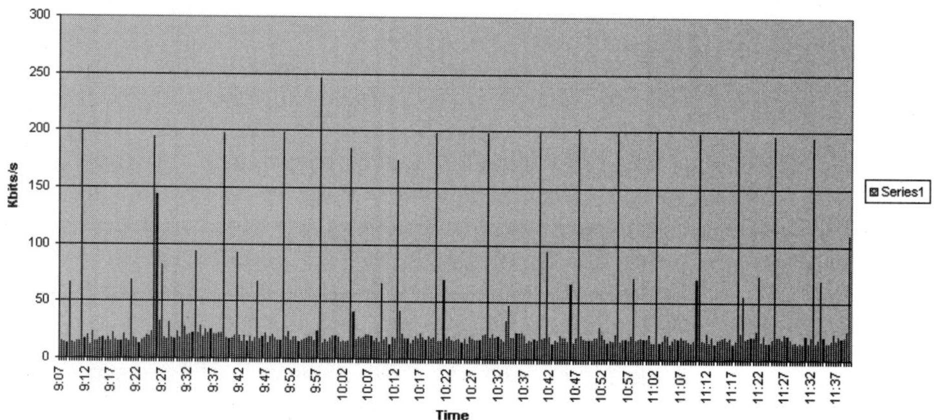

Figure 2.10 Traffic volumes to/from one of the DHCP servers in Kbits/sec.

Server characteristics:

- Total amount of scopes (subnets maintained by a server): 71
- Total addresses: 65130
- Addresses in use: 39884 (61%)
- Addresses available: 25246 (38%)

Traffic to/from a DHCP server consists of IP address leases and other related services provided by the server. For the server examined in this test, it appears that little of its traffic is related to DHCP—around 20-22 Kbits/sec. (8-10 packets/sec.).

This would be considered low traffic on a fast LAN, but it wouldn't make sense to have this kind of "background" administrative traffic on a WAN, where speeds are slower and costs are higher. For this reason, Microsoft offices have local DHCP servers so that users do not have to send IP address requests across the country or around the world. If a local DHCP server fails, requests can be serviced elsewhere on the net, but this is rare.

The sample capture of DHCP-related traffic between 8:30 a.m. and 2.30 p.m. at Microsoft shows an average of 74 requests for IP addresses per minute, each of which creates six small packets (about 2121 bytes total). So the calculations represented on the graph are: 74 requests x 2121 bytes/service x 8 bits/byte divided by 60 seconds/minute = 20.9 Kbits/sec. This has no significant impact on the LAN. The next graph shows only DHCP-related traffic:

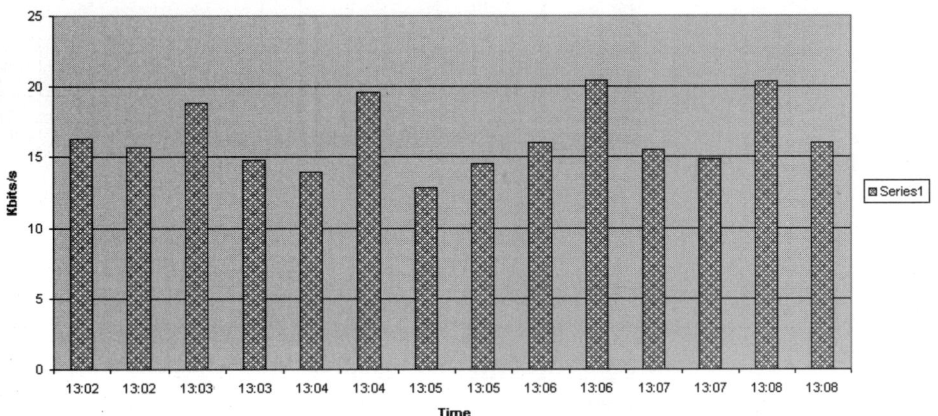

Figure 2.11 DHCP traffic and Kbps.

Spikes on Figures 2.8 and 2.9 can be explained by some additional services, not related to DHCP (browser, database replications between servers, System Management Server operations) running on the analyzed server. These take much more bandwidth than IP address distribution, and the spikes hit 200 Kbits/sec. (35-40 packets/sec.) and higher. Remember that the tool used to produce the graph averaged spikes over the 30-second period, so the graph shows them lower than their actual level, which jumps up to 300-350 Kbits/sec.

Backup Services

Traffic volumes on one of the backup servers looks like this:

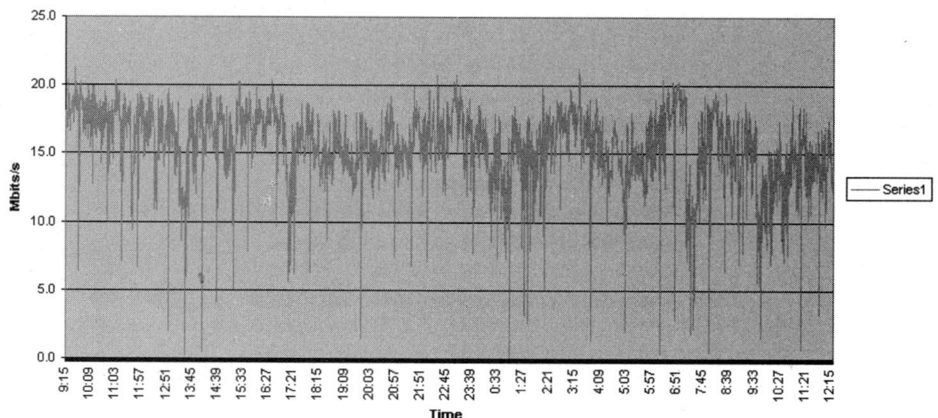

Figure 2.12 Traffic volume on backup server with four tape drives in Mbits/sec.

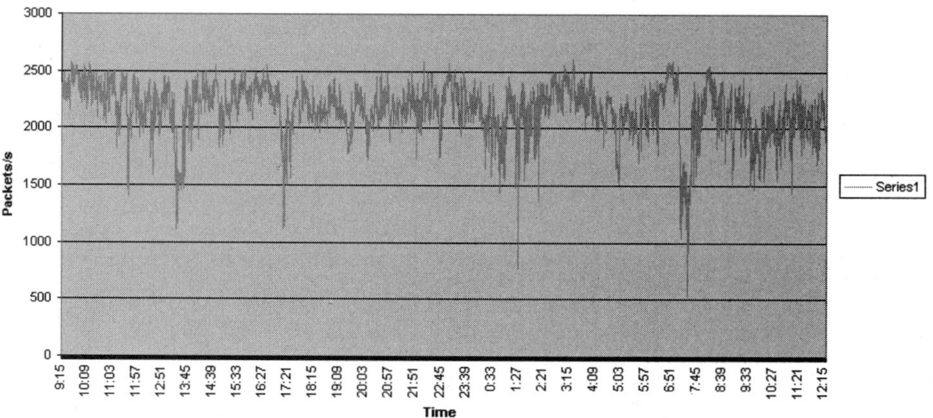

Figure 2.13 Traffic volume on backup server with four tape drives in packets/sec.

The backup services send many full-size packets (1514 bytes) and small acknowledgements (60 bytes) and this distribution (shown in Figure 2.14) is easy to explain: the backup software uses full-size Ethernet packets whenever possible.

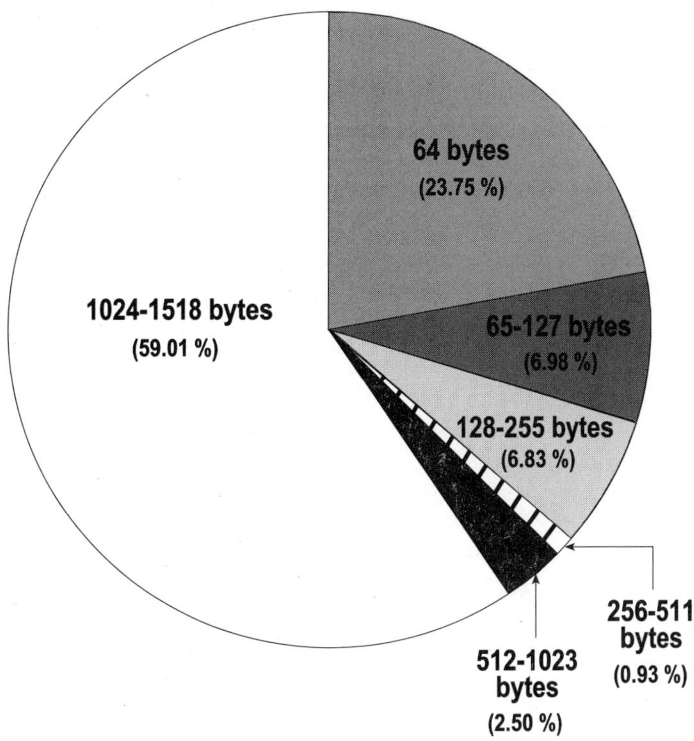

Figure 2.14 Packet size distribution of backup traffic.

Case Studies

If you have ever distributed content on the Internet or moved big batches of data around, you probably have some experience complaining about slow links and long waiting times. Most people immediately think that additional bandwidth will alleviate whatever frustration they are experiencing. Maybe it will, and maybe it won't. What can be done to speed things up without spending money to upgrade bandwidth?

The Copying Process

Suppose you want to move a directory with lots of files across the country from Redmond, WA, to Boston, MA, over a 1.536-Mbps (T1) circuit. How long can you expect it to take?

Here are two ways to effect the move:

1. Go to the command prompt and use the command *copy* *.* to move all the files to their destination.
2. Compress the directory into one file and move it using the same command.

These methods were tested in a lab, using two routers and a WAN simulator to introduce a cross-country delay of 45 ms, 90 ms for a round-trip. The 45 ms is the time required for the electromagnetic wave to "fly" from coast to coast—a propagation speed set by the laws of physics—although the 45 ms includes some delay introduced by multiple network devices on the transmission path. The test copied two files: a Windows NT source directory with 2477 files (53.1 MB total) and a Windows NT source directory ZIPped into a single 49-MB file.

Summary of test results of transferring large files by two methods.

Object transferred	Size	Amount of data on the network	Transfer time	Transfer rate
One file	~49 MB	52.5 Mbytes	~13.5 minutes	516 Kbits/sec.
Windows NT source directory (2477 files)	~53.1 MB	65.5 MBytes	~56.5 minutes	154.4 Kbits/sec.

Obviously, copying multiple files creates significant overhead on the wire (12.4 MB vs. 3.5 MB). This is because the process involves numerous iterations of creating, opening, and closing files, which rapidly increases the number of round trips between source and destination.

Sniff fragment of transferring one file with opening/closing overhead.

Frame	Time (between packets)	Src Name	Dst Name	Protocol	Description
1	0	MyRouter	GNETTOOLS74	SMB	*C transact2 Query path info, File = \ntsource\WOWFAXUI.DL_*
2	0.002	GNETTOOLS74	MyRouter	SMB	*R transact2 - NT error, System, Error, Code = (52) STATUS_OBJECT_*
3	0.099	MyRouter	GNETTOOLS74	SMB	*C NT create & X, File = \ntsource\WOWFAXUI.DL_*
4	0.003	GNETTOOLS74	MyRouter	SMB	*R NT create & X, FID = 0x8806*
5	**0.097**	MyRouter	GNETTOOLS74	SMB	*C write, FID = 0x8806, Write 0x0 at 0x00001C47*
6	0.001	GNETTOOLS74	MyRouter	SMB	*R write, Wrote 0x0*
7	**0.112**	MyRouter	GNETTOOLS74	SMB	*C write block raw, FID = 0x8806, Write 0x10c4 of 0x1c47 at 0x0*
8	0.008	MyRouter	GNETTOOLS74	NBT	SS: Session Message Cont., **1460** Bytes
9	0.001	GNETTOOLS74	MyRouter	TCP	.A...., len: 0, seq: 251972888-251972888, ack: 202967151, win:
10	0.007	MyRouter	GNETTOOLS74	NBT	SS: Session Message Cont., **1440** Bytes

Sniff fragment of transferring one file with opening/closing overhead. *(continued)*

Frame	Time (between packets)	Src Name	Dst Name	Protocol	Description
11	0.001	GNETTOOLS74	MyRouter	SMB	*R write block raw*
12	**0.112**	MyRouter	GNETTOOLS74	NBT	SS: Session Message, Len: 2947
13	0.008	MyRouter	GNETTOOLS74	NBT	SS: Session Message Cont., **1460** Bytes
14	0	MyRouter	GNETTOOLS74	NBT	SS: Session Message Cont., **31** Bytes
15	0	GNETTOOLS74	MyRouter	TCP	.A...., len: 0, seq: 251972929-251972929, ack: 202971542, win:
16	**0.097**	MyRouter	GNETTOOLS74	SMB	*C transact2 Set file info, FID = 0x8806*
17	0.001	GNETTOOLS74	MyRouter	SMB	*R transact2 Set file info (response to frame 16)*
18	**0.097**	MyRouter	GNETTOOLS74	SMB	*C close file, FID = 0x8806*
19	0	GNETTOOLS74	MyRouter	SMB	*R close file*
Total time 0.646 s					

The italicized entries above show overhead during the transfer of one of the NT source files (WOWFAXUI.DL_: 7,239 bytes). It took 0.646 seconds (6 round trips) to complete this transaction ; it takes only 0.025 seconds to copy the same amount of data contained in one big file. Clearly, the number of round trips on the WAN are significant components of transfer time, a fact that is built into file-transfer logic.

Sniff fragment of data transfer without opening/closing overhead.

Frame	Time (between packets)	Src Name	Dst Name	Protocol	Description
1	0	MyRouter	GNETTOOLS74	NBT	SS: Session Message Cont., **1460** Bytes
2	0.001	GNETTOOLS74	MyRouter	TCP	.A...., len: 0, seq: 194679713-194679713, ack: 138262571, win:
3	0.008	MyRouter	GNETTOOLS74	NBT	SS: Session Message Cont., **1460** Bytes
4	0.008	MyRouter	GNETTOOLS74	NBT	SS: Session Message Cont., **1460** Bytes
5	0	GNETTOOLS74	MyRouter	TCP	.A...., len: 0, seq: 194679713-194679713, ack: 138265491, win:
6	0.008	MyRouter	GNETTOOLS74	NBT	SS: Session Message Cont., **1460** Bytes

Total time 0.025 s

Note that the time between packets is 8 ms, which is the time required to put a full-size Ethernet packet (1514 bytes x 8/1536000 = 7.9 ms) on the wire. The actual packet size on the serial side of the router is not exactly 1514 bytes, but the difference is irrelevant in this type of calculation.

Troubleshooting a High Utilization Problem on the WAN

Microsoft has lots of remote offices around the world, and they are connected to the main campus in Redmond, WA, by means of point-to-point links and through hubs and shared WAN links. When one office complained about slow network connectivity, the IT group studied the traffic levels and flavors between the remote site and campus to find out what was going on.

Figuring Out How To Test

To perform this study, Microsoft's IT people used a home-made Web-based tool that reports link utilization parameters for all WAN links in the corporation, and gathers some other statistics that are important for capacity planning. The tool showed that utilization on the 256-Kbps link (the troubled one) stayed high 24 hours a day. This is an immediate and obvious indication that something is out of whack. Utilization during normal business hours was about 100%, which is high, but it was more significant that it stayed at around 30% at night. Obviously, levels should drop significantly after the end of the business day, so this consistently high utilization rate indicated a problem. What was it?

The high levels after regular business hours indicated unknown additional traffic. This meant that traffic analysis during nights or weekends would provide more coherent troubleshooting indicators because the link would be running "clean" (without the usual business applications).

Now that the ITG had decided to ruin a weekend by sitting around sniffing the network, there remained the task of planning the sniff and how to make it. The WAN connection to be examined came directly to Redmond through a router with multiple serial links on the WAN side and a Fiber Distributed Data Interface (FDDI) connection on the LAN side.

This was good news because it meant it was possible to use an old-style Network General sniffer with the FDDI card and 10% beam splitter to see all the traffic coming to the corporate network. The bad news was that the old sniffer was an MS-DOS-based device without good RMON capabilities. This meant two things. The first was that this tool could not be used to gather, save, and adequately format detailed source-destination information over a period of time. The second was that another solution was needed.

After some deliberation, it was decided that Network General's NetXRay would work. This software tool, which loads on top of Windows NT, gathers statistical information that can be very helpful. The next step was to try to insert a PC with the NetXRay and a FDDI network card through the beam splitter. This would simplify things by allowing easy access to all traffic coming in to the campus without looking for another access point on switches "closer" to the backbone. Unfortunately, this attempt was unsuccessful because when information is transmitted by means of light you need a certain power of the incoming light or you can't capture the data, and in this case there was not enough light power for the FDDI card.

The next step was to look higher in the connection hierarchy and finally there was some good luck. As an uplink, the router still had an old shared FDDI hub, which allowed the test devices to be connected to any available port, showing all the traffic that moved through it. (The Microsoft corporate network now has an ATM backbone and traffic analysis (packet sniffing) capabilities on this backbone are significantly reduced. This type of troubleshooting can be accomplished on ATM connections only with very expensive tools.)

Figuring Out the Capture

Once a computer with NetXRay was successfully connected to the shared FDDI hub, all site traffic became visible on the wire. The troubled remote site had two IP address ranges assigned to the Ethernet interface, so the capture had to show all traffic between Redmond and these two IP ranges. Using knowledge of the address ranges, the team identified and isolated the appropriate traffic, and set up the sniff. After several hours the capture was stopped and this is what it showed (in Kbits/sec. and packets/sec.).

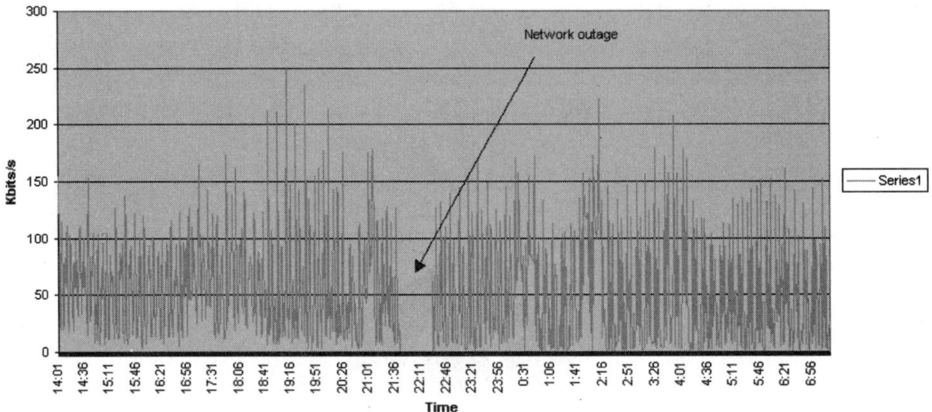

Figure 2.15 Traffic levels to/from a remote site coming to the corporate network in Kbits/sec.

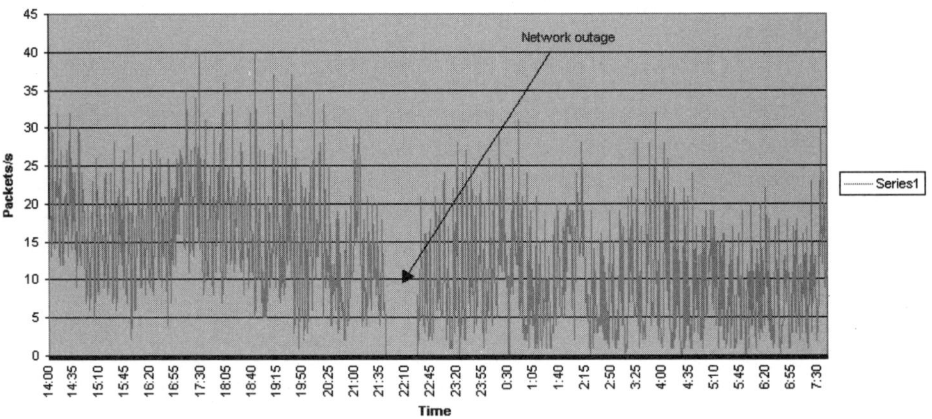

Figure 2.16 Traffic levels to/from a remote site coming to the corporate network in packets/sec.

These graphs verify that traffic levels are a little high for the weekend and night time from Saturday to Sunday. The reason still was not apparent, so a deeper look was arranged into the top 20 pairs of communicating servers between the remote site and corporate campus. The diagram of this distribution is shown in Figure 2.17.

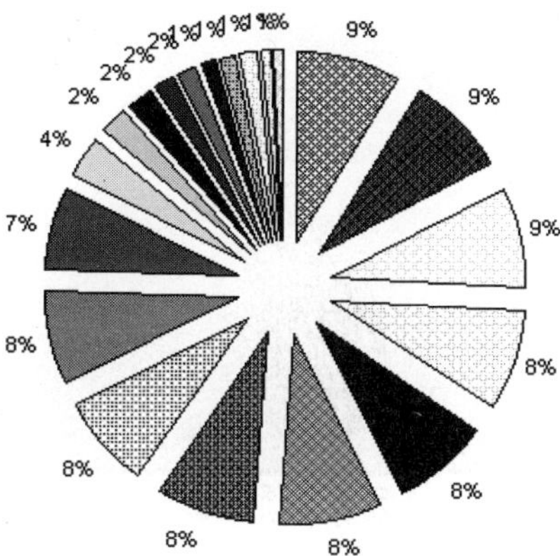

Figure 2.17 Traffic distribution between top 20 server pairs communicating between the remote site and the corporate campus.

A real-life chart should represent bursty and hardly predictable network traffic, so it is startling when one comes out with the pie cut into nice even pieces. It is a sure-fire indication that something is not right. In this case, closer examination of the IP addresses for the communicating pairs showed that the first nine pairs were communicating with only one corporate network server.

Traffic levels between nine servers at the remote site and a single server in Redmond looked like this:

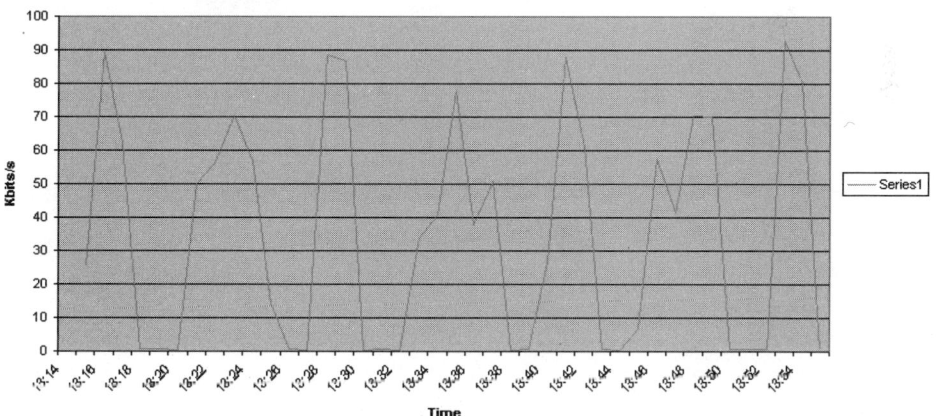

Figure 2.18 Traffic levels between 9 remote servers and a single server on the corporate network.

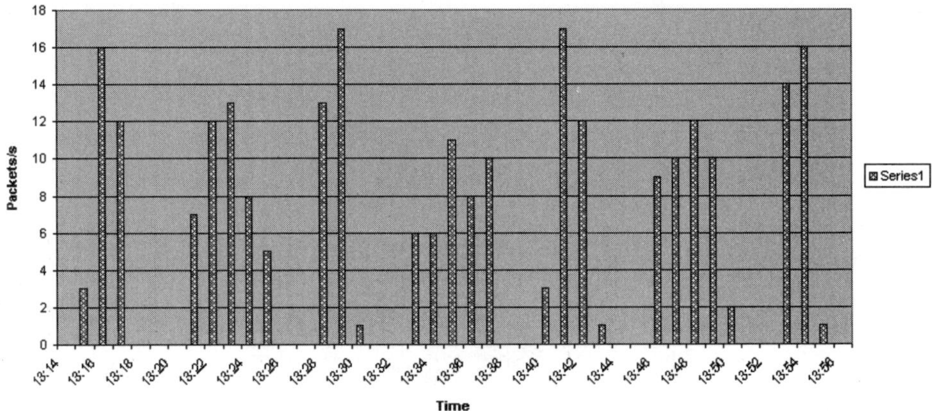

Figure 2.19 Traffic levels between nine remote servers and a single server on the corporate network.

Once this behavior was discovered, a Network Monitor capture showed that nine remote site servers were requesting browser lists from one corporate server. Each request created a response of about 155 full-size Ethernet packets. The transaction took about 22 seconds, which meant that the spike was about 85 Kbits/sec. The screen capture below shows how frequently these requests were coming to the corporate server.

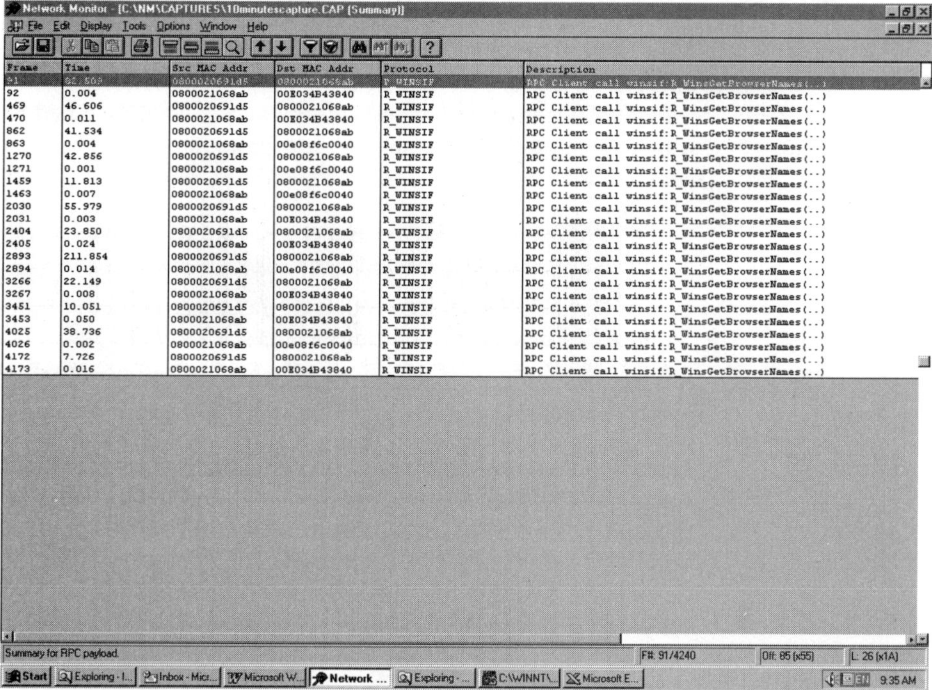

Frame	Time	Src MAC Addr	Dst MAC Addr	Protocol	Description
91	82.509	0800020691d5	0800021068ab	R_WINSIF	RPC Client call winsif:R_WinsGetBrowserNames(..)
92	0.004	0800021068ab	00E034B43840	R_WINSIF	RPC Client call winsif:R_WinsGetBrowserNames(..)
469	46.606	0800020691d5	0800021068ab	R_WINSIF	RPC Client call winsif:R_WinsGetBrowserNames(..)
470	0.011	0800021068ab	00E034B43840	R_WINSIF	RPC Client call winsif:R_WinsGetBrowserNames(..)
862	41.534	0800020691d5	0800021068ab	R_WINSIF	RPC Client call winsif:R_WinsGetBrowserNames(..)
863	0.004	0800021068ab	00e08f6c0040	R_WINSIF	RPC Client call winsif:R_WinsGetBrowserNames(..)
1270	42.856	0800020691d5	0800021068ab	R_WINSIF	RPC Client call winsif:R_WinsGetBrowserNames(..)
1271	0.001	0800021068ab	00e08f6c0040	R_WINSIF	RPC Client call winsif:R_WinsGetBrowserNames(..)
1459	11.813	0800020691d5	0800021068ab	R_WINSIF	RPC Client call winsif:R_WinsGetBrowserNames(..)
1463	0.007	0800021068ab	00e08f6c0040	R_WINSIF	RPC Client call winsif:R_WinsGetBrowserNames(..)
2030	55.979	0800020691d5	0800021068ab	R_WINSIF	RPC Client call winsif:R_WinsGetBrowserNames(..)
2031	0.003	0800021068ab	00E034B43840	R_WINSIF	RPC Client call winsif:R_WinsGetBrowserNames(..)
2404	23.850	0800020691d5	0800021068ab	R_WINSIF	RPC Client call winsif:R_WinsGetBrowserNames(..)
2405	0.024	0800021068ab	00E034B43840	R_WINSIF	RPC Client call winsif:R_WinsGetBrowserNames(..)
2893	211.854	0800020691d5	0800021068ab	R_WINSIF	RPC Client call winsif:R_WinsGetBrowserNames(..)
2894	0.014	0800021068ab	00e08f6c0040	R_WINSIF	RPC Client call winsif:R_WinsGetBrowserNames(..)
3266	22.149	0800020691d5	0800021068ab	R_WINSIF	RPC Client call winsif:R_WinsGetBrowserNames(..)
3267	0.008	0800021068ab	00E034B43840	R_WINSIF	RPC Client call winsif:R_WinsGetBrowserNames(..)
3451	10.051	0800020691d5	0800021068ab	R_WINSIF	RPC Client call winsif:R_WinsGetBrowserNames(..)
3453	0.050	0800021068ab	00E034B43840	R_WINSIF	RPC Client call winsif:R_WinsGetBrowserNames(..)
4025	38.736	0800020691d5	0800021068ab	R_WINSIF	RPC Client call winsif:R_WinsGetBrowserNames(..)
4026	0.002	0800021068ab	00e08f6c0040	R_WINSIF	RPC Client call winsif:R_WinsGetBrowserNames(..)
4172	7.726	0800020691d5	0800021068ab	R_WINSIF	RPC Client call winsif:R_WinsGetBrowserNames(..)
4173	0.016	0800021068ab	00E034B43840	R_WINSIF	RPC Client call winsif:R_WinsGetBrowserNames(..)

Figure 2.20 Network Monitor screen capture showing browser list request periodicity from different servers.

What did this mean in terms of fixing the slow link? It meant that the solution lay in tuning, not additional bandwidth. The remote office has to request browser lists, but configuring them to request over the net was disastrously inefficient. The system was reconfigured so that only one active server communicates with the corporate master browser: the other servers request browser lists locally. This took all the requesting traffic and the responses off the net and dropped line utilization back into an acceptable and understandable range.

The NetMon capture shows another interesting feature: the interpacket delay in the "Time" column indicates that requests from the remote site are coming to the corporate network at irregular intervals. Delays after packets 91, 469, 862, 1270, etc., are very short, but longer delays happen after every other packet. What can cause these short delays?

The search for a cause begins with a closer look at the source and destination MAC addresses. These belong to the routers, which is as it should be. The analysis tool was connected on the corporate network. Packets coming from the remote office crossed several routers on the way, then had to cross one more router to get to the server on the corporate network. Thus, on the MAC level, source and destination addresses should be router MAC addresses, specifically:

- 080002 0691D5 (3Com router)—the MAC address of the WAN router that the remote site packets come from
- 00E034 B43840 (Cisco router)—the MAC address of the router that the destination server is "sitting" behind

So the question is: what is the MAC address (080002 1068AB, another 3Com router) shown for packets 92, 470, 863, 1271, etc.?

Here is what this was found to indicate. Packet 91, for example, comes from the remote site to the corporate network and, instead of being forwarded directly to the Cisco router with MAC address 00E034 B43840, it goes to the 3Com router with MAC address 080002 1068AB. This "mystery" router forwards it to its destination through the Cisco router with MAC address 00E034 B43840, which in turn forwards it to the destination server connected to the corporate network. This means:

- Packets make an additional hop (they are rerouted one more time).
- Packets are delivered with an additional delay varying from 1 ms (packet #1271) to 50 ms (packet 3453), which is equivalent to the propagation delay across the USA—a significant amount of time.
- Packets from the remote site are going through the shared hub twice.
- This "double flow" creates an additional load on the shared hub.

This path is indeed confusing. And it is a reminder that sometimes it makes sense to take a closer look at routing to verify that data streams are going through the correct paths. In a heavily utilized network, false routing (especially through the WAN) can badly affect network utilization and, as a result, application performance.

In this case, however, further investigation proved that there was no mystery and that this *was* a correct path. Ongoing network reengineering had resulted in the concurrent use of old and new backbones and this resulted in a necessary redirection of traffic flow. The "strange" evidence indicated only business as usual.

CHAPTER 3

Strategies in Network Capacity Planning and Network Optimization—AB Pound & Co.

By Anthony Baron, MCS—United Kingdom

Client-server applications need a reliable and available communication channel between systems, so it is critical that the network providing this link be correctly sized to meet capacity requirements. This chapter explores network capacity, offering strategies and best practices that show how to assess its current characteristics and potential, and how to look ahead to its changes and limitations as the network grows.

This chapter explains how to use the ideas and methods discussed in Chapters 1 and 2, to assess the state (current and projected) of your network.

In Focus

Enterprise
A modest but impeccable department store, AB Pound & Co.

Network
AB Pound & Co.'s network consists of two subnets (one on each floor of the building) connected by a backbone.

Challenge
To gather information on network traffic, array it meaningfully, assess it, and use it to plan for a network that can handle normal capacity effectively.

Solution
Categorize traffic (background vs. transactional), discover its patterns as they relate to network use, and use an understanding of general and specific aspects to assess capacity requirements.

What You'll Find In This Chapter

- **A discussion on understanding network capacity.**
- **Ways to assess the sorts of traffic that are moving through your network.**
- **Methods for gauging the relative predictability of different traffic types.**
- **An introduction of Network Monitor, a tool you can use for capacity planning.**

Is this Really Necessary?

Network planning can be compared to designing a town's road system. In both tasks, you need to understand who is using which routes, how large batches of traffic are (and can be), where journeys start, where they stop, and how all of these things vary over time. If a road system doesn't have enough lanes, traffic jams up and people get delayed and testy; if each road has 20 lanes, you can stop worrying about traffic jams and start worrying about bankruptcy or about the possibility that the mere presence of all those extra lanes may encourage more traffic, ultimately causing problems for smaller roads connected to the big ones. If you under-size the network, things slow down and eventually stop. People get delayed and unhappy. If you over-size it, you waste money and invite problems further up the network.

Proper network capacity planning (like road planning) starts with careful capacity measurement. You need to monitor and assess the number and type of vehicles (whether cars or packets) using the system.

Are There Risks of Doing It?

It is part of the rich texture of life that even doing the right thing can have associated risks. When you undertake network capacity planning you need to be confident that your results are correct and reliable. If, for instance, you announce that a network has ten times the capacity it will ever need, you invite users to load anything they want onto the wire.

Some key risks:

- **Getting the figures wrong.** A simple thing such as inaccurately adding up a row of numbers can be expensive if it impels you to upgrade unnecessarily from a 64-K line to a T1.
- **Spending too much time trying to predict the unpredictable.** Sometimes the nature of your business is simply unpredictable. If this is true, it can often cost you more to make misguided attempts at scientific quantification than to guesstimate usage, monitor the network, and tinker.

Are There Risks of *Not* Doing It?

Of course. The network is a critical conduit—if it stops working, the enterprise often stops working as well. It is far better to anticipate problems than simply to encounter them.

Some key risks:

- **Wasting Time.** Not all problems can be solved through capacity analysis. You don't want to waste time looking in the wrong place for a solution, and you may not even know when you don't understand which issues are relevant to which factors.
- **Lost Productivity or Opportunity.** Many businesses, particularly in the securities industry, rely on near instantaneous transaction completion. Delays can be expensive.

Approach

First off, you have to find and examine network traffic. There are two basic types:

- **Background traffic.** This is a by-product of the infrastructure. For example: when you map a drive to a network share, the keep-alive packets between PC and server are background traffic.
- **Transactional/functional traffic.** This is generated when a task is performed. For example: a bank teller enters a deposit for a customer.

There are several ways to categorize network traffic. As you discern types based on other criteria, you need to know if they are background or transactional so that you can understand their frequency and nature.

The Daily Task List

Another category of traffic contains high-level tasks that people perform daily as part of their job. These vary from company to company of course, but to get a feel for the types here is an example—a stock clerk in the Electronics department of the AB Pound & Co. The clerk's high-level objective is to ensure that the department holds enough stock to meet its sales objectives. To accomplish this, he performs these tasks on a typical day:

- Logs on
- Reads e-mail
- Checks task list
- Reviews stock level
- Places stock orders
- Pays suppliers
- Produces standard letters to inform customers that orders are in.
- Reads e–mail
- Logs off

An analysis of this traffic would also look at *when* tasks are completed during a typical day.

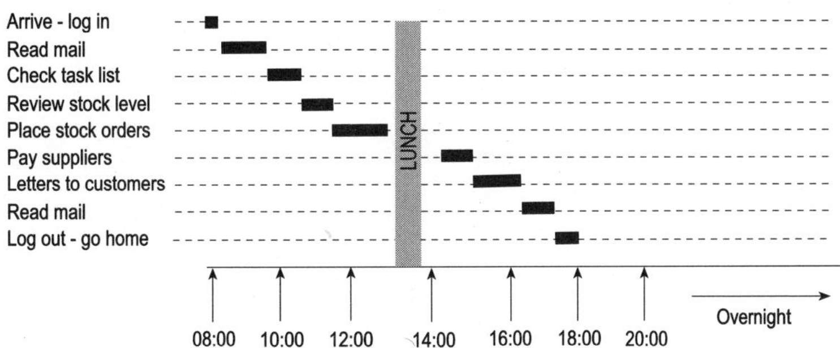

Figure 3.1 Daily tasks that create network traffic—time distribution.

Figure 3.1 profiles one type of user. Now all you have to do is repeat the process for each type of user so that you create a comprehensive set of profiles. AB Pound & Co., for example, has:

- Sales assistants
- Managers
- Stock clerks
- Secretaries
- Human resources workers
- Warehouse personnel
- Maintenance

Once you create a profile for each role, scale them up to the numbers of workers in each role.

AB Pound & Co. user profiles and quantities—in general.

Role	Average Net Traffic p/hour	Total Number of Users	Average Network per Hour
Sales Assistants	700 K	420	294 Mb
Managers	60 K	40	2.4 Mb
Stock Clerks	6 Mb	26	156 Mb
Secretarial	2 Mb	8	16 Mb
Human Resources	4 Mb	6	24 Mb
Warehouse Personnel	400 K	30	12 Mb
Maintenance	20 K	20	400 K
TOTAL			**504.8Mb/hour**
			140k/sec

This is helps you see the average load on the network as a whole, which is important, but you also need to understand how potential traffic flow relates to the location of users, lines, and servers.

It so happens that AB Pound & Co. has two floors, each with a network, and a backbone that runs between them. Now the table can be rewritten this way:

AB Pound & Co. user profiles and quantities—by floor.

AB Pound & Co. user profiles and quantities—by floor.

Floor	Role	Average Net Traffic p/hour	Total Number of Users	Average Network per Hour
One	Sales Assistants	700 K	300	210 Mb
	Managers	60 K	30	1.8 Mb
	Stock Clerks	6 Mb	16	96 Mb
	Secretarial	2 Mb	0	0
	Human Resources	4 Mb	0	0
	Warehouse Personnel	400 K	30	12 Mb
	Maintenance	20 K	20	400 K
	TOTAL Floor 1 Net			**320.2Mb/hour**
				89K/sec

AB Pound & Co. user profiles and quantities—by floor. *(continued)*

Floor	Role	Average Net Traffic p/hour	Total Number of Users	Average Network per Hour
Two	Sales Assistants	700 K	120	84 Mb
	Managers	60 K	10	600 K
	Stock Clerks	6 Mb	10	60 Mb
	Secretarial	2 Mb	8	16 Mb
	Human Resources	4 Mb	6	24 Mb
	Warehouse Personnel	400 K	0	0
	Maintenance	20 K	0	0
	TOTAL Floor 2 Net			**184.6 Mb/hour**
				52K/sec
Backbone	**Server Room**			**504.8 Mb/hour**
	= Floor 1 + Floor 2			**140 K/sec**

This gives a good idea of average network load an hour for each floor. The next question is: when does traffic flow throughout the day? Does it happen at the same time each day or does it vary throughout the day? Throughout the week?

To derive this information, you need to complete the above tables on an hourly basis each day of the week. This can be a huge undertaking and before you get started you should know that, unfortunately, your results may not reflect reality. Very few companies have consistent identifiable hourly traffic patterns that vary in any meaningful way. Not surprisingly, very few companies take the time to take a complete hourly-traffic profile.

It may be useful, however, to take a look at the couple hours in the morning when most people arrive (if this is relevant) and to sample around to see if you can identify any other peaks or valleys in normal usage.

AB Pound & Co., for instance, found a surge on Monday mornings as people came in to shop after reading about sales in the Sunday newspaper. Although traffic often surges in networks on Mondays (particularly after extended weekends) the results in this case proved insignificant in the big picture. This is to say that the increases were neither frequent nor large enough to justify design changes or expensive implementation. The opening salvos on major sale days also showed measurably increased loading, but these figures, too, failed to warrant expansion. Once, a popular local mall experienced problems, and as a result many shoppers came to the more dependable venue of AB Pound & Co., but this, too, was (an unfortunate) anomaly warranting no design accommodation.

If you have a feel for the rhythms of your business you can make intelligent guesses about this kind of thing.

Peak Workload Modeling

An alternative approach is to identify the peak days for each role in each department, measure the traffic, and tabulate it. If you use these figures for capacity planning, the network should then be able to cope with peak traffic in all departments simultaneously. This may be too much capability, depending on the nature of the peaks you observe. Furthermore, actual figures may show that peaks seldom overlap so there is no need to plan for them doing so. AB Pound & Co, for instance, found that:

- Sales assistants are busiest on Saturdays, when they make the most sales and take the most orders.
- Stock clerks are busiest on Mondays, when they place orders with suppliers.
- The warehouse is busiest on Wednesdays, when they take the most deliveries from suppliers.
- Human Resources is busiest at the end of the month, when they pay employees.
- Other roles demonstrate no identifiable peaks.

AB Pound & Co. user profiles and quantities—adjusted totals.

Floor	Role	Average Net Traffic p/hour	Total Number of Users	Average Network per Hour
One	Sales assistants (Saturday)	1Mb	300	300 Mb
	Managers	60 K	30	1.8 Mb
	Stock clerks (Monday)	10 Mb	16	160 Mb
	Secretarial	2 Mb	0	0
	Human Resources (End of Month)	15 Mb	0	0
	Warehouse (Wednesday)	800 K	30	24 Mb
	Maintenance	20 K	20	400 K
	TOTAL Floor 1 Net			**320.2Mb p/hour**
				89k p/sec

AB Pound & Co. user profiles and quantities—adjusted totals. *(continued)*

Floor	Role	Average Net Traffic p/hour	Total Number of Users	Average Network per Hour
Two	Sales Assistants	1 Mb	120	120 Mb
	Managers	60 K	10	600 K
	Stock Clerks (Monday)	10 Mb	10	100 Mb
	Secretarial	2 Mb	8	16 Mb
	Human Resources (End of month)	15 Mb	6	45 Mb
	Warehouse (Wednesday)	800 K	0	0
	Maintenance	20 K	0	0
	TOTAL Floor 2 Net			**184.6 Mb/hour**
				52 K/sec
Backbone	**Server Room**			**504.8 Mb/hour**
	= Floor 1 + Floor 2			**140 K/sec**

Map Tasks to Topology

The next step is to look at the physical IT infrastructure, including the network topology, to get an understanding of where the servers are in relation to the clients that use them. In short: how the network is constructed.

Things begin to get difficult along about now. You know who works in the company, where they are, what they do, and when they do it. You need to map this information onto the network's physical topology so that you can work out which task causes which traffic and how much of the total is background traffic.

The only guarantee is that whatever you work out is at best an approximation and is at worst wrong, so you need to identify and allow for variables that can affect the accuracy of your calculation.

Map Background Traffic

You have to map background traffic (keep-alive packets, replication, etc.) to topology, too. First, identify all existing network services, list them, and identify the locations that use them. Cover at least:

Background traffic types.

Traffic type	Description
DHCP	Traffic generated during IP address acquisition, renewal, and release.
WINS	Traffic generated during NetBIOS name registration, resolution, renewal, and release.
Logon validation	Traffic generated by a user logging on to the network and being validated by a domain controller.
Browser	Traffic generated by a client registering itself as a possible provider of network resources, retrieving a list of backup browsers, a list of servers on the network, and a list of resources on a server.
File session	Traffic generated when two computers set up a session.
Domain Name System (DNS)	Traffic generated by Transmission Control Protocol/Internet Protocol (TCP/IP) hosts during TCP/IP host-name resolution. Usually generated by TCP/IP utilities such as Ping and Telnet, or applications such as Internet Explorer.
Internet browsing	Traffic generated by the Internet Explorer browser application to download pages from a Web site.

Some application traffic, too, runs in the background:

- Exchange
- Microsoft SQL Server
- Microsoft Systems Management Server
- Microsoft SNA Server

There are two basic types: server-to-server and client-to-server. If your configuration isolates servers in a computer room to reduce total cost of ownership (TCO), it is relatively easy to tell one type from the other when you look at the combined traffic.

Example

AB Pound & Co. put all of its servers in a computer room connected to the client systems over a backbone. All server-to-client traffic has to cross the backbone, so it is easy to identify and isolate it. The trick is to link it to a *particular client.* Here's the method for completing the model:

- Size each application that runs on any client.
- Identify which network segment each client is on.
- Calculate the total amount of background traffic generated for each network segment.
- Combine the total of each segment to calculate the total potential load on the backbone.

Adding up the network segment loads to calculate the backbone load doesn't always give an accurate answer, because the true total depends on more than just packets: it also is influenced by network topology, particularly if network segments route onto the backbone and some degree of traffic filtering is applied. However adding segment volumes makes for a useful worst-case scenario. Any variance probably will represent an improvement.

Numerous technical sources supply information you can put to good use when sizing background traffic. Search Microsoft TechNet for the string *capacity planning network traffic*.

To calculate server-to-server background traffic you have to model the applications that run and the amount of background traffic that each produces.

Broadcast Traffic

Broadcast traffic (Internet-Protocol (IP) datagrams sent to all hosts on the subnet) is often overlooked, but it can have a major effect on all client-server systems. Broadcast frames result in hardware interrupts, which result in CPU activity. At some critical CPU loading level, the system seizes up. Short of total breakdown, which is thankfully rare, broadcast traffic merely grinds things down.

When a computer system receives a datagram, hardware makes the first filtering decision. The network interface card discards all frames not carrying its system address, then passes all frames (including broadcasts) that do have this address to the NIC driver through a hardware interrupt. The NIC driver is software, so any frames that make it this far cost some CPU processing time.

Sometimes a network shows very low traffic levels and sufficient capacity to look healthy, but analysis of the broadcast traffic levels shows enough to seriously degrade system performance. A system's ability to cope with broadcast traffic depends on its configuration and what other sorts of traffic it is dealing with at the time.

It is easy to measure how excessive broadcast traffic affects a system. Connect two PCs to an isolated network. Put Microsoft Network Monitor (a tool explained below) on one of the systems to generate broadcast frames, and run Microsoft Performance Monitor on the other to monitor the processor time usage levels and interrupts/sec. You can watch these values climb if you gradually increase the number of broadcast frames. The system running Performance Monitor starts to act sluggish and eventually stops responding altogether.

Bottlenecks

Wouldn't it be nice if there were never any bottlenecks on your way to work? No traffic lights, fender benders, car problems, detours, people pulling out in front of you, four lane highways narrowing down to one lane presided over by a lethargic flagman. Stop wishing: it isn't going to happen. And it's not going to happen with your computer system either. Sooner or later the system will reach its limit and getting data onto the network or through a router will take longer…and longe...

As easy as they are to spot, bottlenecks are not easy to predict, but they generally occur where one network is connected to another network—at a router, hub, switch, or server.

There are two types: those that affect a single client and those that affect multiple clients or network segments. The first type is usually easily identified and solved, because it almost always is the result of a single capacity problem: an overloaded server, a wire so packed with bits that nothing can move, etc.

Multiple-effect bottlenecks are usually harder to find because they may be the result of one problem or many. Figuring one of these out usually requires a lot of investigation and carefully documented results. Part of the effort is required to isolate the problem so it can be predicted (maybe it is the result of a unique or anomalous event) and, if necessary solved. And part of the effort is required to help the network manager to justify the perhaps considerable expenditure needed to solve it.

There are a number of areas to examine when you look for bottlenecks. Are any components between a client and server running at 100% utilization? This is a clear warning of bottleneck potential but does not necessarily mean that there *is* a bottleneck. This usage may represent only a spike, and thus be temporary. And if the max-ed out device is not preventing any other resource from getting its work done—if nothing is waiting for it—then it is not a bottleneck and doubling bandwidth will cost money but will not affect the condition. On the other hand, you can have bottlenecks on devices utilized well below 100 percent.

Trace the paths through the network looking at the points of interconnection. Some examples may be:

- Suppose all the network segments connected to a given router are running well within their capacity but the router simply cannot forward the number of packets it receives. NetMon would not show you this. You would have to run the router management software.
- Look for unacceptable broadcast traffic levels. (See the "Broadcast Traffic" section above.)
- Network contention (more than one system attempting to transmit data onto a network at the same time) can cause problems in Ethernet cables. Look for high collision rates.

A good bottleneck strategy has to vary from network to network, but every one should include a certain degree of monitoring designed to find backups before they cripple the system.

Scalability and Predicting the Future

Capacity planning should, within certain practical limits, help you predict the future. Once you know how your network looks today you can experimentally change some values and work out how it might look in the future, and, more importantly, how well the network might cope with specific changes.

Suppose AB Pound & Co., for instance, expands its store by adding a third floor. This means 150 new client systems and a new server. To calculate how the network will cope, the analysts can try extending the current set of spreadsheets. Some enlightened guesswork can probably help them project network loading, predict traffic patterns, and adapt the infrastructure so as to reduce or avoid bottlenecks. At the very least they can get some idea of how network performance levels will change and how network access can be kept at acceptable levels.

Network Monitor

Capacity planning requires tools. Which tools you need is in part dictated by the approach you plan to take. If your network is business-critical you may need to buy additional packages of analytical tools, but Windows NT provides some very good tools for general analysis. Chief among these is Network Monitor. A scaled-down version of NetMon is packaged with Windows NT; a more robust version ships with Systems Management Server. The differences are discussed in Chapter 1. Complete instructions on using NetMon are in the Windows NT Server *Concepts and Planning Manual*, "Chapter 10: Monitoring Your Network," and the *Windows NT Server 4.0 Resource Kit*, Supplement 1 "Chapter 7: Monitoring Bandwidth and Network Capacity."

You install the NetMon Agent driver onto a network card in a Windows NT system. This sets the card in promiscuous mode, which allows the monitor to watch all network packets that go through the system—even packets for other destination systems are copied and passed up to the NetMon Application.

How can seeing everything that crosses the wire help with capacity planning? Because to plan for capacity you need to understand what traffic the network handles on a continuing basis, and this requires that you analyze background and functional/transactional tasks completely, and NetMon provides the information you need for a full load analysis of each task.

For instance, AB Pound & Co., has approximately 25,850 silk ties on display, so of course a customer must have one that is available, he thinks, but not in one of the cases, he knows. It is a garish thing, but the customer is always right, so the clerk logs onto a PC, enters the stock description, uses it to find the stock code, calls up the on-line order form, fills it out, and submits it. This transaction involves several activities, each of which can generate network traffic:

- a log on (plus authentication)
- a search for a stock item (matching fields from the form to the database)
- a response from the server (with information about the horrid tie in question)
- an order entry/submission (which involve a number of client/server transactions)
- a log-off (maybe)

NetMon can tell you how much traffic is generated at each step, and it can tell you in an extremely specific and accurate way if you perform each activity and trace it separately. From there it is a short extrapolation to calculate average numbers of tasks, at which point you are well on the way to establishing traffic levels and deriving a sense of required network capacity.

Network Monitor Interface

The first NetMon window to appear is the Capture window, which presents the UI menus and toolbar, and four panes of statistics you can use to analyze overall network performance:

Capture Window's four panes.

Pane	Description
Graph	Displays the current activity as a set of bar charts indicating the % of network utilization, the frames per second, bytes per second, broadcasts per second, and multicasts per second during the capture process.
Session Statistics	Displays the summary of the conversations between two hosts, and which host is initiating broadcasts and multicasts.
Total Statistics	Displays statistics for the traffic detected on the network as a whole, the statistics for the frames captured, per second utilization statistics, and network adapter card statistics.
Station Statistics	Displays a summary of the total number of frames initiated by a host, the number of frames and bytes sent and received, and the number of broadcast and multicast frames initiated.

Capturing Data

There are three methods:

- From the **Capture** menu, click **Start**.
- Click the **Start Capture** button on the toolbar.
- Press the F10 function key.

As data is captured, the four panes in the Capture window display current network statistics as well as statistics for the captured data.

To stop the capture, use one of three methods:

- From the **Capture** menu, click **Stop**.
- Click the **Stop Capture** button on the toolbar.
- Press the F11 function key.

You can set a capture filter that describes which frames are to be captured, buffered, displayed, and saved. Filters are commonly configured either for specific types of traffic (protocols), such as IP, IPX, VINES, and so on, or on source or destination addresses—media access control (hardware) addresses or protocol addresses (IP or IPX). You can see the value of being able to filter captures in this way. AB Pound & Co., for instance, wanted to measure server-to-client traffic over the backbone, but was confronted with the problem of figuring which portion of pipeline traffic was for which client. Filtering by address can isolate this type of traffic so that you can observe it as a separate component of overall traffic flow.

If you don't want to analyze data as soon as it is captured, you can save it to a capture file (with suffix .CAP) for later analysis or to create a record of system performance.

Configuring Capture Triggers

When troubleshooting, you may want to configure a capture trigger, which directs NetMon to perform an action in response to a certain event or condition: a buffer being filled completely or to a specified amount, a pattern match, a pattern match then buffer space, or buffer space and then a pattern match. For example, suppose a client computer is having difficulty transferring a file from a server. You capture the session, and the results show that every time a specific data pattern is transferred during the session, the transfer stops. Once NetMon fills its buffers, it overwrites previously collected data, and if you can't find the frames leading up to the suspect data pattern because they have been overwritten (by data captured afterwards) you can set a trigger to stop the capture when it has recorded the event you are interested in. You can also set different responses to triggers: complete an action, capture data, perform a command, notify the administrator, etc.

Displaying Data

There are three methods:

- From the **Capture** menu, click **Display Captured Data.**
- Choose the **Display Captured Data** toolbar button.
- Press the F12 function key.

Summary Pane (Top)

This lists all frames included in the current view of the captured data. When a frame is highlighted in the Summary pane, NetMon displays its contents in the **Detail** and **Hex** panes. You can add colors to highlight specific frames.

You can use mouse clicks to sort, move, and resize the pane's nine columns:

- **Frame**. All frames captured during one session are numbered in the order of capture time. The frame number appears in this column.
- **Time**. The frame's capture time relative to the beginning of the capture process. It can be configured to display the time of day when the frame was captured, or time elapsed since the previous frame capture.
- **Src MAC Addr (Source media access control (MAC) Address)**. The hardware address of the computer that sent the frame.
- **Dst MAC Addr (Destination MAC Address)**. The hardware address of the target computer.
- **Protocol**. The protocol used to transmit the frame.

- **Description**. A summary of the frame's contents. This can show the first protocol used in that frame, the last protocol used, or an automatic selection.
- **Src Other Addr (Source Other Address)**. An additional identifying address for the originator of the frame, other than the MAC address. This might be an IP or IPX address.
- **Dst Other Addr (Destination Other Address)**. The frame's destination.
- **Type Other Addr (Type Other Address)**. The type of address displayed in the previous two columns—IP or Internetwork Packet Exchange (IPX).

Detail Pane (Middle)

This pane displays protocol information for the frame currently highlighted in the Summary pane. When a frame contains several protocol layers, the Detail pane displays the outermost level first.

When you select a protocol in the Detail pane, the frame's associated hexadecimal strings are highlighted (in the same color as that used for the protocol) in the Hex pane. If a protocol has a plus sign (+) beside it, you can display more information in the Detail pane by clicking on the +, by double-clicking the protocol, or by highlighting the protocol, and pressing ENTER. The expanded protocol information shows a line of data for each property associated with that frame.

Hexadecimal Pane (Bottom)

This pane displays in hexadecimal format the content of the selected frame. When information is highlighted in the Detail pane, the hexadecimal equivalent appears highlighted in the Hex pane. You may end up studying this data carefully, especially when you are attempting to determine the application programming interface (API) call used in a transaction.

Highlighting Displayed Data

The Capture Summary window displays a summary of all frames captured, and this sometimes is too much data, making the analysis difficult. There are several ways to highlight specific data.

Adding Color to Frames

You can color specific frames. For example, coloring all browser frames can provide a quick visual scan of how many frames were created by browser announcements. To color captured data:

- On the **Display** menu, click **Colors**.
- The **Protocol Colors** dialog box appears.
- Under **Name**, click the protocol(s) you want to color.
- Under **Colors**, set Foreground or Background to the color of choice.
- Click **OK**.

Implementing a Display Filter

A display separates out frames of interest, such as those from a particular host, or those using a particular protocol. You can configure display filters for protocols, for MAC or protocol addresses, or for unique frame properties (such as source or destination port). To configure:

1. On the **Display** menu, click **Filter**. The **Display Filter** dialog box appears.
2. Click either the **Protocol == Any** or **ANY <-> ANY** expression.
3. Under **Edit**, click **Operator/Expression**. The **Expression** dialog box appears.
4. Click the **Address**, **Protocol**, or **Property** tab.
5. Configure the filter as appropriate for the address, protocol or property.
6. Click **OK** twice. The **Capture Summary** window displays only the data passed by the display filter.

To go back to displaying all captured data, either return the display filter to default (by loading DEFAULT.DF) or on the **Display** menu click **Disable Filter**.

Saving and Printing Captured Data

Network Monitor has built-in saving and printing capabilities. These are useful for any number of reasons. For example, the data does not have to be captured *and* analyzed by the same person. And when you are analyzing how a specific function affects network traffic, you probably will need the results of several captures to make an accurate assessment.

You can always print captures and save them, but data often is more useful (easier to manipulate, for instance) in soft copy, and NetMon gives you several options for saving captured data. If you configure a filter to display only data between a specific client and a specific server, you can save the entire capture or just the data that passes the filter. Or you can save only a specific range of frames. Suppose you are analyzing a large data capture, and you are interested in a specific conversation that occurs in frames 17–21: NetMon allows you to save just those frames in a file that you can analyze later.

To save captured data:

1. On the **File** menu, click **Save As**. The **Save Data As** dialog box appears.
2. Under **File Name**, type a name that represents the data in the capture.
3. If a display filter has been implemented, click **Filtered**.
4. If a range of frames is to be saved, under **Range**, type the **From** and **To** values as appropriate.
5. Click **OK**.

Determining Network Resources

The full version of Network Monitor included with Systems Management Server 1.2 offers more sophisticated features to use when determining network usage:

Finding Top User

The **Find Top Users** option on the **Capture Summary** window's **Tools** menu lists in order the computers that sent or received the highest number of frames in a capture. It also includes the bytes transmitted and received, as well as their percentages of the total.

Finding Top Protocol Distribution

The **Protocol Distribution** option on the **Capture Summary** window's **Tools** menu displays the protocol that generated the most network traffic in the capture, by frames or bytes. This also includes their percentages of the total.

Finding Routers

The **Find Routers** option on the **Capture Summary** window's **Tools** menu scans the capture and determines which network devices are routers, identifying them as Service Advertising Protocol (SAP), Browser, Routing Information Protocol over IPX (RIPX), IP, Open Shortest Path First (OSPF), or Raster Image Processor (RIP). You can invoke an interactive version of this function from the **Network Monitor Capture** window.

Finding MAC Address from Name

The **Resolving Addresses From Name** option on the **Capture Summary** window's **Tools** menu queries the network using Domain Name System (DNS), NetBIOS name resolution, and the local NetMon database to display the MAC address associated with a name. You can also use it to query SAP and Systems Management Server databases. This function is also available on the **Network Monitor Capture** window's **Tool** menu.

Remote Capturing

Normally, routers block traffic from moving between subnets unless destined for another network, so troubleshooting a problem on a remote network can be difficult. But NetMon has two components (application and agent) and by installing the agent on a remote computer, then attaching the application to it, you can see and analyze all traffic that appears on the remote network.

Installing the Agent

Separate NetMon agents allow either a Windows 9*x* or a Windows NT (3.5*x* and later) client to be the agent on a remote subnet.

To install the agent on Windows NT, in Control Panel click **Network** and **Add Network Monitor Agent**. This software is included with Windows NT 3.5*x* and later.

To install the agent on Windows 9*x*, start Control Panel and click **Network**. Click **Add**, and then click **Service**. Under **Manufacturers** click **Microsoft**, and then click **Have Disk**. In the **Install From Disk** dialog box type the path *Admin\Nettools\Netmon* on the Windows 95 compact disc. **Microsoft Network Monitor Agent** will appear as the service name to install.

Starting the Agent

The agent must be started before it can be used to capture network traffic.

On Windows NT, use the **Services** dialog box to start the agent. By default, it is configured for manual starting.

On Windows 9*x*, start System\NMAGENT.EXE whenever the agent is required.

Connecting to the Remote Agent

Once the remote agent has been started, connecting the application to it starts the data capture. The agent buffers the data locally then transmits it to the application when requested.

To connect to a remote agent:

1. On the **Capture** menu, click **Networks**. The **Select Capture Network** dialog box is displayed.
2. Click **REMOTE**, and then click **Connect**. The **Connect To Network Monitoring Agent** dialog box is displayed.
3. In the **Agent Name** box, type the remote computer name, and then click **Connect**. The **Network Monitor Capture** window displays the name of the remote agent computer.

Data is buffered and is not sent from the remote two agent to the local application until the capture is stopped, although (by default) the remote agent sends statistics to the application every two seconds. The updates generate some network activity, which you can decrease by decreasing the update frequency. To return to capturing on the local host, disconnect the remote connection and reconnect to the local network.

Comparing Network Protocols

Protocol can affect how much network traffic a function generates. Some protocols such as NWLink base much of their traffic on broadcasts, while others such as Transmission Control Protocol/Internet Protocol (TCP/IP) use more directed frames. Broadcast traffic can have an impact on a WAN, the severity of which depends on whether broadcasts are forwarded by the routers throughout the enterprise. If they are not, some functions will operate on the local network but not have complete functionality throughout the enterprise; if they are, complete functionality is available but WAN traffic is increased.

Microsoft recommends TCP/IP. Designed to avoid the disadvantages of protocols such as NetBEUI, it reduces traffic by delivering directed datagrams rather than broadcast packets.

Best Practices

How much effort (time and cost) should you invest in capacity planning? The answer to this is fairly straightforward although it takes some thinking: calculate how critical the network is to your organization and then calculate how severely network failure will affect your business. The closer this correlation, the more important capacity planning. If your network is less than critical, live monitoring may provide you with enough information and you can let it go at that.

Regardless of the depth of your analysis and planning effort, here are some practices derived in the field:

- Identify your business requirements and how critical the network is to their realization. Can the organization operate without its network? How long? To what degree will operation be curtailed or compromised?
- Identify the key user tasks. If possible, gather data to build a daily task timetable. With some tinkering, you can take into account hours of operation, days of the week, and other factors to get a fairly accurate look at regular network traffic. You may not understand the network's enterprise role accurately until you look at what is done, by whom, when, and how.
- Use Network Monitor to measure the amount of network activity that occurs for each of these tasks and record the results in a spreadsheet.
- Identify network topology and the location of clients and servers. Calculate the basic background traffic client-to-server and server-to-server, then map these onto a spreadsheet by segment (floors in a building, separate buildings, etc.—some segementation scheme usually, but not necessarily, based on subnets).
- Multiply the total for each task by the number resources completing this task and add these to the spreadsheet.
- If the network is absolutely critical, use peak loading figures. Use average loading figures otherwise.
- Look for bottlenecks.
- Calculate how the network will scale and see if you can identify the point at which you will run out of capacity. Scenarios can help with this task. So can Performance Monitor, a tool you can use to observe network load over periods of time and under varying circumstances.

PART 2

Real-World Network Infrastructure Scenarios

The chapters in this section draw on the experience Microsoft Consulting Services (MCS) has built up through extensive collaboration with enterprise customers. Each chapter begins with a synopsis of the facts of the case study and the challenge presented by the job at hand. The discussion that follows details the technical design and implementation that were developed to optimize network infrastructure. Chapters 4, 5, and 6 explore tuning Windows NT Server for branch offices, dial-on-demand configurations, and satellite networking. Chapter 7 steps back and looks at the broader perspective, examining how to plan for traffic in a wide area network design. Chapter 8 explains how to structure Systems Management Server installation jobs over slow links. Chapter 9 returns to the expertise of Microsoft's Information Technology Group to show how application design can affect network performance and traffic.

CHAPTER 4

Tuning Windows NT Server in Branch Offices at GlobalNet Insurance

By Matthew Storer, MCS—Great Lakes

Today, organizations with branch offices connected by a wide area network (WAN) need an inexpensive distributed computing solution to stay competitive. Although Microsoft Windows NT provides branch offices with low-cost file and print services, Internet and intranet connectivity, and electronic messaging, you may still find that supporting WAN functionality increases your costs.

This chapter shows you how to reduce WAN costs associated with Windows NT networking traffic, reviewing ways to optimize the NetLogon service, Network Basic Input/Output System (NetBIOS) name resolution and browsing, printer browsing, server message block (SMB) connections, and the licensing service.

In Focus

Enterprise
GlobalNet Insurance has branch offices in North America and Europe.

Network
4500 backup domain controllers (BDCs) connected across the WAN using Remote Access Services (RAS).

Challenge
Configuring Windows NT Server for optimal intranet communications in branch offices, reducing the WAN traffic, improving overall WAN throughput, and reducing on-demand line costs such as ISDN and analog.

Solution
To reduce startup costs and the time to deliver a distributed solution based on Windows NT Server, GlobalNet used Windows NT RAS and dial-on-demand routers, connecting branch offices and remote users to the corporate network.

What You'll Find In This Chapter

- **Descriptions of registry settings and their parameters.**
- **Techniques to optimize Windows NT services over the WAN, as implemented by GlobalNet Insurance.**

Warning This chapter makes recommendations for tuning the Windows NT registry using the Registry Editor. Using the Registry Editor incorrectly can cause serious, system-wide problems that require you to reinstall Windows NT. Microsoft cannot guarantee that any problems resulting from the use of Registry Editor can be solved. Use this tool at your own risk.

NetLogon Service Optimization

The NetLogon service automatically synchronizes changes in the Windows NT directory database stored on the primary domain controller (PDC) to all backup domain controllers (BDCs). Based on settings in the registry, the PDC sends timed notices that signal the BDCs to request changes at the same time. When a BDC requests changes, it informs the PDC of the last change it received so that the PDC can determine whether a BDC needs updating. If a BDC is up to date, its NetLogon service does not request changes.

Windows NT Domain Directory Synchronization

The NetLogon service synchronizes three domain directory databases: the security accounts manager (SAM) accounts database, the SAM built-in database, and the Local Security Authority (LSA) license database.

Definition of domain directory databases.

Database	What information it contains
SAM accounts	Microsoft domain user and group accounts that you create. Includes all computer accounts added to the domain, such as domain controllers (DCs) and Windows NT computers.
SAM built-in	Local machine built-in user and group accounts, such as Administrator, Domain Admins, and so forth.
LSA	LSA Secrets that are used for trust relationships and DC computer account passwords. Also includes the account policy settings that you configure.

Synchronization occurs:

- When a backup domain controller is initialized or restarted in the domain.
- When "forced" by a network administrator using Server Manager.
- Automatically by the DCs, depending upon Windows NT registry configuration.

Change Log

The **change log** records changes to the domain-directory databases, including new or modified passwords, user and group and accounts, and group membership and user rights. Its size determines how many changes the log can hold, *and* for how long. Typically the change log holds about 2,000 changes, keeping only the most recent changes, deleting the oldest ones first. When a BDC requests changes, it receives only changes that occurred since the last synchronization.

The NetLogon service checks for updates every five minutes (default). If a BDC does not request changes in a timely way, the entire domain directory must be copied to that BDC. For example, if a BDC is offline for a time (such as for system repair), more changes could occur during that timeframe than can be stored in the change log.

Partial and Full Synchronization

Partial synchronization consists of the automatic, timed replication of directory database changes to all BDCs since the last synchronization. **Full synchronization** copies the entire directory database to a BDC; it takes place automatically when changes have been deleted from the change log before replication, or when you add a new BDC to a domain.

Both the NetLogon Service updates and the change log size ensure that full synchronization does not start up under most operating conditions. In the WAN environment, you can control and refine NetLogon activity, using the Windows NT registry entries and methods described below.

One way to reduce the number of full synchronizations is to build BDCs at the corporate network site so that the full directory database can be quickly transferred from a PDC to BDCs. You can then send the new BDC to the branch office and put it into service as soon as possible (within 3-6 days of dispatch). When the new BDC starts up, it contacts the PDC to obtain any directory database changes that occurred while the BDC was offline.

Modifications to Registry Settings

This section describes changes to registry settings that you can make on the BDC that the network promotes in case the PDC becomes unavailable. (These settings are for the PDC and the BDCs targeted for promotion.) The Windows NT registry settings discussed are located in the subkey:

HKEY_LOCAL_MACHINE\Services\NetLogon\Parameters.

You must restart the domain controller for these changes to take effect.

Warning Using Registry Editor incorrectly can cause serious, system-wide problems that require you to reinstall Windows NT. Microsoft cannot guarantee that any problems resulting from the use of Registry Editor can be solved. Use this tool at your own risk.

ChangeLogSize

ChangeLogSize defines the log size (in bytes). Because the change log exists both in memory and on disk (%SystemRoot%\NETLOGON.CHG), increasing its size consumes more disk space and virtual memory, but causes no other problems. Entries into the log represent changes to the SAM and LSA databases, which are maintained with a circular buffer.

In a large organization with many users who frequently change passwords, the change log can quickly reach its limit (default is 64 KB, about 2000 changes, averaging 32 bytes per change), causing new entries to overwrite changes *not yet synchronized.* This can force a full synchronization to start up, generating excess traffic because more information is copied to BDCs than is necessary.

ChangeLogSize registry parameters.

PDC change	BDC change	Default	Minimum	Maximum
X		65536	65536	4194304

Recommendation:

Set the ChangeLogSize to greater than 65536. For example, setting the ChangeLogSize to 4,194,304 bytes (4 megabytes) supports approximately 131,072 change log entries, and does not degrade DC system performance.

- Increase ChangeLogSize if full synchronization becomes prohibitively expensive.
- Increase ChangeLogSize if you expect that one or more BDCs will not requested a partial synchronization within 2,000 changes.

Pulse

Pulse controls how often a PDC looks for changes to its directory services database and sends synchronization messages to BDCs that need updating. The default value equals five minutes (stored in seconds), which you can increase to a maximum of 17200 (48 hours).

The NetLogon service collects all SAM and LSA changes made within the Pulse period, and sends pulses only to BDCs needing the changes. When the NetLogon service starts up, the PDC sends a pulse to every BDC with a machine account. The PDC also forces a pulse once each period according to the **PulseMaximum** frequency (default 7200 seconds—see the "PulseMaximum" section below), regardless of any other information the PDC has collected about the status of the BDC.

Pulse registry parameters.

PDC change	BDC change	Default	Minimum	Maximum
X		300	60	

Recommendation:

Increase this parameter above 300 to ensure that PDCs do not constantly attempt to contact every BDC. In a branch office environment, such as GlobalNet, you can set the Pulse to its maximum value of 172800 (48 hours).

Issues to consider:

- Increasing the pulse parameter raises the risk of a BDC's machine account password expiring. To resolve this, you can disable the machine account password parameter. See the "DisablePasswordChange" section for more information.
- Setting the value high can result in BDCs that do not synchronize with the PDC for a long period of time, causing a full synchronization to start up or a "gap" in receiving timely security updates.

PulseConcurrency

PulseConcurrency defines the maximum number of simultaneous pulses a PDC sends to BDCs. When the NetLogon service sends pulses to BDCs, each BDC responds asking for any database changes. NetLogon controls the maximum load these responses can place on the PDC by having only the defined number of PulseConcurrency pulses "pending" at one time. You must ensure that PDCs have sufficient power to support concurrent replication remote procedure calls (RPCs) to all BDCs.

PulseConcurrency parameters.

PDC change	BDC change	Default	Minimum	Maximum
X		10	1	500

Recommendation:

Set this parameter to match the maximum number of DCs that can request synchronization at any given time (defined with the directory synchronization tool).

Issues to consider:

- Increasing PulseConcurrency increases the load on the PDC.
- Decreasing PulseConcurrency increases the time it takes for a domain with a large number of BDCs to get SAM and LSA changes to all of the BDCs.

PulseMaximum

PulseMaximum specifies how often a PDC sends a pulse message to BDCs, even if its user accounts database is up-to-date. You can increase the default value of 7200 seconds (two hours) to 86400 (24 hours), reducing the number of pulse messages.

PulseMaximum parameters.

PDC change	BDC change	Default	Minimum	Maximum
X		7200	60	86400

Recommendation:

If your environment has multiple DCs for each domain (as does GlobalNet) increase this parameter to its maximum to ensure the PDC is not constantly contacting every BDC.

Issue to consider:

- Increasing this parameter raises the risk that a BDC's machine account password can expire. To resolve this, you can disable the machine account password parameter. See the "DisablePasswordChange" section for more information.

PulseTimeout1

PulseTimeout1 controls how long a PDC waits for a BDC (default 10 seconds). to respond to the PDC's pulse before it considers them non-responsive. A pulse sent to a non-responsive BDC does not count against the PulseConcurrency limit, allowing the PDC to send a pulse to other BDCs in the domain.

PulseTimeout1 parameters.

PDC change	BDC change	Default	Minimum	Maximum
X		10	1	120

Recommendation:

In a slow-link WAN, increase this parameter to reduce the chance of a PDC evaluating BDCs as non-responsive.

Issues to consider:

- If this number is too large, a domain with a large number of non-responsive BDCs takes a long time to complete synchronization (a partial replication).
- If this number is too small, a PDC falsely evaluates a slow BDC as being non-responsive, so when the BDC finally responds, it starts a partial replication from the PDC, unduly increasing the load on the PDC.

PulseTimeout2

PulseTimeout2 defines how long a PDC waits for a BDC to complete partial replication. After a BDC initially responds to a pulse, it must continue making replication progress, or the PDC evaluates the BDC as non-responsive. Each time the BDC calls the PDC, the BDC receives another PulseTimeout2 pulse, marking a period (default 300 seconds) in which the BDC must respond.

PulseTimeout2 parameters.

PDC change	BDC change	Default	Minimum	Maximum
X		300	60	3600

Recommendation:

Set this parameter to slightly more than the average number of seconds needed to complete a partial directory synchronization to ensure the BDCs retrieve all changes to the SAM and LSA databases. Tuning this setting becomes increasingly important when a single RPC cannot retrieve all changes due to an increased ChangeLogSize.

Issues to consider:

- If this number is too large, a slow BDC (or one that has its replication rate artificially governed) consumes one of the PulseConcurrency slots.
- If this number is too small, the load on the PDC unduly increases because of the large number of BDCs doing a partial synchronization.

ReplicationGovernor

ReplicationGovernor defines the size of the data transferred on calls to the PDC and the frequency of those calls. For example, setting it to 50 percent allocates a 64-KB buffer rather than a 128-KB buffer, and allows BDCs to have outstanding replication calls at only 50 percent of the possible rate. Do not set the ReplicationGovernor too low, or replication may never complete.

You can set different replication rates at different times throughout the day by adjusting the ReplicationGovernor parameter to restart the NetLogon service from within an AT script. However, setting the parameter below 100 percent requires configuring it on each BDC.

ReplicationGovernor parameters.

PDC change	BDC change	Default
	X	100

Recommendation:

Leave this parameter at 100 percent so domain synchronization finishes as quickly as possible and completely replicates SAM and LSA changes. Monitor situations where domain synchronization must work in concert with other WAN application activity and decrease ReplicationGovernor as needed.

DisablePasswordChange

DisablePasswordChange allows a Windows NT computer to maintain its domain membership while being offline for more than six days. A Windows NT workstation is a member of a domain, and it accesses domain resources by using a machine account password. It changes the password automatically every three days, and to do this it must register the new password with the PDC.

If the Windows NT workstation cannot access the PDC, it caches the new password for three more days and continues attempting to register it with the PDC. Eventually, the password on the workstation expires and when the DC tries to authenticate the machine account, the password does not match the one in the security database.

By default, Windows NT does not disable the machine account password. You can disable this security layer that Windows NT uses to protect against computer accounts impersonation through **DisablePasswordChange**.

DisablePasswordChange parameters.

PDC change	BDC change	Windows NT Workstation	Default
0x01	0x01	0x01	

Recommendation:

Do not compromise Windows NT security. Disable machine account password changes only when necessary. Review Windows NT domain design alternatives.

ExpectedDialupDelay

If a dial-up router can take longer (30 to 90 seconds) to make a connection to a remote network than NetLogon can wait by default, NetLogon assumes that no DC is available on the network. NetLogon sends out three broadcast/multicast <1C> frames looking for the DC at 5-second intervals (default). The dial-up router has approximately 15 seconds to make the connection and pass the frame before NetLogon times out and uses cached credentials to validate the user. **ExpectedDialupDelay** provides a mechanism to modify the broadcast intervals.

ExpectedDialupDelay parameters.

PDC change	BDC change	Windows NT Workstation	Default
	X	X	

Recommendation:

Use the following formula to set wait time:

5 seconds + (ExpectedDialupDelay / 3).

Therefore, if you set the ExpectedDialupDelay to 120 seconds, the wait time would be:

5 + (120 / 3) = 45,

that is, a 45-second interval between frames.

Note For Windows NT 3.51, this modification requires Service Pack 5 (SP5) or later.

Directory Synchronization Tool

The final and most important step of the optimization process is to ensure that BDCs properly request only Windows NT domain directory *changes,* not a full copy of the SAM database. By default, the BDC replicates directory changes when it is notified by the PDC and when it first boots. In an on-demand WAN environment, configure the PDC's directory synchronization pulses to go out infrequently or not at all.

You can control the directory synchronization pulses by installing NLTEST (a Windows NT 4.0 Resource Kit NetLogon Service tool) that requests the Windows NT directory changes, when appropriate.

Note Windows NT 3.51 does not have this tool, but if NLTEST is run under Windows NT 4.0, it can request a remote Windows NT 3.51 partial directory synchronization.

NLTEST and Windows NT 3.51

To control the Windows NT domain synchronization process, NLTEST emulates the Windows NT synchronization state from the BDC. Assuming a network connection exists between the PDC and the BDC, the following process takes place:

State 1: Notify NetLogon on the PDC that a new transport has come online.

State 2: Notify NetLogon on the PDC that you wish to replicate.

State 3: Query NetLogon on the PDC to determine if you are still replicating.

A sample of necessary MicrosoftVisual C++ code to perform these NetLogon requests is provided in the "Sample AutoRepl Code" section at the end of this chapter.

NLTEST and Windows NT 4.0

You can create the following command file to call NLTEST. It requires a RAS connection using RASDIAL (also included in the *Microsoft Windows NT Server 4.0 Resource Kit*) to make the connection, and NLTEST to request SAM and LAS updates.

```
:RASDIALOUT
RASDIAL PDCSERVER
IF ERRORLEVEL == 1 GOTO BADRASDIAL
NLTEST /TRANSPORT_NOTIFY
NLTEST /SERVER:BDCLOCAL /REPL
GOTO END
:BADRASDIAL
WAIT 5
GOTO RASDIALOUT
:END
```

Note You can force a full synchronization of the SAM, LSA, and BUILT-IN security databases by using the command line **net accounts /sync**. This requires more bandwidth and execution time because the security databases grow in raw size. You can use NLTEST.EXE to force a full synchronization with this command: **nltest /sync /server:<*BDC_name*>**. See Knowledge Base article Q158148, Title: Domain Secure Channel Utility - NLTEST.EXE for more information.

NetBIOS Name Resolution

NetBIOS defines a software interface and a naming convention, not a protocol. The NetBIOS Enhanced User Interface (NetBEUI) protocol, introduced by IBM in 1985, provides a protocol for NetBIOS applications. However, NetBEUI is a small protocol with no networking layer and because of this it is not a routable protocol suitable for medium to large intranetworks. NetBIOS over TCP/IP (NetBT) provides the NetBIOS programming interface over TCP/IP, extending the reach of NetBIOS client-server programs on the WAN, and allowing interoperability with various other operating systems. NetBT and NetBIOS are illustrated in Figure 4.1.

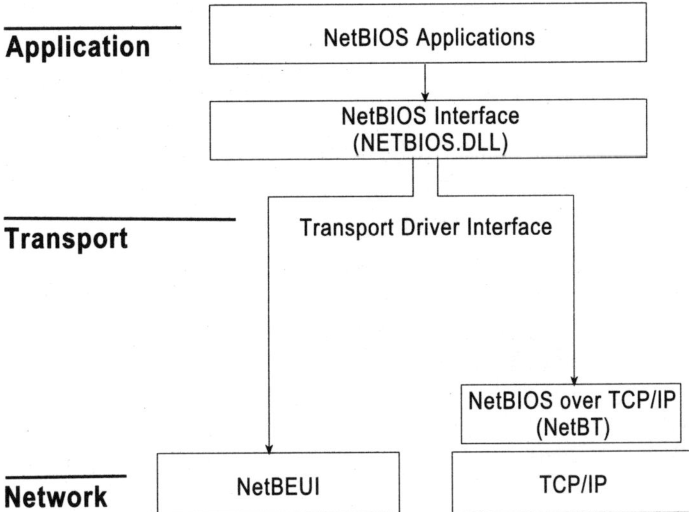

Figure 4.1 Logical relationship of NetBIOS to TCP/IP.

The Windows NT Workstation, Server, Browser, Messenger, and NetLogon services are all direct NetBT clients that use the Transport Driver Interface (TDI) to communicate with NetBT. The NetBIOS namespace is flat, meaning that all names within a network must be unique. Resources are identified by NetBIOS names that are registered dynamically when computers start, services start, or users log on. A NetBIOS Name Query is used to locate a resource by resolving the name to an IP address.

NetBIOS Node Types

NetBIOS name resolution order depends on the node type and computer configuration. The following node types are supported:

- **b-node** (represented in registry by 0x0). Uses broadcasts for name registration and resolution. This is the default for all non-WINS Microsoft TCP/IP clients.
- **p-node** (0x6). Uses only point-to-point name queries to a NetBIOS name server (in this case WINS servers) for name registration and resolution.
- **m-node** (0x4). Uses broadcasts for name registration. For name resolution, it uses broadcasts first, but switches to p-node if no answer is received.
- **h-node** (0x8). Uses NetBIOS name server for both registration and resolution. However, if no name server can be located, it switches to b-node. It continues to poll for nameserver, switching back to p-node when one becomes available. By default, WINS clients are configured as h-node.

For more information on these methods, refer to the *Microsoft Windows NT Server Networking Guide* in the *Microsoft Windows NT 4.0 Resource Kit.*

Tuning the NodeType Registry Setting

You can find the following Windows NT setting in the registry subkey:

HKEY_LOCAL_MACHINE\CurrentControlSet\Services\NetBt\Parameters.

NodeType parameter setting.

PDC change	BDC change	Windows NT Workstation	Default
	x	x	Ox8 h-node

Recommendation:

When using a domain spanning into multiple sites, set the NetBIOS name resolution mode to m-node (broadcasts followed by nameserver) on all servers and workstations in the remote locations (assuming one network segment per branch office). This ensures that a local network resource, such as the BDC, is always contacted first (that is, before trying to contact the PDC).

NetBIOS Browsing

The Windows NT Browser service maintains a list (called the *browse list*) of all available domains and servers. Through Windows NT Network Neighborhood or Explorer, users can view this list provided by a NetBIOS "browser" in the local computer's domain. Windows NT assigns browser tasks to specific computers on the network. Because these computers work together to provide a centralized list of shared resources, they eliminate the need for all machines to maintain their own lists. The Windows NT browser system consists of domain master browsers, master browsers, backup browsers, and browser clients.

Domain Master Browser

Domain master browsers (DMBs) span network segments, collecting computer-name information and storing the domain-wide browse list of available resources. The DMB and cooperating master browsers on each WAN segment provide domain browsing across multiple TCP/IP network segments. The DMB resides on the PDC of a domain. Within a domain, each subnet elects a MB that exchanges a browse list with the DMB every 15 minutes.

Master Browser

The **master browser** collects the information necessary to create and maintain the browse list, including all servers in the master browser's domain or workgroup, and lists of all domains on the network.

When a domain spans multiple network segments, the master browsers for each network segment use a directed datagram called a **MasterBrowserAnnouncement** to announce themselves to the domain master browser. The datagram notifies the DMB that the sending master browser resides in the same domain, and that the domain master browser needs to copy the master browser's list.

The DMB then sends a request to the network segment's master browser to collect a list of that network segment's servers. The DMB merges its own server list with the master browser's server list every 15 minutes, guaranteeing that the DMB has a complete browse list.

Backup Browser

The **backup browser** receives a copy of the network-resource browse list from a master browser and distributes the list upon request to computers in the domain or workgroup. All Windows NT DCs are automatically configured as either master or backup browsers. Computers running Windows NT Workstation, Windows for Workgroups, or Windows 9*x* can serve as backup browsers if fewer than three Windows NT Server computers perform backup-browser functions for the TCP/IP network segment.

Backup browsers call the master every 15 minutes to get the latest copy of the browse list and a list of domains.

Browsing and Windows Internet Name Service

Retrieving a browse list takes approximately six frames: two to determine the list of backup browsers and four to get the list servers and domains in the local domain. On Windows Internet Name Service (WINS)-enabled networks, the Windows NT 3.5*x* or 4.0 browser periodically connects to a WINS server, scans for systems that have registered any new domain name, and adds the domain name and master browser name to its domain/workgroup list. This allows members of one domain to locate the master browser for another domain even when it is on another subnet and the two domains have no “broadcast area” in common.

Tuning Registry Settings

You can find the following Windows NT settings in the registry subkey:

HKEY_LOCAL_MACHINE\CurrentControlSet\Services\Browser\Parameters.

You do not need to restart Windows NT before changes take effect for MasterPeriodicity, but you will need to do so for BackupPeriodicity.

MasterPeriodicity

MasterPeriodicity specifies how frequently a master browser contacts the domain master browser (default 900 seconds—15 minutes). You can add this parameter as a REG_DWORD, and change it dynamically without restarting the computer.

MasterPeriodicity parameters.

PDC change	BDC change	Windows NT Workstation	Default	Minimum	Maximum
	X	X	900	300	FFFFFFFF

Recommendation:

To optimize your WAN, add this parameter on remote network master browsers. Tune master browsers on subnets within a domain because these master browsers must communicate with the domain master browser. You also want to set this value on remote Windows NT workstations in case one of them becomes the subnet's master browser.

BackupPeriodicity

BackupPeriodicity specifies how frequently a backup browser contacts the master browser (default 720 seconds—12 minutes). You can add the parameter as a REG_DWORD and must restart the computer for changes to take effect.

BackupPeriodicity parameters.

PDC change	BDC change	Windows NT Workstation	Default	Minimum	Maximum
	X	X	720	300	FFFFFFFF

Recommendation:

You can leave this parameter at its default value because tuning it does not affect WAN traffic. This broadcast communication remains within a subnet if the network is routing properly.

Printer

Network printer sharing provides users with a great *shared resource*, but can consume network bandwidth with printer data streams, as well as browsing advertisements and simple status notifications. Windows NT print registry settings are in this subkey:

HKEY_LOCAL_MACHINE\CurrentControlSet\Control\Print.

You must restart Windows NT in order for your changes to take effect.

DisableServerThread

DisableServerThread calls other print servers to notify them that a (local) printer exists. When you share a printer in Windows NT, the print spooler broadcasts a message on all of the print server's installed protocols to all Windows NT print servers, announcing the new print share. Print servers add the new share name to their local printer browse list, which they rebroadcast to other print servers every 10 minutes, ensuring that other print servers have current browse lists. This can cause extensive network traffic. You can add this parameter as a REG_DWORD.

DisableServerThread parameter.

PDC change	BDC change	Windows NT Workstation	Default
	X		0 (false)

Recommendation:

Disable the printer browse thread by setting it to 1 (true).

Issue to consider:

- Disabling the thread reduces network traffic, but also keeps the print servers from discovering new print shares.

NetPopup

NetPopup notifies users in real-time of their print job status. The registry setting is under the subkey:

> **HKEY_LOCAL_MACHINE\CurrentControlSet\Control\Print\Providers.**

Add this as a REG_DWORD. Setting the entry to 1 enables NetPopup, and 0 disables NetPopup.

NetPopup parameter.

PDC change	BDC change	Windows NT Workstation	Default
	X	X	1 (enabled)

Recommendation:

Disable the printer notification on both the remote server and workstations by setting it to 0.

Issue to consider:

- Disabling NetPopup eliminates "real-time" user notification of print job status.

Server Message Block (SMB)

The **Server Message Block** (SMB) protocol defines a series of commands used to pass information between networked computers. In a branch office, on-demand WAN environment such as GlobalNet Insurance, a NetBIOS connection should close only when the application or service using the connection completes. Windows NT maintains its SMB connections for 10 minutes before it issues an SMB Tree Disconnect message. If connections do not drop relatively quickly, the on-demand WAN link is brought up for the sole purpose of disconnecting a session.

KeepConn specifies the maximum amount of time that a connection can be left dormant. In a WAN environment, lower this value to approximately 30 seconds on all servers and workstations to prevent establishing a new on-demand connection just to close an SMB connection.

The KeepConn setting is located in the registry subkey:

> **HKEY_LOCAL_MACHINE\CurrentControlSet\Services\LanmanWorkstation\Parameters**.

You do not need to restart Windows NT for these changes to take effect.

KeepConn parameters.

PDC change	BDC change	Windows NT Workstation	Default	Minimum	Maximum
X	X	X	600	1	65535

Recommendation:

Set KeepConn to 30 seconds on the remote server, and also Windows NT workstations (optional).

Issue to consider:

- Changing KeepConn can generate significant SMB overhead. As connections close very quickly, each new connection implies establishing a new SMB connection.

License Management

The Windows NT license service performs licensing replication, moving software license data from BDCs and member servers to the PDCs, and optionally from PDCs to an enterprise server, which maintains licensing information across the whole network. (For more information on enterprise servers, refer to "Keeping an Enterprise Licensing Database" in Chapter 12 of the Windows NT Server *Concepts and Planning Manual.*)

This replication is performed once every 24 hours by default. If for some reason, the BDC cannot connect to the license service on the PDC, the BDC continues to attempt replication once every 15 minutes until it is successful.

The **Start** registry setting disables the Windows NT license service. You can find it in the registry subkey:

HKEY_LOCAL_MACHINE\Services\LicenseService.

You do not need to restart Windows NT for these changes to take effect.

Start parameters.

PDC change	BDC change	Windows NT Workstation	Default
X	X	X	0x2

Where: "disable" = 0x4, "automatic" = 0x2, and "manual" = 0x3.

Recommendation:

Disable the service on all Windows NT machines within the branch office domain, eliminating WAN traffic generated by the license service and reducing the PDC workload.

Issue to consider:

- If you disable this service, Windows NT cannot manage standard Microsoft BackOffice product license information.

Sample AutoRepl Code

The sample skeletal C++ code provided below makes NetLogon SAM update requests.

```
do {
       switch(state) {
       case 0:
              if((rascode = RasDial(...)) != SUCCESS ) {
                     RasHangUp(hRasConn);
              else
                     state++;
              break;

       case 1:
              retcode = I_NetLogonControl2(NULL,

       NETLOGON_CONTROL_TRANSPORT_NOTIFY,
                            1,
(LPBYTE)&Dummy,
&Dummy);

              if(retcode == NO_ERROR)
                     NetApiBufferFree(Dummy);
              state++;
       break;
       case 2:
              retcode = I_NetLogonControl(NULL,
                            NETLOGON_CONTROL_REPLICATE,
                            1,
(LPBYTE *)&Buffer);
              NetApiBufferFree(Buffer);
              if(retcode != NERR_Success) { // LOGON_SERVER not
avail, etc
                     RasHangUp(hRasConn);
                     state = 0;    // start it all over again
```

```
                } else {
                        state++;
                }
        break;

        case 3:
                retcode = I_NetLogonControl(NULL,
                                NETLOGON_CONTROL_QUERY,
                                1,
(LPBYTE *)&Buffer);

                if(retcode != NERR_Success) {
                        NetApiBufferFree(Buffer);
                        RasHangUp(hRasConn);
                        state = 0;    // start it all over again
                } else if((Buffer->netlog1_flags &

        NETLOGON_REPLICATION_IN_PROGRESS) !=
                                NETLOGON_REPLICATION_IN_PROGRESS) {
                        NetApiBufferFree(Buffer);
                        RasHangUp(hRasConn);
                        state = 0;    // start it all over again
                } else {
                        requery = (Buffer->netlog1_flags &
                NETLOGON_REPLICATION_NEEDED);
                        NetApiBufferFree(Buffer);
                        if(!requery)
                                state++;
                }
                break;

        case 4:
                RasHangUp(hRasConn);
                state++;        // were done!!!
                break;
        }
} while(state < 5);.
```

More Information

Refer to these Microsoft Knowledge Base articles for more information:

- Q120151, Title: Browsing a Wide Area Network with WINS
- Q154355, Title: How to Tune Trusts for Dialup Routers in a WAN
- Q152719, Title: WAN and Trust: Traffic on the Wire
- Q163204, Title: Increase Domain Logon Timeout over Network
- Q151259, Title: New Netlogon Registry Entry for Dialup Routers
- Q134985, Title: Browsing & Other Traffic Incur High Costs over ISDN Routers
- Q150350, Title: NetLogon Maximum Value of Pulse Should Exceed 3600

CHAPTER 5

Optimizing for a Dial-on-Demand Network at FoodCo

By Gary Milne, MCS—Minnesota

Maintaining continuous connection over ISDN or analog lines can be expensive, and dial-on-demand networks, which establish connections only when needed, can help reduce communications costs. To maximize these savings with Windows NT, you should specially configure some system services for dial-on-demand configuration to make sure that you minimize unnecessary connection—a seemingly minor problem that can become significant in large networks.

For instance, suppose an average long-distance cost of $0.10/minute. If each of the 3,000 servers in the FoodCo network (on which this chapter is based) initiates one unnecessary dial-up session per day, the cost, even with a five-minute AutoDisconnect setting, would be more than one-half million dollars per year.

In Focus

Enterprise

FoodCo, a large food retailer and wholesaler recently integrated a variety of proprietary systems through growth and acquisition.

Network

The only form of communication and network infrastructure for FoodCo's rural locations is via modem over a PSTN connection.

Challenge

Configuring Windows NT Server for a dial-on-demand network.

Solution

Of the methods researched, only Windows NT Server with the Routing and Remote Access Service (RRAS) update met all of the networking requirements and provided a suitable application platform.

What You'll Find In This Chapter

- **Description of Windows NT Server services that affect dial-up networks.**
- **In-depth look at network communication traces.**
- **Best practices for configuring services for a dial-on-demand network.**
- **Other tips and strategies for tuning network services.**
- **Sample files to implement dial-on-demand policies.**

Warning This chapter makes recommendations for tuning the Windows NT registry using the Registry Editor. Using the Registry Editor incorrectly can cause serious, system-wide problems that require you to reinstall Windows NT. Microsoft cannot guarantee that any problems resulting from the use of Registry Editor can be solved. Use this tool at your own risk.

Customer Profile

FoodCo is a large food retailer and wholesaler with over 3000 distribution and retail centers. Due to its steady growth and competitive acquisitions, it ended up with a mainframe-based environment and a variety of aging proprietary systems that did not meet administrative or customer needs.

Business Need

Initially, sales and inventory reports were delivered to stores in hardcopy—a difficult, costly, and unreliable method, with data sometimes superseded before it could be delivered. FoodCo needed real-time distribution of various electronic reports (most notably invoices), e-mail, corporate information Internet and intranet access, and expandability. This required building a standards-based *push/pull* infrastructure that allowed headquarters to *push* urgent information to the stores, and stores to *pull* information from headquarters regularly. Established applications for report distribution, e-mail, online ordering, etc. were layered on top of the infrastructure. Networking had to be transparent and fully routed so that new applications could be added without changing the network infrastructure.

The solution had to:

- Support *push/pull* information exchange.
- Be transparent to users, and dial automatically when needed.
- Be cost-effective, minimizing phone and support charges.
- Support connection for rural customers via modem over a public switched telephone network (PSTN) connection, which limits capacity and requires time to establish a modem connection.
- Control per-unit costs by offering a single-box solution because of the large number of sites.
- Support addition of workstations.

The Challenge

Although Windows NT Server 4.0 met all of FoodCo's networking requirements, it had to be specially configured for a dial-on-demand network so that servers at branch offices would not unnecessarily activate the dial-on-demand link. The high cost of telecommunication was the most important factor influencing the design: it represented considerable risk in the early design stages and later influenced decisions such as domain design and the name resolution model.

Focusing on Windows NT Services

By studying, understanding, and minimizing the Windows NT operating system services that can cause a dial-on-demand event, you can determine and reduce telecommunication costs as highlighted in the "Custormer Profile" section. This chapter discusses common Windows NT Server services that can affect a dial-on-demand network over Transmission Control Protocol/Internet Protocol (TCP/IP). It briefly describes each service, explains how its configuration affects network traffic, describes strategies to improve the default behavior, and when appropriate, shows how to modify the registry. Although different domain models affect network traffic, the discussion does not include domain planning recommendations. It does, however, cite other sources of information (Microsoft Knowledge Base articles listed at the end of the chapter) and provide illustrative examples of network traces such as the example below:

Network trace example.

Frame	Time	Src MAC Address	Dst MAC Address	Protocol	Description
9	57.947	SERVER	PDC	NBT	NS: Refresh req. for TESTLAB <00>
10	57.954	SERVER	PDC	ARP_RARP	ARP: Reply, Target IP: 10.100.1.21 Target Hdwr Addr: 000083228675

Column definitions:

1. **Frame**. Unique number, starting from 1, assigned to each frame as the network monitor receives it.
2. **Time**. Elapsed time from the beginning of the trace until the frame was received.
3. **Src MAC Address**. Source Media Access Control (MAC) address (unique address) of the network card that placed the frame onto the network. This appears in the table as a mnemonic name associated with the particular MAC address (which is always the same as the computername).
4. **Dst MAC Address**. Destination MAC address to which the frame is sent. This appears in the table as a mnemonic name associated with that particular MAC address.
5. **Protocol**. Highest-level protocol used within the frame.
6. **Description**. Summary of the activity carried by the highest-level protocol.

Dynamic Host Configuration Protocol Server Renewal Requests

In a TCP/IP-based network, the Dynamic Host Configuration Protocol (DHCP) server eliminates most of the effort associated with the configuration and management of a large number of static Internet protocol (IP) addresses that computers use to communicate. A DHCP server leases IP addresses to any DHCP client. Windows NT DHCP clients request a lease renewal from a DHCP server at specific intervals: boot time, 50% of the lease duration (default 3 days), 87.5%, and 100% of the original lease duration until the original DHCP server responds.

This network trace shows the packets that arise from a successful DHCP renewal request—a single directed request followed by a single acknowledgement (ACK).

A successful DHCP renewal request.

Frame	Time	Src MAC Address	Dst MAC Address	Protocol	Description
1	2.307	LAPTOP	LONDON	DHCP	Request (xid=7A074280)
2	2.378	LONDON	SERVER	DHCP	ACK (xid=7A074280)

If DHCP client systems are not powered-off each night, increasing the DHCP lease time reduces the amount and frequency of DHCP-related traffic. An office with 10 computers using the default three-day lease produces, on average, a dial-on-demand event every 3.6 hours.

To reduce the number of DHCP renewal requests:

1. **Set the DHCP lease period for a longer duration** using the Windows NT Server DHCP administration utility, if there are IP addresses available for all computers. Increasing the renewal period lengthens the time to propagate DHCP configuration changes to all DHCP clients (because longer leases delay connection with the server).
2. **Implement a DHCP server on the local area network (LAN) segment**, especially in environments where many clients shut down or regularly reboot. LAN-based DHCP servers require minimal maintenance after configuration and deployment.
3. **In small organizations, use static IP addresses** to eliminate DHCP requests.

Note For larger organizations, using static IP addresses is often undesirable because it can increase costs associated with manually allocating, managing, tracking, and troubleshooting many IP addresses. If software or configurations require static addresses, DHCP may not be an option.

Windows Internet Name Service (WINS) Client

Windows NT Server-based computers connect with one another over the network by obtaining IP addresses of destination computers. A Windows NT Server's WINS client requests a computername and the WINS server returns its IP address. Two types of WINS traffic affect a dial-on-demand environment: *WINS Registration\Renewal Requests* and *WINS Queries*.

WINS Registration\Renewal Requests

Like DHCP clients, WINS clients must renew their registration with a WINS server. By default the WINS server sets the registration renewal period to four days. WINS clients automatically renew registrations at various intervals: halfway through this set period, when users reboot computers, when services stop or start, or when administrators promote a computer from backup domain controller (BDC) to primary domain controller (PDC).

A WINS registration number has 16 digits: the first 15 identify the computername, and the last indicates a particular type of service running on a computer. In the traces below and throughout this chapter, SERVER<XX> refers to a server and its registration number as a two digit hexadecimal value. Common values and their significance are listed in the table below.

Common trace values and their significance.

Frame 9 - TESTLAB <00>.	Name refresh request for the domain name.
Frame 12 - SERVER.	Name refresh request for the SERVER process, equivalent to SERVER <20>.
Frame 14 - SERVER <03>.	Name refresh request for the messenger service for the computer.
Frame 16 - SERVER <00>.	Name refresh request for the workstation process for the computer.

WINS registration requests.

Frame	Time	Src MAC Address	Dst MAC Address	Protocol	Description
9	57.947	SERVER	PDC	NBT	NS: Refresh req. for TESTLAB <00>
10	57.954	SERVER	PDC	ARP_RARP	ARP: Reply, Target IP: 10.100.1.21 Target Hdwr Addr: 000083228675
11	57.954	PDC	SERVER	NBT	NS: Registration (Node Status) resp. for TESTLAB <00>, Success, Owner Addr. 10.100.1.23
12	57.955	SERVER	PDC	NBT	NS: Refresh req. for SERVER
13	57.977	PDC	SERVER	NBT	NS: Registration (Node Status) resp. for SERVER, Success, Owner Addr. 10.100.1.23
14	57.978	SERVER	PDC	NBT	NS: Refresh req. for SERVER <03>
15	58.003	PDC	SERVER	NBT	NS: Registration (Node Status) resp. for SERVER <03>, Success, Owner Addr. 10.100.1.23
16	58.003	SERVER	PDC	NBT	NS: Refresh req. for SERVER <00>
17	58.043	PDC	SERVER	NBT	NS: Registration (Node Status) resp. for SERVER <00>, Success, Owner Addr. 10.100.1.23

The number and type of registrations vary based on the number and type of services running on a computer. For example, the PDC makes more WINS registrations than a member server or workstation. The four registrations shown in the trace above (frames 11, 13, 15, 17) are typical for a Windows NT Workstation or Windows NT Server that is a member of a domain.

To reduce WINS registration\renewal traffic:

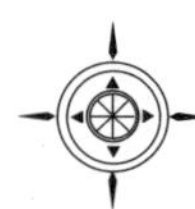

- **Increase the WINS renewal period**. This is the simplest and most effective way to reduce WINS renewal traffic and still provide WINS services.

Note Windows NT Server 4.0-based computers that are multi-homed or that use RAS, refresh their names with a WINS server every ten minutes, instead of using the time-to-live (TTL) value returned by the WINS server. For more information on how to correct this behavior see Knowledge Base article Q164308, Title: Windows NT 4.0 Clients May Refresh WINS Entries Frequently.

- **Avoid using WINS at remote sites.** Use broadcast name resolution to find local resources and an LMHOSTS file to locate remote resources. By using the LMHOSTS #INCLUDE syntax, you can update a single LMHOSTS file at each remote site as needed; the file distribution can be scheduled to piggyback on other business activities.

Warning In this scenario the Windows NT-based workstations at the remote site do not register with any WINS server, and other computers cannot locate them on the network without a static entry being created in some type of name resolution mechanism.

- **Install a local WINS server (small organizations only)**. This avoids transmissions of registrations across the wide area network (WAN).

Note This strategy is recommended only for small networks (2-10 offices). Installing a local WINS server means that WINS replication must be configured between the local WINS server and the headquarters location, which can generate a large amount of network traffic. Typically, Microsoft Technical Support recommends installing fewer, not more, WINS servers to simplify the WINs replication topology.

FoodCo's remote offices use WINS frequently, accessing a small percentage of resources at the headquarters. In turn, the corporate helpdesk and operations staff require WINS infrequently, but immediately, in supporting a large number of field computers. Because an organization needs access to all computers, it cannot eliminate WINS completely, especially when using DHCP. For most branch office environments, the best option is simply to increase the WINS renewal period.

WINS Queries

Whenever a WINS-capable system attempts to locate a resource on the network, it generates a WINS query—a fairly simple process. The workstation directs the WINS server to locate a given computer or resource name, and the server responds by returning the IP address corresponding to the requested name. The following sequence shows a successful lookup on the name VENICE. The lookup query results in two packets on the local network: one request and one response.

Successful WINS query (VENICE).

Frame	Time	Src MAC Address	Dst MAC Address	Protocol	Description
2	2.549	GARYMIL_PC	GLASGOW	NBT	NS: Query req. for VENICE <00>
3	2.552	GLASGOW	GARYMIL_PC	NBT	NS: Query (Node Status) resp. for VENICE <00>, Success

This next trace shows a failed WINS query on the name SICILY.

Failed WINS query (SICILY).

Frame	Time	Src MAC Address	Dst MAC Address	Protocol	Description
1	2.446	GARYMIL_PC	GLASGOW	NBT	NS: Query req. for SICILY <00>
2	2.45	GLASGOW	GARYMIL_PC	NBT	NS: Query (Node Status) resp. for SICILY <00>, Requested
3	3.94	GARYMIL_PC	LONDON	NBT	NS: Query req. for SICILY <00>
4	3.948	LONDON	GARYMIL_PC	NBT	NS: Query (Node Status) resp. for SICILY <00>, Requested
5	5.442	GARYMIL_PC	*BROADCAST	NBT	NS: Query req. for SICILY <00>
6	6.193	GARYMIL_PC	*BROADCAST	NBT	NS: Query req. for SICILY <00>
7	6.945	GARYMIL_PC	*BROADCAST	NBT	NS: Query req. for SICILY <00>

Notice that the workstation contacts both WINS servers in turn in an attempt to resolve the name. This is followed by three broadcasts onto the local network segment at 0.75-second intervals. It takes 4.5 seconds for this name lookup to fail, and it introduces broadcast traffic onto the network.

To reduce WINS queries:

As shown in the successful query above, WINS provides an effective and efficient method for name resolution. In most cases, attempting to modify default behavior yields no benefit because a WINS lookup precedes a network connection attempt.

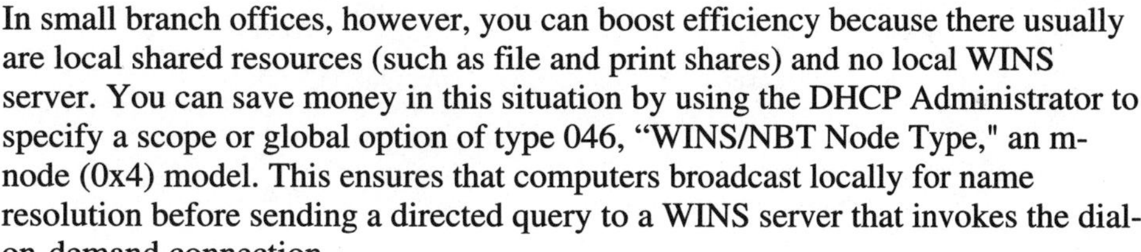

In small branch offices, however, you can boost efficiency because there usually are local shared resources (such as file and print shares) and no local WINS server. You can save money in this situation by using the DHCP Administrator to specify a scope or global option of type 046, "WINS/NBT Node Type," an m-node (0x4) model. This ensures that computers broadcast locally for name resolution before sending a directed query to a WINS server that invokes the dial-on-demand connection.

For details on how to configure name resolution order when DHCP is not used, see Knowledge Base article Q139270, Title: How to Change Name Resolution Order on Windows 95 and Windows NT.

To reduce dial-on-demand traffic and maintain name resolution performance, you can reduce NetBIOS broadcast traffic (amount and timing) by making the following changes.

Reduce the time between successive NetBIOS broadcasts by changing this registry key.

Reduce the time between successive NetBIOS broadcasts.

Registry Path	HKEY_LOCAL_MACHINE\System\CurrentControlSet\Services\NetBT\Parameters
Parameter	BcastQueryTimeout
Type	REG_DWORD
Default Value	750 (milliseconds)
Suggested Value	250 (milliseconds)

Reduce the number of NetBIOS broadcasts before attempting p-node. To do so, change this registry key:

Reduce the number of NetBIOS broadcasts before p-node.

Registry Path	HKEY_LOCAL_MACHINE\System\CurrentControlSet\Services\NetBT\Parameters
Parameter	BcastNameQueryCount
Type	REG_DWORD
Default Value	3
Suggested Value	2

Using the default parameters to locate a remote resource results in a 2.25-second delay before a name query is sent to the WINS server. Using the suggested values reduces this delay to 0.5 seconds.

Depending on the connect time of the dial-on-demand link, you can increase the timeout and retry values for the WINS server lookup, which defaults to 1.5 seconds and three retries, and can timeout before the dial-on-demand connection completes. For more information on how to implement this see Knowledge Base article Q120642, Title: TCP/IP & NBT Configuration Parameters for Windows NT.

Windows NT Browser

The Windows NT Browser service provides administrators with an enterprise-wide view of available network resources. It establishes a hierarchy of computers starting with the PDC as domain master browser followed by a distribution of master and backup browsers throughout the network. These browser services regularly pass data that provides a list of available domains and computers on the network.

Updating Browser Information

In a TCP/IP-based network, each segment (subnet) automatically elects one compuer to function as the master browser, with several other computers operating as backup browsers. By default, each master browser attempts to contact the domain master browser every twelve minutes using a remote procedure call (RPC) over a named pipe to request a new browser list.

If the domain master browser recognizes that the master browser is connecting from a remote subnet (a subnet other than the one to which the domain master browser is directly connected) it will in turn establish a named pipe connection to the calling master browser, request its browse list, and use that information to update its own master browse list. Because the browser uses named pipes to establish a connection and pass information, the default workstation idle timeout period applies (see the "Windows NT Server and Workstation Services" section below for more information).

Reducing Browser Traffic

Establishing a connection every twelve minutes, 365 days per year is a very expensive proposition for any dial-on-demand environment. Fortunately, there are several ways to reduce the impact of the Windows NT browser service:

Reduce browser update frequency. Change the default of 720 seconds to a more reasonable number for a dial-on-demand network. To reduce the frequency at which the master browser attempts to connect to the domain master browser, change the registry key below on all computers that serve as a master browser. For more information on browser services, see Knowledge Base article Q102878, Title: Information on Browser Operation, and Q134985, Title: Browsing & Other Traffic Incur High Costs over ISDN Routers.

Reduce a master browser's update frequency.

Registry Path	HKEY_LOCAL_MACHINE\System\CurrentControlSet\Services\Browser\Parameters
Parameter	MasterPeriodicity
Type	REG_DWORD
Default Value	720 (seconds)
Suggested Value	86400 (seconds—daily)

Note Daily (86400 seconds) is only a suggestion. As with any other decision, you have to evaluate cost against need.

Disable the browser after business hours. You can easily stop and start browser service using the command prompt line NET STOP BROWSER. Use the Windows NT Scheduler to stop browser service after working hours.

Disable the browser completely. If a network doesn't require browser service, you can disable the service, which requires disabling the service on *all* computers in a subnet.

Warning Programs such as Server Manager that provide a "**Select Computer**" menu option do so by using the browse list. If the browser service is disabled, users must type in a computername, and they will not be able to browse all domains.

Windows NT Server and Workstation Services

These services support the client and server connections between two Windows NT-based systems and, under normal conditions, run at all times.

Server Service

This networking service maintains incoming connections for a computer so that it can receive connections from other computers. It generates only low-level browser traffic that announces the presence of the server service on the network.

To tune a dial-on-demand network you can adjust the idle disconnect timeout value (how long a connection to the server can remain idle before disconnecting) by changing or adding the registry key below. For more information on this setting, see Knowledge Base article Q138365, Title: How the Autodisconnect Works in Windows NT, and Q105134, Title: AutoDisconnect Default Incorrect in Online Help.

Reduce the server idle disconnect time.

Registry Path	HKEY_LOCAL_MACHINE\System\CurrentControlSet\Services\LanManServer\Parameters
Parameter	AutoDisconnect
Type	REG_DWORD
Default Value	15 (minutes)
Suggested Value	2 (minutes)

Workstation Service

This service is the outgoing counterpart to the Server service. It allows a computer to connect to a remote server. It creates only low-level browser traffic that announces the presence of the workstation service on the network.

Also like the server service, the workstation service has an idle disconnect parameter. The following trace shows a named pipe connection between two computers for the transfer of browser information. Idle disconnect time was reduced to 60 seconds.

Workstation service traffic trace.

Frame	Time	Src MAC Address	Dst MAC Address	Protocol	Description
1	6.553	GLASGOW	LONDON	TCP	....S., len: 4, seq: 9483601-9483604, ack: 0, win: 8
2	6.554	LONDON	GLASGOW	TCP	.A..S., len: 4, seq: 9537563-9537566, ack: 9483602, win: 8
3	6.555	GLASGOW	LONDON	TCP	.A...., len: 0, seq: 9483602-9483602, ack: 9537564, win: 8
4	6.556	GLASGOW	LONDON	NBT	SS: Session Request, Dest: LONDON, Source: GLASGOW
5	6.558	LONDON	GLASGOW	NBT	SS: Positive Session Response, Len: 0
6	6.56	GLASGOW	LONDON	SMB	C negotiate, Dialect = NT LM 0.12
7	6.563	LONDON	GLASGOW	SMB	R negotiate, Dialect # = 7
8	6.567	GLASGOW	LONDON	SMB	C session setup & X, Username = , and C tree connect & X, Share =
9	6.584	LONDON	GLASGOW	SMB	R session setup & X, and R tree connect & X, Type = IPC
10	6.588	GLASGOW	LONDON	SMB	C transact, Remote API
11	6.609	LONDON	GLASGOW	SMB	R transact, Remote API (response to Frame 10)

Workstation service traffic trace. *(continued)*

Frame	Time	Src MAC Address	Dst MAC Address	Protocol	Description
1	6.553	GLASGOW	LONDON	TCP	....S., len: 4, seq: 9483601-9483604, ack: 0, win: 8
12	6.616	GLASGOW	LONDON	SMB	C transact, Remote API
13	6.632	LONDON	GLASGOW	SMB	R transact, Remote API (response to Frame 12)
14	6.75	GLASGOW	LONDON	TCP	.A...., len: 0, seq: 9484272-9484272, ack: 9538051, win: 8
15	67.615	GLASGOW	LONDON	SMB	C tree disconnect
16	67.621	LONDON	GLASGOW	SMB	R tree disconnect
17	67.622	GLASGOW	LONDON	SMB	C logoff & X
18	67.624	LONDON	GLASGOW	SMB	R logoff & X
19	67.625	GLASGOW	LONDON	TCP	.A...F, len: 0, seq: 9484354-9484354, ack: 9538133, win: 8
20	67.627	LONDON	GLASGOW	TCP	.A...F, len: 0, seq: 9538133-9538133, ack: 9484355, win: 8
21	67.628	GLASGOW	LONDON	TCP	.A...., len: 0, seq: 9484355-9484355, ack: 9538134, win: 8

Frame 8 shows the named pipe connection being initiated; data transfer is finished by Frame 13. Notice however that the connection remains intact until the idle disconnect timeout is reached—an additional 60 seconds. In Frame 15, approximately 60 seconds later, the workstation disconnects from the server.

To reduce the workstation idle disconnect time, add or change the registry key below. For more information on this setting, see Knowledge Base article Q102981, Title: REG: Workstation Service Entries.

Reduce the workstation idle disconnect time.

Registry Path	HKEY_LOCAL_MACHINE\System\CurrentControlSet\Services\LanManWorkstation\Parameters
Parameter	KeepConn
Type	REG_DWORD
Default Value	600 (seconds)
Suggested Value	90 (seconds)

Make sure the idle disconnect parameters for server and workstation services fall within the auto-disconnect value configured on the dial-on-demand routers. Keep the server service AutoDisconnect time higher than the workstation server service, so that the *workstation* initiates disconnection.

Messenger Service

The messenger service receives network messages (such as print notification or administrative alerts) and displays them to the logged-in user through a popup dialog box. The messenger service is required to receive messages, not to send them.

The following trace demonstrates network activity when starting the Windows NT messenger service.

Network activity at start of Windows NT messenger service.

Frame	Time	Src MAC Address	Dst MAC Address	Protocol	Description
16	3.223	SERVER	PDC	NBT	NS: Registration req. for SERVER <03>
17	3.231	PDC	SERVER	NBT	NS: Registration (Node Status) resp. for SERVER <03>, Success
18	3.484	SERVER	PDC	NBT	NS: Registration req. for GARYMIL <03>
19	3.489	PDC	SERVER	NBT	NS: Registration (Node Status) resp. for GARYMIL <03>, Success

The messenger service makes two "<03>" type WINS registrations: the first for the machine name and the second for the logged-on user. A typical startup sequence shows only the machine registration entry when the messenger service starts; it shows the second WINS registration entry when a user logs on.

Whenever users shut down computers, the messenger service stops, and the computer releases its WINS name (Frame 17 below). When users log off computers, WINS releases usernames (Frame 18).

WINS/usernames released at log off.

Frame	Time	Src MAC Address	Dst MAC Address	Protocol	Description
17	4.071	SERVER	PDC	NBT	NS: Release req. for WS001048 <03>
18	4.072	SERVER	PDC	NBT	NS: Release req. for HXGJM0 <03>
19	4.074	PDC	SERVER	NBT	NS: Release (Node Status) resp. for WS001048 <03>, Success
20	4.076	PDC	SERVER	NBT	NS: Release (Node Status) resp. for HXGJM0 <03>, Success

Sending Messages via the Messenger Service

This trace shows the network traffic resulting from a simple NET SEND command.

NET SEND command traffic.

Frame	Time	Src MAC Address	Dst MAC Address	Protocol	Description
4	1.953	SERVER	PDC	NBT	NS: Query req. for EINSTEIN <03>
5	1.964	PDC	SERVER	NBT	NS: Query (Node Status) resp. for EINSTEIN <03>, Success
6	1.965	SERVER	*BROADCAST	ARP_RARP	ARP: Request, Target IP: 10.169.105.34
7	1.966	WKS01	SERVER	ARP_RARP	ARP: Reply, Target IP: 10.169.105.20 Target Hdwr Addr: 0000832B8A77
8	1.966	SERVER	WKS01	TCP	....S., len: 4, seq: 511560177, ack: 0, win: 8192, src: 1590 dst: 139
9	1.967	WKS01	SERVER	TCP	.A..S., len: 4, seq: 4010727, ack: 511560178, win:16064, src: 139 dst: 159
10	1.968	SERVER	WKS01	TCP	.A...., len: 0, seq: 511560178, ack: 4010728, win:16064, src: 1590 dst: 139
11	1.968	SERVER	WKS01	NBT	SS: Session Request, Dest: EINSTEIN <03>, Source: SERVER <01>, Len: 68
12	1.969	WKS01	SERVER	NBT	SS: Positive Session Response, Len: 0
13	1.97	SERVER	WKS01	SMB	C send message, from SERVER to EINSTEIN
14	2.085	WKS01	SERVER	TCP	.A...., len: 0, seq: 4010732, ack: 511560339, win:15903, src: 139 …
15	2.112	WKS01	SERVER	SMB	C send message, reply
16	2.113	SERVER	WKS01	TCP	.A...F, len: 0, seq: 511560339, ack: 4010771, win:16021, src: 1590 dst: 139
17	2.114	WKS01	SERVER	TCP	.A...F, len: 0, seq: 4010771, ack: 511560340, win:15903, src: 139 dst: 159
18	2.115	SERVER	WKS01	TCP	.A...., len: 0, seq: 511560340, ack: 4010772, win:16021, src: 1590 dst: 139

It begins with a name query and response in Frames 4 and 5. After receiving the target address, the server performs a Reverse Address Resolution Protocol (RARP) to retrieve the MAC address for the destination node. A TCP/IP session is established in Frames 8-10. A NetBIOS session is established in Frames 11 and 12. Finally (Frame 13) a workstation sends a message and the server returns a success code (Frame 15).

Messenger Service Strategy

With the exception of receiving print notifications and system alerts, the messenger service provides little benefit to end-users. You can disable it. Even though the messenger service adds minimal network traffic, it has some drawbacks:

- If a LAN has a local WINS server, user logon/logoff on a Windows NT-based computer with messenger service creates minimal network traffic with WINS registration. If the LAN does not have a local WINS server and a local BDC validates user accounts, the messenger service unnecessarily uses the router to send information about the user to a headquarters WINS server.
- The messenger service makes two WINS registrations, one for the computer and one for the user. A network that replicates WINS information across a large number of remote sites effectively doubles the amount of the WINS data that it transfers.
- Use of the NET SEND "Message" /DOMAIN:NAME command can tax the dial-on-demand connection very quickly by tying up all available lines.

License Logging Service (LLS)

The LLS allows a LAN administrator to track the usage of Microsoft BackOffice licenses throughout the enterprise. It stores license usage information locally and periodically rolls it up to a central license-logging server, which by default is the PDC for the domain (although you can use the license manager application to specify a separate server). The LLS is present only on Windows NT-based servers.

License Logging Service Traffic

The LLS creates three types of network traffic identified in the following traces.

- At service start time, the LLS sends its license information to the PDC as shown in the example below, it queries for the domain name (Frames 3-4) and then queries the NETLOGON service for the PDC name. If the LLS reports to an enterprise server, a WINS query resolves the name of that particular computer.

LLS sending license information at start.

Frame	Time	Src MAC Address	Dst MAC Address	Protocol	Description
2	3.54	SERVER	*BROADCAST	ARP_RARP	ARP: Request, Target IP: 10.100.1.21
3	3.54	PDC	SERVER	ARP_RARP	ARP: Reply, Target IP: 10.100.1.23 Target Hdwr Addr: 0000F6181D73
4	3.541	SERVER	PDC	NBT	SERVER NS: Query req. for TESTLAB <1B>
5	3.548	PDC	SERVER	NBT	PDC NS: Query (Node Status) resp. for TESTLAB <1B>, Success
6	3.561	SERVER	PDC	NETLOGON	SERVER Query for Primary DC
7	3.564	PDC	SERVER	NETLOGON	PDC Response to Primary Query

- If the Windows NT Server cannot communicate with the central LLS, it attempts to reconnect every 15 minutes. If an enterprise server regularly receives license information, the server must be available at all times.

Note Because the LLS uses a redirector connection to pass information, it is affected by the workstation service idle disconnect timeout period. Refer to the "Windows NT Server and Workstation Services" section above.

- The LLS replicates license information to the PDC or enterprise server every 24 hours by default. You can use the License Manager to configure this interval (from 1-72 hours) and the start time. By default, Windows NT Server automatically staggers transmission of license information to the PDC to avoid overloading the server.

License Logging Service Strategy

You can disable the LLS without adversely affecting Windows NT operation. If you want to use the service, configure the replication interval and start time to suit your needs. In a LAN environment the LLS replication usually occurs at night. In a dial-on-demand environment, you should configure this time to maximize a connection that has already been established. For example, if there is dial-on-demand connection every night between 4:00 a.m. and 6:00 a.m. for backups, perform LLS replication within that window.

Windows NT Spooler

Windows NT printing services access the network when connecting to printers, printing, and checking printer and job status. Usually client computers are close to their printers and do not generate WAN traffic.

The Windows NT Spooler can cause excess dialing when it distributes information on available printers. It sends out print browser information every 777 seconds as shown in the trace below. Frame 13 shows the initial connection to the SPOOLSS named pipe on the remote server. This connection pattern is then repeated in Frames 98, 175 and 749 at 777-second intervals. Some frames have been omitted for clarity.

Windows NT spooler sending print browser information.

Frame	Time	Src MAC Address	Dst MAC Address	Protocol	Description
7	7.373	LONDON	GLASGOW	NBT	SS: Session Request, Dest: GLASGO, Source: LONDON
8	7.373	GLASGOW	LONDON	NBT	SS: Positive Session Response, Len: 0
9	7.377	LONDON	GLASGOW	SMB	C negotiate, Dialect = NT LM 0.12
10	7.378	GLASGOW	LONDON	SMB	R negotiate, Dialect # = 7
11	7.401	LONDON	GLASGOW	SMB	C session setup & X, Username = , and C tree connect & X, Share =
12	7.406	GLASGOW	LONDON	SMB	R session setup & X, and R tree connect & X, Type = IPC
13	7.411	LONDON	GLASGOW	SMB	C NT create & X, File = \spoolss

Windows NT spooler sending print browser information. *(continued)*

Frame	Time	Src MAC Address	Dst MAC Address	Protocol	Description
14	7.418	GLASGOW	LONDON	SMB	R NT create & X, FID = 0x801
15	7.422	LONDON	GLASGOW	MSRPC	c/o RPC Bind: UUID 12345678-1234-ABCD-EF00-0123456789AB
16	7.428	GLASGOW	LONDON	MSRPC	c/o RPC Bind Ack: call 0x44005C assoc grp 0x394C7A xmit 0x1
17	7.432	LONDON	GLASGOW	R_WINSPOO	Error: Bad Opcode (Function does not exist)
18	7.438	GLASGOW	LONDON	R_WINSPOO	Error: Bad Opcode (Function does not exist)
19	7.441	LONDON	GLASGOW	SMB	C close file, FID = 0x801
20	7.445	GLASGOW	LONDON	SMB	R close file
98	784.562	GLASGOW	LONDON	SMB	C NT create & X, File = \spoolss
175	1807.79	LONDON	GLASGOW	SMB	C NT create & X, File = \spoolss
749	2584.88	GLASGOW	LONDON	SMB	C NT create & X, File = \spoolss

Use REGEDIT.EXE to modify the default print browser parameter as shown in the table below. Disabling the thread reduces network traffic, but prevents the print servers knowing about other print shares on the network. For more information see Knowledge Base article Q131902, Title: Printer Browse Thread May Cause Extensive Network Traffic.

Modify the default print browser parameter.

Registry Path	HKEY_LOCAL_MACHINE\System\CurrentControlSet\Control\Print
Parameter	DisableServerThread
Type	REG_DWORD
Default Value	0 (enabled)
Suggested Value	1 (disabled)

Windows NT Scheduler

Starting and stopping the Windows NT Scheduler service causes no traffic because by default the service runs under the LocalSystem account, which is part of the local security accounts manager (SAM) database and does not have access to the network. It can cause some traffic on startup, though: authentication (if it runs under a domain account) and copying its account to the local computer (if the account has a central profile). And it can create network traffic when a scheduled job uses network facilities for WINS lookups, file copying, and so forth.

Directory Replication

The Directory Replication service synchronizes a directory structure between computers in the domain, primarily the NETLOGON shares between the PDC and all BDCs. The NETLOGON share typically contains all of the scripts associated with the logon process. Although this works well in a LAN environment it can severely tax a dial-on-demand connection.

The default interval for directory replication is five minutes. You can modify this interval using the registry information shown below, up to a maximum interval of 60 minutes.

Modify the Directory Replication interval.

Registry Path	HKEY_LOCAL_MACHINE\System\CurrentControlSet\Replicator\Parameters\Interval
Parameter	Interval
Type	REG_DWORD
Default Value	5 (minutes) Range 1-60
Suggested Value	60 (minutes)

This interval controls the frequency at which the export computer checks its export file system for changes, after which it contacts its partners and notifies them of an update. The replicator service on the export server still attempts to communicate with the replicator service on the import server even if there are no changes in the file system, just to ensure that it is still available. Import computers then contact the export server and copy any directories in which changes are found. If the export server fails to contact the import server within a defined period (*Pulse x Interval*) then the import server initiates communication.

Replication Characteristics

When the Directory Replication service detects a change in the file system, it replicates all of the contents for the directory, including any sub-directories. When there are many files or change is frequent, replication can be time consuming. The Directory Replication service uses the redirector to establish a connection and transfer the files. The idle disconnect parameters described in the "Windows NT Server and Workstation Services" section above apply to directory replication.

Directory Replication Strategy

Because the Directory Replication service severely affects a dial-on-demand network, consider disabling the service. Some options:

- Use the Windows NT Scheduler service to run a batch job on a regular basis that copies any changed files. The Windows NT Server Resource Kit ROBOCOPY.EXE utility provides the ability to synchronize source and destination directories by copying only differences. This method does have some implications.

  The Windows NT Scheduler account must run under a domain account. In a network with standalone domains, without trusts or individual Windows NT-based computers with local logon files, you should use the LocalSystem account for the replicator service. Configure a Null Session Share on the servers hosting the master copy of the logon scripts and give everyone READ access to the share. (See Knowledge Base article Q124184, Title: Service Running as System Account Fails Accessing Network.) The Windows NT Scheduler service on the remote computers should now be able to access all of the files on that share.
- Use the Microsoft Content Replication server.
- Distribute LOGON files with routine business activities.

NETLOGON Service

This provides three primary functions within Windows NT domains:

- On the PDC, it ensures that all BDCs regularly receive copies of all changes made to the domain SAM database.
- On domain controllers, it authenticates domain logon requests against the local copy of the domain SAM database.
- It supports pass-through authentication to other [Trusted] domains.

Only the first function affects dial-on-demand environments. By default the NETLOGON service sends an update pulse every five minutes to all BDCs. You can configure a number of parameters to reduce this activity. TechNet article "NETLOGON Service Entries" documents this configuration.

This next trace illustrates the sequence for providing NETLOGON updates between the PDC (LONDON) and a BDC (GLASGOW) within a domain that was synchronized to ensure that only one change was represented. The changed data is carried in Frame 7.

Sequence of NETLOGON updates showing one change.

Frame	Time	Src MAC Address	Dst MAC Address	Protocol	Description
1	157.360	LONDON	GLASGOW	NETLOGON	Announce Change to UAS or SAM
2	158.036	GLASGOW	LONDON	SMB	C NT create & X, File = \NETLOGON
3	158.073	LONDON	GLASGOW	SMB	R NT create & X, FID = 0x800a
4	158.076	GLASGOW	LONDON	MSRPC	c/o RPC Bind: UUID 12345678-1234-ABCD-EF00-01234567CFFB
5	158.092	LONDON	GLASGOW	MSRPC	c/o RPC Bind Ack: call 0x0 assoc grp 0x8159 xmit 0x1630 re
6	158.095	GLASGOW	LONDON	R_LOGON	RPC Client call logon:NetrDatabaseDeltas(..)
7	158.165	LONDON	GLASGOW	R_LOGON	RPC Server response logon:NetrDatabaseDeltas(..)
8	158.288	GLASGOW	LONDON	TCP	.A...., len: 0, seq: 876161-876161, ack: 1823715, win: 87

Other NETLOGON Traffic

In addition to the NETLOGON functions listed above, other functions can affect a dial-on-demand environment:

- **Establishing a Secure Channel to other Domains**. When a NETLOGON Service starts on a domain controller it immediately attempts to contact a domain controller in each of the trusted domains. The communication establishes a secure channel that allows pass-through authentication to the SAM database with the trusted domains.

Sample environment for establishing a secure channel.

Account Domain – USA	Resource Domain – EUROPE
NEWYORK – PDC	LONDON – PDC
SEATTLE – BDC	PARIS – BDC
CHICAGO – BDC	

In the domain environment represented in the trace below, the resource domain trusts the account domain, therefore the domain controllers in the resource domain must establish a secure channel to a DC in the account domain.

When the NETLOGON service on the PARIS BDC starts, it locates the PDC for its own domain and establishes a connection to the NETLOGON named pipe. PARIS authenticates itself against the PDC (Frames 7-10) so that it can begin to receive SAM updates, then attempts to locate a domain controller in the trusted domain USA by sending out SAM LOGON requests in Frames 11-13.

On a system reboot the computer would typically use WINS to obtain a list of DCs in the trusted domain. The first DC from the account domain to respond is CHICAGO (Frame 14) and it is used to process any pass-through authentication requests. (You can check the status of pass-through authentication by using the Windows NT Resource Kit utility DOMMON.EXE). The BDC then synchronizes the SAM with the PDC by requesting any outstanding changes in Frames 15-18.

Network trace of establishing a secure channel.

Frame	Time	Src MAC Address	Dst MAC Address	Protocol	Description
1	9.276	PARIS	LONDON	NETLOGON	Query for Primary DC
2	9.278	LONDON	PARIS	NETLOGON	Response to Primary Query
3	9.29	PARIS	LONDON	SMB	C NT create & X, File = \NETLOGON
4	9.292	LONDON	PARIS	SMB	R NT create & X, FID = 0x5001
5	9.292	PARIS	LONDON	MSRPC	c/o RPC Bind: UUID 12345678-1234-ABCD …
6	9.293	LONDON	PARIS	MSRPC	c/o RPC Bind Ack: call 0x1 assoc grp 0x9B50 xmit 0
7	9.294	PARIS	LONDON	R_LOGON	RPC Client call logon:NetrServerReqChallenge(..)
8	9.295	LONDON	PARIS	R_LOGON	RPC Server response logon:NetrServerReqChallenge(..)
9	9.296	PARIS	LONDON	R_LOGON	RPC Client call logon:NetrServerAuthenticate2(..)
10	9.301	LONDON	PARIS	R_LOGON	RPC Server response logon:NetrServerAuthenticate2(..)
11	9.303	PARIS	*BROADCAST	NETLOGON	SAM LOGON request from client
12	9.303	PARIS	NEWYORK	NETLOGON	SAM LOGON request from client
13	9.304	PARIS	NEWYORK	NETLOGON	SAM LOGON request from client

Network trace of establishing a secure channel. *(continued)*

Frame	Time	Src MAC Address	Dst MAC Address	Protocol	Description
14	9.305	CHICAGO	PARIS	NETLOGON	SAM Response to SAM LOGON request
15	9.33	PARIS	LONDON	R_LOGON	RPC Client call logon:NetrDatabaseDeltas(..)
16	9.332	LONDON	PARIS	R_LOGON	RPC Server response logon:NetrDatabaseDeltas(..)
17	9.333	PARIS	LONDON	R_LOGON	RPC Client call logon:NetrDatabaseDeltas(..)
18	9.334	LONDON	PARIS	R_LOGON	RPC Server response logon:NetrDatabaseDeltas(..)
19	9.334	SEATTLE	PARIS	NETLOGON	SAM Response to SAM LOGON request
20	9.336	PARIS	LONDON	R_LOGON	RPC Client call logon:NetrDatabaseDeltas(..)
21	9.337	LONDON	PARIS	R_LOGON	RPC Server response logon:NetrDatabaseDeltas(..)

In most cases this sequence poses no problem, but stopping and starting DCs or the NETLOGON service initiates a dial-on-demand event to establish a secure channel to a trusted domain. In some domain designs this behavior could result in numerous dial-on-demand events occurring for every DC that is restarted.

- **Changing Machine and Trust Relationship Passwords**. When you configure a trust relationship for the first time you enter an initial password on both sides to enable the domains to communicate securely. Once established, each PDC establishes a secret account and password with its counterpart. The password is automatically changed every week as shown in the trace below. The actual passwords are set in Frames 24 and 26. Because this information is part of Local Security Authority (LSA) secrets, the domain immediately attempt to synchronize the SAM with all backup domain controllers.

Trust relationships password changed weekly.

Frame	Time	Src MAC Address	Dst MAC Address	Protocol	Description
1	33.634	LONDON	*BROADCAST	NBT	NS: Query req. for NEWYORK
2	33.639	NEWYORK	*BROADCAST	ARP_RARP	ARP: Request, Target IP: 89.0.0.3
3	33.640	LONDON	NEWYORK	ARP_RARP	ARP: Reply, Target IP: 89.0.0.2 Target Hdwr Addr: 0080C7E2168A
4	33.640	NEWYORK	LONDON	NBT	NS: Query (Node Status) resp. for NEWYORK, Success
5	33.642	LONDON	NEWYORK	TCP	....S., len: 4, seq: 604893393-604893396, ack: 0, win:
6	33.643	NEWYORK	LONDON	TCP	.A..S., len: 4, seq: 391927223-391927226, ack: 604893394, win:
7	33.645	LONDON	NEWYORK	TCP	.A...., len: 0, seq: 604893394-604893394, ack: 391927224, win:
8	33.645	LONDON	NEWYORK	NBT	SS: Session Request, Dest: NEWYORK, Source: LONDON
9	33.646	NEWYORK	LONDON	NBT	SS: Positive Session Response, Len: 0
10	33.656	LONDON	NEWYORK	SMB	C negotiate, Dialect = NT LM 0.12
11	33.658	NEWYORK	LONDON	SMB	R negotiate, Dialect # = 7
12	33.717	LONDON	NEWYORK	SMB	C session setup & X, Username = , and C tree connect & X, Share =
13	33.721	NEWYORK	LONDON	SMB	R session setup & X, and R tree connect & X, Type = IPC

Trust relationships password changed weekly. *(continued)*

Frame	Time	Src MAC Address	Dst MAC Address	Protocol	Description
14	33.734	LONDON	NEWYORK	SMB	C NT create & X, File = \NETLOGON
15	33.742	NEWYORK	LONDON	SMB	R NT create & X, FID = 0x800
16	33.755	LONDON	NEWYORK	MSRPC	c/o RPC Bind: UUID 12345678-1234-ABCD-EF00-01234567CFFB
17	33.762	NEWYORK	LONDON	MSRPC	c/o RPC Bind Ack: call 0x3 assoc grp 0xE6F8 xmit 0x1630 re
18	33.809	LONDON	NEWYORK	R_LOGON	RPC Client call logon:NetrServerReqChallenge(..)
19	33.815	NEWYORK	LONDON	R_LOGON	RPC Server response logon:NetrServerReqChallenge(..)
20	33.850	LONDON	NEWYORK	R_LOGON	RPC Client call logon:NetrServerAuthenticate2(..)
21	34.009	NEWYORK	LONDON	TCP	.A...., len: 0, seq: 391927786-391927786, ack: 604894484, win:
22	34.124	NEWYORK	LONDON	R_LOGON	RPC Server response logon:NetrServerAuthenticate2(..)
23	34.291	LONDON	NEWYORK	TCP	.A...., len: 0, seq: 604894484-604894484, ack: 391927886, win:
24	34.650	LONDON	NEWYORK	R_LOGON	RPC Client call logon:NetrServerPasswordSet(..)
25	34.811	NEWYORK	LONDON	TCP	.A...., len: 0, seq: 391927886-391927886, ack: 604894712, win:
26	34.886	NEWYORK	LONDON	R_LOGON	RPC Server response logon:NetrServerPasswordSet(..)
27	34.992	LONDON	NEWYORK	TCP	.A...., len: 0, seq: 604894712-604894712, ack: 391927986, win:

When a Windows NT Server or Workstation is a member of the domain there is a similar activity, but its traffic is one-way. The Windows NT-based computer receives a password that it can use in conjunction with its computer account to provide pass-through authentication to the domain NETLOGON services. This machine password changes weekly.

Note In Windows NT Server domains all changes to the SAM, including machine account information, occur on the PDC.

- **Disabling Machine Account Password Changes**. In an organization with 3000 copies of Windows NT Workstation installed into a large dial-on-demand network the annual cost of this type of traffic alone could be as high as $78,000 (3000 nodes x 52 weeks x 5 minutes per call x $0.10 per minute). To disable the machine account password change on a Windows NT Workstation or Server, edit the registry key below. (For information on disabling machine account passwords, see Knowledge Base article Q154501, Title: How to Disable Automatic Machine Account Password Changes.)

Disable machine account password change.

Registry Path	HKEY_LOCAL_MACHINE\System\CurrentControlSet\Service\NETLOGON\Parameters
Parameter	DisablePasswordChange
Type	REG_DWORD
Default Value	0 (enabled)
Suggested Value	1 (disabled)

- **Replicating LSA Secrets**. One class of security information, LSA secrets, requires that the SAM be synchronized without waiting for the next NETLOGON pulse period. Even when you have correctly configured the NETLOGON parameters ChangeLogSize and Pulse, LSA Secrets replication can increase NETLOGON traffic with:
  - Addition of machine accounts to the domain (but not deletion).
  - Changes in machine account passwords.
  - Changes in account policies.
  - Changes in trust relationships including trust password changes.

The synchronization of LSA secrets uses the same transmission mechanism as all other NETLOGON data except that it happens immediately instead of being deferred until the next NETLOGON pulse. Although administrators cannot alter the behavior of LSA Secrets replication, simple measures such as creating machine accounts in batch mode instead of sporadically throughout the day can reduce unwanted connections.

To reduce NETLOGON traffic:

- Change the default parameters for NETLOGON replication.
- Disable weekly machine account password changes.

  You cannot disable the NETLOGON service. The methods above work for domain designs with distributed or centralized BDCs.

Implementing Windows NT Dial-on-Demand Optimizations

During deployment, you can configure all Windows NT Server-based computers optimally for a dial-on-demand network. It is more challenging, however, to implement recommended changes to an existing network because computers may not follow a standard configuration. This section includes a Windows NT policy file you can use to configure Windows NT 4.0-based computers with a set of parameters.

Implementing Dial-on-Demand Policies in an Windows NT 4.0 Domain

Copy the policy file (DOD.ADM—found on the sample CD in the DialOn folder) to a local file system on a server and name it DOD.ADM. Start the Windows NT Policy Editor and select **Options-Policy Template**, and add the DOD.ADM file. Make the selections that you require and save the file as NTCONFIG.POL. Windows NT Server adds this new policy and automatically applies it to all computers in the domain, guaranteeing that both existing and new computers are optimized with the appropriate dial-on-demand policies. For information on the use and deployment of system policies see the Window NT Server 4.0 documentation or resource kit.

Implementing Dial-on-Demand Policies on Standalone Windows NT 4.0 Workstations or Servers

When Windows NT-based computers are not members of a domain, you can still implement local policies but you have to make a one-time modification to every computer. To implement local policies, open the registry editor and edit or create the following registry values:

One-time modification for standalone computers (a).

Registry Path	HKEY_LOCAL_MACHINE\System\CurrentControlSet\Control\Update
Parameter	UpdateMode
Type	REG_DWORD
Value	2 (manual updates)

One-time modification to standalone computers (b).

Registry Path	HKEY_LOCAL_MACHINE\System\CurrentControlSet\Control\Update
Parameter	NetworkPath
Type	REG_SZ
Value	C:\WINNT\POLICY\NTCONFIG.POL (example only)

To implement this registry or editing step on multiple computers, export this registry key to a .REG file using REGEDIT.EXE. Then merge it on remote computers by using Windows NT Scheduler, Microsoft Systems Management Server, or some other method. Create the NTCONFIG.POL file and save it to a directory. Reboot each computer twice to make sure policies have installed completely. The first reboot applies the policy and changes the registry to reflect the new value; the second makes changes to services that users started before the policies were applied.

Implementing Dial-on-Demand Policies using a REG File

If administrators prefer not to use System Polices in their environments, they can apply the template DOD.REG file (included on the sample CD in the DialOn folder) with Windows NT Scheduler or other software distribution tools. To perform a silent installation of a .REG file, use REGEDIT /S DOD.REG. The settings in the .REG file are the same as the suggested values found throughout this chapter. The .REG file states values in hexadecimal, not decimal. You can use the Windows calculator to convert: on the **View** menu select **Scientific**.

More Information

KB Articles referenced in this chapter:

- Q164308, Title: Windows NT 4.0 Clients May Refresh WINS Entries Frequently
- Q139270, Title: How to Change Name Resolution Order on Windows 95 and Windows NT
- Q120642, Title: TCP/IP & NBT Configuration Parameters for Windows NT
- Q102878, Title: Information on Browser Operation
- Q134985, Title: Browsing & Other Traffic Incur High Costs over ISDN Routers
- Q138365, Title: How the Autodisconnect Works in Windows NT
- Q105134, Title: AutoDisconnect Default Incorrect in Online Help
- Q102981, Title: REG: Workstation Service Entries
- Q131902, Title: Printer Browse Thread May Cause Extensive Network Traffic
- Q124184, Title: Service Running as System Account Fails Accessing Network
- Q154501, Title: How to Disable Automatic Machine Account Password Changes

CHAPTER 6

Configuring Windows NT for Satellite Networking at Coho Winery

By Jim Gowler, MCS—Great Lakes

Enterprise network infrastructure often includes a variety of communication media and links: Ethernet, integrated services digital network (ISDN), frame relay, dial-up lines, and satellite connections. This chapter focuses on using Microsoft Transmission Control Protocol/Internet Protocol (TCP/IP) with Microsoft Windows for Workgroups 3.11, Windows 9*x*, Windows NT Workstation and Server, and Windows 2000 in an Ethernet local area network (LAN) environment communicating to remote sites over satellite connections. The configuration recommendations also apply to wide area networks (WANs) and dial-up connections.

In Focus

Enterprise
Coho Winery, a growing company with vineyards throughout North America and Australia, and international distributorships.

Network
Over 8000 remote offices and distributorships linked to the corporate headquarters based in Napa Valley over satellite connections.

Challenge
Systems administrators must optimize the network for satellite communications, configuring packet transmission latency (lag time), the Server Message Block (SMB) size on Windows NT Server, and the Maximum Transmit Unit (MTU) size of the LAN.

Solution
Satellite links typically impose the highest latency of any media, and they require more complex parameter adjustment to optimize network communications.

What You'll Find In This Chapter

- **How to test, assess, and deal with latency in your network.**
- **How to configure networks effectively for the varying speeds found in networks incorporating satellite links.**
- **How to adjust parameters for replication in large networks and those with multiple-processor PDCs and BDCs. (This discussion also explains which parameters do not require adjustment and why.)**
- **How to incorporate configuration ideas on most Microsoft operating systems (Windows NT Server/Workstation, Windows 2000 Server/Professional, Windows for Workgroups, Windows 9x) and Microsoft server applications such as Microsoft SQL Server and Microsoft Exchange Server.**

Warning This chapter makes recommendations for modifying or adding Windows registry parameters with REGEDIT.EXE or REGEDT32.EXE. Using Registry Editor incorrectly can cause serious, system-wide problems that require you to reinstall Windows NT. Microsoft cannot guarantee that any problems resulting from the use of Registry Editor can be solved. Use this tool at your own risk.

Windows NT setup installs two versions of Registry Editor: REGEDT32.EXE (the Windows NT version) and REGEDIT.EXE (the Windows 9*x* version). Although you can use REGEDIT.EXE to search for keys and values in Windows NT 4.0, *use REGEDT32.EXE to edit the Windows NT registry.*

Enterprise Requirements

The recommendations and best practices in this chapter address some basic networking requirements.

For Windows for Workgroups, Windows 9*x*, Windows NT Workstation, and Windows 2000 Professional, each desktop:

- Uses TCP/IP for network communications.
- Can browse every corporate-supported resource server in the LAN.
- Can browse every corporate-supported resource server in the WAN.
- Communicates over satellite links.

For Windows NT Server, Windows 2000 Server, Microsoft SQL Server, and Microsoft Exchange, each server and service:

- Uses TCP/IP for network communications.
- Has access to every corporate-supported resource server in the LAN.
- Has access to every corporate-supported resource server in the WAN.
- Communicates over satellite links.

Overview of Satellite Communications

A typical network with satellite links includes earth stations (remote sites) that communicate to a hub site (also an earth station) that serves as the main data center in the enterprise. The hub site does not have to be at the same physical location of the main data repository; it can be a remote site with a secure connection to a LAN or a WAN.

An earth station consists of a satellite dish (with a central head) and a digital interface unit (DIU) connected to the local network through a turbo port card. The dish transmits and receives data to the satellite (bird). Dish bandwidths vary from 128 Kbs to 1 Mbs. The available bandwidth to each earth station can be divided (the term is *carved*) into separate channels varying from 9600 baud to 1 Mb.

You can configure the maximum transmit unit (MTU) size of data sent through software and hardware and over satellite links to a maximum of 1500 bytes to match the default size of the DIU. You can also drop the MTU below this figure to match available bandwidth for performance reasons. The circled numbers in the figure apply to the explanation that follows.

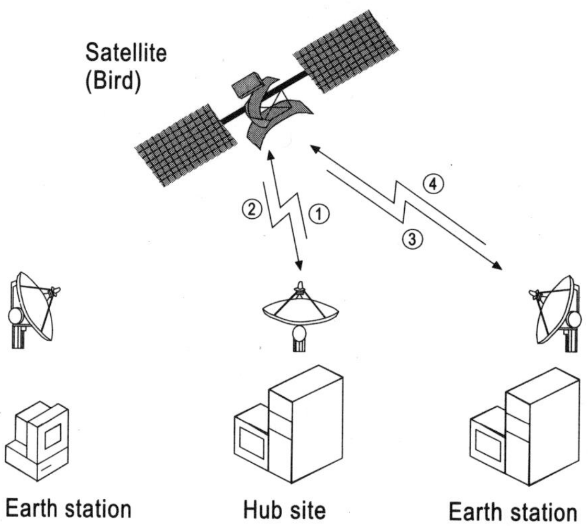

Figure 6.1 Communications between earth stations and the hub site.

The terminology that describes satellite communications is similar to other telecommunications terminology. All communications *from* the hub site are **outbound** transmissions (1), and all communications *to* the hub site are **inbound** transmissions (2). Communications *from* the satellite to the remote earth stations are **outroute** (3), and communications *to* the satellite from the remote earth station are **inroute** (4).

Network administrators must tune three areas to optimize satellite links for networking communications: packet transmission latency (lag time), the Server Message Block (SMB) size of Windows NT Servers, and the LAN's maximum transmit unit (MTU) size. These areas are discussed in the next three sections.

Latency

The following illustrations show the results of using PING.EXE to test latency across network segments. These use baseline measurements set in a test lab; individual measurements and results vary with network design.

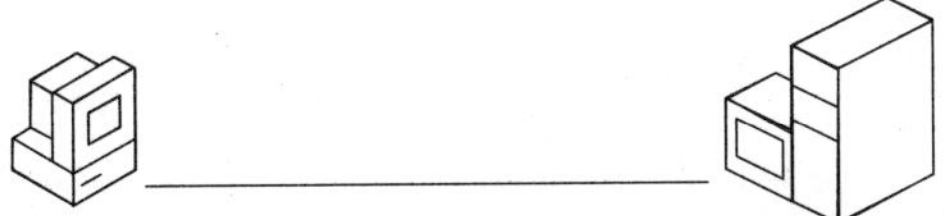

```
Pinging 123.456.789.10 with 32 bytes of data:

Reply from 123.456.789.10: bytes=32 time<10 ms TTL=59
Reply from 123.456.789.10: bytes=32 time<10 ms TTL=59
Reply from 123.456.789.10: bytes=32 time<10 ms TTL=59
Reply from 123.456.789.10: bytes=32 time<10 ms TTL=59
```

Figure 6.2 Checking latency period on a LAN using PING.

Figure 6.2 uses the PING utility to set a reference point for latency in milliseconds (ms). In this example, a local PING reports a latency less than 10 ms.

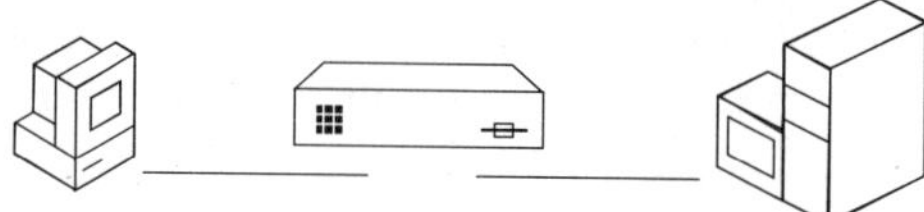

```
Pinging 456.789.123.10 with 32 bytes of data:

Reply from 456.789.123.10: bytes=32 time<10 ms TTL=59
Reply from 456.789.123.10: bytes=32 time<10 ms TTL=59
Reply from 456.789.123.10: bytes=32 time<10 ms TTL=59
Reply from 456.789.123.10: bytes=32 time<10 ms TTL=59
```

Figure 6.3 Checking latency across a local router.

This shows a local router with a latency of 10 ms or less. Latency increases as router load and the number of routers increase.

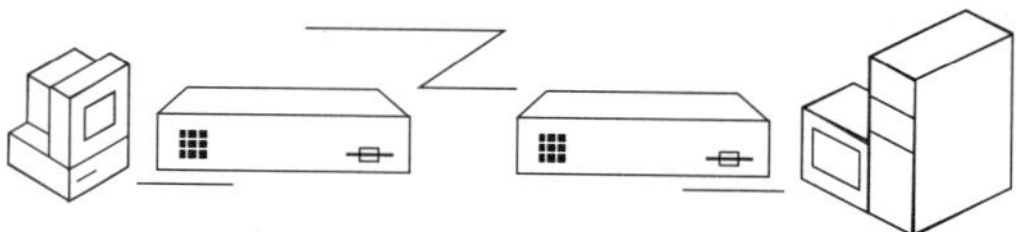

```
Pinging 789.123.456.10 with 32 bytes of data:

Reply from 789.123.456.10: bytes=32 time<110 ms TTL=59
Reply from 789.123.456.10: bytes=32 time<109 ms TTL=59
Reply from 789.123.456.10: bytes=32 time<110 ms TTL=59
Reply from 789.123.456.10: bytes=32 time<112 ms TTL=59
```

Figure 6.4 Checking latency across a remote router or bridge.

Figure 6.4 shows PING results in a WAN environment. Here response time increases substantially from less than 10 ms to more than 110 ms. By default Microsoft's implementation of TCP/IP addresses potential LAN and WAN latency by setting the wait time to 750 ms. This is important, because when latency starts approaching wait time, as it often does over WANs, timeouts (and communications failures) increase.

When sending a PING from the hub site to the satellite (**outbound**) and from there to a remote earth station (**outroute**) the test returns these results (the path is from 1 to 3 in Figure 6.1):

Pinging 123.456.789.10 with 32 bytes of data:

Request timed out.
Request timed out.
Request timed out.
Request timed out.

When using the commands below, the NetBIOS TCP (NetBT) stack also fails when communications travel *outbound* from the hub site, over the satellite, and *outroute* to a remote earth station. Both the PING utility and the NET USE DOS command use a Broadcast Query Time-out value to locate the destination host:

NET VIEW \\SATURN
System error 53 has occurred.

NET USE Z: \\SATURN\NETLOGON
System error 53 has occurred.

To troubleshoot, use the PING utility with the **-w** option to increase the ms time-out value and determine the network latency. The results in this example are:

PING 123.123.123.10 -w 1600

Pinging 197.127.135.10 with 32 bytes of data:

Reply from 123.123.123.10: bytes=32 time=1382ms TTL=32
Reply from 123.123.123.10: bytes=32 time=1331ms TTL=32
Reply from 123.123.123.10: bytes=32 time=1342ms TTL=32
Reply from 123.123.123.10: bytes=32 time=1342ms TTL=32

After you have determined the proper ms time-out value, you can modify the Broadcast Query Time-out values for workstations to accommodate the latency across satellite links.

Configuring BcastQueryTimeout Values

The default value for BcastQueryTimeout is 750 ms (hexadecimal value 2ee). In the previous example, the satellite (123.123.123.10) has a latency period greater than 1300 ms. You can increase this value to 1600 ms, allowing NBT name query to resolve machine names submitted via the NET USE command.

Note The PING.EXE utility only creates its packets: it does not resolve a hostname to an IP address, nor does it use the NBT to do so. Increasing the BcastQueryTimeout parameter does not apply to PING, but does work for all other WINSOCK and NBT programs.

- For Windows for Workgroups 3.11, modify the SYSTEM.INI file:
  [NBT]
  BcastQueryTimeout =
  Default: 750

For Windows 9*x*, edit the BcastQueryTimeout registry subkey:

HKEY_LOCAL_MACHINE\System\CurrentControlSet\Services\VxD \MSTCP

For Windows NT versions through 4.0, and Windows 2000, modify the BcastQueryTimeout parameter:

HKEY_LOCAL_MACHINE\System\CurrentControlSet\Services\NetBT\ Parameters\BcastQueryTimeout

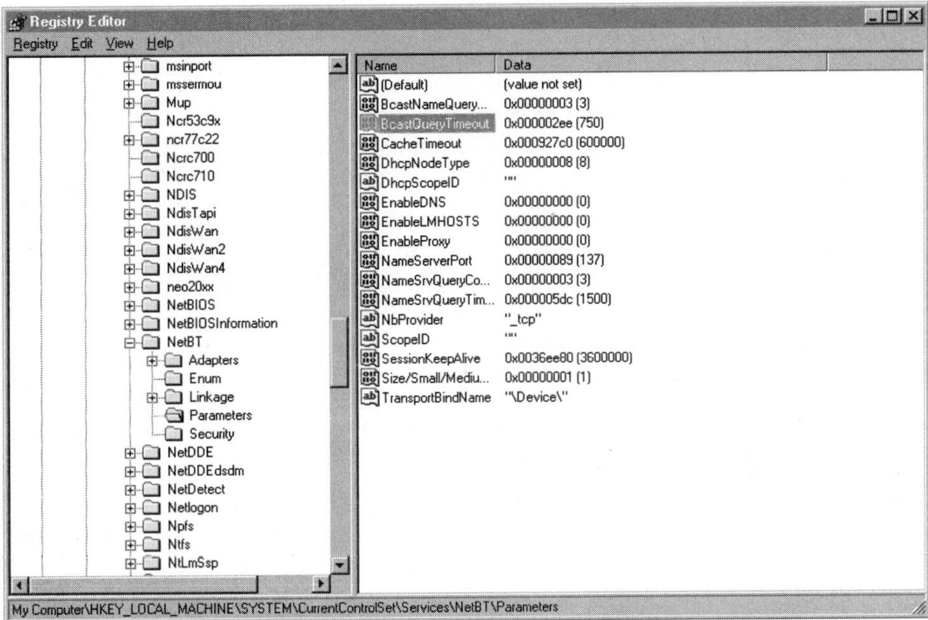

Figure 6.5 Using Registry Editor (REGEDIT.EXE) to configure BcastQueryTimeout in Windows NT.

To modify this setting, double-click on the parameter in the right pane of the Registry Editor window, bringing up the Edit DWORD Value window:

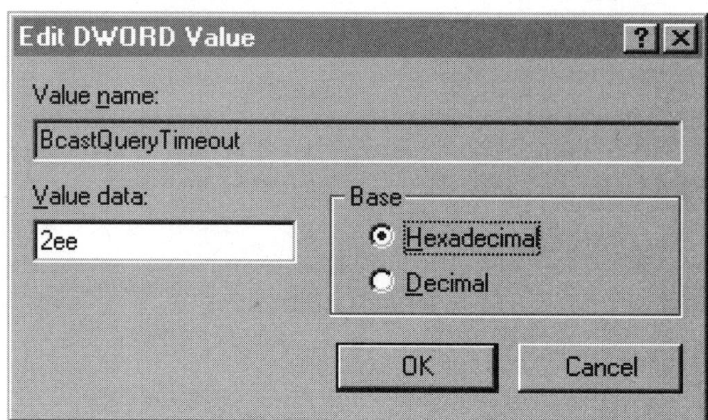

Figure 6.6 Edit DWORD Value window to modify BcastQueryTimeout.

Server Message Block (SMB)

Configuring SizReqBuf for Windows NT Server versions 3.5*x*

Windows NT Server manages input/output by carving data into blocks. When enough memory is available, it operates in *raw* mode, allocating large blocks of data (64 KB). When there is not enough memory, the server uses a request buffer for large- and small-block reads/writes. You can configure these sizes in the **SizReqBuf** parameter (default 4356 bytes, range 512 to 65536).

By increasing the SizReqBuf to match the TCP/IP window for **RawIoTimeLimit**, **EnableRaw**, and **MaxLinkDelay** (discussed in the next section), you can load-balance the system for buffering when there is not enough memory available to run in raw mode. Two common increases are:

- 12288 to match the default transmission size of Windows 95 and Windows for Workgroups 3.11's internal reads/writes buffering of the 32-bit redirector.
- 12548 to create best throughput and support for Windows NT Server, Windows for Workgroups 3.11, Windows 9*x*.

The redirector in Windows NT Server and Workstation can dynamically adjust to operate in raw state or to use the request buffer (SizReqBuf), which does not affect raw requests *from a remote* Windows NT Workstation/Server, Windows for Workgroups 3.11, or Windows 9*x* nodes. It controls the data flow only to nodes with other operating systems.

Windows NT Server and Workstation by default invoke raw mode when requested by other Windows NT computers. When the connection is established, the redirector determines if it is over a slow link and uses SizReqBuf if it is.

To modify the SizReqBuf registry subkey:

1. Start Registry Editor (REGEDT32.EXE).
2. Go to this subkey:

   HKEY_LOCAL_MACHINE\SYSTEM\CurrentControlSet\Services\LanmanServer\Parameters\SizReqBuf

To add the SizReqBuf registry subkey:

1. Create the SizReqBuf value using this information:

   Value name: SizReqBuf

   Data type: REG_DWORD (DWORD)

   Data: 512 to 65536 (bytes in decimal)
2. Close Registry Editor and restart the computer.

For more information on this registry subkey, see Microsoft Knowledge Base article Q177266, Title: Remote Directory Lists Are Slower Than Local Directory Listings.

In a Windows NT 3.5*x* environment, the redirector counts the amount of data in a specified time frame to decide if the connection a slow link. If it is, the operating system switches to request buffer input/output.

Configuring RawIoTimeLimit for Windows NT 3.5*x* (and 4.0)

This Windows NT registry parameter (default 5 seconds) allows you to set the redirector to send data in 64-KB blocks (raw mode) if you are not using Remote Access Service (RAS). Increasing the timing interval "tricks" the operating system into thinking a higher speed connection exists, causing it to shift into raw mode. For example, if you increase the **RawIoTimeLimit** parameter to 20, the redirector switches into raw mode, without having to make special calculations to find a boundary for SizReqBuf.

1. Start Registry Editor (REGEDT32.EXE).
2. Go to this subkey:

   HKEY_LOCAL_MACHINE\System\CurrentControlSet\Services\Rdr\Paramaters\RawIoTimeLimit
3. If this value does not exist, add it using these parameters:

   Value name: RawIoTimeLimit

   Data type: REG_DWORD (DWORD)

   Data range: 0 to 65535 seconds
4. To stop and restart the redirector use the commands **net stop rdr** and **net start rdr** from a command prompt. This puts the new setting into effect.

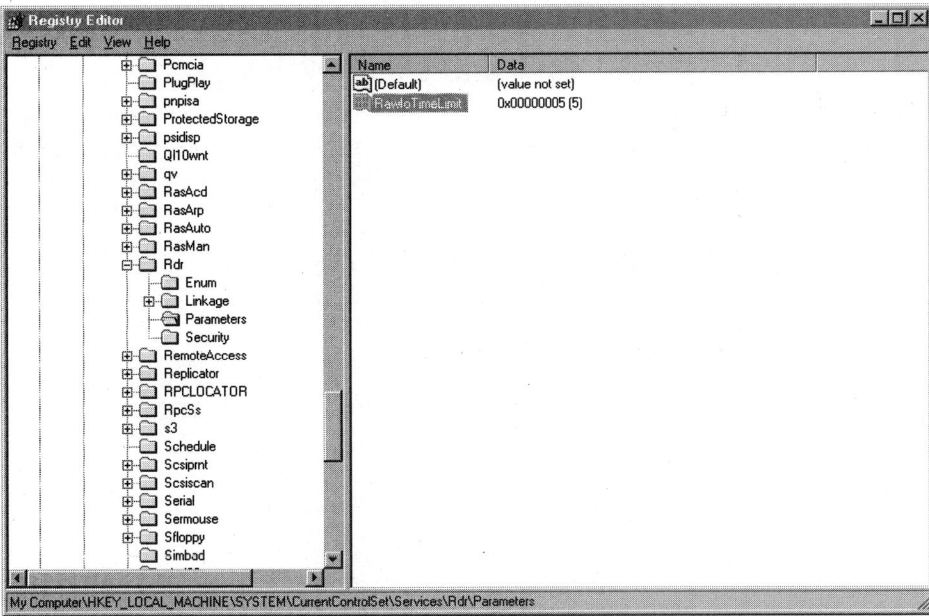

Figure 6.7 Using Registry Editor (REGEDIT.EXE) to search for RawIoTimeLimit in Windows NT.

Warning Although you can use the RawIoTimeLimit parameter to speed up copying from a network server down to the desktop, you cannot use it with RAS because copying data from the desktop up to a RAS server overrides that server's serial line, truncates the copy, and exits. The only error seen on the workstation is *copy failure*. On the server side, the modem reports CRC errors and disconnects the network session.

Configuring Windows NT 4.0 and Windows 2000 (EnableRaw and MaxLinkDelay)

The previous parameter modifications enable raw detection over the WAN with satellite connections. You do not need to implement them on Windows NT 4.0 because processing raw SMBs can impede performance on some networks. You can disable the raw mode by adding the parameter **EnableRaw** and setting it to 0:

> **HKEY_LOCAL_MACHINE\System\CurrentControlSet\Services\LanmanServer\Parameters\EnableRaw**

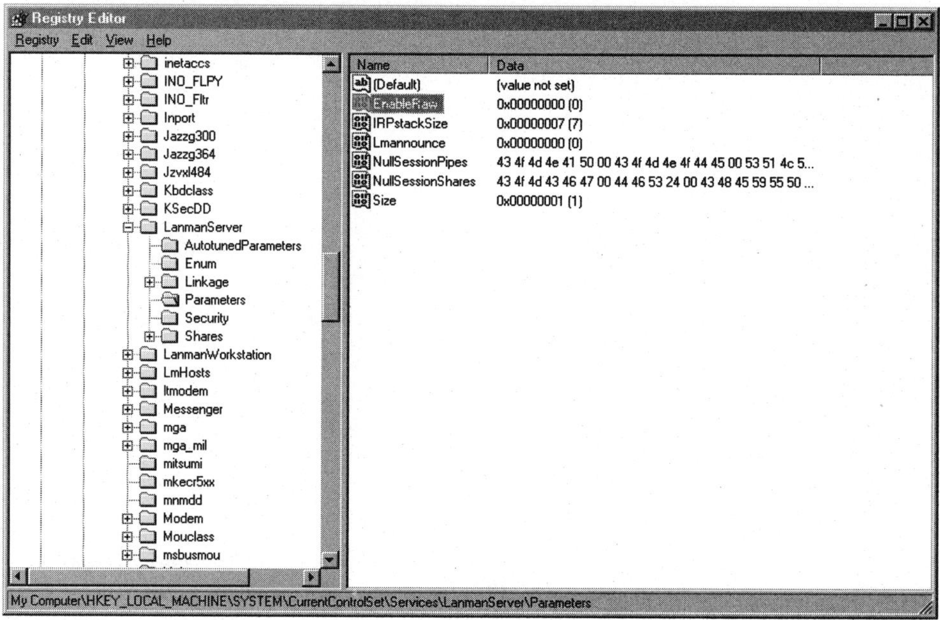

Figure 6.8 Using Registry Editor (REGEDIT.EXE) to search for EnableRaw.

For more information, see Knowledge Base article Q127023, Title: Raw SMB Requests Across Router Results in Session Termination.

MaxLinkDelay specifies the maximum time allowed for a link delay (default 60 seconds) before a server automatically disables raw mode input/output for a connection. Increase the MaxLinkDelay registry subkey to override this feature:

HKEY_LOCAL_MACHINE\System\CurrentControlSet\Services\LanmanServer\Parameters\MaxLinkDelay

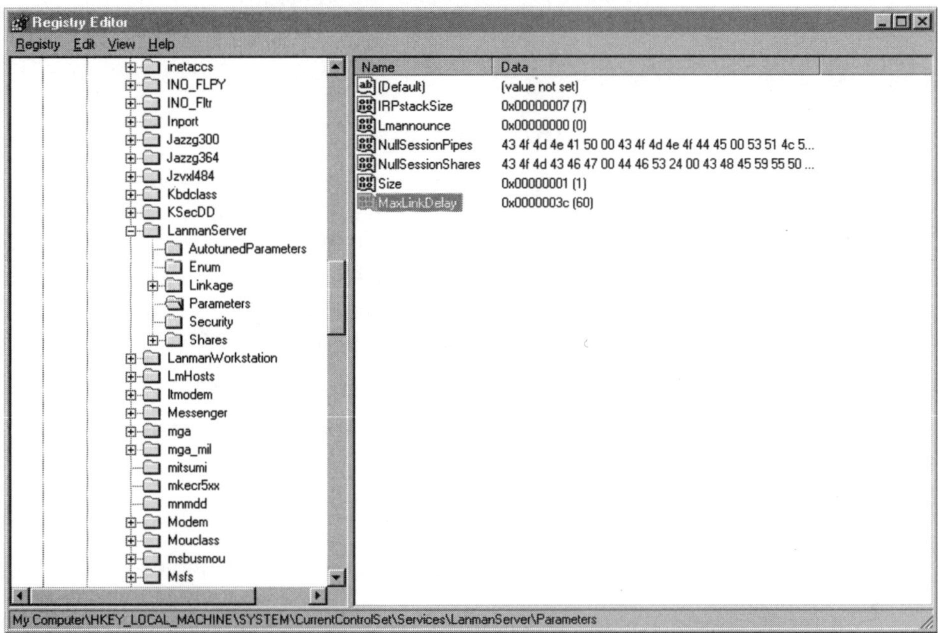

Figure 6.9 Using Registry Editor (REGEDIT.EXE) to search for MaxLinkDelay.

HKEY_LOCAL_MACHINE\System\CurrentControlSet\Services\rdr\Parameters\RawIoTimeLimit

You can modify or add the parameter RawIoTimeLimit to Windows NT 4.0 and Windows 2000 (see the above section "Configuring RawIoTimeLimit for Windows NT 3.5x (and 4.0)") in network configurations using the NetBIOS gateway. When turned on, this setting can increase throughput by 10-15 percent, blocking all other data transfers. By default, RawIoTimeLimit is disabled over slow links speeds of 14,400 BPS (or slower) and enabled (default 5 seconds) over faster links, such as ISDN lines.

For more information, see the *Windows NT Server Networking Supplement Manual*, "Appendix A—RAS Registry Values."

TCP Window Size

Configuring DefaultRcvWindow

The transmission control protocol (TCP) **receive window** specifies the maximum number of bytes a sender can transmit without receiving an **acknowledgment** (ACK). Increasing this value improves performance on networks with high latency. Both sides of a network connection control the TCP receive window size. You can configure receive window size for Windows for Workgroups in the SYSTEM.INI file, and for Windows 9*x* with the DefaultRcvWindow registry entry.

- For Windows for Workgroups 3.11, modify the SYSTEM.INI file:
  [MSTCP]
  DefaultRcvWindow =
  Default: 8192

For Windows 9*x*, modify the DefaultRcvWindow registry subkey in:

HKEY_LOCAL_MACHINE\System\CurrentControlSet\Services\VXD\MSTCP

Windows NT TCPWindowSize

When data blocks greater than the MTU or segment size travel across the network, the TCP Window Size buffers them, returning acknowledgments to notify the sending computer when one block has been received and it is time to send the next one. Larger buffers can accommodate larger blocks of data, allowing more data to flow before reversing direction and sending an acknowledgment. This reduces traffic by generating fewer ACK packets.

Windows NT default TCPWindowSize values.

Registry Parameters	Windows NT 3.1	Windows NT 3.5*x*	Windows NT 4.0	Windows 2000
TCPWindowSize	8192 (1)	8760	8760	16504
	8K	8K	8K	16K

To adjust the TCP Window size, modify or add this registry subkey:

HKEY_LOCAL_MACHINE\System\CurrentControlSet\Services\Tcpip\Parameters\TCPWindowSize

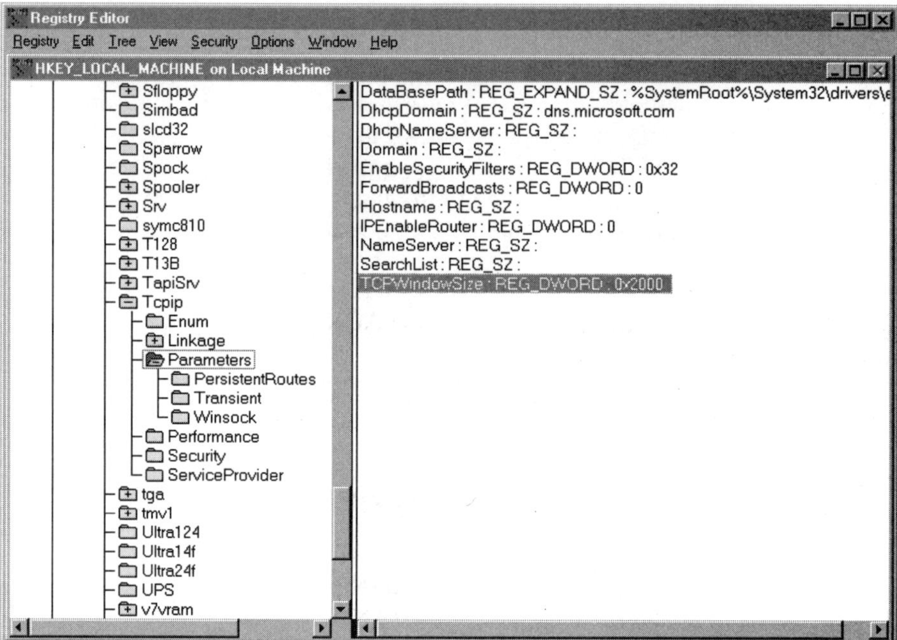

Figure 6.10 Using Registry Editor (REGEDT32.EXE) to modify TCPWindowSize.

Note When a TCP/IP client communicates over a router that imposes a hop-count—which limits the number of subsequent routers a message can pass through—a forced ACK is issued for every two packets. This avoids the *silly window syndrome*, which occurs when the window is so large that it causes a high retransmission rate and system thrashing. This is rare in test labs, but common in production environments. Microsoft TCP/IP does not allow you to disable the forced ACK setting (every two packets over a router).

TCP Window Size in Windows 2000

Windows 2000 addressing performance is optimized for all types of media and WAN connectivity, effectively avoiding *silly window syndrome*. The protocol stack maintains the two-packet recommendation over routers, but it waits for a response rather than reversing the data flow and issuing an ACK. This improves performance over satellite links. Here's a representation:

- Windows 2000:
  DATA==> DATA==> DATA==> DATA==> DATA==> DATA==>
  <==ACK <==ACK <==ACK
- Windows NT:
  DATA==> DATA==> <==ACK DATA==> DATA==> <==ACK DATA==>
  DATA==> <==ACK

Maximum Transmit Unit (MTU) Registry Parameters

Windows NT TCP transport entries govern the segment size of data traveling over the network. **TCPRecvSegmentSize** specifies the maximum receive segment size, and **TCPSendSegmentSize** specifies the maximum send segment size. You can modify or add these parameters (REG_DWORD or DWORD) in:

HKEY_LOCAL_MACHINE\System\CurrentControlSet\Services\TCPIP\Parameters

Windows NT registry parameters for MTU.

Registry Parameters	Windows NT 3.1	Windows NT 3.5*x*	Windows NT 4.0	Windows 2000
TCPRecvSegmentSize	1460	0 (1)	0 (1)	0 (1)
TCPSendSegmentSize	1460	0 (1)	0 (1)	0 (1)
MTU	1500	0 (2)	0 (2)	0 (2)

Notes on Windows NT MTU parameters:

(1) MTU size - 40 = segment size.

(2) Windows NT 3.5 uses the default MTU size of the MAC interface: Ethernet = 1500.

In token ring networks, this value depends on the MAXFRAME size of the token ring card. Because the desktop cannot process transactions larger than 4096 bytes, avoid token ring net cards with hard coded MTU MAXFRAME sizes greater than 4096.

Cautionary Notes

MTU settings can create problems when:

- Sending packets (that require a response) from one token ring site over a satellite to another token ring site with a smaller MTU size.
- Sending packets from one token ring site over frame relay to another token ring site.
- Communicating from one token ring site over Asynchronous Transfer Mode (ATM) to another token ring site.
- Using different media types in any combination.

Use the Ethernet default size of 1500 to avoid these problems.

Configuring MTU Size for Windows NT

- For Windows for Workgroups 3.11, you can set the **MaxMTU** parameter in the SYSTEM.INI file.
  [network_card]
  MaxMTU =
  Default: 0 (use the value supplied by the network adapter manufacturer)

- For Windows 95 and Windows 98, you can configure MaxMTU in the registry subkey:

  HKEY_LOCAL_MACHINE\System\CurrentControlSet\Services\Class\NetTrans\000n

- For Windows NT modify or add the MTU subkey:

  HKEY_LOCAL_MACHINE\System\CurrentControlSet\Services\CENDIS31\Parameters\Tcpip\MTU

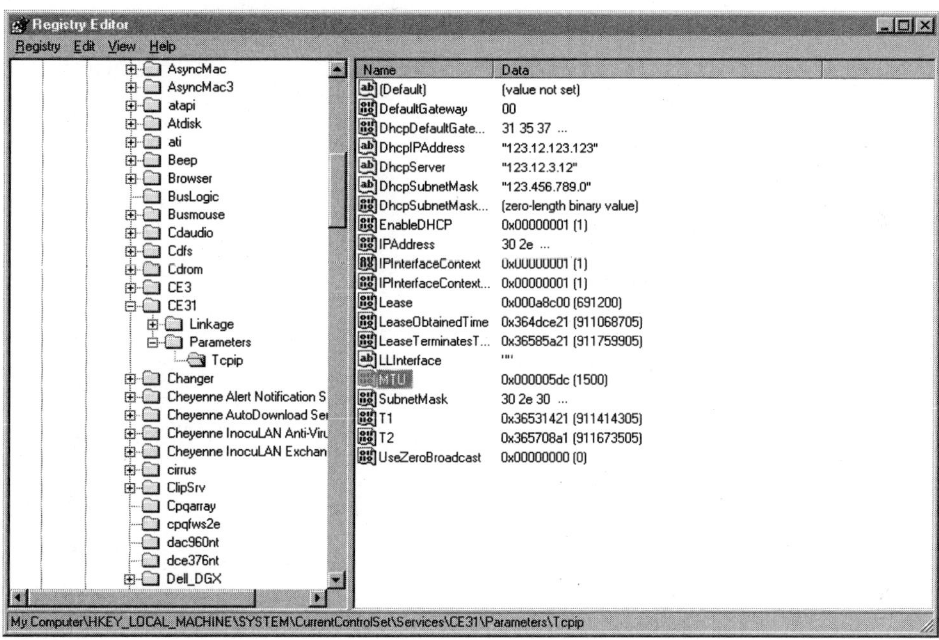

Figure 6.11 Looking for MTU with Registry Editor (REGEDIT.EXE).

Configuring MTU Size for Windows 2000

The redesigned Windows 2000 registry parameters for network services use a component object model (COM) component interface design. COM uses a global unique identifier (GUID) for each component, including network adapter cards. The registry subkey example below is for a Compaq NetFlex network adapter card:

HKEY_LOCAL_MACHINE\System\CurrentControlSet\Services\tcpip\Parameters\interface\F8B40F3E-6F17-11D2-90E1-D0086EA127CB\MTU

The COM component design allows you to disconnect the network interface, change parameters such as the MTU size, and connect the TCP/IP stack to the network interface without rebooting.

Services and Application Transactions

Trust Relationships

Once a trust has been established, primary domain controllers (PDCs) and backup domain controllers (BDCs) locate trusted domains while booting up, establishing a password-protected communications "pipe." The PDC generates a pulse (approximately every day) and changes the internal password on the secure pipe. If domain controllers do not receive this pulse at boot time for internal password changes or initiations of pass-through authentication, then the trust goes dormant for 15 minutes.

Note If a user tries to log on when the trust is inactive, the system uses cached logon accounts. The maximum for the cache is 10 accounts, so if the user is not one of the last 10 accounts to log on, the attempt fails.

Every 15 minutes the domain controller tries to locate the trusted domain. Because of this, a trust may work initially then stop working after 15-30 minutes. In general, using Windows Internet Naming Service (WINS) keeps the trust relationship intact, but WINS server location and link speed (below 128 Kbs) can introduce a resolution latency that causes a trust to fail, rendering the domain dormant until contact is reestablished. You can avoid this by adding the entries described below to the LMHOSTS file on all domain controllers that are connected by slow links:

197.127.137.10 ACCOUNTS1 #DOM:NORTHAMERICA #PRE
197.127.136.11 RESOURCE1 #DOM:RESOURCE_DOMAIN #PRE

Performance Hints and Tips

The trust tries to change its internal secure pipe password, and if it cannot communicate the new password to both sides within a week, the trust breaks and you must delete and re-add it. To disable the password change so that the trust is not automatically broken, you can change the DisablePasswordChange from 0 (default) to 1 in the registry subkey:

HKEY_LOCAL_MACHINE\System\CurrentControlSet\Services\NetLogon\Parameters\DisablePasswordChange

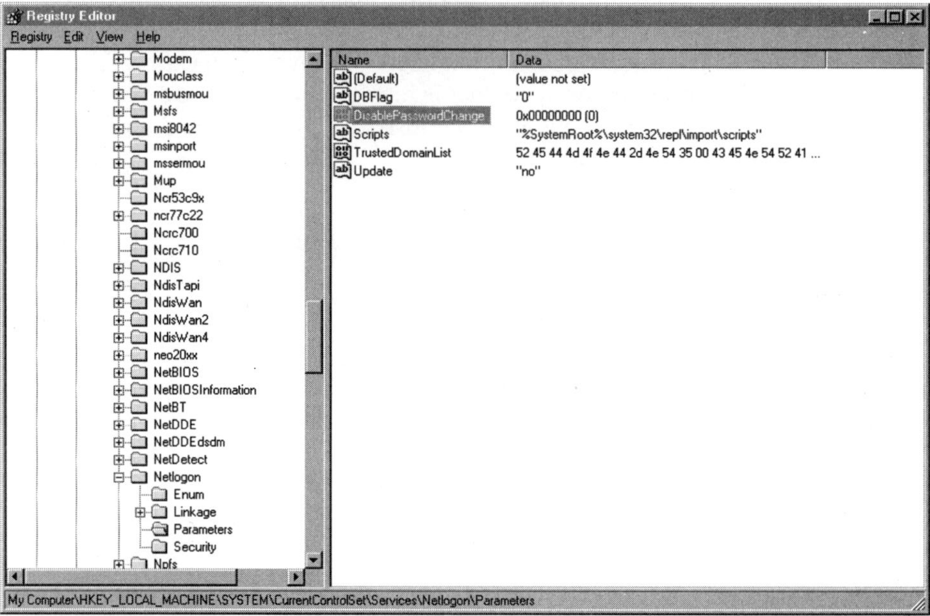

Figure 6.12 Searching for DisablePasswordChange with Registry Editor (REGEDIT.EXE).

Primary Domain Controller (PDC)

Even when using large (5,000 +) account domains, daily change replication from the PDC to the BDCs is small. The NETLOGON service tracks changes in a log which is by default 64 KB (roughly 2,000 changes). In most cases 64 KB is large enough to queue the daily changes, but if it isn't you can increase the log size by changing the ChangeLogSize registry subkey:

HKEY_LOCAL_MACHINE\System\CurrentControlSet\Services\NetLogon\Parameters\ChangeLogSize

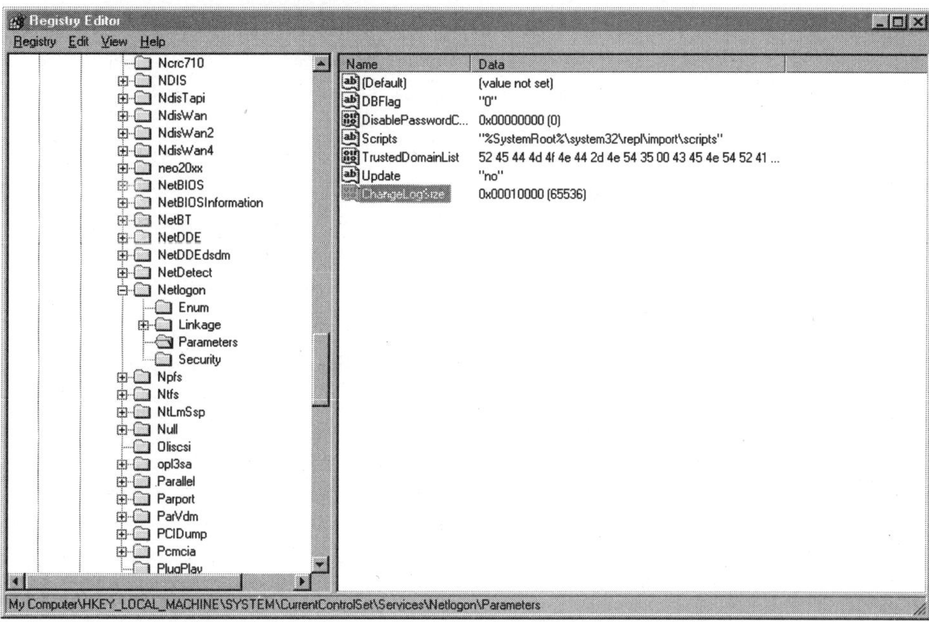

Figure 6.13 Looking for ChangeLogSize with Registry Editor (REGEDIT.EXE).

Replication Issues In Large Networks

Before the replication process starts, the PDC freezes time inside the box, grabs 98% of the CPU processing, and starts calculating what changes go where. In a perfect world this happens without a hitch, but in the real world the *Change Log* sometimes is overrun before all BDCs are synchronized. This forces a full synchronization, which can be a cascading event if all BDCs need a full synchronization instead of just the deltas.

You could increase the *Change Log* size as stated above but it is not really necessary, not even when dealing with large numbers in a single-processor environment. When the PDC freezes time and starts calculating what changes go where, it collects the deltas (changes) into groups of up to 255 deltas for each remote procedure call (RPC) transmission. If the PDC is interrupted during the calculation process (such as to service a bad password check request), the PDC stops all calculations, sends any deltas that have been calculated, services the request, and then resumes calculating what changes go where. This starting and stopping calculation (and thus replication) does not flood the network with RCP transmissions because the network segment with the highest bandwidth is the segment where the PDC is located—and the PDC never floods this segment.

When there is more than one processor, the lowest-order processor works as stated above, exclusively handling all exceptions (service requests) when required. The other processors do not halt—they continue replicating. The lowest-order processor has to start over when the exceptions have been completed but if another processor has meanwhile completed the synchronization, the lowest-order processor backs off rather than duplicate network traffic unnecessarily.

Multiple-Processor Replication Issues in Large Systems

Multiple processors are used only on PDCs, not on BDCs, which simply request data from the PDC. But does a multiple-processor PDC require a multiple-processor BDC for a back up? After all, a backup controller should be able to step in as a new PDC (if needed) and preserve the network topology. Nevertheless, the backup in these cases does not require multiple processors.

Loss of the PDC deprives the system of functions (Enable and Disable Logon Account—Create, and Delete Logon Account—Change Password) that should not break the system over the 15 minutes or so that it takes to promote the backup to PDC (not even if all passwords expire or all accounts are disabled). Users are not even affected, although it may take longer to fully synchronize the entire domain. If you have been diligent with upgrades and maintenance you can promote the backup controller without affecting administrators, telecommunications, support, or users.

With a large number of BDCs (more than 50) the time during which the PDC uses resources increases exponentially with the number of accounts, BDCs, and changes. PDCs are designed to handle this stress and instead of flooding the network with changes they distribute updated information in an orderly fashion.

Although the PDC is designed to calculate replication changes simultaneously for 10 BDCs in Windows NT 3.51 and 20 BDCs in Windows NT 4.0, these figures may be too low to keep large numbers of BDCs updated evenly. In this case, a multiple-processor PDC issues round-robin updates from processor to processor until it reaches the Pulse Concurrency limit (the maximum number of simultaneous pulses a PDC sends to BDCs).

High-Latency Connections

Overall you should not have to change this parameter. Only changes get forwarded through the network so on the last days of a required 90-day password change only passwords are replicated, not the complete user account databases. For slow links, monitor the network traffic and if this traffic causes problems on lines slower than 64 Kbps, use the ReplicationGovernor.

Performance Hints and Tips

- You can configure different replication rates at different times of the day. With the AT command, use a script file containing the path to the **ReplicationGovernor** parameter and the new Registry entries. (For example: net stop netlogon, regini script file, net start netlogon). REGINI.EXE is part of the *Windows NT Resource Kit.*

Dial-up Links

In a dial-up environment you may exercise all of these suggested options but still fail to get the BDC to synchronize with the PDC in a controlled process rather than having it connect all day long across expensive dial-up lines. To make the connection when you want and automate on-demand synchronization, use the command line utility NLTEST.EXE. Combining this utility with RASDIAL you can "batch dial" and synchronize the BDC. Here is an example:

```
:RASDIALOUT
RASDIAL PDCSERVER
IF ERRORLEVEL == 1 GOTO BADRASDIAL
NLTEST /TRANSPORT_NOTIFY
NLTEST /SERVER:BDCLOCAL /REPL
GOTO END
:BADRASDIAL
WAIT 5
GOTO RASDIALOUT
:END
```

The example above is only a sample; below is a complete list of parameters and options. (Refer to the *Microsoft Windows NT 4.0 Resource Kit, Supplement Two* for complete information and examples.)

```
Usage: nltest [/OPTIONS]

   /SERVER:<ServerName> - Specify <ServerName>

   /QUERY - Query <ServerName> netlogon service

   /REPL - Force replication on <ServerName> BDC

   /SYNC - Force SYNC on <ServerName> BDC

   /PDC_REPL - Force UAS change message from <ServerName> PDC

   /SC_QUERY:<DomainName> - Query secure channel for <Domain> on <ServerName>

   /SC_RESET:<DomainName> - Reset secure channel for <Domain> on <ServerName>

   /DCLIST:<DomainName> - Get list of DC's for <DomainName>

   /DCNAME:<DomainName> - Get the PDC name for <DomainName>

   /DCTRUST:<DomainName> - Get name of DC is used for  trust of <DomainName>
```

/WHOWILL:<Domain>* <User> [<Iteration>] - See if <Domain> will log on <User>

/FINDUSER:<User> - See which trusted <Domain> will log on <User>

/TRANSPORT_NOTIFY - Notify of netlogon of new transport

/RID:<HexRid> - RID to encrypt Password with

/USER:<UserName> - Query User info on <ServerName>

/TIME:<Hex LSL> <Hex MSL> - Convert NT GMT time to ascii

/LOGON_QUERY - Query number of cumulative logon attempts

/TRUSTED_DOMAINS - Query names of domains trusted by workstation

/BDC_QUERY:<DomainName> - Query replication status of BDCs for <DomainName>

/SIM_SYNC:<DomainName> <MachineName> - Simulate full sync replication

/LIST_DELTAS:<FileName> - display the content of given change log file

/LIST_REDO:<FileName> - display the content of given redo log file

Performance Hints and Tips

- On the PDC increase the change log so that the transaction log can hold the worst-case number of changes for the time the BDC is off line.
- Use a script file with the AT command to configure different replication rates at different times of the day. See above.
- Use a batch file to dial, connect, and execute NLTEST.EXE.

NETLOGON.BAT (Batch File Execution)

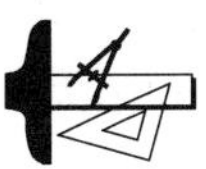

Windows NT provides logon scripts that enforce standards on the desktop. The following example performs a virus check, and links a home directory, a mail drive, a common applications drive, and common printers.

```
@echo off
rem echo netlogon.bat version 01.00.00
echo.
msav /c /r /a
net use h: /HOME
net use m: \\MYSERVER\MAIL
net use s: \\MYSERVER\APPS
net use lpt1: \\MYSERVER\printer1
net use lpt2: \\MYSERVER\printer2
```

You can use the NetLogon feature to impose and enforce standards, but it can create performance issues when executed over slower links. This batch file was created and executed from Windows NT Workstation and a Windows 95 workstation.

```
NETLOGON
@Echo off
Echo netlogon.bat version 01.00.00
Echo.
NET VIEW
```

Network Trace—Windows NT NETLOGON (Remote)

The trace below shows the network traffic generated by NETLOGON.BAT from a remote Windows NT workstation. At the command line the batch file NETLOGON <enter> was used.

- When executed from a Windows NT workstation, 26 packets were generated to "find" the file to execute. The logic used at the command line is to find NETLOGON, then NETLOGON.COM, then NETLOGON.EXE, and finally NETLOGON.BAT. Typing NETLOGON.BAT at the command line avoids the execution of 26 packets of data.
- Echo is used to insert a CR/LF on the screen during execution of a batch file. It makes reading the output more manageable, but generates 4 packets, which really are not required for the execution.
- The net command goes through the same search for the program net, generating extra 14 packets.
- Note that the system is now trying to load the NET.EXE and the DLLs that support the call, even though all the files are in the local search path and the program executes it. The drive off of which NETLOGON was executed is always searched before the search path. Note that this generated over 133 packets.

Network Monitor trace Sat 04/15/98 15:48:18 NT Netlogon (Remote).

Frame	Time	Src MAC Addr	Dst MAC Addr	Protocol	Description
5	4.344	3COM 4CEC95	ANDROMEDAII	SMB	C NT create & X, File = \
6	4.347	ANDROMEDAII	3COM 4CEC95	SMB	R NT create & X, FID = 0x8003
7	4.351	3COM 4CEC95	ANDROMEDAII	SMB	C transact2 FindFirst, File = \netlogon"*
8	4.356	ANDROMEDAII	3COM 4CEC95	SMB	R transact2
9	4.359	3COM 4CEC95	ANDROMEDAII	SMB	C find close, FID = 0x5
10	4.362	ANDROMEDAII	3COM 4CEC95	SMB	R find close

Network Monitor trace Sat 04/15/98 15:48:18 NT Netlogon (Remote). *(continued)*

Frame	Time	Src MAC Addr	Dst MAC Addr	Protocol	Description
11	4.363	3COM 4CEC95	ANDROMEDAII	SMB	C close file, FID = 0x8003
12	4.366	ANDROMEDAII	3COM 4CEC95	SMB	R close file
13	4.369	3COM 4CEC95	ANDROMEDAII	SMB	C NT create & X, File = \
14	4.373	ANDROMEDAII	3COM 4CEC95	SMB	R NT create & X, FID = 0x7804
15	4.377	3COM 4CEC95	ANDROMEDAII	SMB	C transact2 FindFirst, File = \NETLOGON.COM
16	4.382	ANDROMEDAII	3COM 4CEC95	SMB	R transact2 (Error)
17	4.385	3COM 4CEC95	ANDROMEDAII	SMB	C close file, FID = 0x7804
18	4.387	ANDROMEDAII	3COM 4CEC95	SMB	R close file
19	4.391	3COM 4CEC95	ANDROMEDAII	SMB	C NT create & X, File = \
20	4.394	ANDROMEDAII	3COM 4CEC95	SMB	R NT create & X, FID = 0x7006
21	4.397	3COM 4CEC95	ANDROMEDAII	SMB	C transact2 FindFirst, File = \NETLOGON.EXE
22	4.403	ANDROMEDAII	3COM 4CEC95	SMB	R transact2 (Error)
23	4.406	3COM 4CEC95	ANDROMEDAII	SMB	C close file, FID = 0x7006
24	4.408	ANDROMEDAII	3COM 4CEC95	SMB	R close file
25	4.412	3COM 4CEC95	ANDROMEDAII	SMB	C NT create & X, File = \
26	4.415	ANDROMEDAII	3COM 4CEC95	SMB	R NT create & X, FID = 0x8002
27	4.421	3COM 4CEC95	ANDROMEDAII	SMB	C transact2 FindFirst, File = \NETLOGON.BAT
28	4.428	ANDROMEDAII	3COM 4CEC95	SMB	R transact2 FindFirst (response to frame 27)
29	4.431	3COM 4CEC95	ANDROMEDAII	SMB	C close file, FID = 0x8002
30	4.433	ANDROMEDAII	3COM 4CEC95	SMB	R close file

Network Monitor trace Sat 04/15/98 15:48:18 NT Netlogon (Remote). *(continued)*

Frame	Time	Src MAC Addr	Dst MAC Addr	Protocol	Description
31	4.440	3COM 4CEC95	ANDROMEDAII	SMB	C NT create & X, File = \NETLOGON.BAT
32	4.444	ANDROMEDAII	3COM 4CEC95	SMB	R NT create & X, FID = 0x780d
33	4.448	3COM 4CEC95	ANDROMEDAII	SMB	C read & X, FID = 0x780d, Read 0xa4 at 0x0
34	4.450	ANDROMEDAII	3COM 4CEC95	SMB	R read & X, Read 0xa4
35	4.497	3COM 4CEC95	ANDROMEDAII	SMB	C NT create & X, File = \
36	4.500	ANDROMEDAII	3COM 4CEC95	SMB	R NT create & X, FID = 0x8005
37	4.503	3COM 4CEC95	ANDROMEDAII	SMB	C close file, FID = 0x780d
38	4.505	ANDROMEDAII	3COM 4CEC95	SMB	R close file
39	4.507	3COM 4CEC95	ANDROMEDAII	SMB	C transact2 FindFirst, File = \Echo."*
40	4.513	ANDROMEDAII	3COM 4CEC95	SMB	R transact2 (Error)
41	4.516	3COM 4CEC95	ANDROMEDAII	SMB	C close file, FID = 0x8005
42	4.519	ANDROMEDAII	3COM 4CEC95	SMB	R close file
43	4.548	3COM 4CEC95	ANDROMEDAII	SMB	C NT create & X, File = \NETLOGON.BAT
44	4.550	ANDROMEDAII	3COM 4CEC95	SMB	R NT create & X, FID = 0x780d
45	4.554	3COM 4CEC95	ANDROMEDAII	SMB	C read & X, FID = 0x780d, Read 0xa4 at 0x0
46	4.555	ANDROMEDAII	3COM 4CEC95	SMB	R read & X, Read 0xa4
47	4.572	3COM 4CEC95	ANDROMEDAII	SMB	C NT create & X, File = \
48	4.575	ANDROMEDAII	3COM 4CEC95	SMB	R NT create & X, FID = 0x780a
49	4.578	3COM 4CEC95	ANDROMEDAII	SMB	C close file, FID = 0x780d
50	4.580	ANDROMEDAII	3COM 4CEC95	SMB	R close file

Network Monitor trace Sat 04/15/98 15:48:18 NT Netlogon (Remote). *(continued)*

Frame	Time	Src MAC Addr	Dst MAC Addr	Protocol	Description
51	4.583	3COM 4CEC95	ANDROMEDAII	SMB	C transact2 FindFirst, File = \NET"*
52	4.589	ANDROMEDAII	3COM 4CEC95	SMB	R transact2 FindFirst (response to frame 51)
53	4.592	3COM 4CEC95	ANDROMEDAII	SMB	C find close, FID = 0x802
54	4.594	ANDROMEDAII	3COM 4CEC95	SMB	R find close
55	4.596	3COM 4CEC95	ANDROMEDAII	SMB	C close file, FID = 0x780a
56	4.598	ANDROMEDAII	3COM 4CEC95	SMB	R close file
57	4.602	3COM 4CEC95	ANDROMEDAII	SMB	C NT create & X, File = \
58	4.605	ANDROMEDAII	3COM 4CEC95	SMB	R NT create & X, FID = 0x3801
59	4.608	3COM 4CEC95	ANDROMEDAII	SMB	C transact2 FindFirst, File = \NET.COM
60	4.614	ANDROMEDAII	3COM 4CEC95	SMB	R transact2 (Error)
61	4.616	3COM 4CEC95	ANDROMEDAII	SMB	C close file, FID = 0x3801
62	4.619	ANDROMEDAII	3COM 4CEC95	SMB	R close file
63	4.622	3COM 4CEC95	ANDROMEDAII	SMB	C NT create & X, File = \
64	4.626	ANDROMEDAII	3COM 4CEC95	SMB	R NT create & X, FID = 0x4000
65	4.629	3COM 4CEC95	ANDROMEDAII	SMB	C transact2 FindFirst, File = \NET.EXE
66	4.635	ANDROMEDAII	3COM 4CEC95	SMB	R transact2 FindFirst (response to frame 65)
67	4.638	3COM 4CEC95	ANDROMEDAII	SMB	C close file, FID = 0x4000
68	4.641	ANDROMEDAII	3COM 4CEC95	SMB	R close file
69	4.644	3COM 4CEC95	ANDROMEDAII	SMB	C NT create & X, File = \
70	4.648	ANDROMEDAII	3COM 4CEC95	SMB	R NT create & X, FID = 0x6807

Network Monitor trace Sat 04/15/98 15:48:18 NT Netlogon (Remote). *(continued)*

Frame	Time	Src MAC Addr	Dst MAC Addr	Protocol	Description
71	4.650	3COM 4CEC95	ANDROMEDAII	SMB	C transact2 GetFileInfo, FID = 0x6807
72	4.652	ANDROMEDAII	3COM 4CEC95	SMB	R transact2 GetFileInfo (response to frame 71)
73	4.655	3COM 4CEC95	ANDROMEDAII	SMB	C transact2 GetFsInfo
74	4.657	ANDROMEDAII	3COM 4CEC95	SMB	R transact2 GetFsInfo (response to frame 73)
75	4.660	3COM 4CEC95	ANDROMEDAII	SMB	C close file, FID = 0x6807
76	4.663	ANDROMEDAII	3COM 4CEC95	SMB	R close file
77	4.669	3COM 4CEC95	ANDROMEDAII	SMB	C NT create & X, File = \
78	4.673	ANDROMEDAII	3COM 4CEC95	SMB	R NT create & X, FID = 0x800e
79	4.677	3COM 4CEC95	ANDROMEDAII	SMB	C transact2 FindFirst, File = \NET"*
80	4.683	ANDROMEDAII	3COM 4CEC95	SMB	R transact2 FindFirst (response to frame 79)
81	4.687	3COM 4CEC95	ANDROMEDAII	SMB	C find close, FID = 0x805
82	4.689	ANDROMEDAII	3COM 4CEC95	SMB	R find close
83	4.690	3COM 4CEC95	ANDROMEDAII	SMB	C close file, FID = 0x800e
84	4.693	ANDROMEDAII	3COM 4CEC95	SMB	R close file
85	4.696	3COM 4CEC95	ANDROMEDAII	SMB	C NT create & X, File = \
86	4.700	ANDROMEDAII	3COM 4CEC95	SMB	R NT create & X, FID = 0x800b
87	4.703	3COM 4CEC95	ANDROMEDAII	SMB	C transact2 FindFirst, File = \NET.COM
88	4.709	ANDROMEDAII	3COM 4CEC95	SMB	R transact2 (Error)
89	4.711	3COM 4CEC95	ANDROMEDAII	SMB	C close file, FID = 0x800b
90	4.714	ANDROMEDAII	3COM 4CEC95	SMB	R close file

Network Monitor trace Sat 04/15/98 15:48:18 NT Netlogon (Remote). *(continued)*

Frame	Time	Src MAC Addr	Dst MAC Addr	Protocol	Description
91	4.717	3COM 4CEC95	ANDROMEDAII	SMB	C NT create & X, File = \
92	4.721	ANDROMEDAII	3COM 4CEC95	SMB	R NT create & X, FID = 0x780f
93	4.724	3COM 4CEC95	ANDROMEDAII	SMB	C transact2 FindFirst, File = \NET.EXE
94	4.731	ANDROMEDAII	3COM 4CEC95	SMB	R transact2 FindFirst (response to frame 93)
95	4.734	3COM 4CEC95	ANDROMEDAII	SMB	C close file, FID = 0x780f
96	4.736	ANDROMEDAII	3COM 4CEC95	SMB	R close file
97	4.742	3COM 4CEC95	ANDROMEDAII	SMB	C NT create & X, File = \NET.EXE
98	4.744	ANDROMEDAII	3COM 4CEC95	SMB	R NT create & X, FID = 0x6808
99	4.747	3COM 4CEC95	ANDROMEDAII	SMB	C read & X, FID = 0x6808, Read 0x1000 at 0x0
100	4.750	ANDROMEDAII	3COM 4CEC95	SMB	R read & X, Read 0x1000
101	4.751	ANDROMEDAII	3COM 4CEC95	NBT	SS: Session Message Cont., 1460 Bytes
102	4.752	ANDROMEDAII	3COM 4CEC95	NBT	SS: Session Message Cont., 1240 Bytes
103	4.753	3COM 4CEC95	ANDROMEDAII	TCP	.A...., len: 0, seq: 506612, ack: 1100064, win: 8760
104	4.763	3COM 4CEC95	ANDROMEDAII	SMB	C transact2 GetPathInfo, File = \
105	4.767	ANDROMEDAII	3COM 4CEC95	SMB	R transact2 GetPathInfo (response to frame 104)
106	4.791	3COM 4CEC95	ANDROMEDAII	SMB	C NT create & X, File = \
107	4.794	ANDROMEDAII	3COM 4CEC95	SMB	R NT create & X, FID = 0x8803
108	4.797	3COM 4CEC95	ANDROMEDAII	SMB	C read & X, FID = 0x6808, Read 0xa00 at 0xae00
109	4.800	ANDROMEDAII	3COM 4CEC95	SMB	R read & X, Read 0xa00
110	4.801	ANDROMEDAII	3COM 4CEC95	NBT	SS: Session Message Cont., 1164 Bytes

Network Monitor trace Sat 04/15/98 15:48:18 NT Netlogon (Remote). *(continued)*

Frame	Time	Src MAC Addr	Dst MAC Addr	Protocol	Description
111	4.802	3COM 4CEC95	ANDROMEDAII	TCP	.A...., len: 0, seq: 506850, ack: 1104139, win: 8760
112	4.807	3COM 4CEC95	ANDROMEDAII	SMB	C transact2 GetPathInfo, File = \NETAPI32.dll
113	4.810	ANDROMEDAII	3COM 4CEC95	SMB	C transact2 (Error)
114	4.814	3COM 4CEC95	ANDROMEDAII	SMB	C transact2 GetPathInfo, File = \NETAPI32.dll
115	4.817	ANDROMEDAII	3COM 4CEC95	SMB	C transact2 (Error)
116	4.841	3COM 4CEC95	ANDROMEDAII	SMB	C transact2 GetPathInfo, File = \NETRAP.dll
117	4.845	ANDROMEDAII	3COM 4CEC95	SMB	C transact2 (Error)
118	4.849	3COM 4CEC95	ANDROMEDAII	SMB	C transact2 GetPathInfo, File = \NETRAP.dll
119	4.852	ANDROMEDAII	3COM 4CEC95	SMB	C transact2 (Error)
120	4.866	3COM 4CEC95	ANDROMEDAII	SMB	C transact2 GetPathInfo, File = \SAMLIB.dll
121	4.869	ANDROMEDAII	3COM 4CEC95	SMB	C transact2 (Error)
122	4.873	3COM 4CEC95	ANDROMEDAII	SMB	C transact2 GetPathInfo, File = \SAMLIB.dll
123	4.877	ANDROMEDAII	3COM 4CEC95	SMB	C transact2 (Error)
124	4.889	3COM 4CEC95	ANDROMEDAII	SMB	C transact2 GetPathInfo, File = \MPR.dll
125	4.893	ANDROMEDAII	3COM 4CEC95	SMB	C transact2 (Error)
126	4.897	3COM 4CEC95	ANDROMEDAII	SMB	C transact2 GetPathInfo, File = \MPR.dll
127	4.901	ANDROMEDAII	3COM 4CEC95	SMB	C transact2 (Error)
128	4.914	3COM 4CEC95	ANDROMEDAII	SMB	C read & X, FID = 0x6808, Read 0x400 at 0xb800
129	4.916	ANDROMEDAII	3COM 4CEC95	SMB	R read & X, Read 0x400
130	4.969	3COM 4CEC95	ANDROMEDAII	SMB	C read block raw, FID = 0x6808, Read 0x6600 at 0x400
131	4.972	ANDROMEDAII	3COM 4CEC95	NBT	SS: Session Message, Len: 26112
132	4.973	ANDROMEDAII	3COM 4CEC95	NBT	SS: Session Message Cont., 1460 Bytes
133	4.974	ANDROMEDAII	3COM 4CEC95	NBT	SS: Session Message Cont., 1460 Bytes
134	4.975	3COM 4CEC95	ANDROMEDAII	TCP	.A...., len: 0, seq: 507785, ack: 1108459, win: 876

Network Trace—Windows 95 NETLOGON.BAT (Remote)

The next trace shows the network traffic generated by executing NETLOGON.BAT from a remote Windows 95 workstation. At the command line the batch file NETLOGON <enter> was used.

- When executed from a Windows 95 workstation, it takes fewer packets; the search order is netlogon, NETLOGON.BAT.
- Echo does not generate any network traffic.
- Note that loading the NET.EXE off the network generated 207 packets.

Network Monitor trace Thu 04/13/98 19:52:48 Windows 95 Netlogon.bat (Remote).

Frame	Time	Src MAC Addr	Dst MAC Addr	Protocol	Description
1	1.956	WORK1	TXI320	SMB	C search directory, File = \NETLOGON">>>
2	1.959	TXI320	WORK1	SMB	R search directory, Files = 1
3	1.961	WORK1	TXI320	SMB	C search directory, File =
4	1.962	TXI320	WORK1	SMB	R search directory (Error)
5	1.963	WORK1	TXI320	SMB	C search directory, File = \NETLOGON"BAT
6	1.966	TXI320	WORK1	SMB	R search directory, Files = 1
7	2.017	WORK1	TXI320	SMB	C search directory, File = \NET">>>
8	2.021	TXI320	WORK1	SMB	R search directory, Files = 1
9	2.022	WORK1	TXI320	SMB	C search directory, File =
10	2.023	TXI320	WORK1	SMB	R search directory (Error)
11	2.024	WORK1	TXI320	SMB	C open & X, File = \NET.EXE (R -Share Deny None)
12	2.027	TXI320	WORK1	SMB	R open & X, FID = 0x1004, File Size = 0x5b40a

Network Monitor trace Thu 04/13/98 19:52:48 Windows 95 Netlogon.bat (Remote). *(continued)*

Frame	Time	Src MAC Addr	Dst MAC Addr	Protocol	Description
13	2.028	WORK1	TXI320	SMB	C read block raw, FID = 0x1004, Read 0x1000 at 0x0
14	2.032	TXI320	WORK1	NBT	SS: Session Message, Len: 4096
15	2.033	TXI320	WORK1	NBT	SS: Session Message Cont., 1460 Bytes
16	2.034	TXI320	WORK1	NBT	SS: Session Message Cont., 1180 Bytes
17	2.036	WORK1	TXI320	TCP	.A...., len: 0, seq: 6174814, ack: 1323028, win: 8760
18	2.039	WORK1	TXI320	SMB	C open & X, File = \NET.EXE (X -Share Deny W)
19	2.041	TXI320	WORK1	SMB	C lock & X, FID = 0x1004
20	2.042	WORK1	TXI320	SMB	C close file, FID = 0x1004
21	2.044	TXI320	WORK1	SMB	R close file
22	2.045	TXI320	WORK1	SMB	R open & X, FID = 0x1006, File Size = 0x5b40a
23	2.045	WORK1	TXI320	TCP	.A...., len: 0, seq: 6174947, ack: 1324371, win: 7417
24	2.047	WORK1	TXI320	SMB	C read block raw, FID = 0x1006, Read 0xfe00 at 0x2a00
25	2.054	TXI320	WORK1	NBT	SS: Session Message, Len: 65024
26	2.055	TXI320	WORK1	NBT	SS: Session Message Cont., 1460 Bytes
27	2.057	TXI320	WORK1	NBT	SS: Session Message Cont., 1460 Bytes
28	2.058	TXI320	WORK1	NBT	SS: Session Message Cont., 1460 Bytes
29	2.059	WORK1	TXI320	TCP	.A...., len: 0, seq: 6175002, ack: 1327291, win: 8760
30	2.060	TXI320	WORK1	NBT	SS: Session Message Cont., 1460 Bytes
31	2.062	TXI320	WORK1	NBT	SS: Session Message Cont., 1460 Bytes
32	2.063	TXI320	WORK1	NBT	SS: Session Message Cont., 1460 Bytes

Network Monitor trace Thu 04/13/98 19:52:48 Windows 95 Netlogon.bat (Remote). *(continued)*

Frame	Time	Src MAC Addr	Dst MAC Addr	Protocol	Description
33	2.064	WORK1	TXI320	TCP	.A...., len: 0, seq: 6175002, ack: 1330211, win: 8760
34	2.064	TXI320	WORK1	NBT	SS: Session Message Cont., 1460 Bytes
35	2.066	TXI320	WORK1	NBT	SS: Session Message Cont., 1460 Bytes
36	2.067	TXI320	WORK1	NBT	SS: Session Message Cont., 1460 Bytes
37	2.068	WORK1	TXI320	TCP	.A...., len: 0, seq: 6175002, ack: 1333131, win: 8760
38	2.070	TXI320	WORK1	NBT	SS: Session Message Cont., 1460 Bytes
39	2.073	TXI320	WORK1	NBT	SS: Session Message Cont., 1460 Bytes
40	2.074	WORK1	TXI320	TCP	.A...., len: 0, seq: 6175002, ack: 1337511, win: 8760
41	2.076	TXI320	WORK1	NBT	SS: Session Message Cont., 1460 Bytes
42	2.077	TXI320	WORK1	NBT	SS: Session Message Cont., 1460 Bytes
43	2.078	TXI320	WORK1	NBT	SS: Session Message Cont., 1460 Bytes
44	2.079	WORK1	TXI320	TCP	.A...., len: 0, seq: 6175002, ack: 1341891, win: 8760
45	2.082	TXI320	WORK1	NBT	SS: Session Message Cont., 1460 Bytes
46	2.083	TXI320	WORK1	NBT	SS: Session Message Cont., 1460 Bytes
47	2.084	TXI320	WORK1	NBT	SS: Session Message Cont., 1460 Bytes
48	2.087	WORK1	TXI320	TCP	.A...., len: 0, seq: 6175002, ack: 1346271, win: 8760
49	2.089	TXI320	WORK1	NBT	SS: Session Message Cont., 1460 Bytes
50	2.091	TXI320	WORK1	NBT	SS: Session Message Cont., 1460 Bytes
...					
216	2.367	WORK1	TXI320	SMB	C read block raw, FID = 0x1006, Read 0xa00 at 0x2000

Network Monitor trace Thu 04/13/98 19:52:48 Windows 95 Netlogon.bat (Remote). *(continued)*

Frame	Time	Src MAC Addr	Dst MAC Addr	Protocol	Description
217	2.371	TXI320	WORK1	NBT	SS: Session Message, Len: 2560
218	2.372	TXI320	WORK1	NBT	SS: Session Message Cont., 1104 Bytes
219	2.375	WORK1	TXI320	TCP	.A...., len: 0, seq: 6175222, ack: 1525095, win: 8760
220	2.383	WORK1	TXI320	SMB	C tree connect & X, Share = \\TXI320\IPC$
221	2.384	TXI320	WORK1	SMB	R tree connect & X, Type = IPC
222	2.386	WORK1	TXI320	SMB	C transact, Remote API
223	2.399	TXI320	WORK1	SMB	R transact, Remote API (response to frame 222)
224	2.551	WORK1	TXI320	TCP	.A...., len: 0, seq: 6175401, ack: 1525579, win: 8276
225	3.851	WORK1	TXI320	SMB	C tree disconnect
226	3.852	TXI320	WORK1	SMB	R tree disconnect
227	4.056	WORK1	TXI320	TCP	.A...., len: 0, seq: 6175440, ack: 1525618, win: 8237

Network Trace—Windows 95 NETLOGON.BAT (Local)

The next trace shows the network traffic generated by executing NETLOGON.BAT from a local Windows 95 workstation. At the command line the batch file NETLOGON <enter> was used. At the command line the batch file NETLOGON <enter> was used.

- This was executed with the NET.EXE local to the machine. The total number of packets generated during the execution was only 21.

Network Monitor trace Thu 04/13/95 20:19:03 Windows 95 NETLOGON.BAT (Local).

Frame	Time	Src MAC Addr	Dst MAC Addr	Protocol	Description
2	4.955	WORK1	TXI320	SMB	C search directory, File = \NETLOGON">>>
3	4.959	TXI320	WORK1	SMB	R search directory, Files = 1
4	4.960	WORK1	TXI320	SMB	C search directory, File =
5	4.961	TXI320	WORK1	SMB	R search directory (Error)

Network Monitor trace Thu 04/13/95 20:19:03 Windows 95 NETLOGON.BAT (Local). *(continued)*

Frame	Time	Src MAC Addr	Dst MAC Addr	Protocol	Description
6	4.963	WORK1	TXI320	SMB	C search directory, File = \NETLOGON"BAT
7	4.966	TXI320	WORK1	SMB	R search directory, Files = 1
8	4.968	WORK1	TXI320	SMB	C open & X, File = \NETLOGON.BAT (R -Share Deny W)
9	4.972	TXI320	WORK1	SMB	R open & X, FID = 0x1001, File Size = 0x4c
10	4.973	WORK1	TXI320	SMB	C read block raw, FID = 0x1001, Read 0x1000 at 0x0
11	4.974	TXI320	WORK1	NBT	SS: Session Message, Len: 76
12	5.005	WORK1	TXI320	SMB	C search directory, File = \NET">>>
13	5.007	TXI320	WORK1	SMB	R search directory (Error)
14	5.040	WORK1	TXI320	SMB	C tree connect & X, Share = \\TXI320\IPC$
15	5.042	TXI320	WORK1	SMB	R tree connect & X, Type = IPC
16	5.043	WORK1	TXI320	SMB	C transact, Remote API
17	5.056	TXI320	WORK1	SMB	R transact, Remote API (response to frame 16)
18	5.216	WORK1	TXI320	TCP	.A...., len: 0, seq: 5799747, ack: 1319143, win: 8237
19	7.468	WORK1	TXI320	SMB	C tree disconnect
20	7.469	TXI320	WORK1	SMB	R tree disconnect
21	7.591	WORK1	TXI320	TCP	.A...., len: 0, seq: 5799786, ack: 1319182, win: 8198

Performance Hints and Tips

- Try to avoid executing EXE, COM, DLL files over a slow link.
- If you need to execute files, first copy them down to a local drive of the client and then execute them
- When you do execute files over a slow link make sure you include the extensions, TEST.BAT, TEST.EXE, TEST.COM so that the redirector does not have to discover which extension to use.
- Do not use the ECHO. The information it provides can enhance your understanding of batch file execution, but it generates unwanted network traffic.

Copy Command (CMD, WINFILE, Explorer)

Network Trace—Copy Command: Windows 95 Workstation Redirector Requests

Using COMMAND.COM, CMD.EXE, or WINFILE.EXE interfaces to copy files across the network requests the redirector to use large read or writes blocks. By default the Windows 95 workstation redirector requests large read or write blocks (64-K—raw state). The trace below shows that when the system invokes the raw state there is only a single 2-SMB packet for every 64 K of data.

Network Monitor trace Mon 03/13/98 13:36:17 Small / Medium / Large Reads & Writes.

Frame	Time	Src MAC Addr	Dst MAC Addr	Protocol	Description
4	2.597	VOYAGERIX	WANTEST2	SMB	C get attributes, File = \temp\002
5	2.685	WANTEST2	VOYAGERIX	SMB	R get attributes
6	2.689	VOYAGERIX	WANTEST2	SMB	C NT create & X, File = \temp
8	4.065	WANTEST2	VOYAGERIX	SMB	R NT create & X, FID = 0x806
9	4.068	VOYAGERIX	WANTEST2	SMB	C transact2 FindFirst, File = \temp\002

Network Monitor trace Mon 03/13/98 13:36:17 Small / Medium / Large Reads & Writes. *(continued)*

Frame	Time	Src MAC Addr	Dst MAC Addr	Protocol	Description
11	6.075	WANTEST2	VOYAGERIX	SMB	R transact2
12	6.079	VOYAGERIX	WANTEST2	SMB	C NT create & X, File = \temp\002
13	7.418	WANTEST2	VOYAGERIX	SMB	R NT create & X, FID = 0x807
14	7.422	VOYAGERIX	WANTEST2	SMB	C read & X, FID = 0x807, Read 0x1000 at 0x0
15	8.885	WANTEST2	VOYAGERIX	SMB	R read & X, Read 0x1000
16	9.006	VOYAGERIX	WANTEST2	TCP	.A...., len: 0, seq: 2259110, ack: 239873, win:12288
17	9.014	WANTEST2	VOYAGERIX	NBT	SS: Session Message Cont., 1460 Bytes
18	9.115	WANTEST2	VOYAGERIX		SS: Session Message Cont., 1240 Bytes
19	9.117	VOYAGERIX	WANTEST2	TCP	.A...., len: 0, seq: 2259110, ack: 242573, win:12288

Network Trace—Copy Command: Windows NT Clients

By default Windows NT 3.5*x* disables raw mode over slow links from Windows NT client to Windows NT server. But Windows NT Server will service (raw state) over slow links, so you see great performance of Windows 95 connected to a Windows NT server even over a slow link. The Windows NT clients use the default size of **SizReqBuf** of 4292, as shown in this trace. Note that there are 2-SMB packets for every 4292 bytes of data.

Network Monitor trace Sun 03/05/98 12:57:59
Copy Command -COMMAND.COM, CMD.EXE, WINFILE.EXE.

Frame	Time	Src MAC Addr	Dst MAC Addr	Protocol	Description
19	15.191	VOYAGERIX	3COM 8DFB25	SMB	C write & X, FID = 0x801, Write 0x10c4 at 0x0
20	15.194	VOYAGERIX	3COM 8DFB25	NBT	SS: Session Message Cont., 1460 Bytes
21	15.196	VOYAGERIX	3COM 8DFB25	NBT	SS: Session Message Cont., 1439 Bytes
22	16.659	3COM 8DFB25	VOYAGERIX	TCP	.A...., len: 0, seq: 205717, ack: 2468724, win: 8760, src

Network Monitor trace Sun 03/05/98 12:57:59
Copy Command -COMMAND.COM, CMD.EXE, WINFILE.EXE. *(continued)*

Frame	Time	Src MAC Addr	Dst MAC Addr	Protocol	Description
23	17.337	3COM 8DFB25	VOYAGERIX	SMB	R write & X, Wrote 0x10c4
24	17.341	VOYAGERIX	3COM 8DFB25	SMB	C write & X, FID = 0x801, Write 0x10c4 at 0x10c4
25	17.343	VOYAGERIX	3COM 8DFB25	NBT	SS: Session Message Cont., 1460 Bytes
26	17.345	VOYAGERIX	3COM 8DFB25	NBT	SS: Session Message Cont., 1439 Bytes
27	18.864	3COM 8DFB25	VOYAGERIX	TCP	.A...., len: 0, seq: 205768, ack: 2473083, win: 8760, src
28	19.545	3COM 8DFB25	VOYAGERIX	SMB	R write & X, Wrote 0x10c4
29	19.548	VOYAGERIX	3COM 8DFB25	SMB	C write & X, FID = 0x801, Write 0x10c4 at 0x2188
30	19.551	VOYAGERIX	3COM 8DFB25	NBT	SS: Session Message Cont., 1460 Bytes
31	19.553	VOYAGERIX	3COM 8DFB25	NBT	SS: Session Message Cont., 1439 Bytes
32	21.024	3COM 8DFB25	VOYAGERIX	TCP	.A...., len: 0, seq: 205819, ack: 2477442, win: 8760, src
33	21.704	3COM 8DFB25	VOYAGERIX	SMB	R write & X, Wrote 0x10c4
34	21.708	VOYAGERIX	3COM 8DFB25	SMB	C write & X, FID = 0x801, Write 0x10c4 at 0x324c
35	21.710	VOYAGERIX	3COM 8DFB25	NBT	SS: Session Message Cont., 1460 Bytes
36	21.712	VOYAGERIX	3COM 8DFB25	NBT	SS: Session Message Cont., 1439 Bytes
37	23.237	3COM 8DFB25	VOYAGERIX	TCP	.A...., len: 0, seq: 205870, ack: 2481801, win: 8760, src
38	23.254	3COM 8DFB25	VOYAGERIX	SMB	R write & X, Wrote 0x10c4

Network Trace—Increasing SizReqBuf for Windows NT

This trace shows that increasing the **SizReqBuf** from 11504 to 12548 for the Windows NT client and server increases performance. This increase is shown in Figure 6-15 in the Performance Results section at the end of this chapter.

Network Monitor trace Sun 03/05/98 13:49:39 SizReqBuf of 12548.

Frame	Time	Src MAC Addr	Dst MAC Addr	Protocol	Description
66	24.840	VOYAGERIX	WANTEST2	SMB	C write & X, FID = 0x804, Write 0x30c4 at 0x924c
67	24.842	VOYAGERIX	WANTEST2	NBT	SS: Session Message Cont., 1460 Bytes
68	24.844	VOYAGERIX	WANTEST2	NBT	SS: Session Message Cont., 1460 Bytes
69	24.846	VOYAGERIX	WANTEST2	NBT	SS: Session Message Cont., 1460 Bytes
70	24.848	VOYAGERIX	WANTEST2	NBT	SS: Session Message Cont., 1460 Bytes
71	24.850	VOYAGERIX	WANTEST2	NBT	SS: Session Message Cont., 1460 Bytes
72	24.852	VOYAGERIX	WANTEST2	NBT	SS: Session Message Cont., 1460 Bytes
73	26.386	WANTEST2	VOYAGERIX	TCP	.A...., len: 0, seq: 233563, ack: 1293253, win:12288
74	26.389	VOYAGERIX	WANTST2	NB	SS: Session Message Cont., 1460 Bytes
75	26.390	VOYAGERIX	WANTST2	NB	SS: Session Message Cont., 871 Bytes
76	27.072	WANTEST2	VOYAGERIX	TCP	.A...., len: 0, seq: 233563, ack: 1296173, win:12288
77	27.098	WANTEST2	VOYAGERIX	TCP	.A...., len: 0, seq: 233563, ack: 1299093, win:12288
78	27.098	WANTEST2	VOYAGERIX	TCP	.A...., len: 0, seq: 233563, ack: 1300553, win:12288
79	28.421	WANTEST2	VOYAGERIX	TCP	.A...., len: 0, seq: 233563, ack: 1302884, win:12288
80	28.437	WANTEST2	VOYAGERIX	SMB	R write & X, Wrote 0x30c4
81	28.440	VOYAGERIX	WANTEST2	SMB	C write & X, FID = 0x804, Write 0x2cf0 at 0xc310
82	28.442	VOYAGERIX	WANTEST2	NBT	SS: Session Message Cont., 1460 Bytes
83	28.445	VOYAGERIX	WANTEST2	NBT	SS: Session Message Cont., 1460 Bytes
84	28.447	VOYAGERIX	WANTEST2	NBT	SS: Session Message Cont., 1460 Bytes

Network Monitor trace Sun 03/05/98 13:49:39 SizReqBuf of 12548. *(continued)*

Frame	Time	Src MAC Addr	Dst MAC Addr	Protocol	Description
85	28.449	VOYAGERIX	WANTEST2	NBT	SS: Session Message Cont., 1460 Bytes
86	28.451	VOYAGERIX	WANTEST2	NBT	SS: Session Message Cont., 1460 Bytes
87	28.453	VOYAGERIX	WANTEST2	NBT	SS: Session Message Cont., 1460 Bytes
88	28.455	VOYAGERIX	WANTEST2	NBT	SS: Session Message Cont., 1351 Bytes
89	29.986	WANTEST2	VOYAGERIX	TCP	.A...., len: 0, seq: 233614, ack: 1305804, win:12288
90	30.675	WANTEST2	VOYAGERIX	TCP	.A...., len: 0, seq: 233614, ack: 1308724, win:12288
91	30.711	WANTEST2	VOYAGERIX	TCP	.A...., len: 0, seq: 233614, ack: 1311644, win:12288
92	30.711	WANTEST2	VOYAGERIX	TCP	.A...., len: 0, seq: 233614, ack: 1314455, win:12288
93	30.711	WANTEST2	VOYAGERIX	SMB	R write & X, Wrote 0x2cf0
94	30.721	VOYAGERIX	WANTEST2	SMB	C write & X, FID = 0x804, Write 0x30c4 at 0xf000
95	30.723	VOYAGERIX	WANTEST2	NBT	SS: Session Message Cont., 1460 Bytes
96	30.725	VOYAGERIX	WANTEST2	NBT	SS: Session Message Cont., 1460 Bytes
97	30.727	VOYAGERIX	WANTEST2	NBT	SS: Session Message Cont., 1460 Bytes
98	30.729	VOYAGERIX	WANTEST2	NBT	SS: Session Message Cont., 1460 Bytes
99	30.731	VOYAGERIX	WANTEST2	NBT	SS: Session Message Cont., 1460 Bytes
100	30.733	VOYAGERIX	WANTEST2	NBT	SS: Session Message Cont., 1460 Bytes
101	30.735	VOYAGERIX	WANTEST2	NBT	SS: Session Message Cont., 1460 Bytes
102	32.193	WANTEST2	VOYAGERIX	TC	.A...., len: 0, seq: 233665, ack: 1315915, win:12288
103	32.194	VOYAGERIX	WANTEST2	NBT	SS: Session Message Cont., 871 Bytes
104	32.880	WANTEST2	VOYAGERIX	TCP	.A...., len: 0, seq: 233665, ack: 1318835, win:12288
105	32.917	WANTEST2	VOYAGERIX	TCP	.A...., len: 0, seq: 233665, ack: 1321755, win:12288
106	32.917	WANTEST2	VOYAGERIX	TC	.A...., len: 0, seq: 233665, ack: 1324675, win:12288
107	32.917	WANTEST2	VOYAGERIX	TCP	.A...., len: 0, seq: 233665, ack: 1326135, win:12288
108	33.543	WANTEST2	VOYAGERIX	SMB	R write & X, Wrote 0x30c4

Windows NT 4.0/Windows 2000

When using NT 4.0 and Windows 2000 there is no requirement for modifying the **SizReqBuf** parameter. These operating systems have been designed to address the raw mode over high-latency, dial-up, and slow-link connections.

With the introduction of EXPLORER.EXE with Windows NT 4.0 more data is brought across the network while viewing a network drive's resources. Each version of the EXPLORER.EXE has introduced networking savings transactions for attributes, icons, and directories. In order of most-to-least traffic for network drive access, these services are:

1. EXPLORER.EXE
2. WINFILE.EXE
3. FTP command
4. CMD.EXE

Performance Hints and Tips

- See the Performance Results section (at the end of this chapter) for your operating system version.
- Compress the files that you want to move as in WinZip (by Niko Mak Computing, Inc.)
- Using the operating compression bit does not retain compression over the network.

Microsoft Word 97

This network trace is typical network activity running Microsoft Word 97 over the network. Starting at packet 16 you will note that the file TECH01.DOC was accessed multiple times. This is a combination of Windows Explorer and Word. Attributes are being read. If Word is configured to pre-view in the Open pane, even more traffic is generated.

You can see at packet 213 that a file is being generated (~TEXCH01.DOC). Looking closely you will see that there is a lot of write activity to the destination drive. Not shown is read-only of the drive or document. If the share is read-only, attribute read-only, or the document is password protected (so you are prompted for read-only), Word generates a lot of overhead is as it determines how to proceed, where to generate temporary files, and so on. This can be an additional 100 packets or so.

Performance Hints and Tips

- Make sure you do not attempt to load WORD.EXE program over a slow link WORD.EXE program should be loaded locally or off a local network server.
- Make sure to configure Word to generate TEMP files locally and not to generate them on the default drive off of which the document is retrieved.
- Always try to copy the document to a local drive—remember: a copy command is the most efficient method for moving data over slow links.

Network Trace—Typical Network Activity Running Microsoft Word 97 Over the Network

Network Monitor trace Tue 04/11/98 00:20:15 Word.DOC.

Frame	Time	Src MAC Addr	Dst MAC Addr	Protocol	Description
16	24.364	TIGERII	VOYAGERIX	SMB	R session setup & X, and R tree connect & X, Type = A:
17	24.367	VOYAGERIX	TIGERII	SMB	C NT create & X, File = \source\teched
18	24.668	TIGERII	VOYAGERIX	NBT	SS: Session Keep Alive, Len: 0
19	24.801	VOYAGERIX	TIGERII	TCP	.A...., len: 0, seq: 5707630, ack:1893659553, win: 8496
20	25.077	TIGERII	VOYAGERIX	SMB	R NT create & X, FID = 0x3008
21	25.201	VOYAGERIX	TIGERII	TCP	.A...., len: 0, seq: 5707630, ack:1893659660, win: 8389

Network Monitor trace Tue 04/11/98 00:20:15 Word.DOC. *(continued)*

Frame	Time	Src MAC Addr	Dst MAC Addr	Protocol	Description
22	25.459	VOYAGERIX	TIGERII	SMB	C close file, FID = 0x3008
23	25.741	TIGERII	VOYAGERIX	SMB	R close file
24	25.902	VOYAGERIX	TIGERII	TCP	A...., len: 0, seq: 5707676, ack:1893659699, win: 8350
25	45.989	VOYAGERIX	TIGERII		C NT create & X, File = \SOURCE\TECHED\TECH01.DOC
26	46.353	TIGERII	VOYAGERIX	SMB	R NTcreate & X (Error)
27	46.358	VOYAGERIX	TIGERII	SMB	C NTcreate & X, File = \source\teched
28	46.645	TIGERII	VOYAGERIX	SMB	R NTcreate & X, FID = 0x3006
29	46.685	VOYAGERIX	TIGERII	SMB	C transact2 GetPathInfo, File = \SOURCE\TECHED\TECH01.DOC
30	47.054	TIGERII	VOYAGERIX	SMB	R transact2 GetPathInfo (responsc to framc 29)
31	47.236	VOYAGERIX	TIGERII	TCP	.A...., len: 0, seq: 5708060, ack:1893659949, win: 8100
32	47.412	VOYAGERIX	TIGERII	SMB	C transact2 GetPathInfo, File = \SOURCE\TECHED\TECH01.DOC
33	47.756	TIGERII	VOYAGERIX	SMB	R transact2 GetPathInfo (response to frame 32)
34	47.764	VOYAGERIX	TIGERII	SMB	C close file, FID = 0x3006
35	48.010	TIGERII	VOYAGERIX	SMB	R close file
36	48.138	VOYAGERIX	TIGERII	TCP	.A...., len: 0, seq: 5708234, ack:1893660092, win: 7957
37	48.160	VOYAGERIX	TIGERII	SMB	C NT create & X, File = \SOURCE\TECHED\TECH01.DOC
38	48.494	TIGERII	VOYAGERIX	SMB	R NT create & X, FID = 0x3004
39	48.495	VOYAGERIX	TIGERII	SMB	C transact2 GetFsInfo
40	48.798	TIGERII	VOYAGERIX	SMB	R transact2 GetFsInfo (response to frame 39)
41	48.803	VOYAGERIX	TIGERII	SMB	C read & X, FID = 0x3004, Read 0x1000 at 0x0

Network Monitor trace Tue 04/11/98 00:20:15 Word.DOC. *(continued)*

Frame	Time	Src MAC Addr	Dst MAC Addr	Protocol	Description
42	49.513	TIGERII	VOYAGERIX	SMB	R read & X, Read 0x1000
43	49.640	VOYAGERIX	TIGERII	TCP	.A...., len: 0, seq: 5708510, ack:1893661743, win: 8760
44	50.051	TIGERII	VOYAGERIX	NBT	SS: Session Message Cont., 1460 Bytes
45	50.241	VOYAGERIX	TIGERII	TCP	.A...., len: 0, seq: 5708510, ack:1893663203, win: 8760
46	50.353	TIGERII	VOYAGERIX	NBT	SS: Session Message Cont., 1240 Bytes
47	50.357	VOYAGERIX	TIGERII	SMB	C read & X, FID = 0x3004, Read 0x10c5 at 0x1000
48	50.963	TIGERII	VOYAGERIX	SMB	R read & X, Read 0x10c5
108	77.440	VOYAGERIX	TIGERII	TCP	.A...., len: 0, seq: 5709022, ack:1893697723, win: 8760
109	77.453	VOYAGERIX	TIGERII	SMB	C close file, FID = 0x3004
110	77.932	TIGERII	VOYAGERIX	SMB	R close file
111	77.936	VOYAGERIX	TIGERII	SMB	R NT create & X, FID = 0x300a
113	78.393	VOYAGERIX	TIGERII	SMB	C read & X, FID = 0x300a, Read 0x1000 at 0x0
114	79.883	TIGERII	VOYAGERIX	SMB	R read & X, Read 0x1000
115	79.989	VOYAGERIX	TIGERII	TCP	.A...., len: 0, seq: 5709270, ack:1893699329, win: 8760
116	80.405	TIGERII	VOYAGERIX	NBT	SS: Session Message Cont., 1460 Bytes
117	80.590	VOYAGERIX	TIGERII	TCP	.A...., len: 0, seq: 5709270, ack:1893700789, win: 8760
118	80.664	TIGERII	VOYAGERIX	NBT	SS: Session Message Cont., 1240 Bytes
213	118.049	VOYAGERIX	TIGERII	SMB	C NT create & X, File = \SOURCE\TECHED\~$TECH01.DOC
214	118.408	TIGERII	VOYAGERIX	SMB	R NT create & X, FID = 0x3009

Network Monitor trace Tue 04/11/98 00:20:15 Word.DOC. *(continued)*

Frame	Time	Src MAC Addr	Dst MAC Addr	Protocol	Description
215	118.413	VOYAGERIX	TIGERII	SMB	C write, FID = 0x3009, Write 0x0 at 0x36
216	118.493	TIGERII	VOYAGERIX	TCP	.A...., len: 0, seq:1893764536, ack: 5710372, win: 7794
217	118.665	TIGERII	VOYAGERIX	SMB	R write, Wrote 0x0
218	118.721	VOYAGERIX	TIGERII	SMB	C read & X, FID = 0x300a, Read 0xa00 at 0xb6000
219	119.939	TIGERII	VOYAGERIX	SMB	R read & X, Read 0xa00
220	119.940	VOYAGERIX	TIGERI	SMB	C write & X, FID = 0x3009, Write 0x36 at 0x0
222	120.639	TIGERII	VOYAGERIX	TCP	.A...., len: 0, seq:1893767201, ack: 5710609, win: 7557
223	120.753	VOYAGERIX	TIGERII	TCP	.A...., len: 0, seq: 5710609, ack:1893767201, win: 7596
224	120.978	TIGERII	VOYAGERIX	SMB	R write & X, Wrote 0x36
225	121.010	VOYAGERIX	TIGERII	SMB	C read & X, FID = 0x300a, Read 0x1000 at 0xb5000
226	121.318	TIGERII	VOYAGERIX	SMB	R read & X, Read 0x1000
227	121.454	VOYAGERIX	TIGERII	TCP	.A...., len: 0, seq: 5710673, ack:1893768712, win: 8760
228	121.627	TIGERII	VOYAGERIX	NBT	SS: Session Message Cont., 1460 Bytes

Microsoft Excel 97

This network trace shows typical network activity running Microsoft Excel 5.0 over the network. Note that the Excel application is read in a header of the file first—a 4096-byte read. Next it reads a block of data that is defined in the first header, then the next header of 4096 bytes, then the next block of data referenced by the second header. This goes on throughout the trace. This technique is used so the system can recover at any time. This does cause overhead on the network, but helps in any error recovery that may be needed. Towards the end of the action of opening the document, the File TECH01.XLS is opened again to update the workbook and statistics of the file.

Performance Hints and Tips

- Make sure you do not attempt to load EXCEL.EXE program over a slow link. Load EXCEL.EXE locally or off a local network server
- Make sure to configure Excel to generate TEMP files locally and not on the default drive from which the document is retrieved.
- Try to always copy the spreadsheet to a local drive—remember: a copy command is the most efficient method of moving data over slow links.

Network Trace—Typical Network Activity Running Microsoft Excel 5.0 Over the Network

Network Monitor trace Tue 04/11/98 00:18:09 Excel.XLS.

Frame	Time	Src MAC Addr	Dst MAC Addr	Protocol	Description
1	2.442	TIGERII	VOYAGERIX	NBT	SS: Session Keep Alive, Len: 0
2	2.607	VOYAGERIX	TIGERII	TCP	.A...., len: 0, seq: 5996073, ack: 722263424, win: 8097
3	7.042	VOYAGERIX	TIGERII	SMB	C NT create & X, File = \SOURCE\TECHED\TECH01.XLS
4	7.323	TIGERII	VOYAGERIX	SMB	R NT create & X (Error)
5	7.331	VOYAGERIX	TIGERII	SMB	C transact2 GetPathInfo, File = \SOURCE\TECHED\TECH01.XLS
6	8.015	VOYAGERIX	TIGERII	SMB	C transact2 GetPathInfo, File = \SOURCE\TECHED\TECH01.XLS
7	8.448	TIGERII	VOYAGERIX	SMB	R transact2
8	8.521	TIGERII	VOYAGERIX	TCP	.A...., len: 0, seq:1894305079, ack: 5836658, win: 7410
9	8.564	VOYAGERIX	TIGERII	SMB	C transact2 GetPathInfo, File = \SOURCE\TECHED\TECH01.XLS
10	9.919	VOYAGERIX	TIGERII	SMB	C transact2 GetPathInfo, File = \SOURCE\TECHED\TECH01.XLS
11	10.130	TIGERII	VOYAGERIX	SMB	R transact2

Network Monitor trace Tue 04/11/98 00:18:09 Excel.XLS. *(continued)*

Frame	Time	Src MAC Addr	Dst MAC Addr	Protocol	Description
12	10.130	VOYAGERIX	TIGERII	TCP	.A...., len: 0, seq: 5836786, ack:1894305079, win: 8539
13	10.158	TIGERII	VOYAGERIX	SMB	R transact2
14	10.180	VOYAGERIX	TIGERII	SMB	C transact2 GetPathInfo, File = \SOURCE\TECHED\TECH01.XLS
15	10.345	TIGERII	VOYAGERIX	TCP	.A...., len: 0, seq:1894305183, ack: 5836786, win: 7282
16	10.480	TIGERII	VOYAGERIX	SMB	R transact2
17	10.619	VOYAGERIX	TIGERII	TCP	.A...., len: 0, seq: 5836914, ack:1894305287, win: 8331
18	10.757	VOYAGERIX	TIGERII	SMB	C lock & X, FID = 0x4000, Unlocks = 1 (0x2d for 0xff930000)
19	11.016	TIGERII	VOYAGERIX	SMB	R lock & X
20	11.017	VOYAGERIX	TIGERII	NBT	SS: Session Message Cont., 150 Bytes
21	11.521	VOYAGERIX	TIGERII	NBT	SS: Session Message Cont., 150 Bytes
22	11.852	TIGERII	VOYAGERIX	SMB	R lock & X
23	11.946	TIGERII	VOYAGERIX	TCP	.A...., len: 0, seq:1894305373, ack: 5837139, win: 6929
24	12.022	VOYAGERIX	TIGERII	TCP	.A...., len: 0, seq: 5837139, ack:1894305373, win: 8245
25	12.250	TIGERII	VOYAGERIX	SMB	R lock & X
26	12.257	VOYAGERIX	TIGERII	SMB	C close file, FID = 0x4000
27	12.488	TIGERII	VOYAGERIX	SMB	R close file
28	12.595	VOYAGERIX	TIGERII	SMB	C NT create & X, File = \SOURCE\TECHED\TECH01.XLS
29	12.918	TIGERII	VOYAGERIX	SMB	R NT create & X, FID = 0x400f
30	12.928	VOYAGERIX	TIGERII	SMB	C read & X, FID = 0x400f, Read 0x1000 at 0x0
34	20.615	TIGERII	VOYAGERIX	SMB	R read & X, Read 0x1000
35	20.735	VOYAGERIX	TIGERII	TCP	.A...., len: 0, seq: 5837387, ack:1894307022, win: 8760

Network Monitor trace Tue 04/11/98 00:18:09 Excel.XLS. *(continued)*

Frame	Time	Src MAC Addr	Dst MAC Addr	Protocol	Description
36	21.131	TIGERII	VOYAGERIX	NBT	SS: Session Message Cont., 1460 Bytes
37	21.236	VOYAGERIX	TIGERII	TCP	.A...., len: 0, seq: 5837387, ack:1894308482, win: 8760
38	21.416	TIGERII	VOYAGERIX	NBT	SS: Session Message Cont., 1240 Bytes
39	21.420	VOYAGERIX	TIGERII	SMB	C read & X, FID = 0x400f, Read 0x10c5 at 0x1000
69	28.401	VOYAGERIX	TIGERII	SMB	C transact2 FindFirst, File = \SOURCE
71	29.684	TIGERII	VOYAGERIX	SMB	R transact2 FindFirst (response to frame 70)
72	29.690	VOYAGERIX	TIGERII	SMB	C NT create & X, File = \SOURCE
73	29.776	TIGERII	VOYAGERIX	TCP	.A...., len: 0, seq:1894319310, ack: 5837679, win: 7900
74	29.957	TIGERII	VOYAGERIX	SMB	R NT create & X, FID = 0x4801
75	29.961	VOYAGERIX	TIGERII	SMB	C transact2 FindFirst, File = \SOURCE\TECHED
76	30.952	VOYAGERIX	TIGERII	SMB	C transact2 FindFirst, File = \SOURCE\TECHED
77	32.386	TIGERII	VOYAGERIX	SMB	R transact2 FindFirst (response to frame 76)
78	32.390	VOYAGERIX	TIGERII	SMB	C close file, FID = 0x4801
79	32.470	TIGERII	VOYAGERIX	TCP	.A...., len: 0, seq:1894319597, ack: 5837897, win: 7682
80	32.612	TIGERII	VOYAGERIX	SMB	R transact2 FindFirst (response to frame 76)
81	32.612	VOYAGERIX	TIGERII	TCP	.A...., len: 0, seq: 5837943, ack:1894319597, win: 8293
82	32.648	TIGERII	VOYAGERIX	SMB	R close file
83	32.652	VOYAGERIX	TIGERII	SMB	C NT create & X, File = \source\teched
84	32.907	TIGERII	VOYAGERIX	SMB	R NT create & X, FID = 0x4803
85	32.910	VOYAGERIX	TIGERII	SMB	C transact2 FindFirst, File = \source\teched\TECH01.XLS

Network Monitor trace Tue 04/11/98 00:18:09 Excel.XLS. *(continued)*

Frame	Time	Src MAC Addr	Dst MAC Addr	Protocol	Description
86	33.243	TIGERII	VOYAGERIX	SMB	R transact2 FindFirst (response to frame 85)
87	33.248	VOYAGERIX	TIGERII	SMB	C close file, FID = 0x4803
88	33.459	TIGERII	VOYAGERIX	SMB	R close file
89	33.475	VOYAGERIX	TIGERII	SMB	C NT create & X, File = \SOURCE\TECHED\TECH01.XLS
90	33.718	TIGERII	VOYAGERIX	SMB	C lock & X, FID = 0x400f
91	33.720	VOYAGERIX	TIGERII	SMB	C lock & X, FID = 0x400f, Locks = 3 (0x0 for 0xff930000)
92	33.963	TIGERII	VOYAGERIX	SMB	R lock & X
93	33.965	VOYAGERIX	TIGERII	SMB	C lock & X, FID = 0x400f
94	34.209	TIGERII	VOYAGERIX	SMB	R NT create & X, FID = 0x4802
95	34.212	VOYAGERIX	TIGERII	SMB	C read & X, FID = 0x4802, Read 0x200 at 0x0
96	34.517	TIGERII	VOYAGERIX	SMB	R read & X, Read 0x200
97	34.521	VOYAGERIX	TIGERII	SMB	C lock & X, FID = 0x4802, Locks = 1 (0x0 for 0xff920000)
98	34.750	TIGERII	VOYAGERIX	SMB	C lock & X, FID = 0x400f
99	34.858	VOYAGERIX	TIGERII	TCP	.A...., len: 0, seq: 5838688, ack:1894320809, win: 8705
100	35.060	TIGERII	VOYAGERIX	SMB	R lock & X
101	35.062	VOYAGERIX	TIGERII	SMB	C lock & X, FID = 0x4802, Locks = 1 (0x0 for 0xffbb0000)
102	35.297	TIGERII	VOYAGERIX	SMB	R lock & X
103	35.300	VOYAGERIX	TIGERII	SMB	C lock & X, FID = 0x4802, Unlocks = 1 (0x0 for 0xffbb0000)
104	35.524	TIGERII	VOYAGERIX	SMB	R lock & X
105	35.525	VOYAGERIX	TIGERII	SMB	C lock & X, FID = 0x4802, Locks = 1 (0x0 for 0xff940000)
106	35.741	TIGERII	VOYAGERIX	SMB	R lock & X

Network Monitor trace Tue 04/11/98 00:18:09 Excel.XLS. *(continued)*

Frame	Time	Src MAC Addr	Dst MAC Addr	Protocol	Description
107	35.743	VOYAGERIX	TIGERII	SMB	C lock & X, FID = 0x4802, Locks = 1 (0x0 for 0xffa80000)
108	35.959	TIGERII	VOYAGERIX	SMB	R lock & X
109	35.964	VOYAGERIX	TIGERII	SMB	C lock & X, FID = 0x4802, Locks = 1 (0x0 for 0xffbc0000)
110	36.173	TIGERII	VOYAGERIX	SMB	R lock & X
111	36.175	VOYAGERIX	TIGERII	SMB	C lock & X, FID = 0x4802, Locks = 1 (0x0 for 0xffd00000)
112	36.379	TIGERII	VOYAGERIX	SMB	R lock & X
113	36.381	VOYAGERIX	TIGERII	SMB	C lock & X, FID = 0x4802, Unlocks = 1 (0x0 for 0xffa80000)
114	36.566	TIGERII	VOYAGERIX	SMB	R lock & X
115	36.567	VOYAGERIX	TIGERII	NBT	SS: Session Message Cont., 300 Bytes
116	36.837	TIGERII	VOYAGERIX	SMB	R lock & X
117	36.962	VOYAGERIX	TIGERII	TCP	.A...., len: 0, seq: 5839513, ack:1894321199, win: 8315
118	37.176	TIGERII	VOYAGERIX	NBT	SS: Session Message Cont., 129 Bytes
119	37.180	VOYAGERIX	TIGERII	SMB	C lock & X, FID = 0x4802, Locks = 1 (0x0 for 0xff810000)
120	37.380	TIGERII	VOYAGERIX	SMB	R lock & X
121	37.383	VOYAGERIX	TIGERII	SMB	C lock & X, FID = 0x4802, Unlocks = 1 (0x0 for 0xff800000)
122	37.596	TIGERII	VOYAGERIX	SMB	R lock & X
123	37.599	VOYAGERIX	TIGERII	SMB	C read & X, FID = 0x4802, Read 0x80 at 0x400
124	37.920	TIGERII	VOYAGERIX	SMB	R read & X, Read 0x80
125	37.923	VOYAGERIX	TIGERII	SMB	C lock & X, FID = 0x4802, Unlocks = 1 (0x0 for 0xff810000)
126	38.120	TIGERII	VOYAGERIX	SMB	R lock & X
127	38.121	VOYAGERIX	TIGERII	SMB	C lock & X, FID = 0x4802, Unlocks = 1 (0x0 for 0xff940000)

Network Monitor trace Tue 04/11/98 00:18:09 Excel.XLS. *(continued)*

Frame	Time	Src MAC Addr	Dst MAC Addr	Protocol	Description
128	38.318	TIGERII	OYAGERIX	SMB	R lock & X
129	38.320	VOYAGERIX	TIGERII	SMB	C close file, FID = 0x4802
130	38.528	TIGERII	VOYAGERIX	SMB	R close file
131	38.536	VOYAGERIX	TIGERII	SMB	C NT create & X, File = \source\teched
132	38.789	TIGERII	VOYAGERIX	SMB	R NT create & X, FID = 0x400b
133	38.793	VOYAGERIX	TIGERII	SMB	C transact2 FindFirst, File = \source\teched\TECH01.XLS
134	39.027	TIGERII	VOYAGERIX	SMB	R transact2 FindFirst (response to frame 133)
135	39.031	VOYAGERIX	TIGERII	SMB	C close file, FID = 0x400b
136	39.243	TIGERII	VOYAGERIX	SMB	R close file
137	39.346	VOYAGERIX	TIGERII	SMB	C transact2 GetFileInfo, FID = 0x400f
138	39.626	TIGERII	VOYAGERIX	SMB	R transact2 GetFileInfo (response to frame 137)
139	39.629	VOYAGERIX	TIGERII	SMB	C transact2 GetFileInfo, FID = 0x400f
140	39.913	TIGERII	VOYAGERIX	SMB	R transact2 GetFileInfo (response to frame 139)
141	39.921	VOYAGERIX	TIGERII	SMB	C transact2 GetPathInfo, File = \SOURCE\TECHED\TECH01.XLS
142	40.121	TIGERII	VOYAGERIX	SMB	R transact2 GetPathInfo (response to frame 141)
143	40.158	VOYAGERIX	TIGERII	SMB	C read & X, FID = 0x400f, Read 0x1000 at 0x1400
144	40.667	VOYAGERIX	TIGERII	SMB	C read & X, FID = 0x400f, Read 0x1000 at 0x1400
145	41.224	TIGERII	VOYAGERIX	SMB	R read & X, Read 0x1000
146	41.368	VOYAGERIX	TIGERII	TCP	.A...., len: 0, seq: 5840565, ack:1894323821, win: 8760
147	45.040	TIGERII	VOYAGERIX	NBT	SS: Session Message, Len: 57344
148	45.136	TIGERII	VOYAGERIX	NBT	SS: Session Message Cont., 1240 Bytes

Network Monitor trace Tue 04/11/98 00:18:09 Excel.XLS. *(continued)*

Frame	Time	Src MAC Addr	Dst MAC Addr	Protocol	Description
149	45.137	VOYAGERIX	TIGERII	TCP	.A...., len: 0, seq: 5840565, ack:1894326521, win: 8760
150	45.154	TIGERII	VOYAGERIX	TCP	.A...., len: 0, seq:1894326521, ack: 5840565, win: 8000
151	45.157	VOYAGERIX	TIGERII	SMB	C transact2 GetFileInfo, FID = 0x400f
152	45.177	TIGERII	VOYAGERIX	SMB	R read & X, Read 0x1000
153	45.178	VOYAGERIX	TIGERII	TCP	.A...., len: 0, seq: 5840641, ack:1894326521, win: 8760
154	45.189	TIGERII	VOYAGERIX	NBT	SS: Session Message, Len: 57344
155	45.190	VOYAGERIX	TIGERII	TCP	.A...., len: 0, seq: 5840641, ack:1894326521, win: 8760
156	45.194	TIGERII	VOYAGERIX	NBT	SS: Session Message Cont., 1240 Bytes
157	45.195	VOYAGERIX	TIGERII	TCP	.A...., len: 0, seq: 5840641, ack:1894326521, win: 8760,
158	45.683	TIGERII	VOYAGERIX	NBT	SS: Session Message, Len: 57344
159	45.684	VOYAGERIX	TIGERII	TCP	.A...., len: 0, seq: 5840641, ack:1894326521, win: 8760
160	45.761	TIGERII	VOYAGERIX	SMB	R transact2 GetFileInfo (response to frame 151)
161	45.764	VOYAGERIX	TIGERII	SMB	C transact2 GetFileInfo, FID = 0x400f
162	46.044	TIGERII	VOYAGERIX	SMB	R transact2 GetFileInfo (response to frame 161)
163	46.047	VOYAGERIX	TIGERII	SMB	C transact2 GetFileInfo, FID = 0x400f
164	46.275	TIGERII	VOYAGERIX	SMB	R transact2 GetFileInfo (response to frame 163)
165	46.279	VOYAGERIX	TIGERII	SMB	C transact2 GetFileInfo, FID = 0x400f
166	46.493	TIGERII	VOYAGERIX	SMB	R transact2 GetFileInfo (response to frame 165)
167	46.495	VOYAGERIX	TIGERII	SMB	C write, FID = 0x400f, Write 0x0 at 0x3400
168	46.747	TIGERII	VOYAGERIX	SMB	R write, Wrote 0x0
169	46.750	VOYAGERIX	TIGERII	SMB	C transact2 SetFileInfo, FID = 0x400f

Network Monitor trace Tue 04/11/98 00:18:09 Excel.XLS. *(continued)*

Frame	Time	Src MAC Addr	Dst MAC Addr	Protocol	Description
170	47.039	TIGERII	VOYAGERIX	SMB	R transact2 SetFileInfo (response to frame 169)
171	47.042	VOYAGERIX	TIGERII	SMB	C lock & X, FID = 0x400f, Locks = 1 (0x5 for 0xff800000)
172	47.300	TIGERII	VOYAGERIX	SMB	R lock & X
173	47.306	VOYAGERIX	TIGERII	SMB	C write & X, FID = 0x400f, Write 0x1000 at 0x1400
174	47.310	VOYAGERIX	TIGERII	NBT	SS: Session Message Cont., 1460 Bytes
175	47.671	VOYAGERIX	TIGERII	NBT	SS: Session Message Cont., 1243 Bytes
176	47.991	TIGERII	VOYAGERIX	SMB	R lock & X
177	48.112	VOYAGERIX	TIGERII	SMB	C write & X, FID = 0x400f, Write 0x1000 at 0x1400
178	48.184	TIGERII	VOYAGERIX	TCP	.A...., len: 0, seq:1894327053, ack: 5842544, win: 8192
179	48.201	VOYAGERIX	TIGERII	TCP	.A...., len: 0, seq: 5842544, ack:1894327053, win: 8228
180	48.230	VOYAGERIX	TIGERII	NBT	SS: Session Message Cont., 1460 Bytes
181	48.240	VOYAGERIX	TIGERII	NBT	SS: Session Message Cont., 1243 Bytes
182	48.591	TIGERII	VOYAGERIX	TCP	.A...., len: 0, seq:1894327053, ack: 5845247, win: 8192
183	48.639	TIGERII	VOYAGERIX	SMB	R write & X, Wrote 0x1000
184	48.642	VOYAGERIX	TIGERII	SMB	C write & X, FID = 0x400f, Write 0x200 at 0x400
188	48.690	TIGERII	VOYAGERIX	TCP	.A...., len: 0, seq:1894327104, ack: 5845247, win: 8192
189	49.043	TIGERII	VOYAGERIX	SMB	R write & X, Wrote 0x200
190	49.046	VOYAGERIX	TIGERII	SMB	C write, FID = 0x400f, Write 0x0 at 0x3400
191	49.502	TIGERII	VOYAGERIX	SMB	R write, Wrote 0x0
192	49.507	VOYAGERIX	TIGERII	SMB	C transact2 SetFileInfo, FID = 0x400f
193	49.801	TIGERII	VOYAGERIX	SMB	R transact2 SetFileInfo (response to frame 192)

Network Monitor trace Tue 04/11/98 00:18:09 Excel.XLS. *(continued)*

Frame	Time	Src MAC Addr	Dst MAC Addr	Protocol	Description
194	49.805	VOYAGERIX	TIGERII	SMB	C lock & X, FID = 0x400f, Unlocks = 1 (0x5 for 0xff800000)
195	50.080	TIGERII	VOYAGERIX	SMB	R lock & X
196	50.182	VOYAGERIX	TIGERII	TCP	.A...., len: 0, seq: 5846041, ack:1894327303, win: 7978
197	50.367	VOYAGERIX	TIGERII	SMB	C read & X, FID = 0x400f, Read 0x800 at 0x1400
198	50.984	VOYAGERIX	TIGERII	SMB	C read & X, FID = 0x400f, Read 0x800 at 0x1400
199	51.064	TIGERII	VOYAGERIX	SMB	R read & X, Read 0x800
200	51.184	VOYAGERIX	TIGERII	TCP	.A...., len: 0, seq: 5846105, ack:1894328763, win: 8760
201	51.271	TIGERII	VOYAGERIX	NBT	SS: Session Message, Len: 57344
202	51.305	TIGERII	VOYAGERIX	SMB	R read & X, Read 0x800
203	51.306	VOYAGERIX	TIGERII	TCP	.A...., len: 0, seq: 5846105, ack:1894329415, win: 8108
204	51.312	TIGERII	VOYAGERIX	TCP	.A...., len: 0, seq:1894328763, ack: 5846105, win: 7334
205	51.313	VOYAGERIX	TIGERII	TCP	.A...., len: 0, seq: 5846105, ack:1894329415, win: 8108

Microsoft PowerPoint 97

This network trace shows typical network activity running Microsoft PowerPoint 97 over the network. Note that the PowerPoint application reads in larger blocks of data than do other Office applications. Note that PowerPoint opens and closes the TECH01.PPT presentation in large-block increments—a technique that allows the system to recover at any time. This causes overhead on the network, but helps error recovery. In this example the presentation had embedded sounds and special effects that were not installed on the default machine that was reading the file. Notice the extra overhead that was caused over the network looking for "missing DLL support."

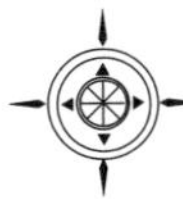

Performance Hints and Tips

- Make sure you do not attempt to load PPOINT.EXE program over a slow link. It should be loaded locally or off a local network server.
- Make sure to configure Excel to generate TEMP files locally and not on the default drive from which the document is retrieved.
- Always try to copy the PowerPoint presentation to a local drive—remember: a copy command is the most efficient method for moving data over slow links.

Network Trace—Typical Network Activity Running Microsoft PowerPoint 97 Over the Network

Network Monitor trace Sun 03/05/98 12:57:59 PowerPoint 97.

Frame	Time	Src MAC Addr	Dst MAC Addr	Protocol	Description
29	3.840	BLACKHOLES	PIONEERV	SMB	R NT transact
30	3.841	PIONEERV	BLACKHOLES	SMB	C NT transact - NT IOCTL
31	3.843	BLACKHOLES	PIONEERV	SMB	R NT create & X, FID = 0x7807
32	3.843	PIONEERV	BLACKHOLES	SMB	C NT create & X, File = \Tech01.ppt
33	3.844	BLACKHOLES	PIONEERV	SMB	R NT transact
34	3.844	PIONEERV	BLACKHOLES	SMB	C NT transact - NT IOCTL
35	3.849	PIONEERV	BLACKHOLES	SMB	C read & X, FID = 0x7807, Read 0x8000 at 0x00000000
36	3.850	BLACKHOLES	PIONEERV	SMB	R read & X, Read 0x8000
37	3.851	BLACKHOLES	PIONEERV	NBT	SS: Session Message Cont., 1460 Bytes
38	3.851	PIONEERV	BLACKHOLES	TCP	.A...., len: 0, seq: 13104926-13104926, ack: 31472886, win:1
39	3.852	BLACKHOLES	PIONEERV	NBT	SS: Session Message Cont., 1460 Bytes

Network Monitor trace Sun 03/05/98 12:57:59 PowerPoint 97. *(continued)*

Frame	Time	Src MAC Addr	Dst MAC Addr	Protocol	Description
40	3.854	BLACKHOLES	PIONEERV	NBT	SS: Session Message Cont., 1460 Bytes
41	3.854	PIONEERV	BLACKHOLES	TCP	.A...., len: 0, seq: 13104926-13104926, ack: 31475806 win:1
42	3.855	BLACKHOLES	PIONEERV	NBT	SS: Session Message Cont., 1460 Bytes
43	3.856	BLACKHOLES	PIONEERV	NBT	SS: Session Message Cont., 1460 Bytes
44	3.857	PIONEERV	BLACKHOLES	TCP	.A...., len: 0, seq: 13104926-13104926, ack: 31478726, win:1
45	3.857	BLACKHOLES	PIONEERV	NBT	SS: Session Message Cont., 1460 Bytes
46	3.859	BLACKHOLES	PIONEERV	NBT	SS: Session Message Cont., 1460 Bytes
47	3.859	PIONEERV	BLACKHOLES	TCP	.A...., len: 0, seq: 13104926-13104926, ack: 31481646, win:1
48	3.860	BLACKHOLES	PIONEERV	NBT	SS: Session Message Cont., 1460 Bytes
49	3.861	BLACKHOLES	PIONEERV	NBT	SS: Session Message Cont., 1460 Bytes
50	3.862	PIONEERV	BLACKHOLES	TCP	.A...., len: 0, seq: 13104926-13104926, ack: 31484566, win:1
51	3.863	BLACKHOLES	PIONEERV	NBT	SS: Session Message Cont., 1460 Bytes
52	3.864	BLACKHOLES	PIONEERV	NBT	SS: Session Message Cont., 1460 Bytes
					...
103	3.907	PIONEERV	BLACKHOLES	SMB	C NT transact - NT IOCTL
104	3.908	BLACKHOLES	PIONEERV	SMB	R close file
105	3.909	PIONEERV	BLACKHOLES	SMB	C close file, FID = 0x7807

Network Monitor trace Sun 03/05/98 12:57:59 PowerPoint 97. *(continued)*

Frame	Time	Src MAC Addr	Dst MAC Addr	Protocol	Description
106	3.910	BLACKHOLES	PIONEERV	SMB	R NT create & X, FID = 0x600a
107	3.910	PIONEERV	BLACKHOLES	SMB	C NT create & X, File = \Tech01.ppt
108	3.911	PIONEERV	BLACKHOLES	SMB	C read & X, FID = 0x600a, Read 0x1000 at 0x00000000
109	3.912	BLACKHOLES	PIONEERV	SMB	R read & X, Read 0x1000
110	3.913	BLACKHOLES	PIONEERV	NBT	SS: Session Message Cont., 1460 Bytes
111	3.914	PIONEERV	BLACKHOLES	TCP	.A...., len: 0, seq: 13105300-13105300, ack: 31536214, win:1
112	3.914	BLACKHOLES	PIONEERV	NBT	SS: Session Message Cont., 1240 Bytes
113	3.979	BLACKHOLES	PIONEERV	SMB	R NT transact
114	3.979	PIONEERV	BLACKHOLES	SMB	C NT transact - NT IOCTL
115	3.980	BLACKHOLES	PIONEERV	SMB	R NT transact
116	3.981	PIONEERV	BLACKHOLES	SMB	C NT transact - NT IOCTL
117	3.983	BLACKHOLES	PIONEERV	SMB	R transact2 Open (response)
118	3.983	PIONEERV	BLACKHOLES	SMB	C transact2 Findfirst, File = \Tech01.ppt
119	3.984	BLACKHOLES	PIONEERV	SMB	R NT transact
120	3.984	PIONEERV	BLACKHOLES	SMB	C NT transact - NT IOCTL
121	3.985	BLACKHOLES	PIONEERV	SMB	R close file
122	3.985	PIONEERV	BLACKHOLES	SMB	C close file, FID = 0x600a
123	3.986	BLACKHOLES	PIONEERV	SMB	R NT create & X, FID = 0x7805
124	3.986	PIONEERV	BLACKHOLES	SMB	C NT create & X, File = \Tech01.ppt
125	3.987	BLACKHOLES	PIONEERV	SMB	R NT transact

Network Monitor trace Sun 03/05/98 12:57:59 PowerPoint 97. *(continued)*

Frame	Time	Src MAC Addr	Dst MAC Addr	Protocol	Description
126	3.987	PIONEERV	BLACKHOLES	SMB	C NT transact - NT IOCTL
127	3.990	PIONEERV	BLACKHOLES	SMB	C read & X, FID = 0x7805, Read 0x1000 at 0x00000000
128	3.991	BLACKHOLES	PIONEERV	SMB	R read & X, Read 0x1000
129	3.992	BLACKHOLES	PIONEERV	NBT	SS: Session Message Cont., 1460 Bytes
130	3.993	PIONEERV	BLACKHOLES	TCP	.A...., len: 0, seq: 13105982-13105982, ack: 31541032, win:1
131	3.993	BLACKHOLES	PIONEERV	NBT	SS: Session Message Cont., 1240 Bytes
132	3.995	PIONEERV	BLACKHOLES	SMB	C read & X, FID = 0x7805, Read 0x600 at 0x0008F000
133	3.996	BLACKHOLES	PIONEERV	SMB	R read & X, Read 0x600
134	3.996	BLACKHOLES	PIONEERV	NBT	SS: Session Message Cont., 140 Bytes
135	3.996	PIONEERV	BLACKHOLES	TCP	.A...., len: 0, seq: 13106046-13106046, ack: 31543872, win:1
136	3.998	PIONEERV	BLACKHOLES	SMB	C read & X, FID = 0x7805, Read 0x1000 at 0x0008D000
137	3.999	BLACKHOLES	PIONEERV	SMB	R read & X, Read 0x1000
138	4.001	BLACKHOLES	PIONEERV	NBT	SS: Session Message Cont., 1460 Bytes
139	4.001	PIONEERV	BLACKHOLES	TCP	.A...., len: 0, seq: 13106110-13106110, ack: 31546792, win:1
140	4.002	BLACKHOLES	PIONEERV	NBT	SS: Session Message Cont., 1240 Bytes
141	4.006	BLACKHOLES	PIONEERV	SMB	R write, Wrote 0x0
142	4.006	PIONEERV	BLACKHOLES	SMB	C write, FID = 0x7805, Write 0x0 at 0x0008F600
143	4.007	BLACKHOLES	PIONEERV	NBT	SS: Session Message Cont., 216 Bytes

Network Monitor trace Sun 03/05/98 12:57:59 PowerPoint 97. *(continued)*

Frame	Time	Src MAC Addr	Dst MAC Addr	Protocol	Description
144	4.007	PIONEERV	BLACKHOLES	SMB	C transact2 Set file info, FID = 0x7805
145	4.008	BLACKHOLES	PIONEERV	SMB	R transact2 Set file info (response to frame 144)
146	4.008	PIONEERV	BLACKHOLES	SMB	C NT transact - Notify Change
147	4.011	PIONEERV	BLACKHOLES	SMB	C write & X, FID = 0x7805, Write 0x1000 at 0x0008D000
148	4.011	PIONEERV	BLACKHOLES	NBT	SS: Session Message Cont., 1460 Bytes
149	4.011	PIONEERV	BLACKHOLES	NBT	SS: Session Message Cont., 1243 Bytes
150	4.012	BLACKHOLES	PIONEERV	SMB	R NT transact
151	4.013	BLACKHOLES	PIONEERV	TCP	.A...., len: 0, seq: 31548461-31548461, ack: 13110498, win:
152	4.014	BLACKHOLES	PIONEERV	SMB	R write & X, Wrote 0x1000
153	4.014	PIONEERV	BLACKHOLES	SMB	C NT transact - Notify Change
154	4.018	BLACKHOLES	PIONEERV	TCP	.A...., len: 0, seq: 31548512-31548512, ack: 13112186, win:
155	4.018	BLACKHOLES	PIONEERV	SMB	R write & X, Wrote 0x600
156	4.018	PIONEERV	BLACKHOLES	SMB	C write & X, FID = 0x7805, Write 0x600 at 0x0008F000
157	4.018	PIONEERV	BLACKHOLES	NBT	SS: Session Message Cont., 143 Bytes
158	4.030	PIONEERV	BLACKHOLES	SMB	C flush file, FID = 0x7805
159	4.091	BLACKHOLES	PIONEERV	SMB	R NT transact
160	4.093	BLACKHOLES	PIONEERV	SMB	R flush file
161	4.093	PIONEERV	BLACKHOLES	SMB	C NT transact - Notify Change
162	4.095	BLACKHOLES	PIONEERV	SMB	R NT transact

Network Monitor trace Sun 03/05/98 12:57:59 PowerPoint 97. *(continued)*

Frame	Time	Src MAC Addr	Dst MAC Addr	Protocol	Description
163	4.095	PIONEERV	BLACKHOLES	SMB	C NT transact - NT IOCTL
164	4.098	BLACKHOLES	PIONEERV	TCP	.A...., len: 0, seq: 31548790-31548790, ack: 13114003, win:
165	4.098	BLACKHOLES	PIONEERV	SMB	R write & X, Wrote 0x600
166	4.098	PIONEERV	BLACKHOLES	SMB	C write & X, FID = 0x7805, Write 0x600 at 0x0008F000
167	4.098	PIONEERV	BLACKHOLES	NBT	SS: Session Message Cont., 143 Bytes
168	4.099	BLACKHOLES	PIONEERV	SMB	R close file
169	4.099	PIONEERV	BLACKHOLES	SMB	C close file, FID = 0x7805
170	4.100	BLACKHOLES	PIONEERV	SMB	R NT transact
171	4.100	PIONEERV	BLACKHOLES	SMB	C NT create & X, File = \Tech01.ppt
172	4.102	BLACKHOLES	PIONEERV	SMB	R NT create & X, FID = 0x780e
173	4.102	PIONEERV	BLACKHOLES	SMB	C NT transact - Notify Change
174	4.103	BLACKHOLES	PIONEERV	SMB	R transact2 NT Get DFS Referral (response)
175	4.104	PIONEERV	BLACKHOLES	SMB	C transact2 Set file info, FID = 0x780e
176	4.104	BLACKHOLES	PIONEERV	SMB	R NT transact - Notify Change (response to frame 173)
177	4.104	PIONEERV	BLACKHOLES	SMB	C close file, FID = 0x780e
178	4.106	BLACKHOLES	PIONEERV	SMB	R close file
179	4.106	PIONEERV	BLACKHOLES	SMB	C NT transact - Notify Change
180	4.107	BLACKHOLES	PIONEERV	SMB	R NT transact
181	4.107	PIONEERV	BLACKHOLES	SMB	C NT transact - NT IOCTL
182	4.108	BLACKHOLES	PIONEERV	SMB	R NT create & X, FID = 0x5809

Network Monitor trace Sun 03/05/98 12:57:59 PowerPoint 97. *(continued)*

Frame	Time	Src MAC Addr	Dst MAC Addr	Protocol	Description
183	4.108	PIONEERV	BLACKHOLES	SMB	C NT create & X, File = \Tech01.ppt
184	4.109	BLACKHOLES	PIONEERV	SMB	R transact2 NT Get DFS Referral (response)
185	4.110	PIONEERV	BLACKHOLES	SMB	C transact2 Set file info, FID = 0x5809
186	4.110	BLACKHOLES	PIONEERV	SMB	R NT transact - Notify Change (response to frame 179)
187	4.110	PIONEERV	BLACKHOLES	SMB	C close file, FID = 0x5809
188	4.113	BLACKHOLES	PIONEERV	SMB	R close file
189	4.113	PIONEERV	BLACKHOLES	SMB	C NT transact - Notify Change
190	4.115	BLACKHOLES	PIONEERV	SMB	R NT transact
191	4.115	PIONEERV	BLACKHOLES	SMB	C NT transact - NT IOCTL
192	4.116	BLACKHOLES	PIONEERV	SMB	R NT create & X, FID = 0x680f
193	4.116	PIONEERV	BLACKHOLES	SMB	C NT create & X, File = \Tech01.ppt
194	4.117	BLACKHOLES	PIONEERV	SMB	R NT transact
195	4.117	PIONEERV	BLACKHOLES	SMB	C NT transact - NT IOCTL
196	4.120	PIONEERV	BLACKHOLES	SMB	C read & X, FID = 0x680f, Read 0x8000 at 0x00000000
197	4.121	BLACKHOLES	PIONEERV	SMB	R read & X, Read 0x8000
198	4.122	BLACKHOLES	PIONEERV	NBT	SS: Session Message Cont., 1460 Bytes
199	4.123	PIONEERV	BLACKHOLES	TCP	.A...., len: 0, seq: 13115300-13115300, ack: 31552891, win:1
200	4.124	BLACKHOLES	PIONEERV	NBT	SS: Session Message Cont., 1460 Bytes
201	4.125	BLACKHOLES	PIONEERV	NBT	SS: Session Message Cont., 1460 Bytes

Network Monitor trace Sun 03/05/98 12:57:59 PowerPoint 97. *(continued)*

Frame	Time	Src MAC Addr	Dst MAC Addr	Protocol	Description
202	4.125	PIONEERV	BLACKHOLES	TCP	.A...., len: 0, seq: 13115300-13115300, ack: 31555811, win:1
203	4.126	BLACKHOLES	PIONEERV	NBT	SS: Session Message Cont., 1460 Bytes
204	4.128	BLACKHOLES	PIONEERV	NBT	SS: Session Message Cont., 1460 Bytes
205	4.128	PIONEERV	BLACKHOLES	TCP	.A...., len: 0, seq: 13115300-13115300, ack: 31558731, win:1
206	4.129	BLACKHOLES	PIONEERV	NBT	SS: Session Message Cont., 1460 Bytes
					...
353	4.494	PIONEERV	BLACKHOLES	SMB	C transact2 Query path info, File = \#96.mci
354	4.711	PIONEERV	BLACKHOLES	TCP	.A...., len: 0, seq: 13116436-13116436, ack: 31679330, win:1
355	6.122	BLACKHOLES	PIONEERV	SMB	R transact2 Open (response)
356	6.122	PIONEERV	BLACKHOLES	SMB	C transact2 Findfirst, File = *
357	6.127	BLACKHOLES	PIONEERV	SMB	R transact2 Open (response)
358	6.128	PIONEERV	BLACKHOLES	SMB	C transact2 Query file system info
359	6.131	BLACKHOLES	PIONEERV	SMB	R find close
360	6.131	PIONEERV	BLACKHOLES	SMB	C find close, FID = 0x1807
					...
512	9.255	PIONEERV	BLACKHOLES	SMB	C transact2 Query path info, File = \mciwave.dll
513	9.259	BLACKHOLES	PIONEERV	SMB	R NT transact

Network Monitor trace Sun 03/05/98 12:57:59 PowerPoint 97. *(continued)*

Frame	Time	Src MAC Addr	Dst MAC Addr	Protocol	Description
514	9.259	PIONEERV	BLACKHOLES	SMB	C NT transact - NT IOCTL
					...
895	12.702	PIONEERV	BLACKHOLES	SMB	C NT transact - NT IOCTL
896	12.703	BLACKHOLES	PIONEERV	SMB	R transact2 - NT error, System, Error, Code = (52)
897	12.703	PIONEERV	BLACKHOLES	SMB	C transact2 Query path info, File = \OLEAUT32.dll
898	12.755	BLACKHOLES	PIONEERV	SMB	R NT transact
899	12.756	PIONEERV	BLACKHOLES	SMB	C NT transact - NT IOCTL
900	12.924	PIONEERV	BLACKHOLES	TCP	.A...., len: 0, seq: 13126675-13126675, ack: 31993906, win:1
901	13.343	BLACKHOLES	PIONEERV	SMB	R NT transact
902	13.343	PIONEERV	BLACKHOLES	SMB	C NT transact - NT IOCTL
903	13.345	BLACKHOLES	PIONEERV	SMB	R transact2 Open (response)
904	13.345	PIONEERV	BLACKHOLES	SMB	C transact2 Findfirst, File = \Tech01.ppt
905	13.456	BLACKHOLES	PIONEERV	SMB	R NT create & X, FID = 0x7006
906	13.456	PIONEERV	BLACKHOLES	SMB	C NT create & X, File = \srvsvc
907	13.458	BLACKHOLES	PIONEERV	SMB	R transact
					...
913	13.465	BLACKHOLES	PIONEERV	SMB	R close file
914	13.465	PIONEERV	BLACKHOLES	SMB	C close file, FID = 0x7006
915	13.625	PIONEERV	BLACKHOLES	TCP	.A...., len: 0, seq: 13127429-13127429, ack: 31996636, win:1
916	13.736	PIONEERV	BLACKHOLES	SMB	C read & X, FID = 0x680f, Read 0x8000 at 0x00018000
917	13.737	BLACKHOLES	PIONEERV	SMB	R read & X, Read 0x8000

Microsoft Outlook 98

Exchange RPC Transport

The Exchange Server provider is based on RPCs. By using RPCs the Exchange client benefits from single-logon authentication, single bit reorder for encryption of mail traffic over the LAN, and protocol independence. The RPC interface includes full functionality for the Exchange client. In addition to the three features above, the client provides a full Messaging Application Interface (MAPI) that provides an automated access for offline and on-line address book. As part of the negotiation, the RPC interface determines if the mailbox has moved and if it has the software automatically reconfigures the client to use the correct Exchange Server. This interface increases performance by compressing e-mail to and from the desktop. RPC connections are session-based: the system logs on only once, which also reduces network traffic.

Message Storage Options

- **On the Exchange Server**. This generates a lot of traffic because all titles must come down the pipe and most users prefer opening mail in auto view, reading the first 20 lines or so, then opening each message as they work through the inbox.
- **Locally in a Personal Store (PST)**. Messages are delivered to the local PST in the background, using Outlook 98's multi-threaded capability.
- **In an Offline Store (OST)**. One copy of the message is stored on the network and one locally. The user can make changes off line and the system synchronizes both stores when the user reconnects to the network.
- **Using the Remote Mail (Dial-up Networking)**. Even without a local modem you can select "use existing connection," connect to the server store, and pick which messages to download rather than downloading them all. This differs from the first option in that only titles are displayed and the tools are optimized for high-latency and lower-speed links.

Short Cuts

The Outlook client's desktop design allows you to create Short Cuts to folders on the Exchange Server. The default configuration has all the mail short cuts referenced over the network. The trace below (Outlook RPC Default) shows Outlook booting up and logging in. While Outlook is loading it must enumerate all the short cuts. To see if Outlook is completely initialized, use the **Tools** option on the pull-down menu. The Outlook client may take a while to respond while initializing all the default short cuts—Inbox, Calendar, Notes, Contacts, Tasks and Public folders.

The second trace below (Outlook RPC Local PST without Short Cuts) shows that only 41 packets were generated (the default configuration generated 176 packets). In a high-latency network, 135 packets can make quite a difference in response times.

Performance Hints and Tips

- For best performance the client should have a local Exchange Server. This shields the user from any high-latency and dial-up issues. (See the Microsoft Exchange Server section below.)
- For best performance over high-latency or slow links, use a local PST to store mail.
- Make sure to remove any toolbar short cut references for use over high-latency or slow links; reference only local folders.
- Frequent connecting and disconnecting create traffic; it is more efficient to connect and stay connected. Users who have to connect frequently can also use the dial-up feature.

Exchange Service Provider

The Exchange Service provider controls the connection order of protocols used by the Exchange RPC Provider. This registry entry lists the current protocols available for RPC connection. Each is tried in the RPC_Bindings_Order until a connection is made.

HKEY_LOCAL_MACHINE\Software\Microsoft\Exhange\Exchange Provider

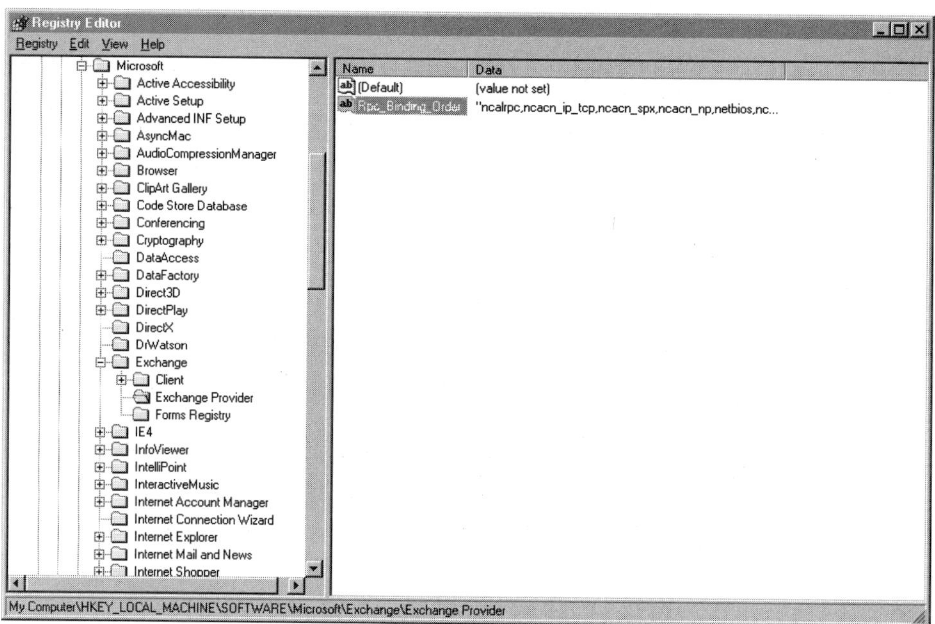

Figure 6.14 Looking for the RPC_Binding_Order with Registry Editor (REGEDIT.EXE).

- **NCALRPC**—Local RPC is the first in the binding order. This is a local RPC internal to the machine; it does not pass over the network.
- **NCACN_IP_TCP**—This binding creates an RPC connection using the TCP transport (a connection state instead of a connectionless state).
- **NCACN_SPX**—This binding creates an RPC connection using the Sequenced Package Exchange (SPX) protocol.
- **NCACN_NP**—This binding creates an RPC connection using a NamePipe interface. When more than one NetBIOS is loaded, the provider tries each in the NetBIOS binding order.
- **NETBIOS**—This binding creates an RPC connection using the NetBEUI protocol.
- **NCACN_VNS_SPP**—This binding creates an RPC connection using the Banyan Vines scalable parallel processing (SPP) protocol (a connection state instead of a connectionless state).

Outlook 98 binding order has been changed from previous versions to optimize performance order, trying first for TCP, the most efficient. If connection cannot be established, the provider tries the next binding. This can have inconvenient consequences. For instance, if you mistype a server name you have to wait for all six bindings to fail or for a security credential mismatch to prompt for a password six times, once for each binding. So while this is a good default configuration for an unknown network, you should consider deleting unsupported protocols from the list when you deploy: it makes for faster error message response and higher user satisfaction.

Performance Hints and Tips

- When using TCP provider for fastest response in a high-latency or dial-up network, use HOSTS file for the Exchange Server.
- When using TCP provider make sure the DNS is configured properly and the Exchange Server is listed in DNS, or you will have to wait up to 3 x 750 ms before an error message is issued or the next bindings are tried.

- When using Name-Pipe over TCP/IP for fastest response in a high-latency or dial-up network, include an LMHOSTS #PRE entry for the Exchange Server.
- When using Name-Pipe over TCP/IP, make sure the WINS is configured properly and the Exchange Server is listed in the WINS database, or you will have to wait up to 3 x 750 ms before an error message is issued or the next bindings are tried.
- Delete unsupported protocols for better performance at connect time.

Network Trace—Outlook RPC Default

Network Monitor trace Fri 11/13/98 23:09:22 \OutlookRPCDefault.

Frame	Time	Src MAC Addr	Dst MAC Addr	Protocol	Description
1	2.774	BLACKHOLES	PIONEERV	TCP	.A..S., len: 4, seq: 116498-116501, ack: 120353, win: 87
2	2.775	PIONEERV	BLACKHOLES	TCP	....S., len: 4, seq: 120352-120355, ack: 0, win:163
3	2.775	PIONEERV	BLACKHOLES	TCP	.A...., len: 0, seq: 120353-120353, ack: 116499, win:163
4	2.777	BLACKHOLES	PIONEERV	MSRPC	c/o RPC Bind Ack: call 0x0 assoc grp 0x187C5 xmit
5	2.777	PIONEERV	BLACKHOLES	MSRPC	c/o RPC Bind: UUID E1AF8308-5D1F-11C9-91A4-
6	2.779	BLACKHOLES	PIONEERV	MSRPC	c/o RPC Response: call 0x1 context 0x0 hint 0x80 cancels 0
7	2.779	PIONEERV	BLACKHOLES	MSRPC	c/o RPC Request: call 0x1 opnum 0x3 context 0x0 hint
8	2.780	BLACKHOLES	PIONEERV	TCP	.A...., len: 0, seq: 116711-116711, ack: 120582, win: 85
9	2.780	PIONEERV	BLACKHOLES	TCP	.A...F, len: 0, seq: 120581-120581, ack: 116711, win:161
10	2.780	BLACKHOLES	PIONEERV	TCP	.A...F, len: 0, seq: 116711-116711, ack: 120582, win: 85
11	2.780	PIONEERV	BLACKHOLES	TCP	.A...., len: 0, seq: 120582-120582, ack: 116712, win:161

Network Monitor trace Fri 11/13/98 23:09:22 \OutlookRPCDefault. *(continued)*

Frame	Time	Src MAC Addr	Dst MAC Addr	Protocol	Description
12	2.790	BLACKHOLES	PIONEERV	TCP	.A..S., len: 4, seq: 116509-116512, ack: 120367, win: 87
13	2.790	PIONEERV	BLACKHOLES	TCP	....S., len: 4, seq: 120366-120369, ack: 0, win:163
14	2.791	PIONEERV	BLACKHOLES	TCP	.A...., len: 0, seq: 120367-120367, ack: 116510, win:163
15	2.792	BLACKHOLES	PIONEERV	MSRPC	c/o RPC Bind Ack: call 0x1 assoc grp 0x1D69C xmit
16	2.793	PIONEERV	BLACKHOLES	MSRPC	c/o RPC Bind: UUID F5CC5A18-4264-101A-8C59-
17	2.794	BLACKHOLES	PIONEERV	R_NSPI	Error: Bad Opcode (Function does not exist)
18	2.794	PIONEERV	BLACKHOLES	R_NSPI	RPC Client call nspi:NspiBind(..)
19	2.858	BLACKHOLES	PIONEERV	TCP	.A..S., len: 4, seq: 116524-116527, ack: 120368, win: 87
20	2.858	PIONEERV	BLACKHOLES	TCP	....S., len: 4, seq: 120367-120370, ack: 0, win:163
21	2.858	PIONEERV	BLACKHOLES	TCP	.A...., len: 0, seq: 120368-120368, ack: 116525, win:163
22	2.861	BLACKHOLES	PIONEERV	MSRPC	c/o RPC Bind Ack: call 0x44 assoc grp 0x1D69C xmit
23	2.861	PIONEERV	BLACKHOLES	MSRPC	c/o RPC Bind: UUID F5CC5A18-4264-101A-8C59-
24	2.867	BLACKHOLES	PIONEERV	TCP	.A...., len: 0, seq: 116657-116657, ack: 120806, win: 83
25	2.868	PIONEERV	BLACKHOLES	TCP	.AP..., len: 198, seq: 120496-120693, ack: 116657, win:162
26	2.868	PIONEERV	BLACKHOLES	R_NSPI	RPC Client call nspi:NspiBind(..)
27	2.874	BLACKHOLES	PIONEERV	R_NSPI	RPC Server response nspi:NspiBind(..)
28	2.931	PIONEERV	BLACKHOLES	TCP	.A...., len: 0, seq: 120523-120523, ack: 116638, win:162
29	2.975	BLACKHOLES	PIONEERV	TCP	.A..S., len: 4, seq: 116529-116532, ack: 120381, win: 87
30	2.975	PIONEERV	BLACKHOLES	TCP	....S., len: 4, seq: 120380-120383, ack: 0, win:163
31	2.975	PIONEERV	BLACKHOLES	TCP	.A...., len: 0, seq: 120381-120381, ack: 116530, win:163

Network Monitor trace Fri 11/13/98 23:09:22 \OutlookRPCDefault. *(continued)*

Frame	Time	Src MAC Addr	Dst MAC Addr	Protocol	Description
32	2.977	BLACKHOLES	PIONEERV	MSRPC	c/o RPC Bind Ack: call 0x0 assoc grp 0x187C6 xmit
33	2.977	PIONEERV	BLACKHOLES	MSRPC	c/o RPC Bind: UUID E1AF8308-5D1F-11C9-91A4-
34	2.978	BLACKHOLES	PIONEERV	MSRPC	c/o RPC Response: call 0x1 context 0x0 hint 0x80 cancels
35	2.978	PIONEERV	BLACKHOLES	MSRPC	c/o RPC Request: call 0x1 opnum 0x3 context 0x0 hint
36	2.979	BLACKHOLES	PIONEERV	TCP	.A...., len: 0, seq: 116742-116742, ack: 120610, win: 85
37	2.979	PIONEERV	BLACKHOLES	TCP	.A...F, len: 0, seq: 120609-120609, ack: 116742, win:161
38	2.979	BLACKHOLES	PIONEERV	TCP	.A...F, len: 0, seq: 116742-116742, ack: 120610, win: 85
39	2.979	PIONEERV	BLACKHOLES	TCP	.A...., len: 0, seq: 120610-120610, ack: 116743, win:161
40	2.990	BLACKHOLES	PIONEERV	TCP	.A..S., len: 4, seq: 116532-116535, ack: 120383, win: 87
41	2.990	PIONEERV	BLACKHOLES	TCP	....S., len: 4, seq: 120382-120385, ack: 0, win:163
42	2.990	PIONEERV	BLACKHOLES	TCP	.A...., len: 0, seq: 120383-120383, ack: 116533, win:163
43	2.993	BLACKHOLES	PIONEERV	MSRPC	c/o RPC Bind Ack: call 0x0 assoc grp 0x1F85A xmit
44	2.993	PIONEERV	BLACKHOLES	MSRPC	c/o RPC Bind: UUID A4F1DB00-CA47-1067-B31F-
45	3.001	PIONEERV	BLACKHOLES	TCP	.AP..., len: 198, seq: 120511-120708, ack: 116665, win:162
46	3.004	BLACKHOLES	PIONEERV	TCP	.A...., len: 0, seq: 116665-116665, ack: 120885, win: 82
47	3.004	PIONEERV	BLACKHOLES	MSRPC	c/o RPC Request: call 0x1 opnum 0x0 context 0x0 hint
48	3.016	BLACKHOLES	PIONEERV	MSRPC	c/o RPC Response: call 0x1 context 0x0 hint 0x9C cancels
49	3.016	PIONEERV	BLACKHOLES	TCP	.A...., len: 0, seq: 120806-120806, ack: 116753, win:161

Network Monitor trace Fri 11/13/98 23:09:22 \OutlookRPCDefault. *(continued)*

Frame	Time	Src MAC Addr	Dst MAC Addr	Protocol	Description
50	3.031	PIONEERV	BLACKHOLES	MSRPC	c/o RPC Request: call 0x2 opnum 0x2 context 0x0 hint
51	3.047	BLACKHOLES	PIONEERV	MSRPC	c/o RPC Response: call 0x2 context 0x0 hint 0xD4 cancels
52	3.064	BLACKHOLES	PIONEERV	MSRPC	c/o RPC Response: call 0x3 context 0x0 hint 0x58 cancels
53	3.064	PIONEERV	BLACKHOLES	MSRPC	c/o RPC Request: call 0x3 opnum 0x2 context 0x0 hint
54	3.212	PIONEERV	BLACKHOLES	MSRPC	c/o RPC Request: call 0x4 opnum 0x2 context 0x0 hint
55	3.214	BLACKHOLES	PIONEERV	MSRPC	c/o RPC Response: call 0x4 context 0x0 hint 0x34 cancels
56	3.219	BLACKHOLES	PIONEERV	MSRPC	c/o RPC Response: call 0x5 context 0x0 hint 0x108 cancels
57	3.219	PIONEERV	BLACKHOLES	MSRPC	c/o RPC Request: call 0x5 opnum 0x2 context 0x0 hint
58	3.225	BLACKHOLES	PIONEERV	MSRPC	c/o RPC Response: call 0x6 context 0x0 hint 0x238 cancels
59	3.225	PIONEERV	BLACKHOLES	MSRPC	c/o RPC Request: call 0x6 opnum 0x2 context 0x0 hint
60	3.230	BLACKHOLES	PIONEERV	MSRPC	c/o RPC Response: call 0x7 context 0x0 hint 0x1C cancels
61	3.231	PIONEERV	BLACKHOLES	MSRPC	c/o RPC Request: call 0x7 opnum 0x4 context 0x0 hint
62	3.305	BLACKHOLES	PIONEERV	MSRPC	c/o RPC Response: call 0x8 context 0x0 hint 0xA0 cancels
63	3.305	PIONEERV	BLACKHOLES	MSRPC	c/o RPC Request: call 0x8 opnum 0x2 context 0x0 hint
64	3.310	BLACKHOLES	PIONEERV	MSRPC	c/o RPC Response: call 0x9 context 0x0 hint 0x1D0
65	3.310	PIONEERV	BLACKHOLES	MSRPC	c/o RPC Request: call 0x9 opnum 0x2 context 0x0 hint

Network Monitor trace Fri 11/13/98 23:09:22 \OutlookRPCDefault. *(continued)*

Frame	Time	Src MAC Addr	Dst MAC Addr	Protocol	Description
66	3.398	BLACKHOLES	PIONEERV	MSRPC	c/o RPC Response: call 0xA context 0x0 hint 0x44 cancels
67	3.398	PIONEERV	BLACKHOLES	MSRPC	c/o RPC Request: call 0xA opnum 0x2 context 0x0 hint
68	3.401	BLACKHOLES	PIONEERV	MSRPC	c/o RPC Response: call 0xB context 0x0 hint 0x58 cancels
69	3.402	PIONEERV	BLACKHOLES	MSRPC	c/o RPC Request: call 0xB opnum 0x2 context 0x0 hint
70	3.463	BLACKHOLES	PIONEERV	MSRPC	c/o RPC Response: call 0xC context 0x0 hint 0x5C cancels
71	3.463	PIONEERV	BLACKHOLES	MSRPC	c/o RPC Request: call 0xC opnum 0x2 context 0x0 hint
72	3.592	BLACKHOLES	PIONEERV	MSRPC	c/o RPC Response: call 0xD context 0x0 hint 0x58 cancels
73	3.592	PIONEERV	BLACKHOLES	MSRPC	c/o RPC Request: call 0xD opnum 0x2 context 0x0 hint
74	3.732	PIONEERV	BLACKHOLES	TCP	.A...., len: 0, seq: 123029-123029, ack: 119705, win:150
75	3.929	BLACKHOLES	PIONEERV	TCP	.A..S., len: 4, seq: 116546-116549, ack: 120385, win: 87
76	3.929	PIONEERV	BLACKHOLES	TCP	....S., len: 4, seq: 120384-120387, ack: 0, win:163
77	3.929	PIONEERV	BLACKHOLES	TCP	.A...., len: 0, seq: 120385-120385, ack: 116547, win:163
78	3.931	BLACKHOLES	PIONEERV	MSRPC	c/o RPC Bind Ack: call 0xA assoc grp 0x187C7 xmit
79	3.931	PIONEERV	BLACKHOLES	MSRPC	c/o RPC Bind: UUID E1AF8308-5D1F-11C9-91A4-
80	3.933	BLACKHOLES	PIONEERV	MSRPC	c/o RPC Response: call 0x1 context 0x0 hint 0x80 cancels
81	3.933	PIONEERV	BLACKHOLES	MSRPC	c/o RPC Request: call 0x1 opnum 0x3 context 0x0 hint
82	3.934	BLACKHOLES	PIONEERV	TCP	.A...., len: 0, seq: 116759-116759, ack: 120614, win: 85
83	3.934	PIONEERV	BLACKHOLES	TCP	.A...F, len: 0, seq: 120613-120613, ack: 116759, win:161
84	3.934	BLACKHOLES	PIONEERV	TCP	.A...F, len: 0, seq: 116759-116759, ack: 120614, win: 85

Network Monitor trace Fri 11/13/98 23:09:22 \OutlookRPCDefault. *(continued)*

Frame	Time	Src MAC Addr	Dst MAC Addr	Protocol	Description
85	3.934	PIONEERV	BLACKHOLES	TCP	.A...., len: 0, seq: 120614-120614, ack: 116760, win:161
86	3.945	BLACKHOLES	PIONEERV	TCP	.A..S., len: 4, seq: 116558-116561, ack: 120400, win: 87
87	3.945	PIONEERV	BLACKHOLES	TCP	....S., len: 4, seq: 120399-120402, ack: 0, win:163
88	3.945	PIONEERV	BLACKHOLES	TCP	.A...., len: 0, seq: 120400-120400, ack: 116559, win:163
89	3.947	BLACKHOLES	PIONEERV	MSRPC	c/o RPC Bind Ack: call 0x0 assoc grp 0x1D69D xmit
90	3.947	PIONEERV	BLACKHOLES	MSRPC	c/o RPC Bind: UUID F5CC5A18-4264-101A-8C59-
91	3.948	BLACKHOLES	PIONEERV	R_NSPI	Error: Bad Opcode (Function does not exist)
92	3.948	PIONEERV	BLACKHOLES	R_NSPI	RPC Client call nspi:NspiBind(..)
93	3.959	BLACKHOLES	PIONEERV	TCP	.A..S., len: 4, seq: 116566-116569, ack: 120402, win: 87
94	3.959	PIONEERV	BLACKHOLES	TCP	....S., len: 4, seq: 120401-120404, ack: 0, win:163
95	3.959	PIONEERV	BLACKHOLES	TCP	.A...., len: 0, seq: 120402-120402, ack: 116567, win:163
96	3.962	BLACKHOLES	PIONEERV	MSRPC	c/o RPC Bind Ack: call 0x44 assoc grp 0x1D69D xmit
97	3.962	PIONEERV	BLACKHOLES	MSRPC	c/o RPC Bind: UUID F5CC5A18-4264-101A-8C59-
98	3.965	BLACKHOLES	PIONEERV	TCP	.A...., len: 0, seq: 116699-116699, ack: 120840, win: 83
99	3.965	PIONEERV	BLACKHOLES	TCP	.AP..., len: 198, seq: 120530-120727, ack: 116699, win:162
100	3.965	PIONEERV	BLACKHOLES	R_NSPI	RPC Client call nspi:NspiBind(..)
101	3.973	BLACKHOLES	PIONEERV	R_NSPI	RPC Server response nspi:NspiBind(..)
102	4.094	BLACKHOLES	PIONEERV	TCP	.A..S., len: 4, seq: 116579-116582, ack: 120416, win: 87
103	4.094	PIONEERV	BLACKHOLES	TCP	....S., len: 4, seq: 120415-120418, ack: 0, win:163
104	4.094	PIONEERV	BLACKHOLES	TCP	.A...., len: 0, seq: 120416-120416, ack: 116580, win:163

Network Monitor trace Fri 11/13/98 23:09:22 \OutlookRPCDefault. *(continued)*

Frame	Time	Src MAC Addr	Dst MAC Addr	Protocol	Description
105	4.095	BLACKHOLES	PIONEERV	MSRPC	c/o RPC Bind Ack: call 0x1 assoc grp 0x187C8 xmit
106	4.095	PIONEERV	BLACKHOLES	MSRPC	c/o RPC Bind: UUID E1AF8308-5D1F-11C9-91A4-
107	4.096	BLACKHOLES	PIONEERV	MSRPC	c/o RPC Response: call 0x1 context 0x0 hint 0x80 cancels
108	4.097	PIONEERV	BLACKHOLES	MSRPC	c/o RPC Request: call 0x1 opnum 0x3 context 0x0 hint
109	4.097	BLACKHOLES	PIONEERV	TCP	.A...., len: 0, seq: 116792-116792, ack: 120645, win: 85
110	4.097	PIONEERV	BLACKHOLES	TCP	.A...F, len: 0, seq: 120544-120644, ack: 116792, win:161
111	4.098	BLACKHOLES	PIONEERV	TCP	.A...F, len: 0, seq: 116792-116792, ack: 120645, win: 85
112	4.098	PIONEERV	BLACKHOLES	TCP	.A...., len: 0, seq: 120645-120645, ack: 116793, win:161
113	4.108	BLACKHOLES	PIONEERV	TCP	.A..S., len: 4, seq: 116590-116593, ack: 120427, win: 87
114	4.108	PIONEERV	BLACKHOLES	TCP	....S., len: 4, seq: 120426-120429, ack: 0, win:163
115	4.108	PIONEERV	BLACKHOLES	TCP	.A...., len: 0, seq: 120427-120427, ack: 116591, win:163
116	4.111	BLACKHOLES	PIONEERV	MSRPC	c/o RPC Bind Ack: call 0x0 assoc grp 0x1F85B xmit
117	4.111	PIONEERV	BLACKHOLES	MSRPC	c/o RPC Bind: UUID A4F1DB00-CA47-1067-B31F-
118	4.114	BLACKHOLES	PIONEERV	TCP	.A...., len: 0, seq: 116723-116723, ack: 120929, win: 82
119	4.114	PIONEERV	BLACKHOLES	TCP	.A...., len: 0, seq: 120556-120556, ack: 116687, win:162
120	4.114	PIONEERV	BLACKHOLES	TCP	.A...., len: 0, seq: 120840-120840, ack: 116795, win:161
121	4.114	PIONEERV	BLACKHOLES	TCP	AP..., len: 198, seq: 120555-120752, ack: 116723, win:162
122	4.114	PIONEERV	BLACKHOLES	MSRPC	c/o RPC Request: call 0x1 opnum 0x0 context 0x0 hint
123	4.128	BLACKHOLES	PIONEERV	MSRPC	c/o RPC Response: call 0x1 context 0x0 hint 0x9C cancels

Network Monitor trace Fri 11/13/98 23:09:22 \OutlookRPCDefault. *(continued)*

Frame	Time	Src MAC Addr	Dst MAC Addr	Protocol	Description
124	4.131	BLACKHOLES	PIONEERV	MSRPC	c/o RPC Response: call 0x2 context 0x0 hint 0xD4 cancels
125	4.131	PIONEERV	BLACKHOLES	MSRPC	c/o RPC Request: call 0x2 opnum 0x2 context 0x0 hint
126	4.333	PIONEERV	BLACKHOLES	TCP	.A...., len: 0, seq: 121105-121105, ack: 117203, win:157
127	5.153	BLACKHOLES	PIONEERV	TCP	.A..S., len: 4, seq: 116594-116597, ack: 120435, win: 87
128	5.153	PIONEERV	BLACKHOLES	TCP	....S., len: 4, seq: 120434-120437, ack: 0, win:163
129	5.153	PIONEERV	BLACKHOLES	TCP	.A...., len: 0, seq: 120435-120435, ack: 116595, win:163
130	5.155	BLACKHOLES	PIONEERV	MSRPC	c/o RPC Bind Ack: call 0x44 assoc grp 0x187C9 xmit
131	5.155	PIONEERV	BLACKHOLES	MSRPC	c/o RPC Bind: UUID E1AF8308-5D1F-11C9-91A4-
132	5.157	BLACKHOLES	PIONEERV	MSRPC	c/o RPC Response: call 0x1 context 0x0 hint 0x80 cancels
133	5.157	PIONEERV	BLACKHOLES	MSRPC	c/o RPC Request: call 0x1 opnum 0x3 context 0x0 hint
134	5.158	BLACKHOLES	PIONEERV	TCP	A...., len: 0, seq: 116807-116807, ack: 120664, win: 85
135	5.158	PIONEERV	BLACKHOLES	TCP	.A...F, len: 0, seq: 120663-120663, ack: 116807, win:161
136	5.158	BLACKHOLES	PIONEERV	TCP	.A...F, len: 0, seq: 116807-116807, ack: 120664, win: 85
137	5.158	PIONEERV	BLACKHOLES	TCP	.A...., len: 0, seq: 120664-120664, ack: 116808, win:161
138	5.170	BLACKHOLES	PIONEERV	MSRPC	c/o RPC Response: call 0x3 context 0x0 hint 0x9C cancels
139	5.170	PIONEERV	BLACKHOLES	MSRPC	c/o RPC Request: call 0x3 opnum 0x0 context 0x0 hint
140	5.173	BLACKHOLES	PIONEERV	MSRPC	c/o RPC Response: call 0x4 context 0x0 hint 0xD4 cancels
141	5.173	PIONEERV	BLACKHOLES	MSRPC	c/o RPC Request: call 0x4 opnum 0x2 context 0x0 hint
142	5.189	BLACKHOLES	PIONEERV	MSRPC	c/o RPC Response: call 0x5 context 0x0 hint 0x1C cancels

Network Monitor trace Fri 11/13/98 23:09:22 \OutlookRPCDefault. *(continued)*

Frame	Time	Src MAC Addr	Dst MAC Addr	Protocol	Description
143	5.189	PIONEERV	BLACKHOLES	MSRPC	c/o RPC Request: call 0x5 opnum 0x4 context 0x0 hint
144	5.296	BLACKHOLES	PIONEERV	MSRPC	c/o RPC Response: call 0x6 context 0x0 hint 0x5C cancels
145	5.296	PIONEERV	BLACKHOLES	MSRPC	c/o RPC Request: call 0x6 opnum 0x2 context 0x0 hint
146	5.435	PIONEERV	BLACKHOLES	TCP	.A...., len: 0, seq: 121745-121745, ack: 117907, win:150
147	8.620	PIONEERV	BLACKHOLES	R_NSPI	RPC Client call nspi:NspiGetHierarchyInfo(..)
148	8.620	BLACKHOLES	PIONEERV	R_NSPI	RPC Server response nspi:NspiGetHierarchyInfo(..)
149	8.668	BLACKHOLES	PIONEERV	MSRPC	c/o RPC Response: call 0xE context 0x0 hint 0xB8 cancels
150	8.668	PIONEERV	BLACKHOLES	MSRPC	c/o RPC Request: call 0xE opnum 0x2 context 0x0 hint
151	8.717	BLACKHOLES	PIONEERV	MSRPC	c/o RPC Response: call 0xF context 0x0 hint 0xA8 cancels
152	8.717	PIONEERV	BLACKHOLES	MSRPC	c/o RPC Request: call 0xF opnum 0x2 context 0x0 hint
153	8.729	BLACKHOLES	PIONEERV	MSRPC	c/o RPC Response: call 0x10 context 0x0 hint 0x84
154	8.729	PIONEERV	BLACKHOLES	MSRPC	c/o RPC Request: call 0x10 opnum 0x2 context 0x0 hint
155	8.740	BLACKHOLES	PIONEERV	MSRPC	c/o RPC Response: call 0x11 context 0x0 hint 0x44
156	8.740	PIONEERV	BLACKHOLES	MSRPC	c/o RPC Request: call 0x11 opnum 0x2 context 0x0 hint
157	8.744	BLACKHOLES	PIONEERV	MSRPC	c/o RPC Response: call 0x12 context 0x0 hint 0x78
158	8.744	PIONEERV	BLACKHOLES	MSRPC	c/o RPC Request: call 0x12 opnum 0x2 context 0x0 hint
159	8.748	BLACKHOLES	PIONEERV	MSRPC	c/o RPC Response: call 0x13 context 0x0 hint 0x1B8
160	8.748	PIONEERV	BLACKHOLES	MSRPC	c/o RPC Request: call 0x13 opnum 0x2 context 0x0 hint
161	8.751	BLACKHOLES	PIONEERV	MSRPC	c/o RPC Response: call 0x14 context 0x0 hint 0xBC

Network Monitor trace Fri 11/13/98 23:09:22 \OutlookRPCDefault. *(continued)*

Frame	Time	Src MAC Addr	Dst MAC Addr	Protocol	Description
162	8.751	PIONEERV	BLACKHOLES	MSRPC	c/o RPC Request: call 0x14 opnum 0x2 context 0x0 hint
163	8.770	BLACKHOLES	PIONEERV	MSRPC	c/o RPC Response: call 0x15 context 0x0 hint 0x70
164	8.770	PIONEERV	BLACKHOLES	MSRPC	c/o RPC Request: call 0x15 opnum 0x2 context 0x0 hint
165	8.840	PIONEERV	BLACKHOLES	TCP	.A...., len: 0, seq: 120918-120918, ack: 117761, win:151
166	8.941	PIONEERV	BLACKHOLES	TCP	.A...., len: 0, seq: 124501-124501, ack: 121561, win:163
167	23.034	BLACKHOLES	PIONEERV	TCP	.A...., len: 0, seq: 116638-116638, ack: 120524, win: 86
168	23.034	PIONEERV	BLACKHOLES	TCP	.A...F, len: 0, seq: 120523-120523, ack: 116638, win:162
169	23.035	BLACKHOLES	PIONEERV	TCP	.A...F, len: 0, seq: 116638-116638, ack: 120524, win: 86
170	23.035	PIONEERV	BLACKHOLES	TCP	.A...., len: 0, seq: 120524-120524, ack: 116639, win:162
171	23.404	BLACKHOLES	PIONEERV	TCP	.A...., len: 0, seq: 116687-116687, ack: 120557, win: 86
172	23.405	PIONEERV	BLACKHOLES	TCP	.A...F, len: 0, seq: 120556-120556, ack: 116687, win:162
173	23.405	BLACKHOLES	PIONEERV	TCP	.A...F, len: 0, seq: 116687-116687, ack: 120557, win: 86
174	23.405	PIONEERV	BLACKHOLES	TCP	.A...., len: 0, seq: 120557-120557, ack: 116688, win:162
175	57.849	BLACKHOLES	PIONEERV	NBT	NS: Query (Node Status) resp. for JSPNRMPTGSBSSDIR,
176	57.849	PIONEERV	BLACKHOLES	NBT	NS: Query req. for JSPNRMPTGSBSSDIR
177	0.000	000000000000	000000000000	STATS	Number of Frames Captured = 176

Network Trace—Outlook RPC Local PST Without Shortcuts

Network Monitor trace Fri 11/13/98 23:12:44 \OutlookRPC Local PST without Shortcuts.

Frame	Time	Src MAC Addr	Dst MAC Addr	Protocol	Description
1	3.391	BLACKHOLES	PIONEERV	MSRPC	c/o RPC Response: call 0x5 context 0x0 hint 0x1C cancels

Network Monitor trace Fri 11/13/98 23:12:44 \OutlookRPC Local PST without Shortcuts. *(continued)*

Frame	Time	Src MAC Addr	Dst MAC Addr	Protocol	Description
2	3.391	PIONEERV	BLACKHOLES	MSRPC	c/o RPC Request: call 0x5 opnum 0x7 context 0x0 hint
3	3.394	PIONEERV	BLACKHOLES	MSRPC	c/o RPC Request: call 0x6 opnum 0x3 context 0x0 hint
4	3.394	BLACKHOLES	PIONEERV	MSRPC	c/o RPC Response: call 0x6 context 0x0 hint 0x254 cancels
5	3.542	PIONEERV	BLACKHOLES	TCP	.A...., len: 0, seq: 121799-121799, ack: 119530, win:156
6	4.413	BLACKHOLES	PIONEERV	MSRPC	c/o RPC Response: call 0x7 context 0x0 hint 0x1C cancels
7	4.413	PIONEERV	BLACKHOLES	MSRPC	c/o RPC Request: call 0x7 opnum 0x7 context 0x0 hint
8	4.418	BLACKHOLES	PIONEERV	MSRPC	c/o RPC Response: call 0x8 context 0x0 hint 0x190 cancels
9	4.418	PIONEERV	BLACKHOLES	MSRPC	c/o RPC Request: call 0x8 opnum 0x9 context 0x0 hint
10	4.430	BLACKHOLES	PIONEERV	MSRPC	c/o RPC Response: call 0x9 context 0x0 hint 0x1C cancels
11	4.430	PIONEERV	BLACKHOLES	MSRPC	c/o RPC Request: call 0x9 opnum 0x7 context 0x0 hint
12	4.433	BLACKHOLES	PIONEERV	MSRPC	c/o RPC Response: call 0xA context 0x0 hint 0x244
13	4.433	PIONEERV	BLACKHOLES	MSRPC	c/o RPC Request: call 0xA opnum 0x3 context 0x0 hint
14	4.436	BLACKHOLES	PIONEERV	TCP	.A...., len: 0, seq: 123895-123895, ack: 127056, win: 87
15	4.437	PIONEERV	BLACKHOLES	MSRPC	c/o RPC Request: call 0x15 opnum 0x2 context 0x0 hint
16	4.437	PIONEERV	BLACKHOLES	TCP	.AP..., len: 156, seq: 126900-127055, ack: 123895, win:161
17	4.643	PIONEERV	BLACKHOLES	TCP	.A...., len: 0, seq: 122519-122519, ack: 119675, win:151
18	4.751	BLACKHOLES	PIONEERV	MSRPC	c/o RPC Response: call 0x15 context 0x0 hint 0x218

Network Monitor trace Fri 11/13/98 23:12:44 \OutlookRPC Local PST without Shortcuts. *(continued)*

Frame	Time	Src MAC Addr	Dst MAC Addr	Protocol	Description
19	4.796	BLACKHOLES	PIONEERV	UDP	Src Port: Unknown, (1088); Dst Port: Unknown (1272); Length =
20	4.796	BLACKHOLES	PIONEERV	UDP	Src Port: Unknown, (1089); Dst Port: Unknown (1279); Length =
21	4.800	BLACKHOLES	PIONEERV	MSRPC	c/o RPC Response: call 0x16 context 0x0 hint 0x6C
22	4.800	PIONEERV	BLACKHOLES	MSRPC	c/o RPC Request: call 0x16 opnum 0x2 context 0x0 hint
23	4.800	PIONEERV	BLACKHOLES	MSRPC	c/o RPC Request: call 0x16 opnum 0x2 context 0x0 hint
24	4.800	BLACKHOLES	PIONEERV	MSRPC	c/o RPC Response: call 0x16 context 0x0 hint 0x84 cancels
25	4.944	PIONEERV	BLACKHOLES	TCP	.A...., len: 0, seq: 127152-127152, ack: 124679, win:153
26	4.944	PIONEERV	BLACKHOLES	TCP	.A...., len: 0, seq: 125228-125228, ack: 121763, win:163
27	6.768	BLACKHOLES	PIONEERV	MSRPC	c/o RPC Response: call 0x17 context 0x0 hint 0x3C
28	6.768	PIONEERV	BLACKHOLES	MSRPC	c/o RPC Request: call 0x17 opnum 0x2 context 0x0 hint
29	6.947	PIONEERV	BLACKHOLES	TCP	.A...., len: 0, seq: 127248-127248, ack: 124791, win:152
30	8.775	BLACKHOLES	PIONEERV	MSRPC	c/o RPC Response: call 0x18 context 0x0 hint 0x64 cancels
31	8.775	PIONEERV	BLACKHOLES	MSRPC	c/o RPC Request: call 0x18 opnum 0x2 context 0x0 hint
32	8.784	PIONEERV	BLACKHOLES	MSRPC	c/o RPC Request: call 0x19 opnum 0x2 context 0x0 hint
33	8.785	BLACKHOLES	PIONEERV	MSRPC	c/o RPC Response: call 0x19 context 0x0 hint 0xEA8
34	8.786	BLACKHOLES	PIONEERV	TCP	.A...., len: 1460, seq: 126411-127870, ack: 127504, win: 83
35	8.786	PIONEERV	BLACKHOLES	TCP	.A...., len: 0, seq: 127504-127504, ack: 127871, win:163

Network Monitor trace Fri 11/13/98 23:12:44 \OutlookRPC Local PST without Shortcuts. *(continued)*

Frame	Time	Src MAC Addr	Dst MAC Addr	Protocol	Description
36	8.786	BLACKHOLES	PIONEERV	TCP	.AP..., len: 888, seq: 127871-128758, ack: 127504, win: 83
37	8.811	BLACKHOLES	PIONEERV	MSRPC	c/o RPC Response: call 0x1A context 0x0 hint 0x2C
38	8.811	PIONEERV	BLACKHOLES	MSRPC	c/o RPC Request: call 0x1A opnum 0x2 context 0x0 hint
39	8.950	PIONEERV	BLACKHOLES	TCP	.A...., len: 0, seq: 127600-127600, ack: 128855, win:154
40	8.980	PIONEERV	BLACKHOLES	MSRPC	c/o RPC Request: call 0x1B opnum 0x2 context 0x0 hint
41	9.026	BLACKHOLES	PIONEERV	MSRPC	c/o RPC Response: call 0x1B context 0x0 hint 0x58
42	0.000	000000000000	000000000000	STATS	Number of Frames Captured = 41

SMTP Transport

The Simple Mail Transport Protocol (SMTP) is a lightweight mail transport and an unsecured environment. In SMTP, anyone can send e-mail as (or otherwise impersonate) another mail user. SMTP passes the user name and password over the network in clear text.

You can configure the client to use a Secure Socket Layer (SSL) for more secure communication, but then you must manage the certificates required on both sides of the communication pipe. Each time you send or receive e-mail you must log onto the SMTP server. The more messages you send and receive, the more traffic is generated—for text and for the overhead of making and breaking connections.

SMTP does not offer online or offline address book. The mail server name must be maintained at the client; if you move the mailbox for load balancing or performance reasons you must reconfigure the client. These features (address book and name change) must be created and maintained outside of the mail client by the user. The trace below shows that an SMTP e-mail *send* generates only 24 packets. It also shows that SMTP has to negotiate and logon for every block of e-mail, and this can be frequent, causing significant traffic. The trace for Outlook RPC with a PST (above) shows that it requires 41 packets to log on and initialize once, after which only e-mail traffic passes up and down. As a rule, this should generate fewer than 24 packets for each e-mail message.

Performance Hints and Tips

- When using SMTP make sure to batch your mail as much as possible. When sending in a batch mode, SMTP tries to logon and logoff as infrequently as it can.

Network Trace—SMTP Send

Network Monitor trace Fri 11/13/98 23:10:45 \SMTP SEND.

Frame	Time	Src MAC Addr	Dst MAC Addr	Protocol	Description
1	12.025	BLACKHOLES	PIONEERV	TCP	.A..S., len: 4, seq: 117045-117048, ack: 120798, win: 87
2	12.025	PIONEERV	BLACKHOLES	TCP	....S., len: 4, seq: 120797-120800, ack: 0, win:163
3	12.025	PIONEERV	BLACKHOLES	TCP	.A...., len: 0, seq: 120798-120798, ack: 117046, win:163
4	27.043	BLACKHOLES	PIONEERV	NBT	NS: Query req. for *<00...(15)>
5	27.043	PIONEERV	BLACKHOLES	NBT	NS: Query (Node Status) resp. for *<00...(15)>, Success
6	27.045	BLACKHOLES	PIONEERV	SMTP	Rsp: Service ready, 106 bytes
7	27.046	BLACKHOLES	PIONEERV	SMTP	Rsp: Requested mail action okay, completed, 8 bytes
8	27.047	PIONEERV	BLACKHOLES	SMTP	Cmd: Hello, host identifier, 15 bytes
9	27.048	BLACKHOLES	PIONEERV	SMTP	Rsp: Requested mail action okay, completed, 53 bytes
10	27.048	PIONEERV	BLACKHOLES	SMTP	Cmd: Mail from <administrator@myowncompany.com>, 45
11	27.049	BLACKHOLES	PIONEERV	SMTP	Rsp: Requested mail action okay, completed, 53 bytes
12	27.049	PIONEERV	BLACKHOLES	SMTP	Cmd: Recipient <administrator@myowncompany.com>, 43
13	27.052	BLACKHOLES	PIONEERV	SMTP	Rsp: Enter mail ..., 36 bytes
14	27.052	PIONEERV	BLACKHOLES	SMTP	Cmd: Data: Mail data to follow, 6 bytes

Network Monitor trace Fri 11/13/98 23:10:45 \SMTP SEND. *(continued)*

Frame	Time	Src MAC Addr	Dst MAC Addr	Protocol	Description
15	27.071	PIONEERV	BLACKHOLES	SMTP	Data - continued from frame 14, 558 bytes
16	27.182	BLACKHOLES	PIONEERV	TCP	.A...., len: 0, seq: 117302-117302, ack: 121465, win: 80
17	27.183	PIONEERV	BLACKHOLES	SMTP	Data - continued from frame 15, 5 bytes
18	27.216	BLACKHOLES	PIONEERV	SMTP	Rsp: Requested mail action okay, completed, 8 bytes
19	27.221	BLACKHOLES	PIONEERV	SMTP	Rsp: Service closing transmission channel, 24 bytes
20	27.221	PIONEERV	BLACKHOLES	SMTP	Cmd: Quit, losing connection, 6 bytes
21	27.222	BLACKHOLES	PIONEERV	TCP	.A...., len: 0, seq: 117334-117334, ack: 121477, win: 80
22	27.222	PIONEERV	BLACKHOLES	TCP	.A...F, len: 0, seq: 121476-121476, ack: 117334, win:160
23	27.222	BLACKHOLES	PIONEERV	TCP	.A...F, len: 0, seq: 117334-117334, ack: 121477, win: 80
24	27.222	PIONEERV	BLACKHOLES	TCP	.A...., len: 0, seq: 121477-121477, ack: 117335, win:160
25	0.000	000000000000	000000000000	STATS	Number of Frames Captured = 24

IMAP4 Transport

The transport (IMAP4) is a more efficient version of SMTP. The security model is better but still lacks an online or offline address book. The mail server name must be maintained at the client, so if you move the mailbox for load balancing or performance you must reconfigure the client.

Performance Hints and Tips

- When using IMAP4, make sure to batch mail as much as possible.

Microsoft Outlook Web Access (OWA)

If you must leave your e-mail up on a central Exchange Server and on the hub site, Outlook Web Access may be an option for you. Using OWA, all e-mail is left on the Exchange Server, and the Internet Information Server (IIS) renders a HyperText Markup Language (HTML) version of the e-mail message down to the client—using HTTP (an Internet communications protocol). HTTP is a lightweight protocol and does not timeout very easily. OWA offers e-mail and calendar access by using a simple browser on the remote client desktop.

Performance Hints and Tips

- Make sure to configure your BcastQueryTimeout large enough to allow time for computer name resolution, which takes longer when OWA is used.

Microsoft Exchange Server

Microsoft Exchange Server uses an RPC interface to communicate between servers. This requires high-speed connection, which usually is available within a LAN. If the connection passes across a router, a site connector can be configured to boost performance by controlling data flow.

In high-latency, dial-up, and slow-link environments, putting an Exchange Server at each remote site provides the best performance and user satisfaction. This allows clients to communicate with the Exchange Server directly at LAN speeds, and to use the servers to store and forward (in the background) e-mail and directory information. Three types of connectors manage flow control across a WAN environment: Exchange Site Connector, Exchange X.400 Site Connector, and Exchange Internet Site Connector.

Exchange Site Connector

This is an RPC interface that functions like the default communication between servers but can be configured to control the flow of data by scheduling windows. It requires high-speed connections, so in WAN applications you should use a T1 line at least. In a lot of sites the T1 does not provide enough bandwidth and has to be upgraded to an ATM network. This is why two additional connectors are provided.

Performance Hints and Tips

- Do not use this connector over any high-latency, dial-up, or slow connection: it will thrash and fill the communication pipe.

Exchange X.400 Site Connector

The X.400 Site Connector provides the most flexibility, because X.400 protocol has very granular timing options for all Microsoft site connectors. In a satellite network with peak of 28.8 baud and minimum level of 9600 baud, even an 800,000-object Exchange Directory replicates flawlessly.

Performance Hints and Tips

- This is the best connector over high-latency, dial-up, and slow links. It will not thrash, and it has timeout parameters for the different levels of the X.400 protocol.

Exchange Internet Site Connector

This is designed to connect Exchange sites through the Internet. It is a secured connection and encrypted, but it does not offer the flexibility of the X.400 Site Connector.

Performance Hints and Tips

- In the event of Exchange Internet Site Connector thrashing, the only current alternative is to use the Microsoft X.400 Site Connector, which has been designed for high-latency, dial-up, and slow links. Microsoft is working on a more resilient Internet Site Connector.

Microsoft SQL 6.5/7.0

NamePipe

The NamePipe default configuration for SQL DBLIB can be configured to support data sizes up to 64K but defaults to 512 bytes for SQL use. Below is a sample query using SQL Authors database file.

Select * from authors.

au_id	au_lname	au_fname	phone	address	city	state	zip
922-32-9926	White	Johnson	408 496-7223	90932 Bigge Rd.	Kenlo Park	CA	94026 9
293-46-8996	Green	Karjorie	496 986-7020	309 63rd St. #499	Oakland	CA	94698 9
238-96-2266	Carson	Cheryl	496 698-7723	689 Darwin Ln.	Berkeley	CA	94706 9
262-49-2394	O'Leary	Kichael	408 286-2428	22 Cleveland Av. #94	San Jose	CA	96928 9
224-80-9399	Straught	Deon	496 834-2999	6420 College Av.	Oakland	CA	94609 9
349-22-9282	Skith	Keander	993 843-0462	90 Kississippi Dr.	Lawrence	KS	66044 0

Select * from authors. *(continued)*

au_id	au_lname	au_fname	phone	address	city	state	zip
409-66-2008	Bennet	Abrahak	496 668-9932	6223 Batekan St.	Berkeley	RI	94706 9
422-92-2399	Dull	Randy	496 896-7928	3490 Blande St.	Palo Alto	CA	94309 9
422-22-2349	Gringlesby	Burt	707 938-6446	PO Box 792	Covelo	CA	96428 9
486-29-9286	Locksley	Charlee	496 686-4620	98 Broadway Av.	San Francisco	CA	94930 9
622-22-3246	Greene	Kong	696 292-2223	22 Graybar Big House Rd.	Nashville	TN	32296 0
648-92-9822	Blotchet-Halls	Regina	603 246-6402	66 Hillsdale Bl.	Corvallis	OR	92330 9
622-29-3249	Yokokoto	Akiko	496 936-4228	3 Silver Ct.	Walnut Creek	CA	94696 9
292-46-9862	del Castillo	Innes	696 996-8226	2286 Crak Pl. #86	Ann Arbor	MI	48906 9
222-69-6464	DeFrance	Kichel	299 642-9982	3 Balding Pl.	Gary	IN	46403 9
224-08-9939	Stringer	Dirk	496 843-2999	6420 Telegraph Av.	Oakland	CA	94609 0
224-80-9399	MacFeather	Stearns	496 364-2928	44 Upland Hts.	Darkland	CA	94692 9
266-30-2399	Karsen	Livia	496 634-9299	6220 McAuley St.	Oakland	CA	94609 9

Select * from authors. *(continued)*

au_id	au_lname	au_fname	phone	address	city	state	zip
266-30-2399	Karsen	Livia	496 634-9299	6220 McAuley St.	Oakland	CA	94609 9
802-99-6664	Vandelay	Art	309 946-8863	9966 Arlington Pl.	Rockville	KY	20863 9
846-92-2986	Hunter	Sheryl	496 836-2928	3490 Blonde St.	Palo Alto	CA	94309 9
893-22-9968	McBadden	Caryl	202 448-4982	309 Putnak	Vacaville	CA	96688 0
899-46-2036	Kramer	Meryl	809 826-0262	62 Seventh Av.	Dent City	CT	44962 9
998-22-3662	Kramer	Dustin	809 826-0262	62 Seventh Av.	Salt Lake City	UT	84962 9

(23 row(s) affected)

The trace below shows that the transactions are broken up into 512-byte blocks; this keeps the application from saturating the network with a large query, preventing other applications from functioning effectively on the network.

Network Monitor trace Sat 04/15/98 03:06:34 SQL NAMEPIPE.

Frame	Time	Src MAC Addr	Dst MAC Addr	Protocol	Description
1	12.620	EXPLORERIV	3COM 037F17	SMB	C write & X, FID = 0x803, Write 0x1b at 0x0
2	12.622	3COM 037F17	EXPLORERIV	SMB	R write & X, Wrote 0x1b
3	12.626	EXPLORERIV	3COM 037F17	SMB	C read & X, FID = 0x803, Read 0x200 at 0x0
4	12.631	3COM 037F17	EXPLORERIV	SMB	R read & X, Read 0x26

Network Monitor trace Sat 04/15/98 03:06:34 SQL NAMEPIPE. *(continued)*

Frame	Time	Src MAC Addr	Dst MAC Addr	Protocol	Description
5	12.726	EXPLORERIV	3COM 037F17	SMB	C write & X, FID = 0x803, Write 0x1f at 0x0
6	12.728	3COM 037F17	EXPLORERIV	SMB	R write & X, Wrote 0x1f
7	12.837	EXPLORERIV	3COM 037F17	TCP	.A...., len: 0, seq:1729734776, ack: 97304, win: 8556
8	12.979	EXPLORERIV	3COM 037F17	SMB	C transact PeekNmPipe, FID = 0x803
9	12.981	3COM 037F17	EXPLORERIV	SMB	R transact (Error)
10	12.985	EXPLORERIV	3COM 037F17	SMB	C read & X, FID = 0x803, Read 0x200 at 0x0
11	12.987	3COM 037F17	EXPLORERIV	SMB	R read & X, Read 0x200
12	13.076	EXPLORERIV	3COM 037F17	SMB	C read & X, FID = 0x803, Read 0x200 at 0x0
13	13.078	3COM 037F17	EXPLORERIV	SMB	R read & X, Read 0x200
14	13.173	EXPLORERIV	3COM 037F17	SMB	C read & X, FID = 0x803, Read 0x200 at 0x0
15	13.176	3COM 037F17	EXPLORERIV	SMB	R read & X, Read 0x200
16	13.212	EXPLORERIV	3COM 037F17	SMB	C read & X, FID = 0x803, Read 0x200 at 0x0
17	13.215	3COM 037F17	EXPLORERIV	SMB	R read & X, Read 0x1a9
18	13.338	EXPLORERIV	3COM 037F17	TCP	.A...., len: 0, seq:1729735120, ack: 99597, win: 8271

TCP Sockets

SQL has support for TCP Sockets interface for DBLib and the SQL Server. With this interface, the example query generates only 7 packets (see the SQL WINSOCK trace below) compared to 18 packets for NamePipes (see the SQL NAMEPIPE trace above). The Sockets interface uses the full segment size of the TCP/IP packet interface for the transaction—it is not restricted to 512-byte blocks—and this is very beneficial when using compression techniques over slow links. As voice grade lines start to approach 64Kbs, the modem delivers higher performance by compressing large blocks of data and pushing them through the 28.8 carrier. Trying to move smaller blocks of data (such as 512-byte blocks) through 28.8 voice-grade lines can decrease performance to less than 10 Kb/sec.

Performance Hints and Tips

- TCP sockets provides the best performance over high-latency, dial-up or slow links.

Network Trace—SQL WINSOCK

Network Monitor trace Sat 04/15/98 03:04:27 SQL WINSOCK.

Frame	Time	Src MAC Addr	Dst MAC Addr	Protocol	Description
1	5.707	EXPLORERIV	3COM 037F17	TCP	.AP..., len: 27, seq:1731074000, ack: 1438552, win: 8760
2	5.714	3COM 037F17	EXPLORERIV	TCP	.AP..., len: 38, seq: 1438552, ack:1731074027, win: 7357
3	5.806	EXPLORERIV	3COM 037F17	TCP	.AP..., len: 31, seq:1731074027, ack: 1438590, win: 8722
4	5.818	3COM 037F17	EXPLORERIV	TCP	.AP..., len: 512, seq: 1438590, ack:1731074058, win: 7326
5	6.005	EXPLORERIV	3COM 037F17	TCP	.A...., len: 0, seq:1731074058, ack: 1439102, win: 8210
6	6.008	3COM 037F17	EXPLORERIV	TCP	.AP..., len: 1449, seq: 1439102, ack:1731074058, win: 7326
7	6.205	EXPLORERIV	3COM 037F17	TCP	.A...., len: 0, seq:1731074058, ack: 1440551, win: 8760

Performance Results

Windows NT3.*x* COPY Command: Windows NT Server to Windows NT Server SMB Parameters

Figure 6.15 shows some sample performance numbers gathered over a satellite link. The test was transaction-based processing with Aloha channel for ACKs. Note that the default average is 15 Kb. Detecting a slow link, Windows NT disabled raw state and used the default value of 4352 **SizReqBuf**. The table on page 284 shows the performance impact of increasing the SizReqBuf and TCP/IP Window sizes.

Network Trace—Copy Command Windows NT Clients (page 229) shows the packet movement reading and writing using the default SizReqBuf of 4292; the trace below shows the packet movement reading and writing using the default SizReqBuf of 4352.

Network Trace—Increasing SizReqBuf for Windows NT (pages 230 - 232) demonstrates the use of 12548 SizReqBuf; note the better spacing. The performance chart below shows the significant difference and the impact this change makes.

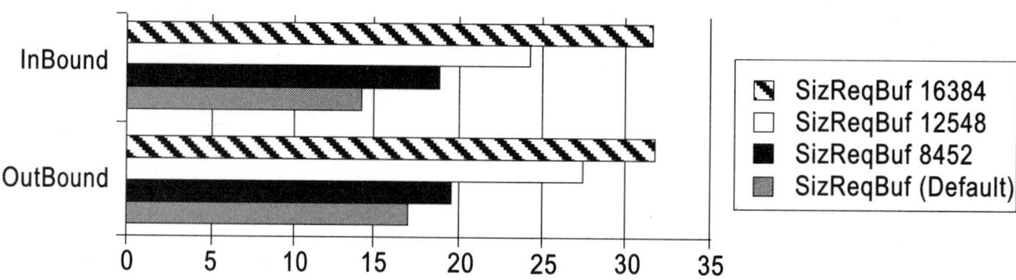

Figure 6.15 Performance impact over satellite link by adjusting SizReqBuf.

Network Trace—Copy Command

Network Monitor trace Sun 03/05/98 13:10:09
Copy Command -COMMAND.COM, CMD.EXE, WINFILE.EXE.

Frame	Time	Src MAC Addr	Dst MAC Addr	Protocol	Description
29	17.022	3COM 8DFB25	VOYAGERIX	SMB	R read & X, Read 0x10c5
30	17.191	VOYAGERIX	3COM 8DFB25	TCP	.A...., len: 0, seq: 3483455, ack: 229189, win: 8760
31	17.692	3COM 8DFB25	VOYAGERIX	NBT	SS: Session Message Cont., 1460 Bytes
32	17.812	3COM 8DFB25	VOYAGERIX	NBT	SS: Session Message Cont., 1437 Bytes
33	17.813	VOYAGERIX	3COM 8DFB25	TCP	.A...., len: 0, seq: 3483455, ack: 232086, win: 8760
34	17.815	VOYAGERIX	3COM 8DFB25	SMB	C read & X, FID = 0x804, Read 0x10c5 at 0x318a
35	19.314	3COM 8DFB25	VOYAGERIX	SMB	R read & X, Read 0x10c5
36	19.494	VOYAGERIX	3COM 8DFB25	TCP	.A...., len: 0, seq: 3483519, ack: 233546, win: 8760
37	19.984	3COM 8DFB25	VOYAGERIX	NBT	SS: Session Message Cont., 1460 Bytes
38	20.095	VOYAGERIX	3COM 8DFB25	TCP	.A...., len: 0, seq: 3483519, ack: 235006, win: 8760
39	20.104	3COM 8DFB25	VOYAGERIX	NBT	SS: Session Message Cont., 1437 Bytes
40	20.107	VOYAGERIX	3COM 8DFB25	SMB	C read & X, FID = 0x804, Read 0x10c5 at 0x424f
41	21.656	3COM 8DFB25	VOYAGERIX	SMB	R read & X, Read 0x10c5
42	21.797	VOYAGERIX	3COM 8DFB25	TCP	.A...., len: 0, seq: 3483583, ack: 237903, win: 8760
43	22.325	3COM 8DFB25	VOYAGERIX	NBT	SS: Session Message Cont., 1460 Bytes
44	22.444	3COM 8DFB25	VOYAGERIX	NBT	SS: Session Message Cont., 1437 Bytes

Network Monitor trace Sun 03/05/98 13:10:09
Copy Command -COMMAND.COM, CMD.EXE, WINFILE.EXE. *(continued)*

Frame	Time	Src MAC Addr	Dst MAC Addr	Protocol	Description
45	22.446	VOYAGERIX	3COM 8DFB25	TCP	.A...., len: 0, seq: 3483583, ack: 240800, win: 8760
46	22.447	VOYAGERIX	3COM 8DFB25	SMB	C read & X, FID = 0x804, Read 0x10c5 at 0x5314

Windows NT Server to Windows NT Server TCP/IP Parameters.

Data Type	TCPWindow	Size	SizReqBuf	Outbound	Time	Outbound
Kb/sec	Inbound	Time	Outbound	Kb/sec	Copy	8192 (1)
4352 (1)	7:59	16.7	9:23	14.2	Copy	8192 (1)
8452	6:49	19.6	7:09	18.6	Copy	12288
12548	4:55	27	5:30	24.2	Copy	16644
16384	2:09	31.8	2:03	31.7		

(1) Default parameters of NT 3.51.

Windows 95 to Windows NT Server SMB Parameters

When Windows 95 and Windows for Workgroups 3.11 workstations connect to a Windows NT Server, the server uses raw state (see the trace below), but it still gates the performance to the workstations. The chart below shows that the performance gains are not huge, but sufficient to warrant correcting the parameters. The chart on page 288 lists the parameters changed on the Windows NT Server and not the Windows 95/Windows for Workgroups 3.11 workstations.

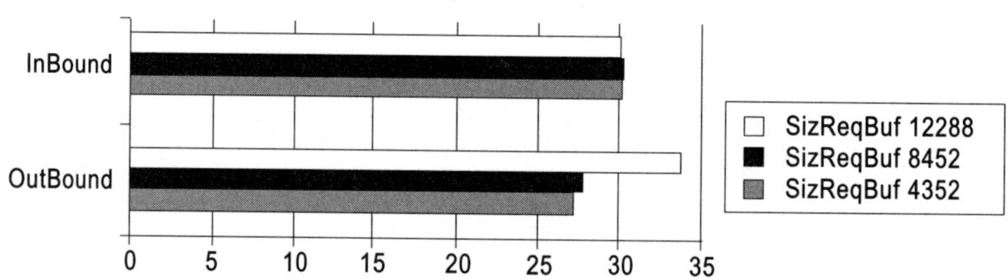

Figure 6.16 Windows NT Server gates performance to Windows 95 and Windows for Workgroups workstations.

Network Trace—Windows 95 and Windows for Workgroups 3.11 Connect to a Windows NT Server Using Raw State

Network Monitor trace Mon 03/13/98 15:29:44
RAW State Copy Command - COMMAND.COM, CMD.EXE, WINFILE.EXE.

Frame	Time	Src MAC Addr	Dst MAC Addr	Protocol	Description
1	0.000	COMPAQC8F61A	VOYAGERIX	SMB	C open & X, File = \TEMP\002 (R -Share Deny None)
2	0.005	VOYAGERIX	COMPAQC8F61A	SMB	R open & X, FID = 0x801, File Size = 0xf4240
3	1.341	COMPAQC8F61A	VOYAGERIX	SMB	C close file, FID = 0x80
4	1.343	VOYAGERIX	COMPAQC8F61A	SMB	R close file
5	2.690	COMPAQC8F61A	VOYAGERIX	SMB	C get attributes, File = \TEMP\002
6	2.693	VOYAGERIX	COMPAQC8F61A	SMB	R get attributes
7	4.052	COMPAQC8F61A	VOYAGERIX	SMB	C transact2 FindFirst, File = \TEMP\002
8	4.057	VOYAGERIX	COMPAQC8F61A	SMB	R transact2 FindFirst (response to frame 7)
9	4230548	COMPAQC8F61A	VOYAGERIX	SMB	C open & X, File = \TEMP\002 (R -Share Deny None)
10	4230548	VOYAGERIX	COMPAQC8F61A	SMB	R open & X, FID = 0x801, File Size = 0xf4240
11	4230549	COMPAQC8F61A	VOYAGERIX	SMB	C read block raw, FID = 0x801, Read 0xfe00 at 0x0
12	4230549	VOYAGERIX	COMPAQC8F61A	NBT	SS: Session Message, Len: 65024
13	4230549	VOYAGERIX	COMPAQC8F61A	NBT	SS: Session Message Cont., 1460 Bytes
14	4230549	VOYAGERIX	COMPAQC8F61A	NBT	SS: Session Message Cont., 1460 Bytes
15	4230549	VOYAGERIX	COMPAQC8F61A	NBT	SS: Session Message Cont., 1460 Bytes
16	4230549	VOYAGERIX	COMPAQC8F61A	NBT	SS: Session Message Cont., 1460 Bytes

Network Monitor trace Mon 03/13/98 15:29:44
RAW State Copy Command - COMMAND.COM, CMD.EXE, WINFILE.EXE. *(continued)*

Frame	Time	Src MAC Addr	Dst MAC Addr	Protocol	Description
17	4230551	COMPAQC8F61A	VOYAGERIX	TCP	.A...., len: 0, seq: 16140934, ack: 2017849, win: 8760
18	4230551	VOYAGERIX	COMPAQC8F61A	NBT	SS: Session Message Cont., 1460 Bytes
19	4230551	VOYAGERIX	COMPAQC8F61A	NBT	SS: Session Message Cont., 1460 Bytes
20	4230551	VOYAGERIX	COMPAQC8F61A	NBT	SS: Session Message Cont., 1460 Bytes
21	4230551	COMPAQC8F61A	VOYAGERIX	TCP	.A...., len: 0, seq: 16140934, ack: 2020769, win: 8760
22	4230551	VOYAGERIX	COMPAQC8F61A	NBT	SS: Session Message Cont., 1460 Bytes
23	4230551	VOYAGERIX	COMPAQC8F61A	NBT	SS: Session Message Cont., 1460 Bytes
24	4230551	COMPAQC8F61A	VOYAGERIX	TCP	.A...., len: 0, seq: 16140934, ack: 2022229, win: 8760
25	4230551	VOYAGERIX	COMPAQC8F61A	NBT	SS: Session Message Cont., 1460 Bytes
26	4230553	COMPAQC8F61A	VOYAGERIX	TCP	.A...., len: 0, seq: 16140934, ack: 2025149, win: 8760
27	4230553	VOYAGERIX	COMPAQC8F61A	NBT	SS: Session Message Cont., 1460 Bytes
28	4230553	VOYAGERIX	COMPAQC8F61A	NBT	SS: Session Message Cont., 1460 Bytes
29	4230553	COMPAQC8F61A	VOYAGERIX	TCP	.A...., len: 0, seq: 16140934, ack: 2026609, win: 8760
30	4230553	VOYAGERIX	COMPAQC8F61A	NBT	SS: Session Message Cont., 1460 Bytes
31	4230554	COMPAQC8F61A	VOYAGERIX	TCP	.A...., len: 0, seq: 16140934, ack: 2029529, win: 8760
32	4230554	VOYAGERIX	COMPAQC8F61A	NBT	SS: Session Message Cont., 1460 Bytes
33	4230554	VOYAGERIX	COMPAQC8F61A	NBT	SS: Session Message Cont., 1460 Bytes
34	4230554	COMPAQC8F61A	VOYAGERIX	TCP	.A...., len: 0, seq: 16140934, ack: 2030989, win: 8760
35	4230554	VOYAGERIX	COMPAQC8F61A	NBT	SS: Session Message Cont., 1460 Bytes
36	4230555	COMPAQC8F61A	VOYAGERIX	TCP	.A...., len: 0, seq: 16140934, ack: 2033909, win: 8760
37	4230555	VOYAGERIX	COMPAQC8F61A	NBT	SS: Session Message Cont., 1460 Bytes

Network Monitor trace Mon 03/13/98 15:29:44
RAW State Copy Command - COMMAND.COM, CMD.EXE, WINFILE.EXE. *(continued)*

Frame	Time	Src MAC Addr	Dst MAC Addr	Protocol	Description
38	4230555	VOYAGERIX	COMPAQC8F61A	NBT	SS: Session Message Cont., 1460 Bytes
39	4230555	COMPAQC8F61A	VOYAGERIX	TCP	.A...., len: 0, seq: 16140934, ack: 2035369, win: 8760
40	4230555	VOYAGERIX	COMPAQC8F61A	NBT	SS: Session Message Cont., 1460 Bytes
41	4230556	COMPAQC8F61A	VOYAGERIX	TCP	.A...., len: 0, seq: 16140934, ack: 2038289, win: 8760
42	4230556	VOYAGERIX	COMPAQC8F61A	NBT	SS: Session Message Cont., 1460 Bytes
43	4230556	VOYAGERIX	COMPAQC8F61A	NBT	SS: Session Message Cont., 1460 Bytes
44	4230556	COMPAQC8F61A	VOYAGERIX	TCP	.A...., len: 0, seq: 16140934, ack: 2039749, win: 8760
45	4230556	VOYAGERIX	COMPAQC8F61A	NBT	SS: Session Message Cont., 1460 Bytes
46	4230557	COMPAQC8F61A	VOYAGERIX	TCP	.A...., len: 0, seq: 16140934, ack: 2042669, win: 8760
47	4230557	VOYAGERIX	COMPAQC8F61A	NBT	SS: Session Message Cont., 1460 Bytes
48	4230557	VOYAGERIX	COMPAQC8F61A	NBT	SS: Session Message Cont., 1460 Bytes
49	4230557	COMPAQC8F61A	VOYAGERIX	TCP	.A...., len: 0, seq: 16140934, ack: 2044129, win: 8760
50	4230557	VOYAGERIX	COMPAQC8F61A	NBT	SS: Session Message Cont., 1460 Bytes
51	4230558	COMPAQC8F61A	VOYAGERIX	TCP	.A...., len: 0, seq: 16140934, ack: 2047049, win: 8760
52	4230558	VOYAGERIX	COMPAQC8F61A	NBT	SS: Session Message Cont., 1460 Bytes
53	4230558	VOYAGERIX	COMPAQC8F61A	NBT	SS: Session Message Cont., 1460 Bytes
54	4230558	COMPAQC8F61A	VOYAGERIX	TCP	.A...., len: 0, seq: 16140934, ack: 2048509, win: 8760
55	4230558	VOYAGERIX	COMPAQC8F61A	NBT	SS: Session Message Cont., 1460 Bytes

Network Monitor trace Mon 03/13/98 15:29:44
RAW State Copy Command - COMMAND.COM, CMD.EXE, WINFILE.EXE. *(continued)*

Frame	Time	Src MAC Addr	Dst MAC Addr	Protocol	Description
56	4230559	COMPAQC8F61A	VOYAGERIX	TCP	.A...., len: 0, seq: 16140934, ack: 2051429, win: 8760
57	4230559	VOYAGERIX	COMPAQC8F61A	NBT	SS: Session Message Cont., 1460 Bytes
58	4230559	VOYAGERIX	COMPAQC8F61A	NBT	SS: Session Message Cont., 1460 Bytes
59	4230559	COMPAQC8F61A	VOYAGERIX	TCP	.A...., len: 0, seq: 16140934, ack: 2052889, win: 8760
60	4230559	VOYAGERIX	COMPAQC8F61A	NBT	SS: Session Message Cont., 1460 Bytes
61	4230560	COMPAQC8F61A	VOYAGERIX	TCP	A...., len: 0, seq: 16140934, ack: 2055809, win: 8760
62	4230560	VOYAGERIX	COMPAQC8F61A	NBT	S: Session Message Cont., 1460 Bytes

Windows 95 to Windows NT Server TCP/IP Parameters

TCP/IP parameters.

Data Type	TCPWindow	Size	SizReqBuf	Outbound	Time	Outbound
Kb/sec	Inbound	Time	Outbound	Kb/sec	Copy	8192 (1)
4352 (1)	4.49	27.7	4.25	30.2	Copy	8192 (1)
8452	4:45	28	4.24	30.3	Copy	12288
12548	3.56	33.9	4.25	30.2		

(1) Default parameters of Windows NT 3.51.

Copy Command: Windows 2000 to Windows 2000 SMB Parameters

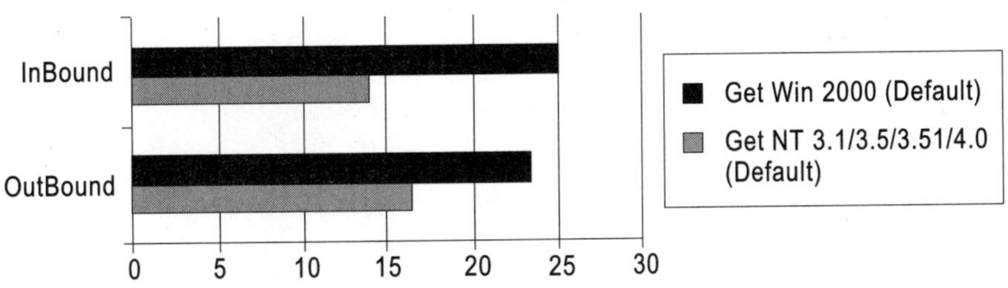

Figure 6.17 Windows 2000 Post BETA 2 default parameters.

Windows NT to Windows NT/Windows 2000 to Windows 2000 FTP Parameters

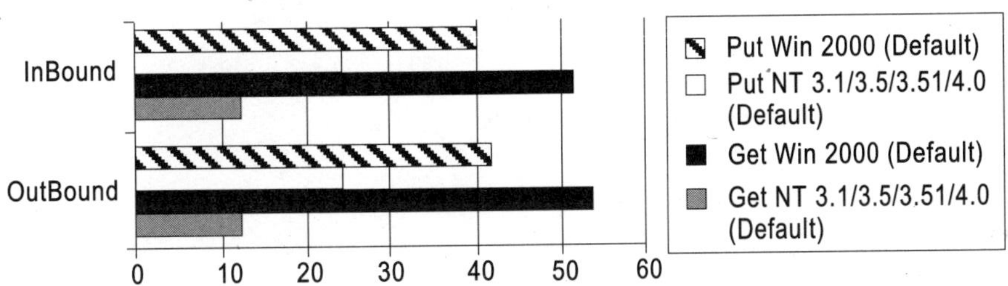

Figure 6.18 Windows 2000 Post BETA 2 default parameters.

CHAPTER 7

WAN Design at Shinozaki Automotive Corp.

By Thomas Schenkman, Michael Shinozaki, MCS—New York

The procedure for acquiring a dynamically assigned Transmission Control Protocol/Internet Protocol (TCP/IP) address is widely documented, as are other networking services such as Windows Internet Naming Service (WINS) and the Internet's Domain Name Service (DNS). Not much has been written, however, about how to implement these network services together while designing an enterprise wide area network (WAN). This chapter is designed to fill the gap, although it obviously cannot cover every topic and technology needed to design a fully redundant, high performance enterprise network. Still, through explanation and examples of network topology, it should help you understand and overcome some of the more common design problems.

In Focus

Enterprise
Shinozaki Automotive, Corp., a reseller of automotive parts, rebuilt engines, and transmissions, headquartered in Lindenhurst, NY.

Network
The Shinozaki network consists of 750 retail offices, four regional warehouses, and a headquarters site.

Challenge
Develop a WAN design that connects the offices in such a way as to provide network capabilities relevant to the sites' various line-of-business applications and practices.

Solution
A frame relay inter-exchange carrier, a centralized infrastructure design for DNS and for WINS (with a primary and a backup WINS server at headquarters), and a single user account domain model with centralized administration.

What You'll Find In This Chapter

- **Methods for implementing network services together to achieve a WAN design sensitive to your specific business needs.**
- **How to gather information from your enterprise and use it to assess various configuration and carrier options to create a design that meets business needs, and is affordable, practical, and manageable.**
- **A discussion of the major network services, their processes and characteristics so that you can better understand the criteria and tradeoffs involved in network design.**

The Wide Area Network

The first section of this chapter focuses on the WAN and the subject of topologies, using an example case study to demonstrate some of the methods and concepts used in WAN design.

The big topic in WAN implementation is cost. Many enterprises have already upgraded their local area networks (LANs) from 10 Mbps Ethernet to 100 Mbps Ethernet, and boosted their infrastructures with new switching technologies. When a single network segment can no longer support higher packet transmission rates, the segment can simply be divided, reducing the number of nodes and lowering segment utilization. For most LAN upgrades cost is easy to measure: you add up the best prices you can get on hubs, switches and routers. Once you pay for the equipment and implement it, the upgrade is mostly paid for.

When you "step outside," to WAN design, things change, first of all by becoming more expensive. WANs are too distributed to be served by the less expensive LAN technologies such as Ethernet and Token Ring. Instead, WANs require costlier high-speed transmission, so to contain WAN costs, architects must carefully analyze available technologies, plan exactly where to place systems, and implement the correct WAN topologies.

Case Study: Shinozaki Automotive

To provide you with a working example of the challenges of efficient WAN design, the first part of this chapter focuses on the fictional Shinozaki Automotive Corporation, a reseller of automotive parts, rebuilt engines, and transmissions, headquartered in Lindenhurst, NY. Shinozaki has 15 retail stores in each state, and one warehouse in each of four regions: Northeast, Northwest, Southeast, and Southwest.

Shinozaki employs approximately 19,500 full and part-time employees. Most of the executive staff, finance, and procurement departments (about 3,000 people) are at the Lindenhurst headquarters. Each regional warehouse employs about 350 people to take inventory, and to receive, track, price, and ship products. They use networked personal computers. Each retail office employs about 20 people, who perform tasks ranging from sales to automotive technical assistance. Each retail office has about 20 Windows NT Workstations and one local Windows NT Server for file and print services. These systems are connected to their regional warehouse for technical specifications, product availability, and purchasing.

Needs Analysis—Defining a Method and an Approach

To perform a technical needs analysis of data communications you need to understand what services and connectivity users (and systems) need to perform day-to-day functions productively and cheaply. A good place to start is the enterprise's availability requirements, and you can understand them by looking at how physical sites relate *logically*. From this point of view Shinozaki's 755 physical sites are of only three types: headquarters (1), retail offices (750), and regional warehouses (4).

Large-enterprise WAN design is not as straightforward as calculating server utilization or LAN transmission speeds, because most WANs require you to analyze many if not all of the enterprise's systems and users. Here is the logical process Shinozaki used:

- Discovery of needed network services: messaging, file and print, fax, database
- Discovery of needed protocols: Systems Network Architecture (SNA), TCP/IP, Internetwork Packet Exchange/Sequenced Packet Exchange (IPX/SPX—used by Novell Netware)
- Discovery of systems maintenance traffic: login, password changes, Dynamic Host Configuration Protocol (DHCP), WINS, replication

- Discovery of LAN locations
- Review of connectivity requirements
- Review of systems management requirements
- Review of available/potential WAN technologies: Integrated Services Digital Network (ISDN), Asynchronous Transfer Mode (ATM), frame relay
- Topology and general service design
- Carrier selection

Discovery of Needed Network Services

Retail Office Discovery

Shinozaki's retail offices need local file and print services. They do not yet have electronic messaging, but are planning to in the near future. Each retail office client requires Internet access. Each retail office manager needs access to the payroll and human resource databases once a week to update employee payroll information. Retail office sales people need access to their regional warehouse's system to check on product availability. And retail offices send daily accounting and sales summaries to headquarters.

Retail office needs summary:

- **Electronic messaging**. Messaging, calendar, and workflow applications during all business hours.
- **File and print services**. Large files and technical diagrams must be stored on local file and print server. File and print services do not require much connectivity, but user profiles and account administration must be centralized.
- **Internet access**. Connectivity to vendors' technical Web sites, sales systems, etc., during all business hours.
- **Human resources systems**. Connectivity for weekly payroll data transmission.
- **Warehouse connectivity**. Access to warehouse databases during business hours.
- **Accounting and sales**. Connectivity for daily transmission of summary files.
- **Systems management**. Remote control of routers, hubs, workstations, and servers via WAN links for troubleshooting and upgrading system components.

Regional Warehouse Discovery

Regional warehouses need essentially the same connectivity as retail offices. Retail office users need access to the warehouses' parts and stock availability databases. Warehouse users need Internet connectivity, electronic messaging, file and print services, and access to the headquarters databases.

Regional warehouse needs summary:

- **Retail office connectivity**. See retail office list.
- **Electronic messaging**. Messaging, calendar, and workflow applications during all business hours.
- **File and print services**. Each warehouse has a data center for file and print servers, stock and order databases, etc.
- **Internet access**. For numerous warehouse systems during all business hours.
- **Human resources systems**. Connectivity for weekly payroll data transmission.
- **Accounting and sales**. Connectivity for daily transmission of summary files.
- **Systems management**. Remote control of routers, hubs, workstations, and servers via WAN links for troubleshooting and upgrading system components.

Headquarters Discovery

The headquarters location needs to meet the data requirements of the retail locations and the warehouse locations, which use connectivity to headquarters for the line of business applications described above. Headquarters systems and clients also need Internet connectivity.

Note In many enterprise WANs, various systems split T1 circuits and channels to supply voice and data over the same connection for services such as voice over frame relay. Applications of this type are not discussed in this chapter, although you may need to consider these services during your needs analysis.

Discovery of Network Protocols

The fewer protocols you implement over the WAN, the less it costs to manage and troubleshoot component systems. In a perfect world, you could simply choose a protocol (such as TCP/IP) that is available on most network operating systems, and services would accommodate it. It seldom works out this simply in the real world, however, where designers are confronted with a complex mix of legacy systems, broadcast technologies, and hardware/software technologies.

Although a single routable protocol simplifies management, it is not a requirement for enterprise systems, where gateways and tunneling can encapsulate protocols into a single routable WAN technology. You need to weigh the benefits of these solutions against the cost of managing a more complex system. No matter how many protocols you use, you need to calculate the network transmission speeds of the various communicating systems.

Shinozaki was happy to find that it could use only TCP/IP for application connectivity.

Discovery of Systems Maintenance Traffic

To calculate the maintenance traffic required in most Windows NT networks, you need to calculate the traffic associated with WINS, DNS, DHCP, and the browser service. (The method described in this section is covered fully in the Microsoft Windows NT Enterprise course.)

All systems maintenance and management traffic is important at this level of implementation. Although in a small network Simple Network Management Protocol (SNMP) may place few demands on the network, at a company the size of Shinozaki it represents the traffic of over 750 connected offices and nodes. Other services such as Novell Service Advertising Protocol (SAP) can also create considerable traffic on this scale.

This chapter focuses on topology and implementation of services. For explanations of network traffic considerations and calculations, see the Microsoft Windows NT Enterprise course and chapters 1 – 3 of this book.

Discovery of LAN Locations

Not all segments of the telecommunications world are created equal. You have to analyze each site to see what services are available. This becomes more difficult but equally important in international enterprises, where branch offices may be located in regions with fewer connectivity options. Exchange carriers can help you during this phase. The AT&T G-INOS service, for instance, allows you to access a database, enter the phone numbers of each of your branch offices, then see various connectivity technologies, prices, and topologies. If you have to discuss options or negotiate arrangements with exchange carriers, start the process early in the design phase.

Review of Connectivity Requirements

Understanding the connectivity requirements is crucial to WAN design. The Shinozaki study has so far identified key service connectivity requirements. Some of these services require connectivity only periodically (for example, the retail office weekly payroll update) and others (for example, messaging) require constant connectivity during business hours. To meet these needs, Shinozaki has a choice: use separate technologies—dial-in access for payroll, and a dedicated service for the Internet and messaging systems—or design the WAN to supply enough access for all services and reduce the number of systems to manage.

A primary need is that certain services (such as T1 and frame relay) require continuous connectivity. You need to identify these services and calculate the traffic they can be expected to generate. You also need to calculate traffic for foreseeable network expansion, such as upgrading to Windows 2000, messaging applications, and client-server applications, and provide for this increase in the communications capability.

How can you do this? Often, you can derive estimates by analyzing services currently in place. For example, if your branch offices have local file and print servers, you can calculate the potential authentication traffic by analyzing a baseline of the current login volume. If these locations currently dial in to an Internet Service Provider (ISP) for Web connectivity, you can further assess potential traffic by tracking what Web sites are used and how often. This data can also help you lower the expected Web traffic by incorporating products such as proxy servers in the design.

Review of Systems Management Requirements

System management concerns itself with servers, workstations, WAN links, and software maintenance. These tasks generate costs and requirements that you need to consider when creating a network design. Numerous vendors supply management tools: Cisco Systems and 3COM corporation offer products for managing routers, hubs, and switches, and carriers such as AT&T and Bell Atlantic provide tools and techniques for analyzing systems utilization, maintenance, and downtime.

How management is implemented can vastly affect the uptime and management costs of these systems. How management systems are designed and implemented in the topology will determine their overall performance and effectiveness. You can consider centralizing management at headquarters or regionalizing it by having management nodes and personnel in selected locations.

Review of Available WAN Technologies

When the needs analysis is complete, you can begin reviewing and assessing WAN technologies such as ATM and frame relay. There are plenty of books and online sources that explain how these technologies work and how much they cost. And you should work with local carriers to see how their implementations can serve your organization's needs. Technologies are discussed in more detail in later sections.

Topology and General Service Design

If you haven't gathered the data discussed so far, you will probably have a hard time defining the shape or topology of the enterprise network you need. Technology and need have driven each other forward in this area, as they have in so many others. Not too long ago, the dedicated links needed to connect offices across the country into a large distributed enterprise would have been prohibitively costly. Multi-drop topologies were used to reduce the cost of specific designs until X.25 and frame relay came along and made reliable connection distance-insensitive. As the need for connectivity evolved, so did technology, which in turn impelled designers to distribute processes and data even more, and so on.

Carrier Selection

Talk to carriers. Investigate their costs, how well their solutions will integrate with other services (voice and video), their quality of service, and their management. Carrier services are discussed in later sections.

The Wide Area Network Technologies

Now it's time to look at technologies and examples of how to use them to implement a large distributed system that meets your organization's requirements.

Review of WAN Topologies

Most large-enterprise WANs comprise many different technologies ranging from dial-up networking with analog modems to high-speed ATM backbones. These technologies are discussed below.

Point-to-Point and Point-to-Many Connections

Point-to-point topologies connect two locations using a carrier's network. This technology was one of the few available in the early 1970s and 1980s, and is still widely used in WANs. Here is an example of point-to-point connection:

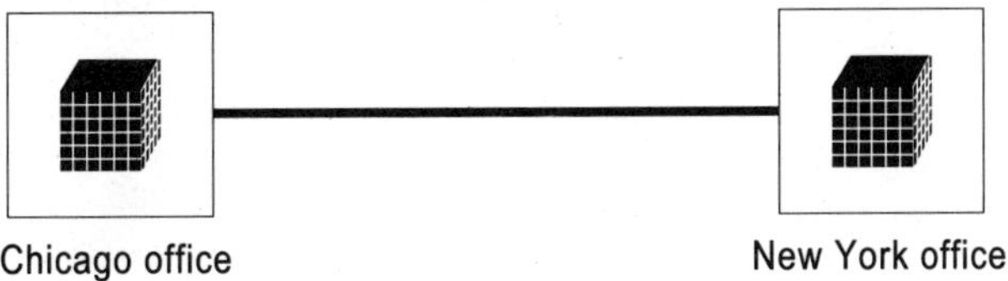

Figure 7.1 Point-to-point topology.

Point-to-many topologies connect a single location to multiple locations, usually via a packet switched cloud such as X.25 or frame relay, as illustrated below:

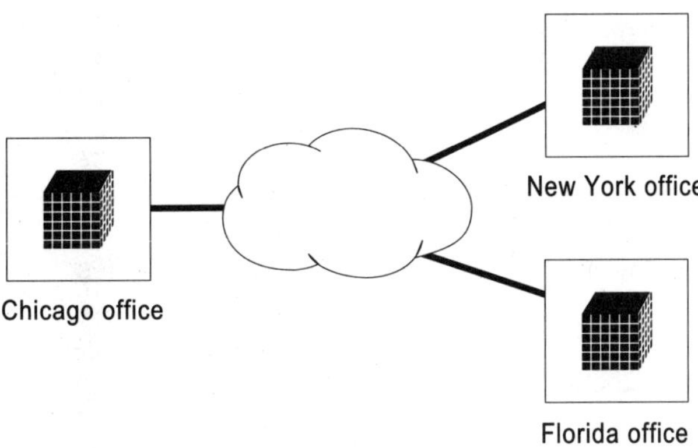

Figure 7.2 Point-to-many topology.

Dedicated Links

Dedicated links are typically point-to-point connections ranging from 56 Kbps to 274 Mbps. They tend to be distance sensitive—the larger the distance between connecting networks, the higher the connection cost. Choosing the correct topology can lower costs associated with dedicated links as illustrated below:

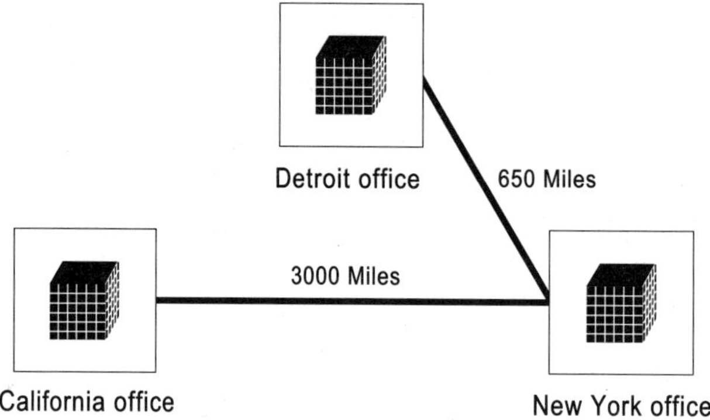

Figure 7.3 Dedicated links.

In this example, the Detroit and California offices connect by dedicated line to the New York office. If the carrier charges per-mile this may be significantly more expensive than the following topology.

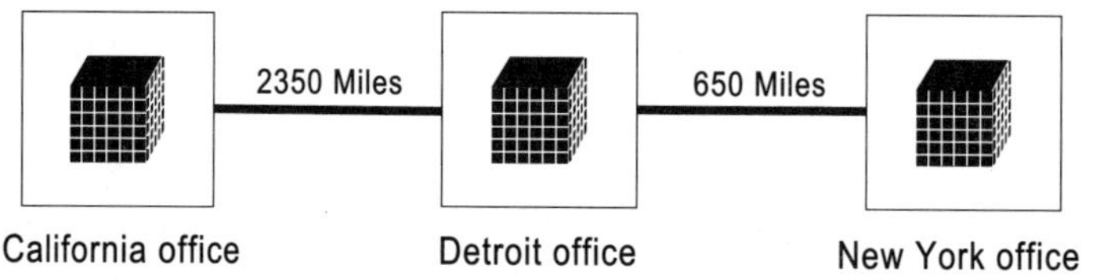

Figure 7.4 Multi-drop topology (a).

At first glance this appears to be cost effective, but there are other things to consider. The Detroit–New York link now has to provide transmission speed appropriate to the California office, too. This is often referred to as a multi-drop topology. Another example, illustrated below, shows two offices (California and Seattle) connecting to New York through the Detroit office. The Seattle and California links are each purchased for 64 Kbps; the Detroit–New York link is purchased as a fractional T1 of 512 Kbps.

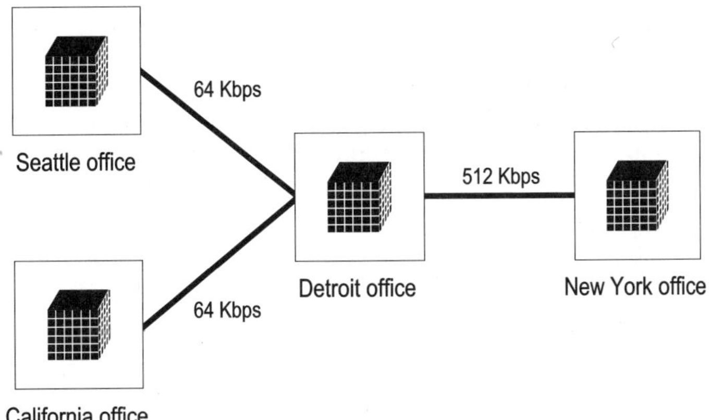

Figure 7.5 Multi-drop topology (b).

Commonly used dedicated link speeds.

	Carrier Line	Speed
DS-0		64 Kbps
DS-1	T1	1.544 Mbps
DS-3	T3	44.736 Mbps

Packet Switched Services

Services such as frame relay, X.25, and ATM provide permanent connectivity similar to that of dedicated 64 Kbps and T1 links. Various customers share the carrier network using virtual circuits to connect customer locations and provide them with a private network. Since the carrier can share out the services backbone (also known as a cloud) this arrangement usually costs less than a dedicated link.

Frame Relay

Frame relay and X.25 Services are very similar. A frame relay network uses nodes (processors) to route packets of user data to their destination within the frame relay cloud. Each location is connected to the frame relay carrier by dedicated services such as T1. This is usually far less expensive than a dedicated connection to distant locations, because carriers' frame relay clouds are usually distance insensitive—meaning that you do not pay more to move data further.

The connection to the frame relay cloud (T1 and 64 Kbps) is referred to as a port, and the ports for the sites in the network are connected via a private virtual circuit (PVC).

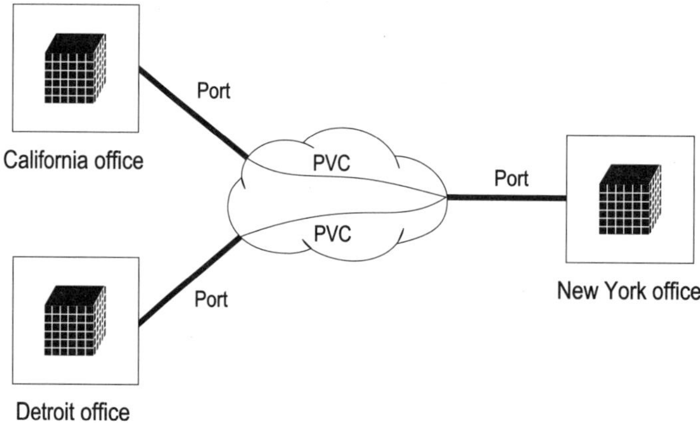

Figure 7.6 PVCs and ports in frame relay WAN configuration.

When you are assessing PVCs as WAN design possibilities you need to know their *burst rate* (how much they can carry at one time) and the committed information rate (CIR)—the minimum transmission rate guaranteed by the carrier. The CIR tells you the lowest rate you can expect when the frame relay network is congested. If you can live with that, you know the worst case will be OK, and when the network is *not* congested you can achieve higher transmission rates.

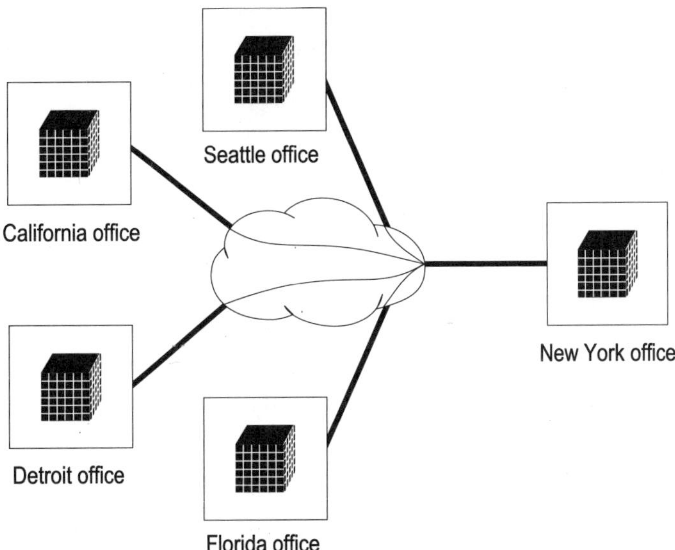

Figure 7.7 Frame relay cloud WAN configuration without PVCs.

The single most common mistake in designing a frame relay network is oversubscription, which is when the sum of PVC's and their CIR's exceed the connecting rate of the destination port.

To notify end-nodes of congestion, the Forward Explicit Congestion Notification (FECN) and Backward Explicit Congestion Notification (BECN) bits are used. These are useful if receiving and sending nodes can throttle transmission rates, but not all routers/protocols can do this.

TCP/IP is another factor. It sometimes resends transmitted packets, not aware that the network is congested. This can exacerbate the problem, with the original retransmissions and then with the transmission of management and raster image processor (RIP) packets to re-discover what appears to be disconnected routers and nodes. These problems can flood WAN links, making them temporarily inoperable.

Inter-Exchange Vs Intra-Exchange Carriers

Some WANs span a state, others span the globe. Inter-exchange carriers can connect sites outside of their geographic range; intra-exchange carriers usually cannot, but they usually offer a low cost solution for WANs within their range. Often, the most cost-effective solution is to combine inter- and intra-exchange carriers although this can complicate troubleshooting and management. The next section reviews some potential design solutions for the Shinozaki WAN.

Review of Connectivity Needs

Shinozaki sites belong to three categories: retail offices, headquarters, and regional warehouses. All sites need connectivity during business hours for messaging, database, and Internet access (not yet considered). Messaging and database needs require WAN connectivity. At Shinozaki, calculations of basic remote management services showed that each retail office needed a WAN connection averaging 96 Kbps.

Regional warehouses need messaging and database access to headquarters, but they have generally larger data access requirements with 350 persons per site. The baseline calculation for each of these sites is about 2300 Kbps.

(Details on establishing baselines are in the *Microsoft Windows NT Enterprise* course.)

Connectivity of the Retail Office Locations

For the 750 retail office locations, frame relay is probably the most efficient connectivity method. This decision is based on analyzing the expected cost of dedicated lines in various topologies, then calculating equipment and maintenance costs. Further, the frame relay should be one of two topologies.

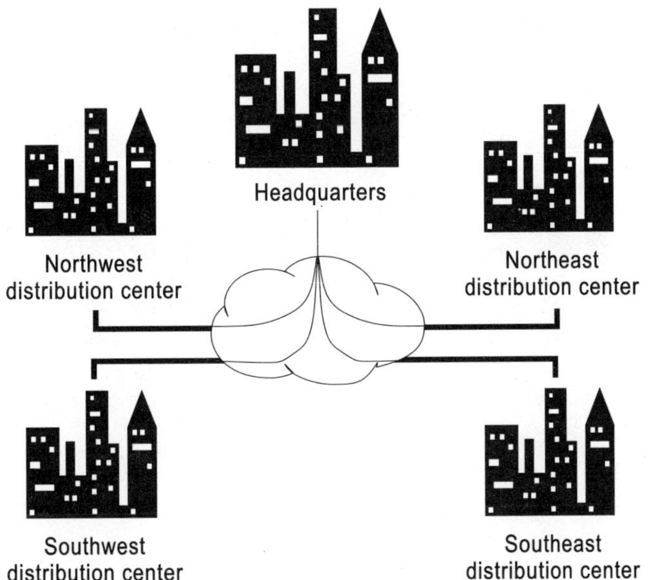

Figure 7.8 Shinozaki regional warehouse configuration.

- Use PVCs to connect the retail offices to their respective regional warehouse, and either larger PVCs or a high-speed backbone (ATM or SONET) to connect warehouses to headquarters. Transmissions from the retail offices to headquarters are routed via the links connecting the warehouses and headquarters.

- Use PVCs to connect each retail office and regional warehouse directly to headquarters. Requests from retail offices to their respective regional warehouses would be routed through headquarters. Because requests destined to the warehouses do not require higher levels of connectivity, this may significantly improve costs and performance for a company as large as Shinozaki by lowering the requirements on certain WAN links.

Here is what the second topology looks like:

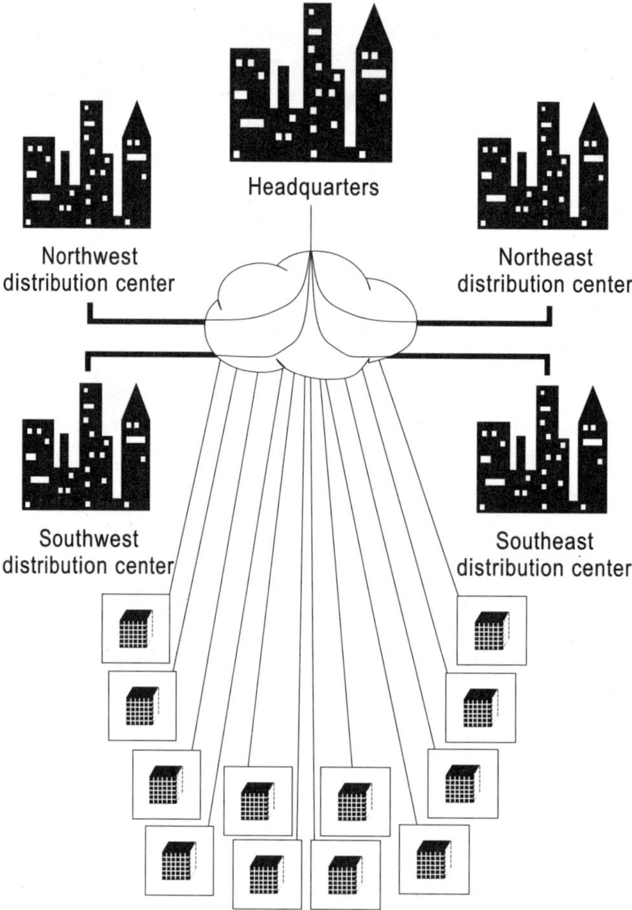

Figure 7.9 Shinozaki retail office configuration.

The first topology segments the corporate network into more connectivity points than does the second, making it easier to provide higher levels of redundancy. Redundancy can be engineered into either topology, of course, by using multiple PVC connections for each office, dial-on-demand backup links, etc.

Case Study Design

After weighing volume pricing and service options, Shinozaki decided to use the topology shown above—a frame relay inter-exchange carrier. Each retail office connects via 96 Kbps CIR PVCs with a 128 Kbps port to the headquarters site. The regional warehouse locations each connect directly with headquarters. ATM or T3 links will support the high traffic volumes generated by retail offices routing through headquarters.

Dynamic Host Configuration Protocol

The second part of this chapter discusses implementation details regarding specific Microsoft network services such as WINS, DHCP, and Windows NT domains.

Administrators have to assign and maintain IP address information and help users who are unable to configure their own computers for internetworking. DHCP was established to relieve this burden by providing reliable, simple TCP/IP network configuration, preventing address conflicts, and helping to conserve the use of IP addresses by centralizing address allocation management. DHCP dynamically configures computer IP addresses; the system administrator controls IP address use by assigning lease durations that specify how long a computer can hold an assigned IP address before having to renew the lease with the DHCP server.

The DHCP client and server services for Windows NT are implementations of Request for Comments (RFCs) 1533, 1534, 1541, and 1542. The DHCP process has four primary stages: discovery, offer, request, and acknowledgment. (Renewal is a repeat of the last two stages.)

Network Design Issues

Access

The first major design issue is to make sure client workstations can access the DHCP server. Workstations broadcast an IP datagram to discover the DHCP server, and this requires that they be on the same segment, because most IP routed environments do not forward broadcast messages across router links. To avoid this, the DHCP server must either be directly connected to the workstation's segment (multi-homed device) or the intervening router must support the DHCP Relay Agent protocol (RFC 1542).

Security

While DHCP eases some TCP/IP administrative effort, it does expose the network to a *denial-of-service* threat (which is non-destructive). A misconfigured or maliciously configured DHCP (rogue) server can issue incorrect configuration information to DHCP clients, causing them to lose IP connectivity. A misconfigured host cannot contact a default router, causing clients to receive *host unreachable* messages. You can find out if this is happening by executing "IPCONFIG /ALL" from the command line. If the IP configuration information is incorrect, disable the rogue server, then issue an "IPCONFIG /RELEASE" and "IPCONFIG /RENEW" command to obtain correct information. In a widely distributed network, it may then take several replication cycles to flush all of the "bad" address information from the WINS system.

You can also provide authentication of the source and contents of DHCP messages. For example, clients may be subject to denial of service attacks through the use of bogus DHCP servers, or may simply be misconfigured due to unintentionally instantiated DHCP servers. Some administrators constrain the allocation of addresses to authorized hosts to avoid denial of service attacks in "hostile" environments where the network medium is not physically secured, such as wireless networks or college residence halls. (For more information, see "Authentication for DHCP Messages," 11/22/1996, http://ds.internic.net/internet-drafts/draft-ietf-dhc-authentication-03.txt.)

One Segment, One Subnet

This configuration has a single network segment with a single defined IP subnet. The DHCP server and client are both on the segment.

Two Segments, Two Subnets (Routed), Internal Router

This configuration uses a multi-homed Windows NT Server (connected to more than one segment) and an external router that connects the local segments to the WAN. The server must be configured with the DHCP relay agent. This is because the DHCP server process binds to one adapter only, so the relay agent is used to forward the request internally to the other adapter. This permits the DHCP server to service DHCP broadcast requests without using resources on the main router. Windows NT Server 4.0 provides an internal DHCP relay agent.

Two Segments, Two Subnets (Routed), External Router: (DHCP RELAY*)*

This configures the router as a DHCP relay agent. A relay agent conforms to RFC 1542 and relays DHCP packets to the remote side even though they are broadcast packets. Before relaying a DHCP message from a DHCP client, the agent examines the gateway IP address (GIADDR) field. If the field has an IP address of 0.0.0.0, the agent fills it with the router's IP address. All communications between the relay agent and the DHCP server are directed User Datagram Protocol (UDP)-datagrams; the communications between the DHCP client and its DHCP relay agent are IP broadcast datagrams.

When the DHCP server receives the message, it examines the Relay IP address field to see if it has a DHCP scope (a pool of IP address) that can be used to supply an IP address lease. If the DHCP server has multiple scopes, the address in the Relay IP address field identifies the correct scope from which to offer an IP address lease. This process allows one DHCP server to manage different scopes for subnets.

When the DHCP server receives the DHCPDISCOVER message, it sends a DHCPOFFER directly to the relay agent identified in the GIADDR field, and the agent relays the message to the DHCP client. The client's IP address is still unknown, thus it has to be a broadcast on the local subnet. Similarly, a DHCPREQUEST message is relayed from client to server and a DHCP message is relayed from server to client, according to RFC 1542.

If you use the Cisco Systems BOOTP relay's "IPHELPER Address" to forward both BOOTP and DHCP requests, you must include the "No IP Forward UDP Port 137" and "No IP Forward UDP Port 138" commands in the interface configuration.

Multiple Subnets per Segment

When multiple subnets are cast on a single segment, the DHCP server cannot dynamically assign IP addresses to multiple subnets.

The most common situation in which multiple subnets per segment are employed is when a router link connects a bridged or switched series of segments to a routed network. Now the downstream bridged or switched segments represent a single logical segment at the subnet level and must exceed the maximum available host count on a given subnet. You should subnet a physical segment space rather than casting multiple subnets on it. If you cannot avoid this, then you can implement DHCP by using supernetting, a proposed extension of the DHCP protocol that allows you to bind multiple address scopes to a single receiving interface or relay agent GIADDR, then chooses an address randomly from the available scopes.

DNS Compatibility

The second major DHCP issue is architectural conflict with the Domain Name System (DNS). DNS employs a statically defined resource table that associates IP addresses with host names. In a DHCP environment where IP addresses are pooled and randomly assigned to any host on a given subnet, the DNS rapidly diverges from the actual IP-name relationship. You can fix this by either permanently assigning IP addresses to hosts in the DHCP server configuration or by devising a method by which the host-to-IP-address relationship can be dynamically learned. One of the proposals for Dynamic DNS links the DHCP server with the DNS database. Now, instead of each workstation registering itself with a name resolver such as WINS, the DHCP server registers the device when the IP address is issued. (For more information, see http://ds.internic.net/internet-drafts/draft-ietf-dhc-dhcp-dns-02.txt).

Q and A: Operational Implementation

Do I have to use DHCP?

No. DHCP merely eases many of the administrative burdens involved with TCP/IP-based networks.

How many DHCP servers do I need?

This depends on the number of arriving requests, the rate at which the server can process them, and the available network bandwidth between the clients and the server. If you configure fewer, centrally managed servers, you reduce server resource consumption but increase network bandwidth consumption. The DHCP server can process 600 lease requests per minute.

Where should I put them?

Placing DHCP servers in branch offices reduces the WAN bandwidth utilization, but each DHCP server consumes a baseline amount of server resources. The number and placement of DHCP servers is entirely based upon the individual environmental constraints. If you have plenty of WAN bandwidth, then you can configure fewer servers and maintain and control then centrally; if you are short on WAN bandwidth, you can distribute servers to the field, but be prepared for additional administrative burdens. The balance must be found case-by-case.

Lease Management

[This is excerpted from the *Microsoft Windows NT Resource Kit*]

To define appropriate values for lease duration, you should consider the frequency of these events for your network:

- Change to DHCP options and default values
- Network interface failures
- Computer removals for any purpose
- Subnet changes by users because of office moves, laptop computers docked at different workstations, and so on

These types of events cause IP addresses to be released by the client or cause leases to expire at the DHCP server. In either case, the IP addresses are returned to the free address pool to be reused.

Another important factor is the ratio between connected computers and available IP addresses. For example, the demand for reusing addresses is low in a network where 40 computers share a class C address (with 254 available addresses), so a long lease time, such as two months, is appropriate. But if 230 computers share the same address pool, demand for available addresses is much greater, so a lease time of a few days works better. Short lease duration requires that the DHCP server be available when the client seeks to renew the lease. Backup servers are especially important when using short durations.

Although infinite leases are allowed, use them cautiously. Even a relatively stable environment has a certain amount of turnover among clients: portable computers are added and removed, desktop computers are moved from one office to another, and network cards are replaced. If a client with an infinite lease is removed from the network, and the DHCP server is not notified, that IP address can't be reused. A long lease duration, such as six months, is better, because it ensures that addresses are ultimately recovered.

DHCP conversation summary.

Src Addr	Dst Addr	Protocol	Description	Src IP Addr	Dst IP Addr
DHCP-C	*BROADCAST	DHCP	**Discover** (xid=5DBE14EA)	0.0.0.0	IP Broadcast
DHCP-S	*BROADCAST	DHCP	**Offer** (xid=5DBE14EA)	DHCP-S	IP Broadcast
DHCP-C	*BROADCAST	DHCP	**Request** (xid=1EFC37B4)	0.0.0.0	IP Broadcast
DHCP-S	*BROADCAST	DHCP	**ACK** (xid=1EFC37B4)	DHCP-S	IP Broadcast

Case Study DHCP Design

Shinozaki saw that DHCP traffic generated over the WAN links for client address leases would be relatively small in comparison to the WAN utilization of Internet and database services. After comparing the WAN costs for centralized DHCP services and the administrative costs of managing DHCP on local servers in each location, they decided on a centralized infrastructure design.

In a centralized DHCP approach clients cannot acquire/renew IP addresses when either the DHCP server or the WAN links between the remote LAN and the centralized DHCP servers are unavailable. Shinozaki reduced this risk by making sure that lease durations did not exceed potential DHCP server or WAN link downtime. Centralized servers at headquarters provide addresses for requesting clients at retail offices, regional warehouses, and headquarters.

Windows Internet Name Service

WINS registers NetBIOS names, challenges those names for uniqueness, replies to names queries, and replicates the names database between WINS servers. NetBIOS naming provides a user-friendly method for identifying network resources—users are much better at remembering server names than they are at remembering IP addresses. A names resolver (NBNS) resolves NetBIOS names to the underlying transport protocol (TCP/IP, IPX, etc.) and an address resolution protocol resolves the transport protocol to the media access control (MAC) address.

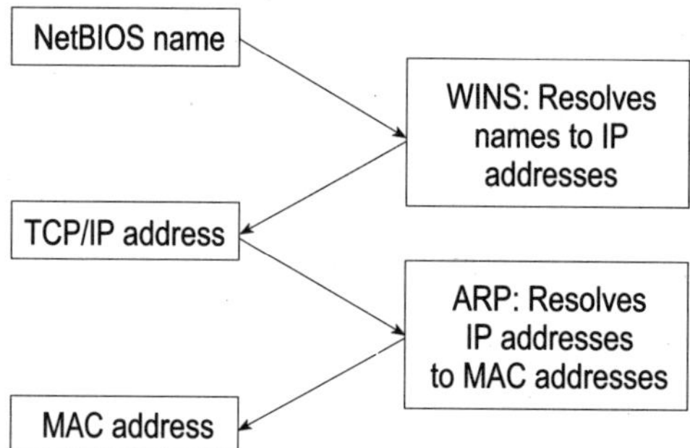

Figure 7.10 Windows Internet Naming Service (WINS) process.

NetBIOS over TCP/IP and NetBIOS Names Service (NBNS)

Windows NT networking is based on a NetBIOS programming interface encapsulated in the TCP/IP, IPX/SPX, or 802.2 LLC (NetBEUI) packets. The NBNS provides name registration and resolution. Registration establishes a unique name for each network node; resolution resolves a TCP/IP address for a NetBIOS name. Hosts register a NetBIOS name with the NBNS either on startup or by subsequent broadcast message to the NetBIOS name cache on each LAN machine. RFCs 1001 and 1002 describe how NetBIOS over TCP/IP (NBT) is implemented.

Name types registered by hosts.

Name Type	Description
Unique	Single entry pair with a name and address.
Group	Addresses a group of machines on a subnet via the broadcast address.
Internet Group	Registers 25 name/address pairs under a single group name (for example, domain name): the PDC address, the most recently locally learned 24 name pairs, then any entries replicated from other WINS servers. This is significant in WINS network design issues, because you can configure this list to optimize domain controller communications within a domain..
Multi-homed	Registers 25 addresses under a single name. The receiving client matches first on the subnet, then the network, then chooses randomly from the returned addresses.

A Windows NT computer can use one or more of the following methods to resolve host names in TCP/IP networks.

Windows Internet Name Service

Windows NT computers can use WINS if one or more WINS servers are available that contain a dynamic database mapping computer names to IP addresses and if the NBT names resolver is WINS-enabled. WINS servers provide point-to-point name resolution services that can overcome subnet broadcast limitations and avoid global broadcasts.

Broadcast Name Resolution

Windows NT computers can also use IP-level broadcasts for name resolution services on the network, which is a mode of operation (NetBIOS over TCP/IP) defined in RFC 1001/1002 as b-node. Each computer in the broadcast area has to challenge attempts to register a duplicate name and respond to name queries for its registered name.

WINS Proxy

In a mixed environment of WINS and non-WINS enabled devices, a WINS proxy agent can relay broadcast name registration/resolution requests to a WINS server. WINS proxies do not save WINS registration information, nor do they participate in PUSH/PULL replication. They can, however, cache data that results from proxy activity.

DNS Name Resolution

DNS provides a way to look up name mappings when connecting a computer to foreign hosts using NetBIOS over TCP/IP or Windows Sockets applications such as File Transfer Protocol (FTP). DNS is a distributed database designed to relieve the traffic problems that arose with the exploding growth of the Internet in the early 1980s.

The NBT node defines the order in which names services are utilized. These are:

- **b-node**, which uses broadcasts to resolve names.
- **p-node**, which uses point-to-point communications with a name server to resolve names in this sequence: NetBIOS Name Cache, WINS, LMHOSTS, HOSTS, DNS.
- **m-node**, which uses b-node first, then (if the broadcast fails) p-node, in this sequence: NetBIOS Name Cache, broadcast, WINS, LMHOSTS, HOSTS, DNS.
- **h-node (default)**, which uses p-node first for name queries, and then b-node if the name service is unavailable or if the name is not registered in the WINS database, in this sequence: NetBIOS Name Cache, WINS, broadcast, LMHOSTS, HOSTS, DNS.

WINS Implementation

Performance

In one minute, a WINS server can typically service 1500 name registrations and about 4500 queries. This is no built-in limit to the number of records that a WINS server can replicate or store. Using these numbers, and planning for large-scale problems (such as a power outage) where many computers will come back on line simultaneously, the conservative recommendation is to include one WINS server and a backup for every 10,000 computers on the network.

Performance studies for registrations and queries show that 10,000 totally random name registrations on a table with two indices takes about 70 secs (7 msec/registration) and totally random name queries take up around 20 msec (2 msec/query). Also, it takes from 2 - 4 seconds to scan the entire database sequentially using an index. The performance of the database engine should continue to improve as buffer cache management and other aspects of the JET engine are refined. Logging can be expected to slow the registration by another 10%.

Two factors can particularly enhance WINS server performance: using two processors on the computer and using NT File System (NTFS) as the file system.

After you establish WINS servers in the network, you can adjust the renewal interval (in the WINS Server Configuration dialog box). Setting it to reduce the number of registrations can boost server response time.

Network Design Issues

In previous versions of WINS, it was not recommended to run a WINS server on a multi-homed machine. This is now recommended provided that:

- Windows NT Server 3.51 with SP4 or greater is installed.
- All attached subnets are not on disjoint networks. Clients must be able to use any of the IP addresses from WINS. MS-DOS Transmission Control Protocol (TCP) clients use only the first address in a list.
- WINS replication initiates replication using the Windows Sockets (Winsock) interface. A replication session can occur on any of the interfaces depending on IP routing. For this reason you need to define each interface as a replication partner.

The Internet Group Lists have a 25-entry limit. When there are more than 25 backup domain controllers (BDCs), a workstation can discover and set up its initial secure channel with a non-local domain controller (that is, across the WAN). This happens if the local domain controller is no longer on the current top 24 Internet group list and the BDC is on a different local subnet than the requesting workstation.

Replication Design

Simple

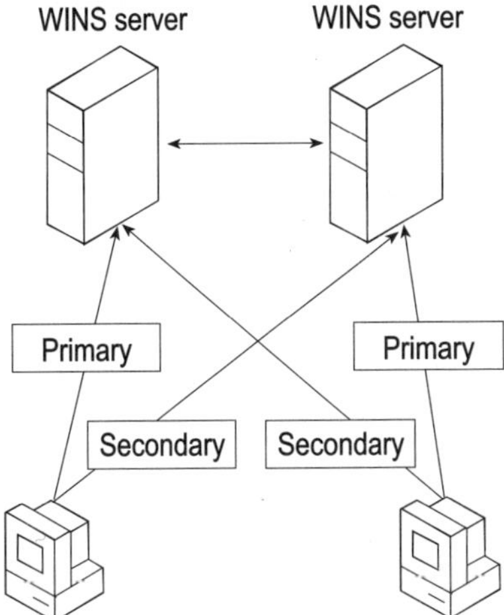

Figure 7.11 "Simple" replication design.

The simple configuration has two WINS servers, each serving half the workstation population for primary and secondary WINS addressing. This provides fault tolerance and load sharing WINS service for 5,000 well connected workstations.

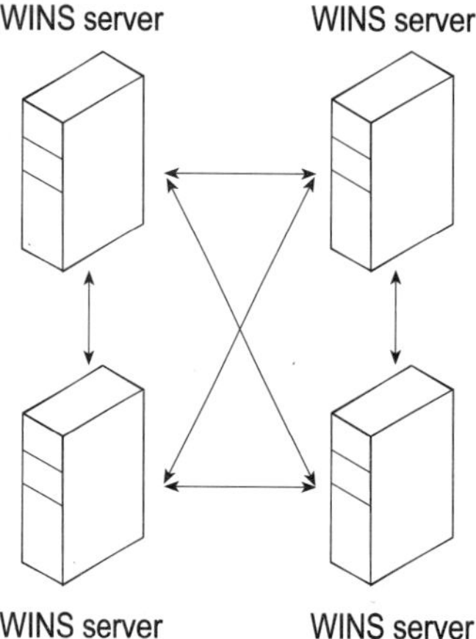

Figure 7.12 Mesh replication design.

In a fully meshed model, each WINS server replicates directly with every other WINS server, so every server contains a complete copy of the WINS database. Thus a single WINS server failure does not prevent other servers from replicating. This works well for a small number of WINS servers (fewer than 7), but as servers increase it becomes difficult to maintain the large number of replication paths. The more replication partners there are, the harder it is to troubleshoot in the event of a failure.

Hub

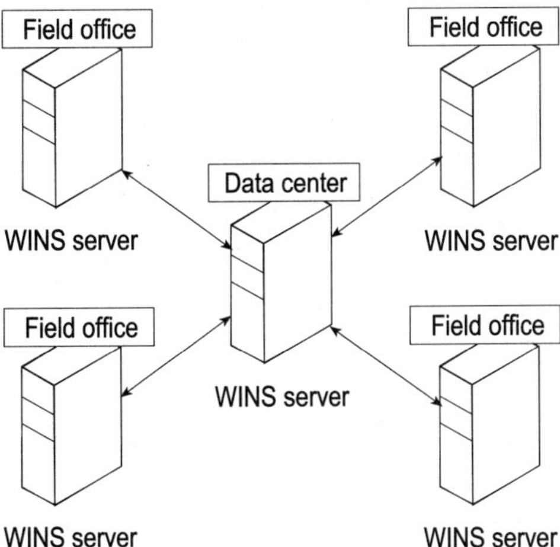

Figure 7.13 Hub replication design.

A hub-based model minimizes the number of hops needed to replicate data to each server. This creates less WAN traffic than the full mesh, but it provides a single failure point for replications and introduces a hop to the replication system that increases the time required to come to convergence.

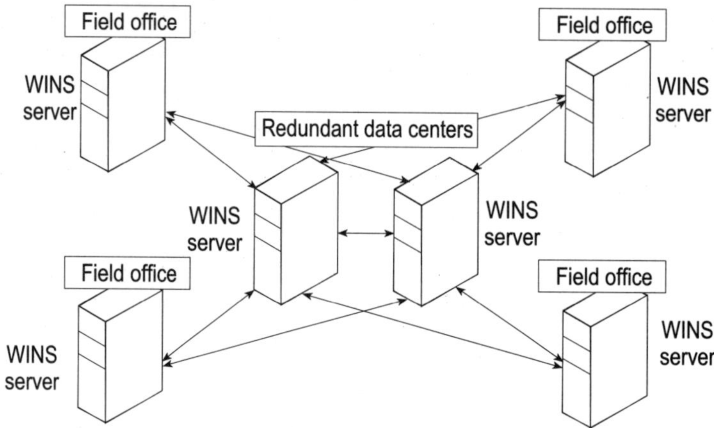

Figure 7.14 Hub with redundancy replication design.

The simple hub's weakness is overcome by the hub with redundancy design, which adds a second central hub that provides a primary and backup replication path for each local WINS server. You can set the replication pull time on the primary paths to a shorter time interval than is used on the backup path.

Multi-tiered

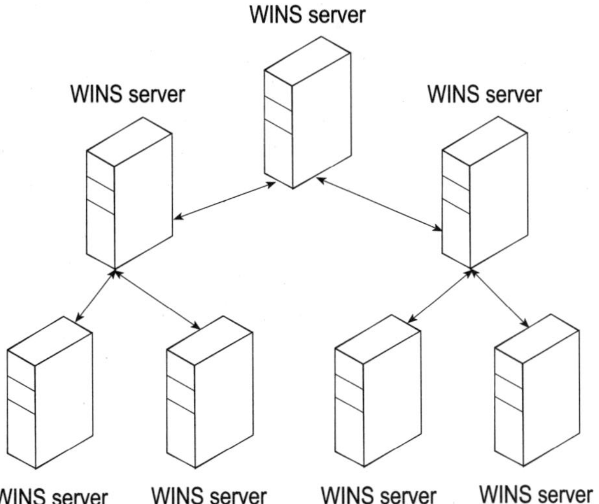

Figure 7.15 Multi-tiered replication design.

A multi-tiered design uses a central WINS hub to provide replication to regional WINS hubs, which can fan out to local site WINS servers if needed.

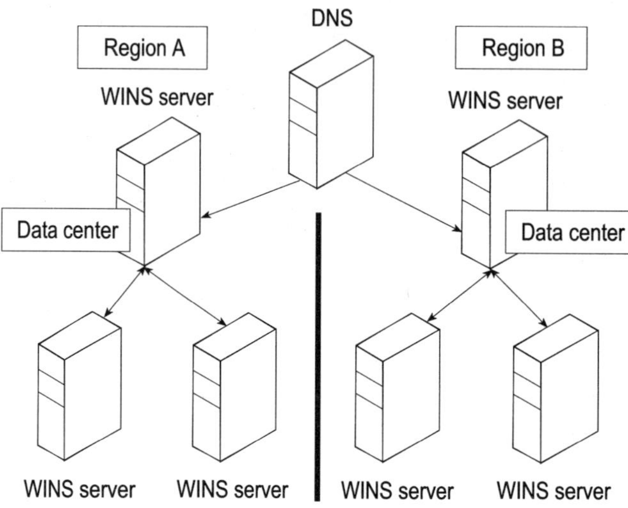

Figure 7.16 DNS non-replicating WINS design for massive environments.

This design is intended to support massive environments (>100,000). The local WINS server replicates only with the regional WINS servers and there is no inter-regional replication. All workstations are pointed to the lowest level WINS server as their primary and to the regional WINS server as their secondary. This model assumes little or no inter-field office connectivity, so any inter-field office traffic must pass through the regional centers. Workstations must be DNS-enabled to make cross-region names queries.

The Data Center tier WINS servers can be replaced with DNS servers by implementing DNS sub-domains. Multiple DNS hierarchies can be constructed for extremely large international corporations. Regionalizing the WINS system reduces the resource requirements on the overall WINS environment (database size, replication traffic, etc.) by segmenting the WINS namespace.

The DNS segmentation must be coordinated with the Windows NT domain structure, because WINS servers do not replicate data across regional lines. This means the domain Internet Group Name would contain and return only entries that exist within a regional WINS database. If the domain crossed regional lines, each region would contain only a partial list of domain controllers for the split domain.

Administration

Members of the Account Operators group and the Server Operators can view the WINS database and add or delete static mappings, but only members of the Administrators Local group can configure the server. To prevent affecting WINS server performance, other users cannot browse the database.

WINS replication is independent of the Windows NT Security Model. Replication partners do not need to be in the same domain or a trusted domain. The ability to replicate with a partner is determined by the replication partner setting. If the *replicate only with partner* option is set (default), the partner server must have a predefined IP address. A decentralized WINS management allows problems to fall through the cracks.

In contrast, a DNS environment is usually managed in a distributed fashion where each organizational unit manages its own delegated zone. WINS is a flat namespace, so central coordination is essential.

The database backs up to the local backup directory every 24 hours. Normal file system backups cannot copy the WINS database while the WINS service is active. The backup copy must be on a local drive. Administrators have to log on to the local WINS server to initiate backup from the WINSADMN tools menu.

Q&A: WINS

How many servers do I need?

Each WINS server can effectively serve 10,000 clients with low demands on both network bandwidth and server resources. Every WINS environment (even with fewer than 10,000 clients) should have at least two WINS servers—a primary and a secondary (as backup).

Case Study WINS Design

After studying all these details and relationships, Shinozaki decided to implement a centralized WINS server solution with a primary and a backup WINS server at headquarters. The WAN topology means that clients and servers will lose connectivity to resources in both the regional warehouses and the headquarters if the WAN link becomes unavailable, and this means no name resolution. Choosing m-node, however, both reduces connectivity issues locally during link failure and prevents name resolution over the WAN link (via WINS) for local resources.

Browser Service

The browsing facility collects, views, and distributes a list of all available domains and servers. The server process running on workstations and servers releases a subnet broadcast message (for example, *announce packet*) received by each subnet's master browser (MB). The MBs report their browse lists to the Domain Master Browser on the domain's PDC, which consolidates all the MB lists and returns new items to each MB. Thus each MB maintains a complete browse list for its network and domain. Since the browser system provides only a list of server names, a name-to-address resolution system is still required.

The browser is designed to speed query resolution and to provide a cache from which to fill the list boxes from network browsing utilities such as Server Manager. Without the browsing system, computers can still be accessed by manually entering a computer name in the drop-down list box of most utilities. The name-to-IP address resolution is then handled in the normal manner (WINS, etc.).

Viewing available network resources is known as browsing. When a user selects "Connect Network Drive" from File Manager, the File Manager code requests a list of available network resources from an available browser server. Any computer running the browser service (Windows NT, Windows for Workgroups, etc.) can be a browser server. A non-browser server periodically announces itself to the MB, with a directed mailslot write to <DOMAIN><1D>. Initially, each non-browser announces itself every minute; as the server runs, the announcement time extends to 12 minutes.

There are five defined types of browser servers.

Potential Browser Server

These represent the vast majority of browser servers. They can be promoted to either backup browser (by the local MB) or master browser status, but by default they remain dormant in the domain.

Backup Browser

Backup browser servers maintain a list of servers retrieved from the MB server, calling the MB every 12 minutes to get the latest browse and domain lists and forcing an election if they cannot find the MB. They cache these lists and return the list of servers to any clients that send them a remote *NetServerEnum* application programming interface (API) call.

Local Master Browser

Local master browsers (LMBs) receive server announcements from Windows NT Workstation and Server, Windows for Workgroups, and LAN Manager servers. They also return lists of local subnet backup browsers to clients. When a computer with its *MaintainServerList* parameter set to Auto starts, the LMB tells it whether to become a backup browser.

When a browser server is elected to LMB status and its browse list is empty, it can force all servers to register with it by broadcasting an *AnnouncementRequest* packet. All computers with a server component that receive this packet must answer within a 30-second period that is randomized to prevent flooding the LMB (losing replies) and the network.

LMBs must announce their domain, which they do by broadcasting a *WkGroupAnnouncement* request to <01><02>_MSBROWSE_<02><01>. This announcement contains the domain name and the name of the domain MB.

Preferred Master Browser Server (PMB)

Any browser server can be configured as a preferred master browser (PMB) server. PMBs function as normal backup MBs, but they force a browser election when the browser is started. If conditions are equal, PMBs are given an advantage in elections. This allows administrators to configure several computers as DMBs and to pick a set of computers that can be DMBs.

Domain Master Browser (DMB)

The browser service running on the PDC in a Windows NT Server domain has a special role—domain master browser (DMB). All DMBs register a unique browser name of <DOMAIN><1B> with the WINS server, which uses the name to build a table of all WAN domains. DMBs periodically query the WINS server for a list of the members of <DOMAIN><1B>, using a two-part process: an API call asking for the domain controller on each <DOMAIN><1B> name, followed by an attempt on <DOMAIN><1C>. The returned list contains both the domain names and the associated DMB names.

Each DMB merges this list into its local domain browse list, which it then propagates to the LMBs on each subnet via the normal replication mechanism. If the DMB did not collect, consolidate, and re-distribute browsing information across subnet boundaries, LMBs would contain only the information that they have directly learned from their subnet.

The LMB for each subnet announces itself to the PDC using a directed datagram that identifies the LMB by name. The PDC sends it a *NetServerEnum* API to collect its subnet list of servers.

Browser Implementation

Network Design Issues

The highest ranked potential browser server, as determined by election, serves as the segment's LMB. The DMB on the PDC coordinates the browse lists of the LMBs on each subnet. The LMBs update the backup master browsers (BMBs) on their local subnets. On TCP/IP-based networks, the browsing facility determines the list of devices on a local subnet by using a subnet broadcast datagram requesting a local announcement. If subnet broadcasts on UDP port 138 are forwarded to a remote device (any device not on the local subnet), then that device is included in the list of local subnet devices. If the remote device has a higher browser value than any local device (for example, it's the PDC), then it attempts to become the MB for the local segment even though it does not actually exist on the local segment.

You can detect this situation by looking for excessively long browsing query times and incomplete or incorrect browsing lists. Standard diagnostic tests for improperly sealed subnet boundaries are:

- Check the actual router configuration files for UDP forwarding (or flooding) of subnet broadcasts on UDP ports 137 and 138.

  Cisco systems' routers forward to these ports by default when the DHCP relay agent configuration *ip helper address* option is used. To disable this feature, use the *no ip forward UDP port 137* and *no ip forward UDP port 138* interface commands on every interface on which the *ip helper* command is also applied.
- If you don't know the router configuration or the protocol implementation, you can determine the UDP forwarding state with a protocol trace. Use Network monitor on the workstation, filter a capture for BROWSER protocol packets, and check for *MasterAnnounce* or *GetBackupServer* responses (which are subnet broadcast packets) originating from the PDC (which is not on the local subnet).

Multi-homed Servers

The browser system can be multi-homed as long as the PDC is not multi-homed and parallel to other domain controllers. The PDC has a hard coded preference to win the browser election. If you put the PDC in the position occupied by a BDC, it attempts to be the LMB on every segment and the DMB for the environment. You can use a NetMon trace to see if this is happening: every time a workstation needs the browse list, the trace will show three unanswered requests for the GetBackupServer list, followed by an election request.

Browser Implementation Recommendations

- Reduce the number of potential browser servers on any given subnet by setting the *MaintainServerList* value to **No**. Make sure that devices configured for browser operations are generally available (application servers, etc.).
- Reduce the number of protocols on each workstation. A browser name is registered for each protocol.
- Reduce the number of browser entries by hiding the server service on workstations. Issue the **net config server /hidden: YES** command from a command prompt. The server will stay hidden until the command is re-issued and set to **NO**.

Domain Name Service

Domain Name Service (DNS) and Berkeley Internet Naming Daemon (BIND) are the standard name-to IP-address resolution methods used on the Internet. DNS provides a naming hierarchy based on the concepts of Scope-of-Authority (SOA), zones, domains, and delegation.

Each node in this hierarchy has a DNS that is authoritative for its zone. This primary DNS is known as a primary master. A zone contains all devices that are directly defined under that DNS server's SOA. All zones under a node constitute its domain. For example, on the Internet, *Microsoft* is a member of the *com* domain.

Delegation of authority allows nodes below a particular node be authoritative for their zone. The "Microsoft" DNS is authoritative for all nodes below it. The "Microsoft" domain administrator registers its name and addresses with the administrator of the "com" domain. The administrator of the ".com" DNS places a pointer to the "Microsoft" domain in its database and the administrator of the "Microsoft" domain places a pointing record to the ".com" domain in its database.

When someone in "microsoft.com" requests service from a device in "ds.internic.net" (for example, FTP an RFC), they send a DNS query to their defined DNS server, which makes a query on behalf of the requesting workstation to the "com" DNS which refers the local DNS to the address of the "root." The local DNS server then queries "root," which refers to the address of "net" and so on. In practice, the resolution process is more direct since many of these addresses are cached.

There are two types of queries:

- The called DNS server returns a reference to another DNS ("I don't know, but I know someone who does").
- The called DNS server makes the referral query on behalf on the calling DNS ("I don't know, but I'll forward your query to someone who does")

The DNS database is basically two flat files, one containing the names-to-address records and the other containing address-to-name records. (There are also some other records such as mail records, alias records, DNS pointers, etc). The DNS administrator creates and maintains these files. For more information on the theory and usage of DNS, see the white paper on **http://www.microsoft.com** called "DNS and Microsoft Windows NT4.0" by Scott B. Suhy and Glen Wood.

The DNS system defines domains and subdomains of host namespace. The master name server is authoritative for the domain. Primary name servers originate source data for the global name service via boot and database files. Secondary name servers obtain copies of the zone information by a file copying process called a *zone transfer*. Name servers can also obtain data from cache entries that are learned from responses to queries forwarded to other name servers.

The DNS system's *primary* records are explained below.

Name Server (NS)

- List of other DNS servers to which queries should be delegated, including name servers that exist both above and below the current DNS tree node (parents and children).
  <domain> IN NS <nameserver>
  Example: @ IN NS nameserver1.microsoft.com
- Mail Exchange (MX):
  Pointer to the mail server.
  <domain> IN MX <preference><mailserver host>
  Example: @ IN MX 1 mailserver1
- Host
  Standard name to address record.
  <host> IN A <ip address>
  Example: rhino IN A 157.55.200.43
- Canonical Name or Alias (CNAME):
  The CNAME allows the DNS administrator to alias a hostname.
  <host name> IN CNAME <host name>
  Example: ftp CNAME fileserver2
- Pointer Record (PTR)
  Static map of IP addresses to host name within the reverse lookup file.
  <address in reverse order>in-addr.arpa IN PTR <host name>
  e.g. 51.200.55.157.in-addr.arpa IN PTR mailserver1.microsoft.com

1. WINS:
   Static map to a WINS server to which WINS NetBIOS names queries should be delegated.
   <domain> IN WINS <IP address of WINS server>
   Example: @ IN WINS 157.55.200.81
2. WINS Reverse lookup (WINS-R):
   Static map to a WINS server for reverse address to name resolution.
   <domain> IN WINS-R <domain to append to returned NetNBIOS Name>
   Example: @ IN WINS-R microsoft.com

Integration of the DNS and WINS

The DNS can be configured with a special $WINS directive that instructs it to pass through WINS server queries for names that can't be found in the DNS database. The algorithm for passing through queries is:

DNS attempts to resolve the name to an IP address using standard DNS records.

If that fails, the domain suffix is stripped off, and a NetBIOS name is formed by space padding the hostname and appending 0x00 as the 16th character. The WINS server configured for the host running the DNS software is then sent a standard NetBIOS name query for that name.

The WINS server returns a Name Query Response, and if it was successful the DNS returns a standard DNS response to the original client using the information obtained from WINS.

Here is an example:

1. Host "A" sends a DNS query for beetle.microsoft.com to the DNS. The DNS checks its records and finds no match.
2. The DNS sends a NetBIOS Name Query to its WINS server for "BEETLE<00>" (BEETLE followed by 9 spaces and hex 00).
3. The WINS server locates the (dynamically registered) IP address for BEETLE and returns it to the DNS in a NetBIOS Name Query Response.
4. The DNS returns the resource record to Host "A" as a DNS response.

The WINS name service is dynamic, which allows it to extend the DNS and provide relief from some of the manual labor normally associated with DNS administration.

Q&A: Name Service

Why use WINS when DNS is available?

First, when DHCP is used, the relationship between the host name and the underlying IP address can change at any time. Second, the Microsoft networking facility currently registers more than just host names for resource location in the name server: user names (used by the messenger service), domain names (which are mapped to a group ID containing all of the DCs). WINS is the recommended NetBIOS Name Service.

Domain Architecture Planning

Domain architecture planning is more than simply choosing a domain structure—it is defining a framework in which to implement complex distributed computing. It involves balancing distributed data storage and bandwidth, control and flexibility, and security and openness. Some basic information must be available to various systems (network addresses, names, user IDs, etc.) so the designer must decide whether the information should be consolidated, which increases remote bandwidth requirements, or distributed, which increases remote resource utilization and administration of data replication. The primary factors influencing the domain design are:

- Business model (user activity profile and network administration)
- processing load
- Processing capacity

Domain Processing Overview

People often get tied up in the Windows NT domain planning and excessively complicate the process. The Windows NT domain system is merely a distributed transactional database that happens to store and distribute security information. It performs two basic functions: distributed transactional authentication, and single-master database replication. This database (like every distributed database) has several engineering parameters:

- CPU: Cryptographic algorithms are numerically intensive
- CPU: Compression algorithms are numerically intensive
- Storage requirements: How much disk space?
- Memory Requirements: How big is the working set?
- Transaction load: authentication/sec, database updates
- Replication: How much data to how many systems?

Authentication Modeling

If everyone in a 20,000-user "enterprise" logs on in a 30 minute period, and the requests are fairly evenly distributed, the network load generated is approximately 11 logons/sec, 220 Kb/sec. (no profiles, single-master domain). Network I/O determines the latency of the challenge-response process, packet acknowledgments, and SID return sets, and network latency affects not only the arrival rate but the holding time as well.

SAM Replication Modeling

The Windows NT domain system is a replicated single-master database (single master in database terms, one authoritative source with one or more read-only replicas). The resource load generated by domain replication is characterized by:

- Single-master database hierarchy
- Non-partitioned database—full replicas in each system
- Both full and record-wise partial replication
- Configurable number of simultaneous replication processes

- Configurable available bandwidth throttling
- Max additions during original system load
- Max changes on Mondays (or after holiday weekend)

SAM replication is driven by two factors. The frequency of periodic data refresh (which is controlled by the configured user account expiration interval and the 7-day machine account expiration interval) and administrative actions (such as user/machine account additions/subtractions/modifications, and manually ordered replications).

Basic capacity modeling requires determining the size of the full SAM (plus an engineering "pad"), then calculating the time required to complete full replication to all BDCs with varying available bandwidth and varying concurrent replication partners. If the replication can be completed in the administrative window available for SAM replication, then the normal partial replication should occur without difficulty.

For example, if you have calculated (or measured) a 20-MB SAM and you assume 56 Kbps to 200 field offices taken 10 at a time:

((20,000 KB x 1.2 (overhead) x 8 bits/byte)/56 Kbps)/60 sec/min = 57 min or ~1 hr/10 offices ~ 20 hours

Physical transmission requirements for a 20 MB file replication.

SAM Size	Link Speed	Offices	Concurrent	Time
20 MB	56 Kb	200	10	20 hrs
20 MB	128 Kb	200	10	8.3 hrs
20 MB	56 Kb	200	20	10 hrs
20 MB	128 Kb	200	20	4.2 hrs

This displays the physical transmission requirements for any 20-MB full file replication. The time column indicates that you should avoid domain replication during the heaviest transaction period, and schedule it around the heaviest loading periods for authentication and business traffic.

Startup Traffic

Both workstation and servers generate startup traffic. This basic process can be viewed by focussing on workstation startup traffic, assuming that servers tend to remain on and that there are significantly fewer servers than workstations. When a workstation first starts up, it must initiate a series of actions to join the network community. If the network uses DHCP, the workstation must obtain or confirm an IP lease from a DHCP server. Then it must register its NetBIOS names with the network (each share and service requires a NetBIOS name registration). Once the workstation is registered with the network, it begins a NetLogon sequence that enables the user to register with a domain server.

The startup process involves two separate logons, one between the workstation and its resource domain controller, and the other between the user and the authentication domain (in a single domain the resource and the authentication domains are the same). When the workstation's NetLogon process starts, it discovers the domain controller, establishes the secure channel, and performs a NULL user logon (~12KB). When the user performs an interactive logon (Ctrl-ALT-DEL prompt), the user credentials are passed to the authentication domain along this secure channel (~3KB).

This much of the process generates workstation traffic between 15,000 and 20,000 bytes (depending on certain factors such as number of permanent connections, shares, etc.).

Amount of traffic for service during startup.

Service	Generated Traffic
DHCP	3084 bytes
Name registrations	856 bytes
Browser announcements	2000 bytes
Null user logon (wrkstn)	6637 bytes
User logon	3000 bytes
Permanent drive map	1634 bytes per drive

This number is affected by the number of shares on the workstation, the number of permanent connections (shares) that the workstation must establish, the number of protocols running on the workstation, and whether the workstation participates in browsing. If users are configured to use server-based, non-cached profiles, then additional network resources are required to transfer the profiles at startup. If the workstation runs more than one protocol, more time is required because NetBIOS names need to be registered with each running protocol.

Various combinations of services can be divided between local and remote servers. For example:

Single Domain with no local BDC:

- All startup traffic traverses the WAN.

Single Domain with local BDC:

- All startup traffic is local but complete domain SAM must be replicated to the local BDC. The replication traffic can be minimal with partial replication and low user account volatility.

Master Domain with local resource controller:

- 15 K of the startup traffic remains local, 3 K traverses the WAN. The resource domain replication traffic is minimal if the computer account base is stable.

Planning the Network

Before planning the network, you need to account for the expected business traffic and the peak operating loads, and to keep in mind that the bottleneck is the available capacity of the slowest link in the path. If analysis shows that the maximum throughput of the network for business traffic will be 32 Kb/sec., and the network will be implemented using 56 Kbps lines, then you have about 24 Kbps of bandwidth available during business hours. Of course, at times when the network is not busy (evenings, weekends, holidays), you can use the entire bandwidth for maintenance work. It's a good idea to plan major migrations, updates, and modifications during these off-peak hours.

Case Study Domain Model

Shinozaki designed its domain model with centralized administration. Though user account domain controllers are in the branch offices, most domain controllers are at headquarters, with the exception of one domain controller at each of the regional warehouses. It is a relatively large enterprise but it can still be designed into a single user account domain.

More Information

- *Microsoft Windows NT Server 4.0 Enterprise Technologies Training.* by Microsoft Press. ISBN 1-57231-710-8.
- *Enterprise Networking,* by Daniel Minoli. ISBN 0-89006-621-3.
- *The Simple Book,* by Marshall T. Rose. ISBN 0-13-451659-1.
- *DNS and BIND,* by Paul Albitz and Cricket Liu. ISBN 1-56592-236-0.
- *How to Manage Your Network Using SNMP,* by Marshall T. Rose and Keith McCloghrie.
- *The Basics Book of Frame Relay,* by Motorola Press University. ISBN 0-201-56377-0.
- *The Open Book,* by Marshall T. Rose. ISBN 0-13-643016-3.
- *TCP/IP Explained,* by Phillip Miller. ISBN 1-55558-166-8.
- RFC 1001 and RFC 1002: Protocol Standard for a NetBIOS Service on a TCP/UDP Transport.
- RFC 1541: Dynamic Host Configuration Protocol.

CHAPTER 8

Software Distribution over Slow Links at Macadam & Grabbo Consulting

By Nigel Cain, MCS—United Kingdom

Sending updates to client software is the most network-intensive task you can perform with Systems Management Server. Initially, most organizations make little use of this feature; new client workstations tend to come pre-installed with the corporate desktop and applications software. There's little need to use software distribution other than to update anti-virus software and corporate data files. But inevitably there comes a time when you have an installed base of client workstations and need to install a new application or perform a software upgrade.

In Focus

Enterprise
Macadam & Gabbro Consulting, an international firm specializing in IT growth and management. Its dynamic consulting force is often on the road, traveling worldwide.

Network
Corporate headquarters in London, 24 branch offices throughout Europe, North America and Asia that support their own Windows NT domains, and over 11,000 mobile users who connect remotely.

Challenge
Distributing application software and updates to client workstations over the wide area network (WAN) and slow links.

Solution
You can use Microsoft Systems Management Server to manage and schedule package distribution over the network.

What You'll Find In This Chapter

- **Review of how SMS distributes software between sites.**
- **Tips for using management information format (MIF) files.**
- **How to use Package Launcher effectively over slow links.**
- **How to allow users to defer mandatory installations.**
- **Descriptions of code samples included on the sample Microsoft TechNet CD along with a package launcher application.**

Warning This chapter makes recommendations for tuning the Windows NT registry using the Registry Editor. Using the Registry Editor incorrectly can cause serious, system-wide problems that require you to reinstall Windows NT. Microsoft cannot guarantee that any problems resulting from the use of Registry Editor can be solved. Use this tool at your own risk.

Quick Overview

To help you get the best from Systems Management Server, this chapter looks at how software is distributed between sites and within a site, how you can improve status reporting, and how to manage client workstations connected over a dial-in (remote access) line. Before looking at the process in depth, it's worth reviewing how a software package moves from the site server to the distribution points and then onwards to the client workstations. This circled numbers in Figure 8.1 are explained on the next page.

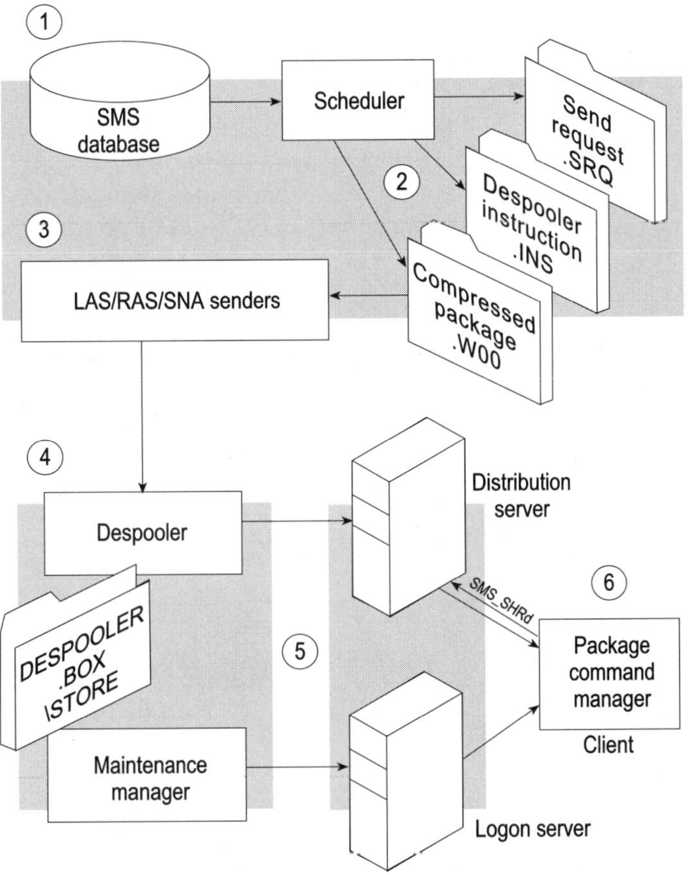

Figure 8.1 A software package moves from the site server to client workstations.

The first step is to create the workstation *package* and *job* using the SMS Administrator UI (1). Once you have done this, the **Scheduler** creates the *package*, *instruction*, and *send* request files, and compresses the package source directories (2). The compressed files and instructions are then sent to the target sites (3). When the package reaches the target site, the **Despooler** decompresses the source files and instructions (4). The source files and package instructions are put on the distribution servers and then on the logon servers (5). Finally (6) Package Command Manager (PCM) on the client reads the instructions from the Logon server, creating a list of packages to install. When the user executes a job, PCM connects to a distribution server and executes the command line.

Package Transfer Between Sites

Typically, you want to ensure that users aren't going to be affected by administrators distributing software during working hours. The two main ways of achieving this are to use Sender Manager to limit the network bandwidth used, and use outbox scheduling to restrict the types or priority of jobs that can be sent during business hours.

In the example below, the point is to ensure that only high-priority jobs can be sent during core business hours, medium during the rest of the business day, and low priority jobs at all other times. You also need to make sure that normal business activities can take place uninterrupted, so you must restrict the network bandwidth available to SMS.

Network bandwidth restriction at Macadam & Grabbo Consulting.

Time	Mon – Friday	Sat – Sun	Max Transfer rate (% of bandwidth)
00:00 – 08:00	**Low**	**Low**	**80**
08:00 – 10:00	**Disabled**	**Medium**	**40**
10:00 – 18:00	**High**	**Medium**	**40**
18:00 – 20:00	**Medium**	**Low**	**40**
20:00 – 00:00	**Low**	**Low**	**80**

During peak periods (08:00 – 10:00) you want to make sure that it's not possible for any software distribution tasks to be carried out, because this could affect users who are trying to logon and gain access to their applications. You can achieve this by closing (disabling) the senders.

Sender Manager

You can use the Sender Manager application to define the total number of concurrent connections that can be opened at any one time, the maximum number of concurrent connections to a single site, and the percentage of bandwidth that can be utilized. All of these settings can be specified on an hour-by-hour basis throughout the day. In the example below, the idea is to limit the bandwidth to 40% during the business day and 80% at all other times.

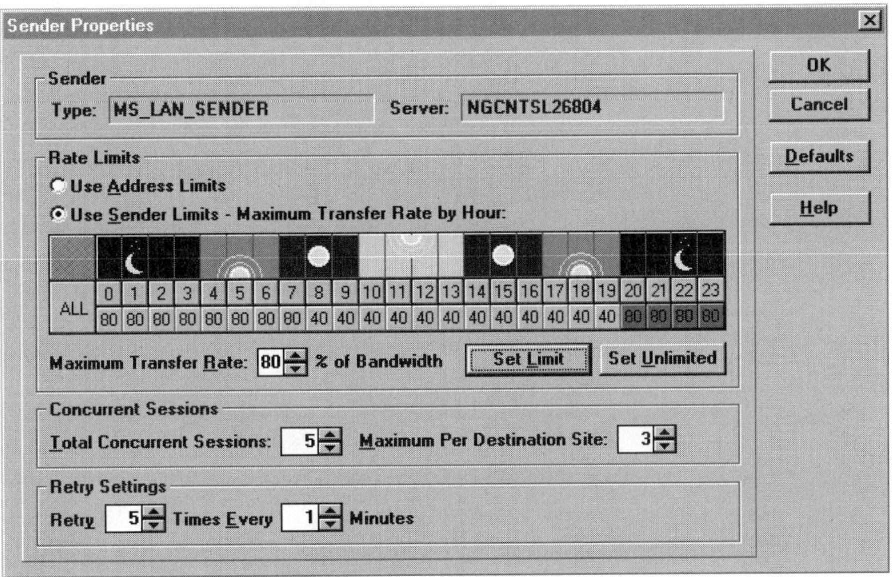

Figure 3.2 Using Sender Manager to control bandwidth use during certain periods.

In the above dialog, the bandwidth restrictions have been placed on the site address. This makes sure that no matter how many senders you configure to communicate with the site, bandwidth use won't exceed the specified limit. If necessary, you can configure different restrictions and line speeds for each type of sender.

Outbox Scheduling

You can use outbox scheduling to control job priority for each site sender. The ideal situation is to send out only small business-critical files during business hours, saving software applications and upgrades processing for when the network is quiet. Of course, there are always going to be times when you need to distribute a large application or set of business files during the working day. All you need to do in this case is set the job as high priority or temporarily lift the outbox restriction for that sender. You may also have to lift the bandwidth restriction (with Sender Manager) or file distribution could take too much time.

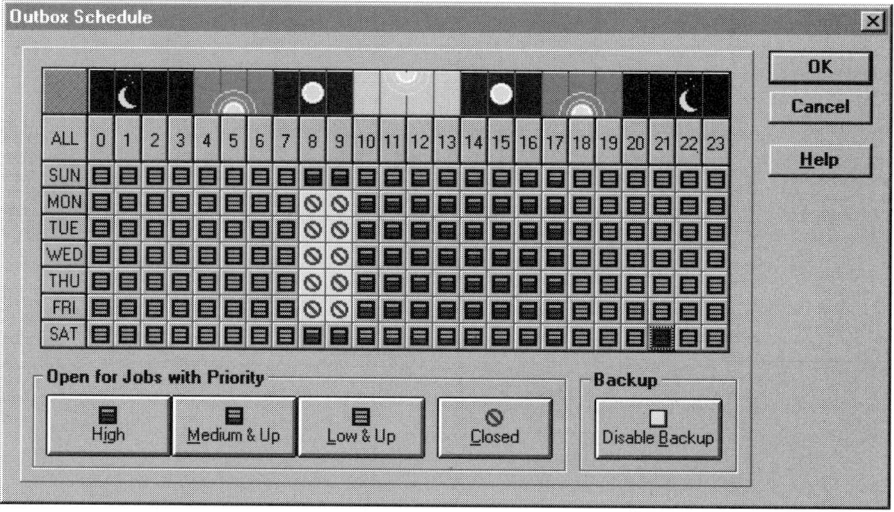

Figure 8.3 Outbox Scheduler window.

Figure 8.3 shows the Outbox Schedule dialog for the MS_LAN_SENDER as per the table above. The sender is closed during peak business hours, so no software distribution can take place. The Disable Backup option has also been set for peak periods. This option prevents SMS from overriding priority restrictions when other senders to that site are busy or closed.

Compression Algorithm

To minimize the time needed to send a package from one site to another, SMS compresses the source files before sending them. A number of different compression algorithms are available. The default offers minimal compression, but it also creates minimal CPU overhead and this can prove useful at busy site servers. To change the compression algorithm, you need to change the following registry key:

**HKEY_LOCAL_MACHINE\SOFTWARE\Microsoft\SMS\Compression\
"Compression Level" (DWORD)**

The compression setting ranges from 1 to 7 but there may be a considerable performance impact as you increase compression from the default. You may also see only a minimal reduction in file size from one setting to another. To work out the best compromise between file compression and processor overhead in your environment, you need to perform a number of tests with different compression ratios and file sizes. The Network Monitor and Performance Monitor tools should help with this. You must tune this setting on each site server because physical hardware, site services and installed systems software may be different.

It is also interesting to note that file compression is used only *between* SMS site servers. This is based on the assumption that within most sites there is sufficient network bandwidth to transmit uncompressed files without affecting performance significantly.

Distribution in a Complex Environment

When creating software distribution jobs, administrators commonly create the package at the central site and send it out to all sub-sites in the hierarchy. Initially, this seems the right thing to do; indeed SMS encourages this way of thinking by leaving the **Limit to Sites** checkbox unselected.

The problem with this approach is that it causes the central site server to act like a distribution hub, sending a full copy of the compressed source files to each SMS site in turn, taking no account of the structure or hierarchy you've designed. The central site server can become exceptionally busy during this time, especially in a large environment, and there are also considerable implications for both LAN and WAN performance. Remember, you can set limitations on the bandwidth and restrict the type (priority) of job that can be sent during the day. These limitations, combined with the way SMS uses the central site as a distribution hub, may mean that it takes considerably longer to distribute files than you might think.

There is an alternative for complex SMS hierarchies (that is, more than two layers). Instead of sending the job to all sites in the hierarchy (default), send it to the sites immediately (one layer) below the central site server. Then use the primary site servers at this level to send the package to those at layer two and so on though the structure. The fan-out distribution method, though requiring manual intervention, has the dual benefit of reducing network traffic and improving performance at the central site. It is also similar to the automatic fan-out distribution method used in the next version of SMS.

(See Chapter 2 in the companion book *Managing a Microsoft Windows NT Network* for a case study on Systems Management Server infrastructure deployment.)

Package Transfer Between Sites

Once the site server has successfully received and uncompressed the package source files, it updates the local distribution servers. Systems Management Server doesn't make use of sender technology within a site because it assumes that network links between a site server and any distribution servers are fast and reliable. You cannot control the network bandwidth used at this point or schedule the priority of distribution tasks. As mentioned earlier, the source files are uncompressed before transmission within a site, and you should make every effort to keep distribution servers as close to the site server as possible. If you have to place a distribution server across a slow WAN link, consider using an SMS secondary site instead.

Installation at the Workstation

In an ideal world, you could distribute a software application using SMS, and all client workstations would install it at the same time. In the real world, if you send a job to all clients within an organization the effect on the network and site services can be catastrophic.

It's far better to group client workstations together into more manageable numbers, either by department or physical location. The ideal number of workstations in a group really depends on the available network bandwidth, physical network topology, number of distribution points and, most importantly, the number of support staff able to assist with user queries and migration problems. In SMS, you can create a machine group or an SMS query to collect workstations.

Once you've decided on the optimum number of client workstations, the next step is to decide whether the job should be mandatory. Most of the time, you want it to be mandatory because this forces the user to run it. The temptation here is to set the **Mandatory After** field to the present date and time. After all, you have a tight deadline to meet and if you're using groups, this is only a small number of client workstations.

Although this may be true, consider the impact on network performance if a number of users install the application at the same time. Rather than forcing users to run the job, it may be far better to allow them a grace period during which they can choose to run it. Some installation tasks, of course, require special workstation privileges or considerable network bandwidth per client. Where possible, create these as system (background) tasks and schedule them to run when the network is quiet. If client workstations can be left switched on overnight, it helps significantly.

What Does SMS 1.2 Provide Out of the Box?

Installing Software at the Client

So far, a number of ways to improve software distribution with SMS have been discussed, with an emphasis on the need to minimize network traffic when possible. It should be possible to target software upgrades so they reach only the workstations that really need them, and to provide a service to remote (dial-in) clients that enables them to defer an installation whenever they're connected over a slow link. The next section looks at how to achieve this using status management information format (MIF) files and a custom written launcher program.

Software Upgrades

To apply a software upgrade, you need to find out which machines are running previous version(s) of the application. In SMS, you can write a query to retrieve the information you need, but first you must find some way of recording it in the database. Out of the box, you can use the Software Inventory and Software Auditing tools to do this. The two methods work in a similar manner, scanning the hard disk for files (and file properties) that uniquely identify a particular software application. Software Auditing is normally run less frequently than Software Inventory because it takes considerably longer to run at the client workstation, although it does enable you to scan for a number of applications at the same time.

Typically, however, you want to know more about an installation than these two tools can tell you, especially when you're concerned with the impact software distribution has on your network. If you're aware, for example, of the delay between the time when a software distribution job is created and when it is installed, you can set user and management expectations accordingly.

Software Installation and Slow Network Links

Whenever you create a mandatory job, you set a date after which the package will run whether the user wants it to or not. This works very well in most cases but you don't want to force the job to run when the user is connected by a slow (dial in) link and can take hours to complete. Though a checkbox in the job definition window seems to indicate that you can make the job optional over slow network links, this doesn't actually work effectively and the job executes anyway.

In SMS Service Pack 4, the **Not Mandatory Over Slow Links** checkbox was removed from the job definition window. You can find more information on this in Knowledge Base article Q191317, Title: SMS: "Not Mandatory Over Slow Link" Check Box Has Been Removed.

Improving Package Installation

The solution to both of these problems lies in the use of management information format (MIF) files. Systems Management Server uses these formatted text files to load hardware and software inventory details into the database and to provide detailed status information on each stage of the software distribution process. They can also be used to customize the database to include information about printers, modems, and other items not normally detected by SMS.

As each **Run Package on Workstation** job executes, a status MIF file must be created that contains details about the client workstation, the application being installed, and whether the user is permitted to defer the installation. Creating and maintaining this file is the responsibility of a new program, Package Launcher, run instead of the normal setup executable. If you like, Package Launcher can also prompt the user to defer the installation.

Using Package Launcher

Technique 1: Record Status Information

Assuming that the **Mandatory After** date is set far enough into the future, laptop users will have had plenty of time to install the application while connected to the network. There's little need to offer them the ability to defer the installation after the mandatory date, as most if not all of them will have done so by then. You can also create two separate distribution jobs: one for laptop users and another for office-based workstations that assumes a permanent connection to a fast and reliable network. In these scenarios, the Package Launcher has only to record the date of installation and some details about the software application, before running the setup executable.

To achieve this, place a copy of the Package Launcher program in the application's source directory, together with a configuration file (NEWPKG.INI). The file is used to populate a status MIF and should contain details about the application, its name and version number, together with an intended installation date. In the example below, for Microsoft Office 97, notice how the **Defer Allowed** option has been set to No to prevent the user from delaying the installation.

```
[Package]
PackageName="Microsoft Office 97"
VersionNumber=8.0
InstallBy=01011999
DeferAllowed=No
CommandLine=setup.exe
```

Once the configuration file has been created, use an SMS job to distribute the source files and install the application on the target workstations.

The example below shows the result of using the Package Launcher program to install Microsoft Office 97. Notice that the installation date, time, and the name of the logged on user have also been recorded in the database. You can use the information obtained in this to target future software upgrades, provide a contact name for queries about the installation, and help with management reporting.

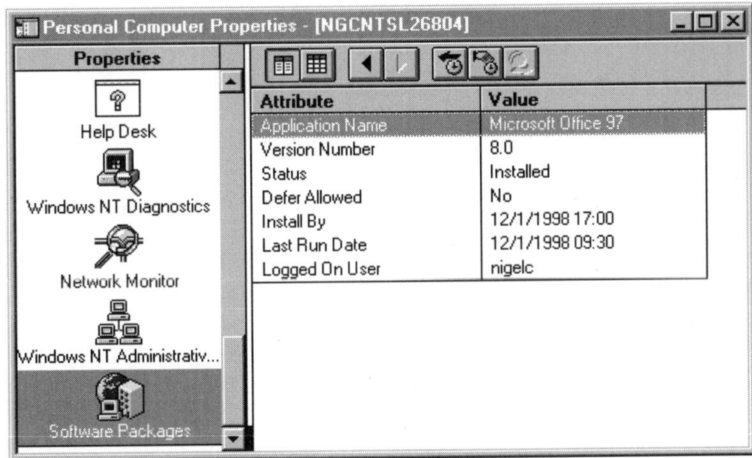

Figure 8.4 Using Package Launcher to install Microsoft Office 97.

You can add as much information to the SMS database as you need by modifying the Package Launcher program. Don't add too much unnecessary detail, or you may have to increase the SMS database's size.

Technique 2: To Defer a Mandatory Job

The **Mandatory After** setting on the job definition dialog allows you to set a date after which a job will run regardless of the user's wishes. These jobs tend to be for updates to systems software and line-of-business-applications, so why would you want to allow the user to postpone the installation?

The answer to this question depends on the systems administrator and the type of software application. In most cases, you want the job to run as quickly as possible so you set the **Mandatory After** field to the present date and time. This makes the job run as soon as the client workstation reads the updated instruction file (*workstation_unique_ID*.INS).

Users may not want this to happen for a number of reasons: they may be running a mission critical application, working on time sensitive data, or (of primary interest in this chapter) be connected over a slow network or remote access link. The current version of SMS, as mentioned previously, doesn't allow you to prevent mandatory jobs executing when the network is slow. If you make Microsoft Office 97 a mandatory job, *all* users, including those on dial-in connections, will be forced to install it.

The tables below provide a rough guide to the length of time needed to download a sample application over different network speeds. The calculations are based on the amount of bits transferred per second and do not take packet headers, footers, compression, or other control information into account. In a real-world situation, there may well be a significant difference between expected and elapsed time.

Time needed to download sample file sizes over network speeds.

		Local Area Network Speed			
		100 Mbit	**16 Mbit**	**10 Mbit**	**4 Mbit**
Job Size	**Size (Bytes)**	**Expected (hh:mm:ss)**	**Expected (hh:mm:ss)**	**Expected (hh:mm:ss)**	**Expected (hh:mm:ss)**
1 Mb	1,048,576	00:00.00	00:00.01	00:00.01	00:00.02
10 Mb	10,485,760	00:00.01	00:00.05	00:00.08	00:00.20
100 Mb	104,857,600	00:00.08	00:00.50	00:01.20	00:03.20

The transfer of files on a local area network happens relatively quickly, as you can see from the table above. Try to transfer the same files across ISDN or normal telephone lines and the picture is very different.

There will be times, of course, when you have to run an SMS job over a slow network link. In these cases you have to tell users how long the operation will take.

Can This be Done in Systems Management Server 1.2?

What is needed is a method of allowing users to delay a mandatory installation for a short time. It must remind them that the job is outstanding, and it must force the job to run when the grace period expires. Systems Management Server assumes that a job is complete once it runs the command line specified in the package definition window. Regardless of whether it ran successfully, what action the user takes as a result, or even if the application was installed, it will not force the user to re-run the job. The Package Launcher program may allow the user to defer the installation, but without additional work nothing more will happen.

The procedure for reminding the user that the installation is still outstanding and, where necessary, forcing the installation, is significantly more complicated than a normal software distribution task. You should consider it only when you have to distribute software upgrades or new applications to mobile (laptop) users.

Put a copy of the Package Launcher program in the application's source directory, together with the configuration file (NEWPKG.INI). Since the idea is to allow users to defer an installation, set **DeferAllowed** to "Yes." The **InstallBy** setting indicates the end of the grace period, after which the job will run regardless of network speed or user wishes. The example below shows a NEWPKG.INI file for Internet Explorer 4.0. Installation can be deferred until December 1. Notice that the date in line 4 is entered in European format (day/month/year).

```
[Package]
PackageName="Microsoft Internet Explorer 4.0"
VersionNumber=4.72.2106.8
InstallBy=01121998
DeferAllowed=Yes
CommandLine=setup.exe
```

Once the configuration file has been created, use an SMS job to distribute the source files and run the Package Launcher on the target workstations. Make the job mandatory after a short time, almost immediately. Assuming that the InstallBy date hasn't been reached, the user can choose to install the application immediately or defer it. In either case, a status MIF file will be created and used to update the database. In the example below, installation of Internet Explorer 4.0 was deferred on November 5 at 9:30 am.

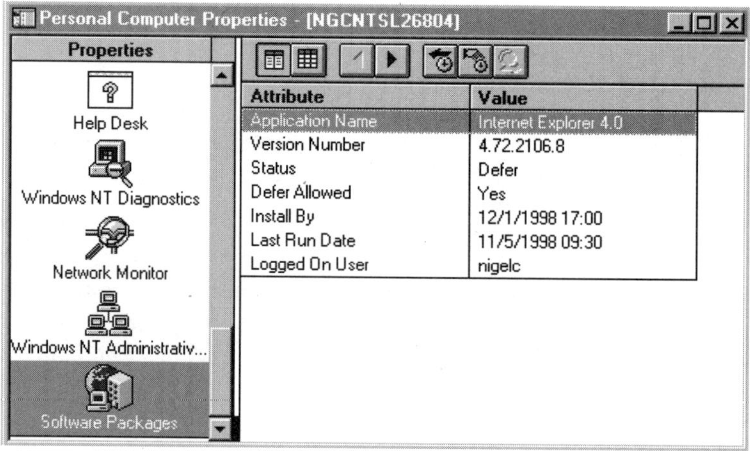

Figure 8.5 Deferral of installation.

Systems Management Server sees the original job as successfully completed; no further action is required. A new job must be created to remind the user that the installation is still outstanding.

This job should run the same package and package command line as the one created previously, but that's where the similarity ends. The new job should be configured to run each day (repeat) and target those workstations where the user deferred installation. You can target workstations by creating an SMS query that looks at the status of the installation, as shown in the example below:

```
MICROSOFT | SOFTWARE_PACKAGES|1.0:Application Name is
'Internet Explorer 4.0'
AND
MICROSOFT | SOFTWARE_PACKAGES|1.0:Status is 'Defer'
```

You should also set the job to *execute only*, by disabling the send and distribute phases, since there's no need for it to send the source files to the SMS site and distribution servers.

As the job repeats each day, the number of records returned by the query cannot be determined. In some cases, the job will fail with SMS error 323 (no records returned). This is no guarantee that all workstations have successfully installed the application. You should allow the repeating job to execute for at least a month; management should decide when to cancel it.

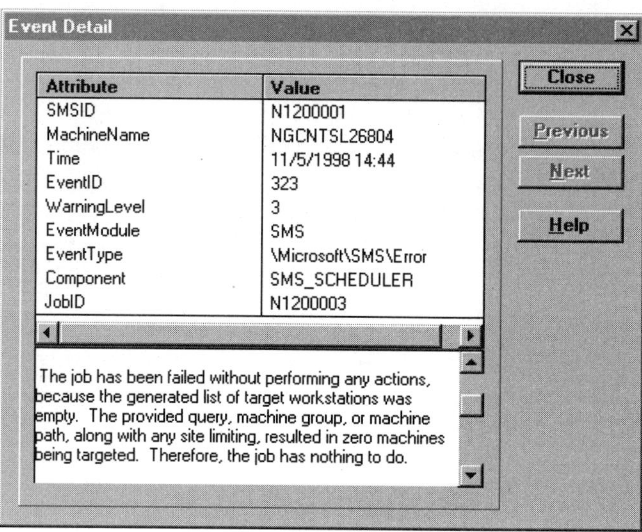

Figure 8.6 Event Detail for a repeating job.

When users defer a package installation and then do not log onto their machine for a significant period of time, a number of SMS jobs may be offered to that client, each for the same software application. To avoid prompting the user with a countdown timer for each mandatory job shown in the PCM window, you should remove the mandatory job countdown timer. A method for doing this is described in Knowledge Base article Q185805, Title: SMS: Disabling The Mandatory Countdown Timer in PCM.

Potential Issues

Job Management

The recurring nature of this solution may complicate your work with the SMS UI. In a large environment there could well be a large number of jobs shown in the job management window. Trying to determine which jobs refer to which application will be difficult unless you complete the job comments field and maintain a log of repeating jobs. You can, however, use a job filter to restrict the display so that only certain types of jobs are shown.

Security Rights

To install many software applications, users need more rights to their workstation than administrators would normally grant. The application setup may need to write to the registry, change system files, or perform other changes to the workstation that are not allowed when running in a user context. In many organizations, it's not possible or even desirable to change the level of access.

In order to provide users with the ability to defer the job when connected over a slow network, split the installation into two portions, one of which runs in a user context (requiring few system rights) and the other in an administrator context. The latter should be relatively small, consisting of registry changes and amendments to system files and should run as a mandatory system (background) task which executes regardless of network link speed. The user portion, which can be deferred, should be distributed to client workstations once the system portion has been installed successfully.

Package Command Manager Service

On Windows NT clients, the Package Command Manager service is often used to run SMS jobs in the background. These jobs typically run under the security context of an administrator account and have little (or no) way of interacting with the logged-on user. In these cases, you can't offer the user the option to defer—the job will run regardless of user preference or network speed. By amending the Package Launcher program so that it detects a remote access or slow network link, you may be able to defer installation automatically. This approach would help in organizations where workstation users are unable to install software due to security restrictions.

Package Launcher

The Package Launcher can be an SMS installer script, Visual Basic, or Visual C++ program that runs instead of the setup executable. Its purpose is to provide the user with an option to defer installation, if the administrator allows this to happen, and to record status information for management reports. The following flowchart shows the processing logic in overview.

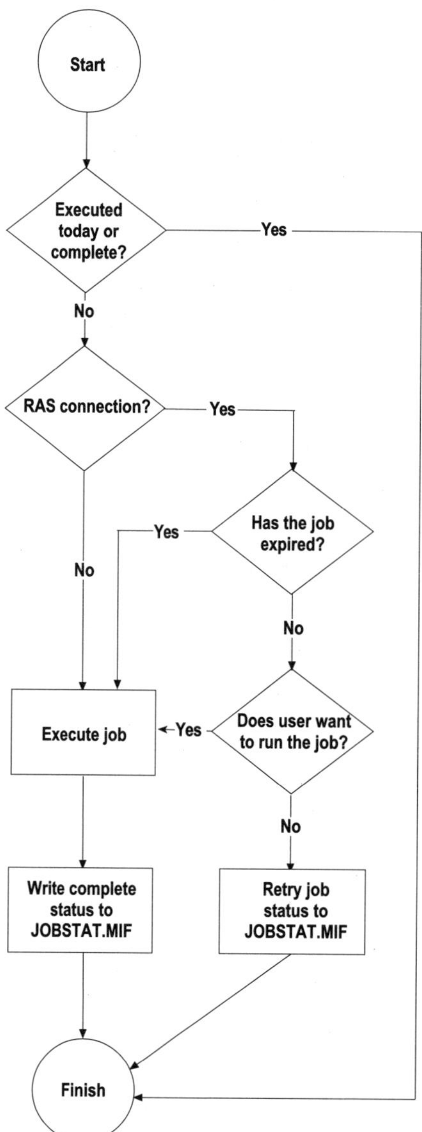

Figure 8.7 Package Launcher processing logic overview.

The next section presents a more detailed look at the package launcher from a programming perspective. You can use this with the flowchart and the code samples provided on the sample TechNet CD in the back of this book (in the \SMSPackage folder) to develop a program more suited to your environment. Read the file "SMS Package.installer.doc" for information on how to set up the utility.

Read SMS.INI and Extract Required Entries

The SMS.INI file is present on all SMS v1.2 client workstations. It contains basic configuration information and specifies file locations for installed client components such as remote tools and package command manager. Package Launcher should use this file to build the identification part of an IDMIF file. There is an example SMS.INI file on page 363.

Read INSTPKG.MIF file from C:\MS\SMS\IDMIFS Directory (If It Exists)

The package launcher creates a new entry in this file for each application. It should be used to determine the status of the installation and record how many days the user has left before the installation becomes mandatory. There is an example INSTPKKG.MIF file on page 365.

Read NEWPKG.INI file from Package Source Directory

This file is created by the administrator and is used to specify the application's name, its version number, and whether the user has the option to defer installation.

Has the Application Been Installed or Has the User Deferred Installation Already Today?

As mentioned above, the INSTPKG.MIF should be used as a reference point. If the application status field indicates that the application has already been installed, then the program has nothing to do and should close. It should also close if the user ran the package earlier in the day and decided to defer the installation. In this case, the **Status** field will be set to Defer and the **Last Run Date** to today.

IF This is the First Time the Package has been Run (No Entries in INSTPKG.MIF)

A new record should be added to INSTPKG.MIF based on the information supplied in NEWPKG.INI. If users have the option to defer the installation, then a dialog should be displayed allowing them to do so. If they decide to install or aren't allowed to defer installation, then the Package Launcher should run the command line specified in NEWPKG.INI.

OTHERWISE Install Status is Set to "Defer" and Installation is Still Pending

The **InstallBy** setting in the NEWPKG.INI file indicates when the installation should become compulsory, regardless of network link speed. The Package Launcher needs to check this date to determine whether installation should proceed without prompting the user. If users still have time available, then a dialog should be displayed which allows them to defer installation if they wish to do so.

Update Installed Package File

The INSTPKG.MIF file will need to be updated with details from SMS.INI and new information from the installation process. Once this has been done, the file should be written back to the C:\MS\SMS\IDMIFS folder where it will be read during the next inventory cycle. Inventory may run only once every seven days, so you need to use a different method of getting the information into the SMS database.

Place a copy of the updated file in the IDMIF folder on the logon server *<Logon Server Name>*\SMS_SHR\ISVMIF. Systems Management Server checks this directory at intervals controlled through the site's service response setting.

Error Handling

All errors encountered by the Package Launcher, such as missing or invalid configuration files, should be written to a log file in the C:\MS\SMS\LOGS directory. For Windows NT, an entry should also be made in the Windows NT event log.

SMS.INI file

This file is created automatically by SMS 1.2 whenever a client is installed, and updated whenever the user logs onto the network and runs the RUNSMS.BAT or SMSLS.BAT batch files. The entries of interest to the Package Launcher are shown in **bold** in the extract below. These entries are used to form the identification section of the INSTPKG.MIF file.

[SMS]
SMS Unique ID=L1200001
[Servers]
Domain=REDMOND
[Local]
NetCardID=00:80:C7:15:C7:99
MachineName=NGCNTSL26804
SystemRole=Server
SystemType=X86-based PC

[LogonHistory]
LastLoggedUser=nigelc

Occasionally, the LogonHistory section will be missing and the Package Launcher will need to perform an API call to determine the name of the currently logged-on user.

NEWPKG.INI file

This file should be distributed with any new software application. It provides the name of the software, the version number, and whether the administrator will allow the user to defer the installation. It also defines the point at which the installation will become compulsory and the command line (and parameters) needed to start the application's setup program. Notice that the date in line 4 is entered in European format (day/month/year).

[Package]
PackageName="Microsoft Internet Explorer 4.0"
VersionNumber=4.72.2106.8
InstallBy=01121998
DeferAllowed=Yes
CommandLine=setup.exe

INSTPKG.MIF file

Whenever the Package Launcher executes, it first checks the INSTPKG.MIF file to determine whether the application has already been installed (or installation was deferred), then, later during the process, updates it with new information. A copy of the file should be created or updated (if it exists) in the C:\MS\SMS\IDMIF directory and a second copy placed in the logon server's \SMS_SHR\ISVMIF folder. This file should be called SMSID.MIF, which refers to the machine unique identifier in the SMS.INI file. In this example, the file is called L1200001.MIF

The attributes in the **workstation** component can all be obtained or derived from the information in the SMS.INI file.

```
Start Component
Name = "Workstation"
      Start Group
            Name = "Identification"
            ID = 1
            Class = "MICROSOFT|IDENTIFICATION|1.0"
            Key = 1,3,2
            Start Attribute
                  Name = "SMSID"
                  ID = 1
                  Access = READ-ONLY
                  Storage = SPECIFIC
                  Type = String(8)
                  Value = "N1200001"
            End Attribute
            Start Attribute
                  Name = "Name"
                  ID = 2
                  Access = READ-ONLY
                  Storage = SPECIFIC
                  Type = String(64)
                  Value = "NGCNTSL26804"
            End Attribute
```

```
Start Attribute
      Name = "NetCardID"
      ID = 3
      Access = READ-ONLY
      Storage = SPECIFIC
      Type = String(18)
      Value = "00:80:C7:15:C7:99"
End Attribute
Start Attribute
      Name = "Domain"
      ID = 4
      Access = READ-ONLY
      Storage = SPECIFIC
      Type = String(16)
      Value = "REDMOND"
End Attribute
Start Attribute
      Name = "Site"
      ID = 5
      Access = READ-ONLY
      Storage = SPECIFIC
      Type = String(3)
      Value = "N12"
End Attribute
Start Attribute
      Name = "SMSLocation"
      ID = 6
      Access = READ-ONLY
      Storage = SPECIFIC
      Type = String(64)
      Value = "N12|REDMOND|NGCNTSL26804"
End Attribute
```

```
            Start Attribute
                  Name = "SystemRole"
                  ID = 7
                  Access = READ-ONLY
                  Storage = SPECIFIC
                  Type = String(12)
                  Value = "Server"
            End Attribute
            Start Attribute
                  Name = "SystemType"
                  ID = 8
                  Access = READ-ONLY
                  Storage = SPECIFIC
                  Type = String(32)
                  Value = "X86-based PC"
            End Attribute
            Start Attribute
                  Name = "LogOn Name"
                  ID = 9
                  Access = READ-ONLY
                  Storage = SPECIFIC
                  Type = String(48)
                  Value = "nigelc"
            End Attribute
      End Group
      Start Group
            Name = "Architecture"
            ID = 2
            Class = "MICROSOFT|ARCHITECTURE|1.0"
            Start Attribute
                  Name = "ArchitectureName"
                  ID = 1
                  Access = READ-ONLY
                  Storage = SPECIFIC
                  Type = String(18)
                  Value = "Personal Computer"
            End Attribute
      End Group
```

```
Start Group
      Name = "Software Packages"
      Class = "MICROSOFT|SOFTWARE_PACKAGES|1.0"
      Key = 1
      Start Attribute
            Name = "Application Name"
            ID = 1
            Storage = COMMON
            Type = String(30)
            Value = "Internet Explorer 4.0"
      End Attribute
      Start Attribute
            Name = "Version Number"
            ID = 2
            Storage = COMMON
            Type = String(20)
            Value = "4.72.2106.8"
      End Attribute
      Start Attribute
            Name = "Status"
            ID = 3
            Type = String(16)
            Value = "Defer"
      End Attribute
      Start Attribute
            Name = "Defer Allowed"
            ID = 4
            Type = String(3)
            Value = "Yes"
      End Attribute
      Start Attribute
            Name = "Install By"
            ID = 5
            Type = Date
            Value = "19981201170000.000000-000"
      End Attribute
```

```
            Start Attribute
                  Name = "Last Run Date"
                  ID = 6
                  Type = Date
                  Value = "19981105093000.000000-000"
            End Attribute
            Start Attribute
                  Name = "Logged On User"
                  ID = 7
                  Type = String(20)
                  Value = "nigelc"
            End Attribute
      End Group
      Start Table
            Name = "Software Package List"
            Class = "MICROSOFT|SOFTWARE_PACKAGES|1.0"
            ID = 51
            {"Microsoft Office 97", "8.0", "Installed", "No",
"19981201170000.000000-000", "19981201093015.000000-000",
"nigelc"}
      End Table
      End Component
```

This file's format differs somewhat from the standards defined in the DMI45 document supplied on the SMS CD. While the table format is supported and used to generate one record per software application, a value must be supplied for each attribute definition in the **template** or SMS rejects the MIF file. This means that the first software application installed must be used as the template default values (indicated in bold); subsequent applications appear as rows in the **table**.

Each table instance, (for example, Internet Explorer 4.0) should appear on a single line—the example above has been wrapped for readability.

More Information

Refer to these Microsoft Knowledge Base articles for more information:

- Q191317, Title: SMS: "Not Mandatory Over Slow Link" Check Box Has Been Removed.
- Q185805, Title: SMS: Disabling the Mandatory Countdown Timer in PCM.
- Q191441, Title: Systems Management Server 1.2 Service Pack 4 Fixlist.

CHAPTER 9

Application Profiling—A Microsoft Network Perspective

Alexander Levin, Microsoft Information Technology Group—Network and Systems Analysis

The study of applications as network components is relatively new among IT professionals, but it is rapidly increasing. One reason for this growth of interest is the significant increase of WAN usage, especially with browser-based applications. Connection to a WAN makes it easier to create large-scale networks, but to what avail if applications perform poorly over them? Another reason is money. Bandwidth can be expensive, and it is important to realize that more bandwidth is not always the only (or even the best) way to improve application performance. This realization, of course, is based on a growing understanding of how applications and networks cooperate and coexist—a profitable knowledge that impels a more systematic study of applications and how they work (or don't work) over networks.

So these ideas have been worked out relatively recently. Meanwhile, down in the trenches, users watch their applications limp along, grind down, or hang up, and their natural inclination is to blame the network, and by extension its architects, for what seems to be bad network design and worse performance. Of course more bandwidth will move things along at an acceptable rate. Anyone knows that. But suppose you spend a lot of dollars to add a lot of throughput only to find that application performance still is unacceptable. *Now* what?

In Focus

Enterprise
An inside view of some network analysis done by Microsoft's Information Technology Group.

Network
This discussion contains a collection of best practices and recommendations derived from studies of the performance of intranet applications put into production on Microsoft's corporate network.

Challenge
Build corporate intranet applications with efficient WAN performance in mind—a design concept that is not difficult to incorporate.

Solution
Improving the performance of a Web-based or Visual Basic application, especially over the wide area network.

What You'll Find In This Chapter

- **Framework for understanding network application communication.**
- **What poor transaction performance over a network looks like.**
- **What network communication looks like for a well-designed application.**
- **Tips on how performance can be enhanced, and other implementation considerations.**

What Exactly *Is* the Problem?

In this context, complaints about an application's performance are really complaints about the performance of a large system consisting of hardware (workstations and servers), software (applications), and internetworking infrastructure. Each component introduces a delay in the response after the user clicks a mouse button then sits back and waits for something to happen.

Performance is not simply a function of the application design, although that can be an important component. And it is not simply a function of network architecture, although it, too, is significant. As with most things, the answer is at once simpler and more complicated. Much of it has to do with the relationship between application and network designs, and some has to do with the simple physical limitations on moving things around.

The Round Trip

So while the user is thumb twiddling, the request initiated by the mouse-click is moving through multiple layers of the operating system doing lots of things. The instruction goes through the network card onto the wire, goes through the hubs, switches, and routers on the way to a destination that can be anywhere in the world. Eventually, the request arrives at that destination computer, which often puts it in the queue for service, processes it after some time, then sends it back across the network to the requestor. This is a simplified explanation of the request-response process but even so it takes you some time to read it: in real life time is likewise spent at every device along the way to the server and back.

To Speed Things Up

If this process simply takes too long, the first step is to upgrade the computer. Now the client's portion of a Visual Basic application (for example—if it is local on the computer) or Internet browser loads faster and the request to the server gets out of the client computer faster. But the target server is far away, somewhere on the WAN, across the country perhaps. A new machine won't speed up the transmission process, nor can you assume that assigning more bandwidth to the network will fix communication latencies. The response still takes a relatively long time.

The frustrated user's next request is to upgrade the network, but this is where jaws start to drop—and well they should because this can be an extremely costly proposition.

A More Detailed Itinerary

Let's follow the request again and see what can be sped up and what can't. After the user's request (a network packet) is sent onto the network it may pass through a shared Ethernet connection, where, if there is high network usage, it may have to wait until a wire is accessed. This is the first delay. The good news is that this is a network problem and networking people can remove or alleviate it by segmenting the network, reducing broadcast levels, removing "chatty" protocols, or introducing a switched environment and assigning each user a switched port.

Once it is on the Ethernet wire the packet can get moving again. If it has been sent out on a large enterprise network, it now has to cross several switches and routers (with possible media changes—between 1514-byte Ethernet packets and 4500-byte FDDI packets, for example) until it reaches the edge router, which connects the LAN to the WAN. Getting to the edge router of course takes time, and how much depends on device performance and network utilization on the wire, but normally this route is traveled quickly because LANs tend to have high bandwidth available.

That's good news, but in such an interconnected environment you can expect a downside even to good news and here it is: LAN speed is much higher than WAN speed, so the packet often is delivered quickly to a place where it has to wait. If the WAN link about to be entered is highly utilized there probably will be a queuing delay on the router. Right here, the five-lane freeway dumps its traffic into a one-lane residential road.

Still, corrective actions are possible. IT specialists can monitor the depth of the queue and the number of discards, and can make adjustments. When a router discards too many packets either it has insufficient performance for its position in the traffic flow or the WAN link on the other side is too slow and just cannot accommodate the required amount of data. These things can be fixed relatively easily, usually with money: installing a more powerful router or upgrading the link, and so on.

Sooner or later, the packet passes through the queue and is placed on the wire. The faster the circuit speed, the quicker the packet gets on the wire. For example, a T1 circuit (1.536 Mbps) takes about 7.8 ms to get a full-size Ethernet packet (1514 bytes) onto the wire. A 512-Kbps circuit, takes about 22.9 ms. (Other factors, such as TCP window size and circuit utilization, influence transmission performance, but they are not in the scope of this chapter.) The time it takes to get the packet onto the wire is significant, but bigger delays lie ahead. Specifically, if after all this travel the application is inefficiently designed, the process gets into double jeopardy, where the scores can *really* change.

At last, the bits are on the wire. They have to fly to the other end of the circuit. This they do at the speed of light, regardless of the speed of the circuit connecting the two end-points. No way to speed things up here, and anyone reading this who knows of one should please contact NASA.

While the packet flies along the wire, let's talk about application architecture.

What About the App?

A significant factor when you are assessing performance is how applications function in a distributed environment where a physical distance separates information requestor (client computer) and provider (server).

From this perspective, there are two types of applications: custom designs with client and server software portions (for example, Microsoft Visual Basic-type applications), and designs based on a standard Web browser (such as Microsoft Internet Explorer), residing on the client and having no additional specially designed software. Both types function the same way: the client portion of the application or browser has to be loaded and then has to access a remote server to get information.

In the simplest case of, say, a Visual Basic application, there are two computers in the communication path: the client and, say, a Microsoft SQL Server. The browser-based application has a more complex path. Its client computer communicates with the front-end (say a Microsoft Internet Information Server computer) which in turn communicates with the SQL server on the back-end.

Information Delivery and Application Design

The process by which instructions (the packets on the wire) are moved across the network and the information is delivered is (or should be) a crucial consideration in any application design. Although the process is hidden from the user, it is obvious to the network specialist. What the application developer has to consider is essentially a simple fact: information is not delivered in a continuous stream. (except for streaming applications). It is delivered in packets, controlled by the application and protocol logic, and the client and the server "discuss" this process.

In the case of a poorly written application, this "discussion" can be as diffuse as cocktail party chatter. In the figure below, each line from left to right or back represents a single packet being moved from source to destination. To move each packet over the WAN takes time: to move it from Boston, MA, to Redmond, WA, for instance, takes 45 ms; between Redmond, WA, and Sydney, Australia, takes 270 ms. Even the larger of these figures is a very small amount of time when you are talking about one request and one response, but it accrues into a some genuine and actual time when you perform enough trips between sites, and this accrual is what makes slow application performance. Figure 9.1 shows how.

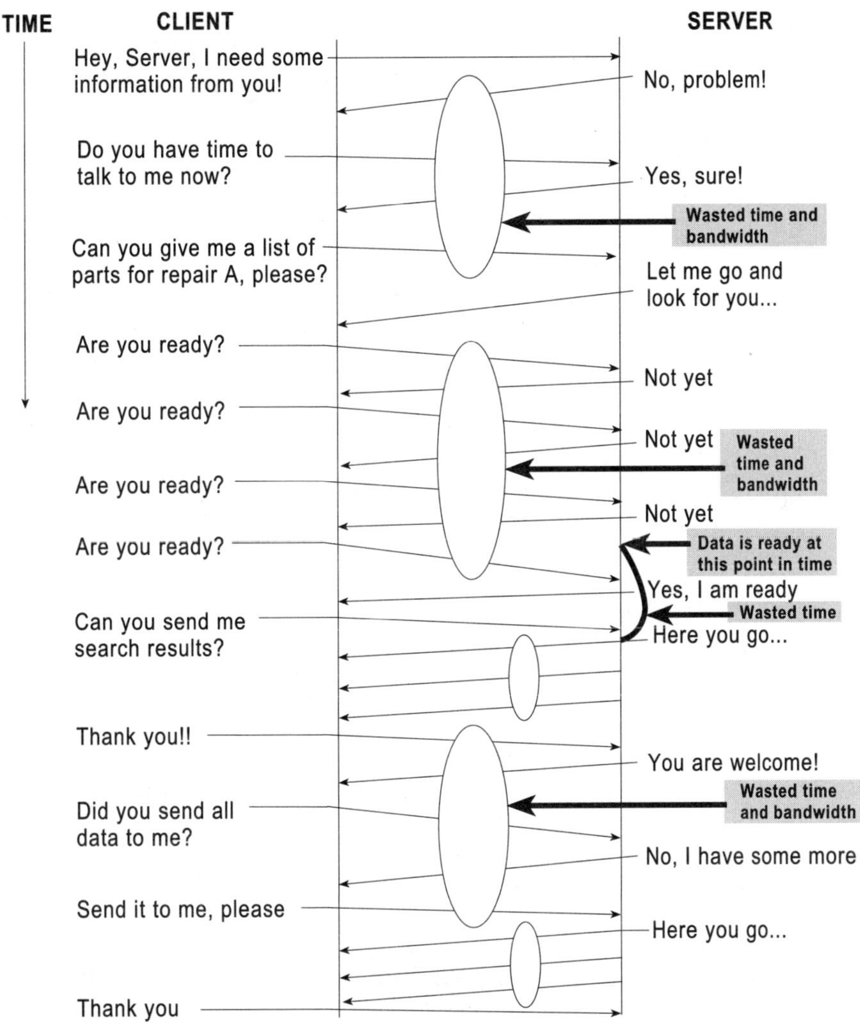

Figure 9.1 Schematic of network communication for a poorly-designed application.

Notice how much time and bandwidth are wasted by the passing back and forth of pleasantries instead of information. On the other hand, a well-written application (Figure 9.2) handles the exchange as if it were delivering marching orders:

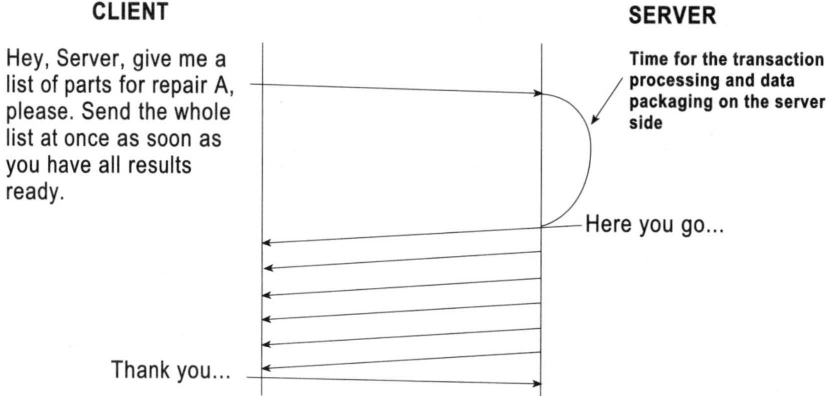

Figure 9.2 Schematic of network communication for a well-designed application

What To Do

Even a poorly written application won't frustrate users by performing slowly if it is run only on a LAN, especially if the network is fast and underutilized. On an extremely fast LAN, an application can be a model of inefficiency and still escape notice and the usual abusive comments. Put it out on the WAN however, and people will quickly spot it for the sloth that it is. When this happens, here are some things to examine in the application profile:

- **HTTP protocol version**. Older browsers are based on the HTTP 1.0, which is inefficient on a network because it unnecessarily opens and closes TCP connections, initiating additional round trips on the network.
- **Persistent connection**. Stay connected to the server during the transaction. Inefficient logic in the application can cause repeated connection.
- **Smooth information delivery from the server**. The requested material should be sent from the server as a single stream of packets. The client requests the information but should not control its delivery. Only TCP and window size should control the flow.

- **Server location**. In a large computer system round-trip time can be reduced by creating local servers or adding servers closer to the client (if possible).
- **Local storage**. For client-server applications (not browser-based ones) storing the client's portion *on the client* rather than downloading it *from the server* speeds things up.
- **Cache screen designs**. This applies to Visual Basic applications, which require that the server deliver screens. Inefficient applications bring the whole screen design down from the server with every query. Caching it reduces traffic.
- **Remember distance**. When the application is communicating over the WAN (not just the LAN) and the (IIS) server front-end and the (SQL) server back-end are far apart and the dialog between them is not optimized, performance can be severely degraded.
- **Reduce exchanges**. For non-multimedia applications, which have different requirements, network exchanges should be kept to a minimum. Putting more into one request avoids sending additional details later on. Use full-size packets.

Application redesign is expensive. The time to think about an application's WAN behavior is before coding. Either way, the characteristics below, which should be considered when creating efficient distributed applications, can also help explain poor performance in inefficient ones. Consider:

- **Location**. Where are the clients and servers with respect to each other? Is an application executing over the net frequently when it could be stored and run locally, with only results sent over the network?
- **Mode**. How is the application used? If it is for real-time (say for customer support) its response should be optimized. Other applications can afford to take longer. Every application should work efficiently, but not all need to be lightning bolts across the PC screen.

- **Distribution**. Sometimes it makes sense to distribute databases. A heavily used application can be helped by placing a lightweight database server on site to provide fast access and speed up response. This server can be synchronized with the main database
- **Timing**. Take some administrative steps to bring data closer to users by moving it over the WAN during off-hours (night is the obvious choice) when network usage is lower.

PART 3

The *Future* Scenario—Windows 2000 Networking Traffic

Plan today what you want to build tomorrow—a simple adage but a challenging one as technology rapidly evolves. Part 1 of this book explained network traffic basics, and Part 2 gave you the hands-on, real-world experience to manage network traffic in your current Windows NT network. Part 3 takes a close look at Windows 2000 Active Directory architecture and database replication to help you plan your future implementation of Windows 2000 *with traffic in mind.* Because database size is a crucial element in directory replication, Chapter 10 uses tests based on real-world samples to show you how to size the Active Directory database. Chapter 11 then introduces the replication architecture and presents network traffic statistics and test results that can help you build an effective replication topology.

CHAPTER 10

Active Directory Database Sizing

By Andreas Luther—Microsoft Enterprise Services

The Microsoft Windows 2000 Active Directory provides new ways for businesses to use directory services. Previous versions of the Windows NT network operating system restricted directory use in some network administration functions such as administrating users and user groups. The Windows 2000 Active Directory extends these functions and other capabilities, and opens the use of the directory as a data store and as a means for network services or directory-enabled applications to publish information in an enterprise-wide network.

The Active Directory uses a database as the information store and the same database engine that is used in Microsoft Exchange Server 5.5. The Active Directory is an enterprise-level directory service, meaning that the system scales for deployment across an enterprise-wide network, integrates with existing directories through synchronization, and supports enterprise-class applications. To keep the Active Directory database up to date, domain controllers generate replication network traffic.

For network administrators, this brings up two questions: How do you size server hard-disk space needed by growth of the directory service? And how does the replication traffic affect overall network performance? This chapter addresses the first question; Chapter 11 "Active Directory Replication Traffic" examines Windows 2000 Active Directory functionality to address the second.

What You'll Find In This Chapter

- **An architectural overview of Windows 2000 Active Directory.**
- **Description of the Active Directory database structure, and how it works.**
- **Walkthrough of database sizing tests.**
- **Scenario-based tests that give you a sense of how database sizing works in practice.**
- **Guidelines for assessing Active Directory database size.**

Active Directory Database Architecture and Components

Besides network administration, you can use Active Directory as a back-end for applications. To take advantage of this, some applications that used to use proprietary directories will, in new versions, move their directory-related information to the Active Directory. For example, the next version of Microsoft Exchange Server (codename *Platinum*) and SAP's R3 business applications will integrate with the Active Directory.

To understand the impact on hard disk sizing, you have to know how the database manages information storage. The explanation below begins with a brief overview of the database's architecture, then presents statistics on the directory database size.

General Structure

The Windows 2000 Active Directory service runs in the protected trusted domain as part of the Local Security Authority process (LSASS.EXE) which manages authentication packages and authenticates users and services. Running within LSASS.EXE allows Active Directory to securely manage secrets such as account passwords.

The Active Directory implementation has three layers: the Core Directory Service Agent (DSA), the Database layer (DB), and the Extensible Storage Engine (ESE). Additional components on top of these layers provide communication with other internal or external services. The LDAP interface (which conforms to RFC 2222) provides access for LDAP clients such as Windows 2000 workstations or Windows 9*x* workstations with the Active Directory client package. The replication interface provides directory replication with other Active Directory domain controllers. The SAM interface provides security services.

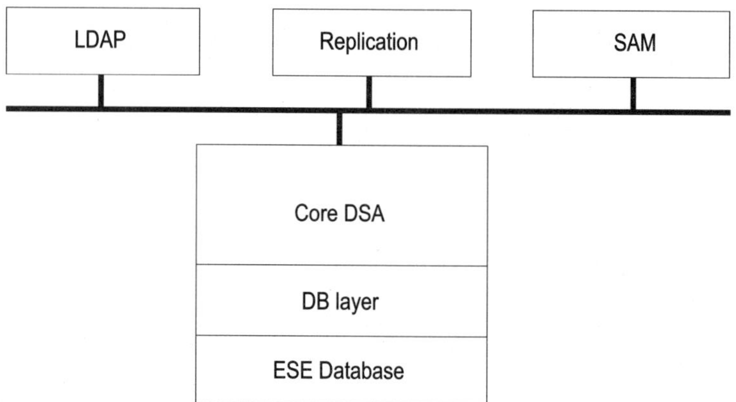

Figure 10.1 Active Directory functional layers.

The core DSA enforces directory semantics, maintains the schema, guarantees and maintains object identity, and enforces data types on attributes. It is also responsible for the class structural and semantic rules, including class inheritance (from abstract and structural classes), auxiliary classes, and enforcement of mandatory properties. All access control routines are implemented as part of the DSA.

Because the ESE database is flat, with no hierarchical namespace, the database layer provides it with the abstraction of an object hierarchy.

A directory objects is named by a **distinguished name** (DN) that contains the components of the domain name system (DNS) name of the domain where the object resides. The **relative distinguished name** (RDN) of an object is the object's name relative to its parent. Each database object has an ObjectGUID (Global Unique Identifier), that is globally unique and immutable (can't be changed after the object is created).

The LDAP interface exposes objects through their distinguished names. Some attributes contain references to other Active Directory objects, such as a user's *manager* attribute. Internally, the value of these attributes is the ObjectGUID of the object they reference. This ensures that a reference always points to the same object, even if that object is renamed or moved. The LDAP interface automatically converts these references to the distinguished name, so when an LDAP client reads these attributes it gets back a distinguished name, not an ObjectGUID.

The ESE database consists of two tables: the data table and the link table. The data table contains a relatively small number of *fixed* columns where storage is allocated for the column on every row, and a large number of *tagged* columns, meaning that storage is allocated only if a value is present. The fixed columns are used to maintain the structure of the directory and are generally invisible to clients; the tagged columns contain the attributes that clients see and care about.

Database Structure

It would take too long to identify an object within a data table if the system always had to store and compare bulky GUIDs, so every object is also identified by a **distinguished name tag** (DNT). This 4-byte DWORD value is incremented when a new object is created in the store (thus it represents the object's database row number). It is an example of a fixed column. Each object's parent relationship is stored as a **parent distinguished name tag** (PDNT, also a DWORD). Resolution of parent-child relationships is optimized because the DNT and PDNT are indexed fields in the database.

The Active Directory Database (NTDS.DIT) contains three tables:

Schema table, containing data that represents the Active Directory schema: the types of objects that can be created in the Active Directory, relationships between them, and the optional and mandatory attributes on each type of object. This table is fairly static and much smaller than the data table, so it is not discussed further.

Link table, containing data that represents linked attributes, which contain values referring to other objects in the Active Directory (for example the *MemberOf* attribute on a user object, which contains values that reference groups to which the user belongs), This is also far smaller than the data table and not discussed further.

Data table, containing the rest of the information in the Active Directory: users, groups, application-specific data, and any other data stored in the Active Directory after its installation. In most installations this is far larger than the link and schema tables, so it is discussed in detail in the rest of this chapter.

The data table can be thought of as having rows (each representing an instance of an object, such as a *user*) and columns (each representing an attribute in the schema, such as *GivenName*). For each attribute in the schema, the table contains a column, also called a *field*. Field sizes can be *fixed* or *variable*. Fixed-size fields contain an integer or long integer as data type; variable-size fields typically hold string types (for example, Unicode strings). The database allocates only as much space as a variable-size field needs—16 bits for a 1-character Unicode string, 160 bits for a 10-character Unicode string, and so on.

The table below shows a reduced data-table with eight tagged columns (of the approximately 800 attributes currently available with the default schema).

Column headers for data table with eight tagged columns.

Cn	Description	EmployeeID	Object Class	ObjectGUID	ObjectSID	Operating System	UserPass Word

The example below shows one row for a user object and one for a directory computer object. An object's type is defined by its *class attribute* (the ObjectClass column below). Note that the data table does not indicate structural rules, such as what attributes can be set on a user object or on a computer object. This abstraction is done by the DSA in conjunction with the schema table, so there are columns below for attributes that don't apply for users (such as OperatingSystem) and columns that don't apply to computer objects (such as EmployeeID). Values cannot be set for these attributes, so the database allocates no storage space for them.

Data table with eight tagged columns.

Cn	Description	EmployeeID	Object Class	Object GUID	ObjectSID	Operating-System	UserPass Word
Aluther	PM ITI	12345	Top# per son# organ izationalPer son# user	xf7 x7e x59 xfc x8e xbe xd1 x11 xbf x84 xa5 x70 x00 x8e x75 x29	S-1-5-21-997912322-3573987441-1172670995-4212 = x01 x05 x00 x00 x00 x00 x00 x05 x15 x00 x00 x00 x02 xef x7a x3b x71 xb8 x06 xd5 x13 x8a xe5 x45 xed x10 x00 x00		******

Data table with eight tagged columns. *(continued)*

Cn	Description	EmployeeID	Object Class	Object GUID	objectSID	Operating-System	UserPass Word
NTRickV	Rick's WS		Top# person# organizational Person# user# computer	xb4 xd5 x2b xc8 x1d xbd xd1 x11 xbf x80 xd5 xcc x44 xdc xcb x29	x01 x05 x00 x00 x00 x00 x00 x05 x15 x00 x00 x00 x02 xef x7a x3b x71 xb8 x06 xd5 x13 x8a xe5 x45 xee x10 x00 x00	Windows NT 5.0	*******

The database space used to store an object depends on the number of attributes for which values are set and the size of the values. For instance, if the administrator creates two user objects (User1 and User2) and sets only the minimum attributes on them, then later adds a 10-character description to User2, the User2 space ends up 20 bytes bigger than the User1 space.

Database records cannot span database pages, so each object is limited to 8 KB. However, some attribute values of an object don't count fully against this limit. Long, variable-length values can be stored on a different page than the object record, leaving behind only a 9-byte reference. In this way, an object and all its attribute values can be much larger than 8 KB.

Changes to the Database

The Active Directory database is stored in a file named NTDS.DIT. When the directory service needs to access data, LSASS.EXE loads pages from the database file into memory. It reserves a pool of memory for these operations and moves the pages between the database and the pool on a *least recently used* (LRU) basis. Some pages in the memory and in the database file get out of synch whenever the DSA performs a write operation on an object. To correct this condition, all pages in the memory are flushed to the database file every time the database shuts down. The domain controller also swaps pages from the memory back to the hard disk (in the background) whenever it is in an idle or low-load state.

Changes are made to in-memory copies of objects. The act of committing a transaction is what writes the changes to the log file first. Writing the changes to the log file is much faster than writing them to the database and this helps makes sure that the change operation is recorded and not lost if the database crashes at that moment. As part of its background work, the database engine continually updates the database file with recently committed changes, getting them from memory directly (not from the log files).

When you perform bulk load operations in the directory (for instance, for performance or scalability tests), you will see that the LDASS.EXE process grows bigger and bigger. This is caused by the database system's memory buffer allocation. The database continues to allocate more memory until the operating system prevents making more buffers available. This can happen when the system approaches its physical memory limitations, or if the administrator restricted the memory that is available for the directory in the registry. But in order to operate as fast as possible, the database tries to get as much memory as it can. When the database is updated later, the memory buffers are released again, and LSASS.EXE shrinks.

If the domain controller cannot shut down in an orderly fashion (which usually means a power failure) the database is left out-of-date because the most recent in-memory pages could not be written to the disk. Transaction logs are used to recover the database. Any change made to the database is also appended to the current log file, and its disk image is always kept up to date. The database change process is:

1. LSASS.EXE writes the change to the log file
2. LSASS.EXE writes the change to a database page in the memory buffer
3. LSASS.EXE confirms the transaction
4. The change is written to the disk (at shutdown, or at idle time)

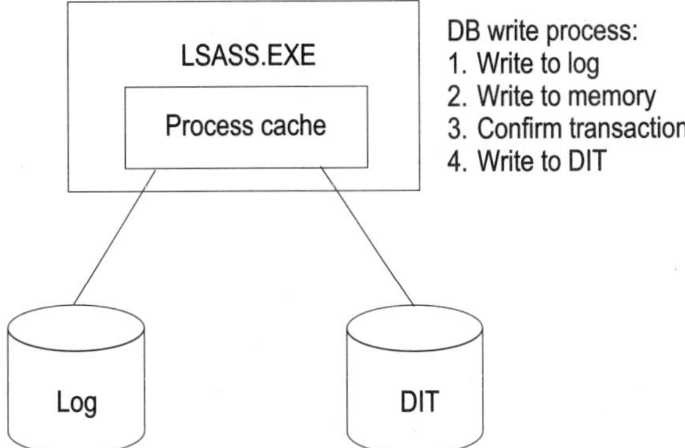

Figure 10.2 Database change process.

If a directory service halt prevents the database file from being successfully flushed to disk, the database performs a recovery on the next restart. Essentially, the database reads through the log files in order and reapplies changes until the database is once again consistent and up-to-date.

The ESE can create a new log file when the current one fills up (**non-circular logging**) or it can overwrite the oldest file when the log reaches a specified number of files (**circular logging**). Non-circular logging uses disk space until you manually delete old log files after a backup or a restart, but it saves *all* database changes and never deletes log files automatically. The Active Directory Service default is non-circular logging. You can overwrite this default with the registry key:

> **HKEY_LOCAL_MACHINE\CurrentControlSetServices\NTDS\Parameters\CircularLogging**
>
> Where: 1 = circular logging; 0 = non-circular logging.

Performing database-sizing tests requires a method to determine the size of the NTDS.DIT file. If you monitor the size of the NTDS.DIT file while an Active Directory domain controller performs a high number of write operations, you will see that the database file size seems not to change. This is because NTFS records the size of a file when the file is opened and does not refresh before the file is closed again. The Active Directory opens the database file when the domain controller boots up, and does not close it again until the machine shuts down. Therefore, you cannot use the size of the NTDS.DIT file reported by Windows Explorer or a command prompt to find out how big the file actually is.

You need another method to determine how big the NTDS.DIT file is. Two are available:

- You can reboot the domain controller, which closes the file. It is reopened when the directory service restarts and NTFS reports the correct file size.
- You can use the Windows Explorer **Properties** dialog on the partition containing the NTDS.DIT file: it always reports the correct available space. Record the available space both before and after the test to easily compute the correct file size (and test delta).

To enhance performance on domain controllers that must handle high request rates, you should hold the Windows 2000 operating system on one hard drive, the Active Directory database file on a second, and the log files on a third. Always use mirrored drives on domain controllers to prevent data loss from a hard-drive crash.

Garbage Collection

Garbage collection is a housekeeping process. It runs on every domain controller (after every continuous 12 hours of operation) deleting objects and files no longer needed by the directory service. This means that if a domain controller is rebooted continuously at intervals less than 12 hours, the database and log files continue to grow, so you should not reboot unnecessarily. Garbage collection has three tasks.

Deleting Unneeded Log Files

A log file is unneeded once all changes (and all previous log files) have been written to the database file.

Deleting Tombstones

Rather than physically delete objects from the database, the directory service removes most attributes and tags the object as being in the **tombstone** state to alert replication partners that the object was deleted. The database removes tombstones after a configurable interval (the **tombstone lifetime**, default 60 days). You should not change this default: tombstones are used to replicate object deletions. If you restore a directory server from a backup tape older than the tombstone lifetime, the server does not learn of some deletions, leading to inconsistencies between domain controllers. (The Restore utility tries to prevent this, but it can't prevent you from changing tombstone lifetime.) To accommodate occasional disruption of replication due to communication failures, keep tombstone lifetime substantially longer than the expected replication latency.

Database Defragmentation

To update the database file, the database system uses the quickest way, which is not always the most efficient way to fill database pages. **Defragmentation** rearranges how the data is written in the database. Online defragmentation does not reduce database file size, but it makes more space available for new objects.

You can also defragment the database file offline. Take the domain controller offline, boot it into directory services repair mode (use the F8 key at system start-up), and use NTDSUTIL.EXE. This creates a second, defragmented version of the database file that is considerably smaller than the original database file. You can at this point choose which database file you want to use on the domain controller.

Recommendation: Use offline defragmentation only when you know database contents have shrunk considerably (for instance, when a global catalog server becomes a normal domain controller) and you need to reclaim space for other uses. Keep the original NTDS.DIT file until the domain controller has restarted with the defragmented file. Once you have no doubts that the directory database is in a consistent state, you can delete the original (fragmented) database file.

To test how the database grows when a specific set of objects is loaded, you have to remember:

1. When the directory is loaded with objects, the database is in a fragmented state, making it impossible to tell how much space the objects really consume in the database file.
2. Online defragmentation makes space available, but does not shrink the database file. However, the result of the defragmentation is the real space consumption.
3. Only offline defragmentation gives you a clear picture of the space consumption.

In a production environment, you should always select online defragmentation: it leads to the same results as the offline process and does not require taking the machine offline. For database growth testing, however, you should defragment the directory database offline after a bulk load of objects, because only the offline defragmented version of the directory database allows you to assess how much space is consumed. To stress these differences, some of the following database load tests show results for both the fragmented and the offline defragmented versions of the database file.

Directory Database Sizing Tests

This section shows the results of tests that load objects into the Active Directory. In general, two different kinds of tests were performed. The first series loaded the database with a large number of identical objects to show how the database grows when objects are loaded, and how much space is consumed for these object types. For a more real-life approach, the second series created a blueprint of a company with user objects, group objects and files shares. It was designed to show how big the database grows for small, medium, and large companies.

Most of the tests used several steps for the object load operation. The empty database size was recorded, then the first set of objects was loaded. An offline defragmentation was performed, then the fragmented and the defragmented versions of the database were measured. The fragmented version was used when the next set of objects was loaded.

Single Object Type Loads

The single object load tests concentrated on finding out how database size increases relative to increase in attribute value size. As pointed out above, the database engine consumes space only for attributes for which values are set, so the number of attributes that have values for an object makes a big difference in that object's size. In the tests for user and organizational unit (OU) objects, only mandatory attributes were set. These are attributes that must contain value(s) so that the directory service can create the object. Subsequent tests show how adding attributes to an object affects object size.

User Objects

Obviously, user objects play a big role in any directory deployment, so if you want to know how big the database will grow you need know how big these objects are. The test loaded the database (**DB** in the table columns) with up to 500,000 users, in increments of 100,000 users.

User object results table.

	Fragmented database			Defragmented database		
#Users	**Kbytes/DB**	**Growth**	**Bytes/User**	**Kbytes/DB**	**Growth**	**Bytes/User**
0	10,256			10,256		
100,000	516,064	505,808	5,179	364,560	354,304	3,628
200,000	899,088	383,024	4,551	720,912	356,352	3,639
300,000	1,294,352	395,264	4,383	1,079,312	358,400	3,649
400,000	1,675,280	380,928	4,262	1,435,664	356,352	3,649
500,000	2,060,328	385,048	4,199	1,792,016	356,352	3,649

Results graph.

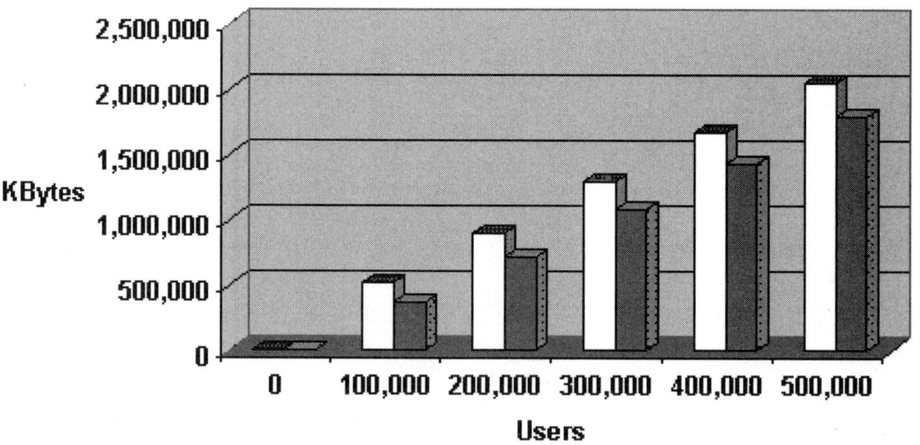

Figure 10. 3 Database file growth as function of user objects.

The database file growth pattern is linear. The growth between two load operations is always almost identical: approximately 385,000 Kbytes in the fragmented version, and approximately 356,000 Kbytes in the defragmented version. The only exception to this linear growth is the load operation in the first step, when the first 100,000 users were loaded. Here the jump is much bigger, around 516,000 Kbytes.

This example shows very well how the online defragmentation works. In this test, the first set of objects (100,000 users) was added, and the file size was checked the next day. Meanwhile, online defragmentation had kicked in and rearranged the objects in the database. This did not shrink the database file size, but it made space available for new objects. Therefore, the file size is much bigger in step one for the fragmented version. When the next set of objects was loaded, the database file space freed up by the defragmentation could be used, so the additional growth is not much different from the growth of the defragmented database version.

Loading 500,000 users (with only mandatory attributes set) in the Active Directory takes about 1.8 GB. To compute the size of one user object, subtract the size of an empty store, then divide the store size by the number of users. In this case, one user object is 3,649 bytes.

Organizational Units

User objects in the Active Directory are larger than most other objects because they contain many mandatory attributes.

Information in the Active Directory is organized in a hierarchy using organizational units (OUs). The table below illustrates the effect of OU objects on database size.

OU test results table.

	Fragmented database			Defragmented database		
#Users	**Kbytes/DB**	**Growth**	**Bytes/User**	**Kbytes/DB**	**Growth**	**Bytes/User**
0	10,256			10,256		
2,000	12,304	2,048	1,049	10,256	0	
4,000	16,440	4,136	1,583	12,304	2,048	524
6,000	18,448	2,008	1,398	14,352	2,048	699
8,000	20,496	2,048	1,311	18,448	4,096	1,049
10,000	24,592	4,096	1,468	20,496	2,048	1,049
12,000	26,640	2,048	1,398	22,544	2,048	1,049
14,000	28,688	2,048	1,348	24,592	2,048	1,049
16,000	32,784	4,096	1,442	26,640	2,048	1,049

The table shows that the growth pattern again is very linear. The size of one organizational unit is 1,049 Bytes.

Adding Attributes

The next series of tests enlarged the user objects with extension Attributes 1 to 10. These attributes are defined in the schema as string value attributes. Each string was filled with 10 characters.

The test began with a store containing 100,000 user objects with only the mandatory attributes set. The server was demoted to a non-domain controller, promoted back, and loaded with 100,000 user objects again, this time with one extension attribute. This was repeated with two attributes and so on.

Extension attributes with user object results table.

# ExtAttr.	Kbytes/DB	Bytes/User	DB/Defrag	Bytes/User	Bytes/Attr.
0	522,256	5,242	364,560	3,627	
1	413,712	4,130	364,560	3,627	0
2	413,712	4,130	364,560	3,627	0
3	485,392	4,864	382,992	3,816	63
4	663,568	6,689	405,520	4,046	105
5	698,384	7,045	405,520	4,046	84
6	706,576	7,129	407,568	4,067	73
7	704,528	7,108	444,432	4,445	117
8	702,480	7,087	444,432	4,445	102
9	497,680	4,990	444,432	4,445	91
10	497,680	4,990	444,432	4,445	82
11	497,680	4,990	444,432	4,445	74

The fragmented version of the database performs big jumps in size at some steps, and smaller jumps at others. This is caused by how the database engine allocates space for new pages. Note that this never happens for the defragmented version.

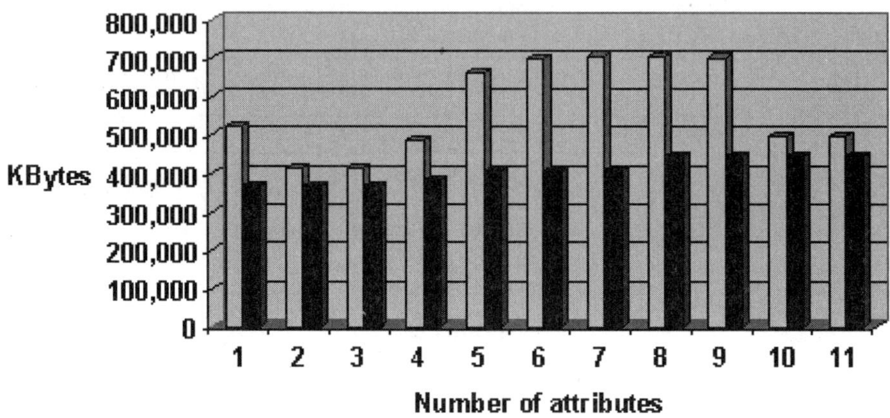

Figure 10.4 Adding attributes to user objects.

The growth of the defragmented database is very linear again. On average, an additional attribute with a string size of 10 characters adds approximately 100 bytes to the object size.

Storing Public Key Certificates in the Active Directory

Many users will want to use public key certificates for authentication and secure e-mail. Public keys are often much larger than any other attribute in the directory and it is not unusual to find users with more than one public key, each serving a different purpose (one for e-mail, another for authentication, etc.). For this reason, it is very important to consider public key support in determining database size in your enterprise.

The next test shows how much bigger user objects grow when Public Keys are deployed. For this test a store was loaded with 100,000 users, then an X.509 v3 certificate was deployed. The store size before and after the deployment is shown. A Windows 2000 Certificate Server issued this certificate; the size of the certificate stored as a file is 1,294 bytes.

Objects used to test growth with Public Keys.

Object	Size
Fragmented store before certificate deployment	522,256 Kbytes
Fragmented store after certificate deployment	657,424 Kbytes
Defragmented store before certificate deployment	364,560 Kbytes
Defragmented store after certificate deployment	525,353 Kbytes
User in defragmented store before certificate deployment	3,626 bytes
User in defragmented store after certificate deployment	5,283 bytes

The growth of the user object is slightly bigger than the size of the certificate, 1,657 bytes compared to 1,608 bytes.

Sample Company

Modeling a customer database provides a more real-life look at these changes in database size. The sample company in these tests consists of the following directory objects: users, groups, organizational units, and volumes (file shares) in this ratio:

Sample company objects.

Object	Number
Computers	90,000
Users	100,000
Groups/distribution lists	30,000
Average number of members per group/distribution list	100
OUs	100
Average number of users/OU	1000
Average number of groups/OU	300
Volumes	2000
Volumes/OU	10

The objects were loaded with different attribute sets: mandatory in the first tests, and additional attributes in subsequent tests. To simulate real-world variation in value size, the attributes were assigned a random number of characters between 1 and 100.

Sample Company with Minimum Properties

Test #1 looked at the growth pattern of the sample company loaded in stages, with minimum properties. Each stage represents 10% of the sample company (10% represents 10,000 users, 9,000 workstation accounts, 3,000 groups with 100 members each, and 200 volumes). Since the growth pattern is so linear, the test was stopped after 50% of the store was populated.

Minimum properties growth test results table.

	Fragmented database		Defragmented database	
	Kbytes/DB	**Growth**	**Kbytes/DB**	**Growth**
Empty	10,256		10,256	
10%	137,232	126,976	102,416	92,160
20%	239,632	102,400	194,576	92,160
30%	344,080	104,448	286,736	92,160
40%	444,432	100,352	376,848	90,112
50%	548,880	104,448	469,008	92,160

Again, database growth is linear and thus predictable. In the fragmented state, the growth for a 10% increase is around 102,400 Kbytes. In the defragmented state, it is around 92,160 Kbytes (even slightly smaller in one case).

The next table shows the effect of adding attributes. For user objects, 30 attributes were chosen (first name, last name, office number, phone number, and so on). For workstations, 6 attributes were added; for groups, 8 attributes were added, and for volumes 3 attributes were added. All attributes were filled with strings of a random size between 1 and 100 characters. For a complete list of the attributes used, see the table at the end of this chapter.

Custom properties results table.

	Fragmented database		Defragmented database	
	Kbytes/DB	**Growth**	**Kbytes/DB**	**Growth**
Empty	10,256		10,256	
10%	198,672	188,416	147,472	137,216
20%	356,368	157,696	284,688	137,216
30%	512,016	155,648	432,952	148,264
40%	669,712	157,696	561,168	128,216
50%	825,360	155,648	700,432	139,264
60%	981,008	155,648	839,696	139,264
70%	1,140,752	159,744	976,912	137,216
80%	1,296,400	155,648	1,116,176	139,264
90%	1,452,048	155,648	1,253,392	137,216
100%	1,609,744	157,696	1,392,656	139,264

Again: linear growth—no database explosion. In the graphic representation below, the left bar in each pair shows the database size in KB; the smaller bar shows database growth from step to step.

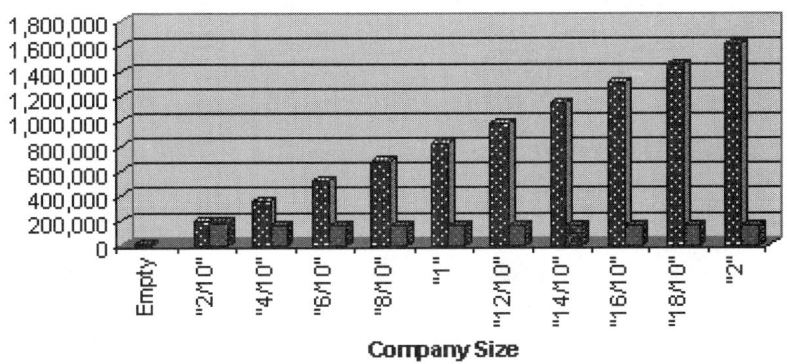

Figure 10. 5 Custom properties results graph.

Access Control Entries

The Active Directory uses **static inheritance** for access control entries. This means that every object contains the access control list (ACL) that applies to it. When a new set of access control entries (ACEs) or deny ACEs are set on a container level, they are pushed from the container level down to all child objects that are configured to inherit ACEs from their parent. It is obviously much faster to get access rights from the object itself than to traverse a whole tree; the effect of this is that the objects take up slightly more space in the directory.

A good practice is to delegate access rights on directory objects only to *user groups* and not to *single users*. This way only a single ACE is written to objects that inherit from their parent. When an additional user needs to receive the same rights on children of an OU, the user is added to the group that already has the necessary rights—no additional ACE is written to the children of the OU.

For the following tests, a domain controller was loaded with 100 OUs, 100 groups, and 100,000 users. Next, full access control on all objects in the whole domain was granted to one group. Then the resulting size of the database was noted. In the next step, the same delegation was repeated, this time to a different group, and so on. The tests went up to 22 access control entries. The table below shows a subset of the results:

Access control entry growth results table (extract).

	Fragmented database			Defragmented database		
#ACEs	**Kbytes/DB**	**Bytes/Users**	**Bytes/ACE**	**/Kbytes/DB**	**Bytes/Users**	**Bytes/ACE**
0	514,064	5,158		366,608	3,648	
1	536,592	5,389	230	372,752	3,711	63
2	536,592	5,389	115	372,752	3,711	31
3	557,072	5,598	147	393,232	3,921	91
4	557,072	5,598	110	393,232	3,921	68
5	557,072	5,598	88	393,232	3,921	54
6	585,744	5,892	122	419,856	4,193	91
10	626,704	6,311	115	458,768	4,592	94
14	628,752	6,332	84	458,768	4,592	67
18	698,384	7,045	105	526,352	5,284	91
22	698,384	7,045	86	526,352	5,284	74

The defragmented version of the database shows that user object growth averaged about 80 bytes per access control entry. This is less than 5% of the size of a user object that is filled with mandatory attributes only. Adding even one attribute requires more space (100 bytes).

Reclaiming Space in the Database

As pointed out above, when objects are deleted in the directory service, the data is not released from the database immediately; instead the deleted object is transformed into a tombstone. When tombstones expire (after the tombstone lifetime), the space can be reused. Although online defragmentation makes the space available again, the database size still does not shrink unless offline defragmentation is used.

The next test examines how space is made available for new objects again. It had four steps:

1. Thc databasc was loadcd with a full copy of the sample company
2. 50% of the company was deleted
3. The database was loaded again in 10% steps until it reached the original size
4. An additional 10% was loaded

For all cases, it was interesting again to look at the size of the fragmented and defragmented data store.

Reclaimed space results table.

	Fragmented database		Defragmented database	
	Kbytes/DB	**Growth**	**Kbytes/DB**	**Growth**
	10,256		10,256	
10%	198,672	188,416	147,472	137,216
20%	356,368	157,696	284,688	137,216
30%	512,016	155,648	432,952	148,264

Reclaimed space results table. *(continued)*

	Fragmented database		Defragmented database	
	Kbytes/DB	**Growth**	**Kbytes/DB**	**Growth**
40%	669,712	157,696	561,168	128,216
50%	825,360	155,648	700,432	139,264
60%	981,008	155,648	839,696	139,264
70%	1,140,752	159,744	976,912	137,216
80%	1,296,400	155,648	1,116,176	139,264
90%	1,452,048	155,648	1,253,392	137,216
100%	1,609,744	157,696	1,392,656	139,264
50% of the store deleted				
50%	1,654,800		700,432	
60%	1,654,800	0	839,696	139,264
70%	1,654,800	0	976,912	137,216
80%	1,654,800	0	1,116,176	139,264
90%	1,662,942	8,142	1,296,400	180,224
100%	1,662,942	0	1,435,664	139,264
110%	1,847,312	184,370	1,572,880	137,216

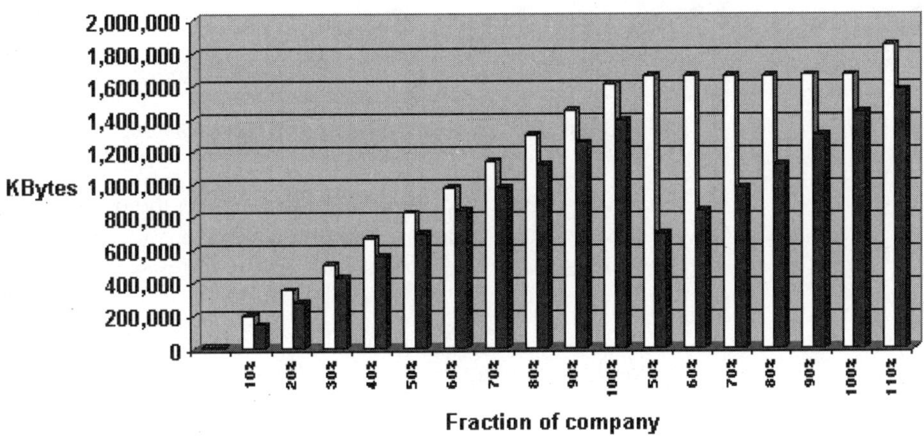

Figure 10.6 Reclaimed space test results.

The results demonstrate that after the delete operation, the database retains its size even though a huge number of objects are loaded again. There is only a small growth before the original size is reached again.

The defragmented version of the database shrinks by 50% percent after the delete, then grows following the same pattern as for the original load. When more loads are performed over 100%, space is consumed in the same manner.

What does this mean for directory service administrators? In a domain controller's first 60 days (60 is the default tombstone lifetime), the database will only grow, even if a large number of objects are deleted. After 60 days, the database will either stay the same size or grow slightly. The fact that the file doesn't shrink after objects are deleted does not mean, however, that new space has not been made available.

Summary of Database Sizing Tests

Guidelines for assessing Active Directory database size:

1. Find the size for your company in the chart and note the database size given there.
2. Compare the objects you want to use with the number of objects used in the tests. If you have additional objects that are security principals, add 3600 bytes per instance; if they are not security principals (such as OUs) add 1,100 bytes per instance.
3. Compare the number of attributes you set on the objects with the test numbers. For additional attributes, add 100 bytes per attribute. For binary data, such as pictures, add the file size, plus a spare buffer of 25% of the file size.
4. To be prepared for additional objects in the future and for tombstones, at least ***double*** your estimate now. In fact, if you are thinking about deploying applications in the future that use the Active Directory as a data store, a factor of 3x or 4x seems to be more appropriate. Remember, adding a certificate to users adds 1,500 bytes. Some messaging applications might add SMIME certificates. Buying more server hardware up front might be expensive, but adding hardware later can be even more painful.
5. Access control entries add around 70 bytes per entry to each object. Consider using groups for access delegation, then add users only to the predefined groups.

Global Catalog Servers

The next test investigates the additional storage resources a domain controller requires when it serves as a **global catalog** (GC) server. A global catalog server is a domain controller that holds a partial replica of all naming contexts in the enterprise, in addition to the standard three: schema, configuration, and domain. The schema defines what attributes are included in global catalog server replication.

Any domain controller can be promoted to a global catalog server. Although it makes no real difference which domain or site the GC server belongs to, deploying them along site boundaries supports faster search and logon operations.

Universal groups publish the group memberships in the global catalog, so their use highly affects the additional load on GC servers. Global groups and local domain groups replicate only their existence to the global catalog (like any other object in the Active Directory), not their group memberships. The test, therefore, needs to examine the additional costs of global catalogs for both cases—universal groups only, and global domain groups only.

Global Catalog Servers with Universal Groups

This test investigates how GC and non-GC server growth compare when universal groups are used. The following environment was used for the test:

There is a small domain tree that consists of a child domain with one domain controller, and a parent domain with one domain controller, which is a GC server. For the tests, the parent and the child domain were loaded with the same objects. Again, the sample company was used, with the usual increments, and with only mandatory attributes set. All groups had 100 members.

The results show a size comparison based on percentages: What percentage bigger is a global catalog server, compared to a normal domain controller? Or, in other words: what percentage of its domain naming context does a domain controller replicate to a global catalog server?

Note These numbers are worst-case scenarios for two reasons: only universal groups were used, and only the mandatory properties were set. Values set for additional attributes aren't included in global catalog server replication (as long as the schema is unchanged) and this would improve the percentages.

Also note that the parent domain and the child domain always have the same number of objects loaded. If the child domain had a smaller number of objects (which would be the norm), the additional load on the global catalog would obviously be much less significant.

GC (parent) and normal (child) controller results table.

	GC	GC defragmented	Child domain	CD defragmented
Empty	10,256	10,256	10,256	10,256
10%	217,104	170,000	137,232	102,416
20%	399,376	331,792	239,632	194,576
30%	581,648	426,000	344,080	286,739
40%	765,698	440,336	444,432	376,848
50%	946,192	546,832	548,880	469,008

Normal and universal GC results table.

	Child Domain	Universal GC.	Percentage
Empty	10,256	10,256	0.00
10%	102,416	170,000	65.99
20%	194,576	331,792	70.52
30%	286,739	426,000	48.57
40%	376,848	440,336	16.85
50%	469,008	546,832	16.59

The results are somewhat surprising. While the first series of tests show the expected result (a growth of approximately 50% to 60%), the later tests show numbers that are very low compared to the prediction. Apparently, the data is stored very efficiently in the Active Directory database.

Global Catalog Servers with Global Groups

Global Groups do not publish the group members in the global catalog, so in this case additional load should be smaller than in the case using only universal groups. The test scenario is basically the same as above.

GC servers with child domain results table.

	GC	GC defragmented	Child domain	CD defragmented
Empty	10,256	10,256	10,256	10,256
10%	188,432	147,472	137,232	102,416
20%	344,080	284,688	239,632	194,576
30%	503,824	423,952	344,080	286,739
40%	659,472	516,112	444,432	376,848
50%	817,168	548,880	548,880	469,008

GC servers with global domain groups results table.

	Child domain	Global domain, groups	Percentage
Empty	10,256	10,256	0.00
10%	102,416	147,472	43.99
20%	194,576	284,688	46.31
30%	286,739	423,952	47.85
40%	376,848	516,112	36.95
50%	469,008	548,880	17.03

Again, the numbers look good for the first tests, but too low for the later tests. The additional load is significantly smaller when global domain groups are used.

Remember that these results indicate *generally* what will happen in a real case. Many factors determine the additional load on global catalogs:

- Are universal groups the most commonly used group type?
- Are global groups the most commonly used group type?
- How many group members are included in universal groups, if universal groups are used?
- How many additional attributes are loaded (besides the mandatory attributes, which won't be replicated to the GC)?
- Is the schema changed to include attributes in partial replication?
- Are applications installed that change the schema in order to extend partial replication?

There are only a few guidelines for the use of the global catalog server:

- Use universal groups or global groups for enterprise-wide access-right operations (granting or denying access to globally available resources, such as Active Directory objects).
- Keep the number of group members in universal groups as low as possible. Typically, all members of universal groups should be global groups.
- Keep changes in the universal groups as infrequent as possible. You can do this by requiring all members of universal groups to be global groups, and making individual membership changes in the global groups.
- Before replicating additional attributes to GC servers, evaluate thoroughly whether the additional load on the GC is required or just "nice to have."
- When deciding on GC hardware, keep future applications that use the GC in mind. Upgrading servers later is more expensive than investing in more hardware when machines are first selected.

Summary

The storage requirements of the Active Directory database are very predictable. Many companies may not achieve a 100,000-user directory for some time, so it is appropriate to note that (from the perspective of disk-space usage) domain controller hardware requirements are not breathtaking—in most cases the directory database remains significantly below 1 GB. However, in order to lower cost of ownership of these systems in the future, you should plan on 3x to 4x the expected size of the database.

Some additional recommendations: use mirrored drives to protect against the loss of a hard-disk device, and for big domain controllers or GCs hold the database and the log files on separate hard drives to isolate them from the operating system partition.

Complete List of Attributes Used in Tests

Attributes used in tests.

Object	UI Tab	Properties	Common
Computer	General	Computer Name	X
		Description	
		Network Address	
		Role	X
		Operating System	X
		Version	X
	Managed By	Service Pack	X
		Managed By	X
Contact	General	First Name	X
		Last Name	X
		Description	
		Office	X
		Telephone	X
		E-Mail	X
		Home Page	
	Organization	Title	X
		Department	X
		Company	X
		Manager	X
		Direct Reports	X
	Member Of	Member of Groups	X

Attributes used in tests. *(continued)*

Object	UI Tab	Properties	Common
Organizational unit	General	Description	X
		Street	X
		City	X
		State/Province	X
		Zip/Postal Code	X
	Managed By	Managed By	X
Group	General	Description	X
		E-Mail	X
		Group Type	X
		Security Enabled	X
		Comments	
	Members	Members	X
	Member Of	Member Of	X
		Primary Group	X
	Managed By	Managed By	X

Attributes used in tests. *(continued)*

Object	UI Tab	Properties	Common
User	General	First Name	X
		Last Name	X
		Description	
		Office	X
		Telephone	X
		E-Mail	X
		Home Page	
	Address	Street	X
		PO Box	X
		City	X
		State/Province	X
		Zip/Postal Code	X
		Country	X

Attributes used in tests. *(continued)*

Object	UI Tab	Properties	Common
	Account	Logon User as NT5	X
		Logon User as NT4	X
		Logon Hours	
		Logon User To	
		User Must Change Password	
		User Cannot Change Password	
		Password Never Expires	
		Save Password as Encrypted Clear Text	
		Account Disabled	
		Account Locked Out	
		Account Expires	
	Profile	Profile Path	X
		Logon Script	X
		Local Path	
		Connect Home Drive to this Letter	X
		Connect Location of Home Drive	X

Attributes used in tests. *(continued)*

Object	UI Tab	Properties	Common
	Telephone/Notes	Home Number	X
		Other Home Number	
		Pager Number	X
		Other Pager Number	
		Mobile Number	X
		Other Mobile Number	
		Fax Number	X
		Other Fax Number	
	Organization	Comments	
		Title	X
		Department	X
		Company	X
		Manager	X
	Certificates	Direct Reports	X
	Member Of	X.509 certificates	
		Member Of	
		Primary Group	X

Attributes used in tests. *(continued)*

Object	UI Tab	Properties	Common
	RAS Dial In	Grant Dial-in Permission	X
		Dial-in Group Profile	X
		Verify Caller-ID	X
		Callback Options	
		Static IP Address for this User	
		Static Routes	
Printer		Location	X
		Model	X
		Color	X
		Staple	X
		Double-sided	X
		Speed	X
		Resolution	X
		Description	X
Volume	General	Description	X
		UNC Name	X
	Managed By	Managed by	X

CHAPTER 11

Active Directory Replication Traffic

By Andreas Luther—Microsoft Enterprise Services

The Windows 2000 Active Directory extends the replication model introduced in Microsoft Exchange Server 4.0—a directory based on a database and a flexible replication engine. The new Active Directory model uses an updated replication architecture to meet the needs for an enterprise directory service. The new design results in finer replication granularity and an architecture that allows administrators to tune replication for specific environments, controlling what is replicated to whom, how, and when. Active Directory replication is designed to work well without tuning, but if you have to perform tuning you'll need a solid understanding of the architecture and the resulting network traffic.

This chapter introduces the new Active Directory replication architecture, shows how to detect network packets that are caused by replication, and presents some network traffic statistics that will help you define an efficient replication topology. It is not a complete discussion of this topic—that level of detail is available in other sources—but is instead intended as a functional overview useful for implementation planning.

What You'll Find In This Chapter

- **An overview of the Active Directory replication architecture.**
- **How replication topology works.**
- **How to measure replication traffic.**
- **Examples of real-world replication test samples.**

Replication Architecture

The Active Directory is made up of one or more **naming contexts** or partitions. A naming context is a contiguous sub-tree of the directory (such as the directory schema) that is a unit of replication. In the Active Directory each domain controller always holds at least three naming replicas:

- The schema
- The configuration (replication topology and related metadata)
- One or more domain naming contexts (sub-trees containing the actual objects in the directory)

The **schema** container defines the objects (such as users) and attributes (such as telephone numbers) that can be created in the Active Directory, and the rules for creating and manipulating them. Schema information (which attributes are mandatory for object creation, what additional attributes can be set, and what attribute data types are used) is replicated to all domain controllers to ensure that objects are created and manipulated in accordance with the rules.

The **configuration** container includes information about the Active Directory as a whole—what domains exist, what sites are available, what domain controllers are running in the particular sites and domains, and what additional services are offered. All enterprise domain controllers need this information to make operational decisions (such as choosing replication partners) so it is replicated to all of them.

A **domain** naming context holds objects such as users, groups, computers, and organizational units. A full domain naming context replica contains a read-write replica of all information in the domain—all objects and attributes. A domain controller holds a full replica of its domain naming context. A partial domain naming context replica contains a read-only subset of the information in the domain—all objects, but only selected attributes. A domain controller that's a global catalog (GC) server contains a partial replica of every other domain in the forest (and a full replica of its own domain.)

GC servers speed up enterprise-wide directory searches by acting as indexers for the enterprise, holding in their database a copy of selected attributes for all enterprise objects—a small set of common object attributes typically meaningful in searches: first and last names for user objects, locations for printers, etc. Thus the GC optimizes a search for, say, a specific color-printer, by consulting its database. Even if the specific attribute is not found in the GC database, the user or application can at least find out which domain controllers to contact for more information.

Besides that, global catalogs are also needed for logon operations. GCs servers map user principal names (*FredG@Acme.com*) to accounts (*HQ.Acme.com\FredG*). Only GC servers know all user memberships in universal groups, so the logon process must communicate to a GC to add the security IDs (SIDs) of the universal groups to the user's access token, if the user is a member of a universal group.

Normal replication mechanisms keep GC server partial domain replicas up to date. When Active Directory builds a replication topology for a naming context, it includes the partial domain replicas. Thus, a partial domain replica cannot act as a replication source for a full domain replica, because the partial domain replica only knows about a subset of attributes. A partial domain replica can act as a replication source for another partial domain replica. This allows for very low-cost topologies.

Object Model

Objects in the Active Directory are defined by their attributes' types and values. An object receives its identity from its Global Unique Identifier (GUID—the only attribute that cannot be changed). It keeps track of a system object in the Active Directory even after a move between domains changes its distinguished name (DN).

As noted, the schema defines which attributes can be used on objects. The Active Directory's Extensible Storage Engine (ESE) reserves space only for attributes with *actual values* set on them (attributes containing values). This helps conserve database space because user objects have more than 100 defined attributes, but only 20 to 30 are commonly used. Using this model, the replication engine minimizes traffic by replicating only object attributes that have values assigned, and only attributes with values that have changed since the last replication.

Multi-Master Replication

The Windows 2000 Active Directory uses a multi-master replication topology that allows you to use any domain controller to manipulate the domain database and to replicate changes to its replication partners.

Domain controllers use update sequence numbers (USNs) to see if replication partners are up to date. In the case of collisions (when the same attribute of the same object is manipulated on two domain controllers at the same time) the last writer wins. To determine last writer status, an algorithm checks: attribute version number, then attribute timestamp, then the GUIDs of the domain controllers that performed the write operation. This ensures that the attribute value is determined consistently and locally, reducing communication between domain controllers.

Replication Topology

Replication efficiency is enhanced by a flexible replication topology that can reflect the structure of an existing network. The Active Directory's replication topology generator runs as part of the **Knowledge Consistency Checker** (KCC). You feed the KCC information on the cost of sending data from one location to another, and which domain controllers are running in the same location. Using this, the KCC builds an inter-site replication topology that is a spanning tree based on low-cost routing decisions between remote locations, and a more strongly connected intra-site topology. You can disable the KCC topology generator and manually create the connection objects required for replication. During this process, the Active Directory logging mechanism identifies domain controllers that appear to be isolated from the enterprise-wide replication.

Note Using replication topology generator is strongly recommended: it simplifies a complex task, has a flexible architecture that reacts to failures and to changes you make later in the network topology, and helps compute the lowest-cost topology.

The next sections discuss essential replication concepts.

Connection Objects

The fact that one domain controller uses another as a source for replication information is expressed as a **connection object** in the Active Directory. These define incoming replication only. For example, if domain controller DC1 has a connection object to DC2, then DC1 can use all naming contexts on DC2 as a source for updated information, but DC2 *cannot* use DC1 unless it creates a connection object that defines DC1 as a source. Once a connection object has been created, it can be used to replicate information from all naming contexts.

Sites

Used in the Active Directory to express proximity of network connection, a **site** is defined as an IP subnetwork—a concept used in all routed TCP/IP network environments. A legal definition of a site could be 177.177.177.0/24, where 177.177.177.0 describes the IP subnet, and 24 tells how many bits are used to define it. The remaining bits of an IP address (32 – 24 = 8 bits in this example) can be used to define hosts.

A site consists of one or more subnets (unique network segments). For example, in a network with three subnets in Redmond and two in Paris, the administrator can create two sites: one in Redmond and one in Paris, and add the subnets to the local sites.

The Active Directory uses site information in these ways:

- The KCC generates a replication topology more strongly-connected within a site than between sites (adds some traffic but reduces intra-site replication latency).
- Does not compress intra-site replication messages (adds some traffic but reduces CPU utilization on DCs).
- Intra-site DC replication is change-based; inter-site DC replication is scheduled.
- Client machines use site information to find nearby DCs for logon operations.
- The Active Directory uses site information to help users find the closest machine that offers a needed network or a third-party service.

Intra-Site Replication

Intra-site replication (between domain controllers in the same site) attempts to complete in the fewest CPU cycles possible. Because domain controllers should be able to serve clients quickly for logons, searches, etc., the network connection between them is assumed to have lots of available bandwidth and reliable connection.

Replication is a trade off: data should be as accurate as possible on all domain controllers, which means that latency should be as small as possible, which means fast updates, which means frequent replication. On the other hand, frequency doesn't always equal efficiency. For instance, if there is a bulk import of directory objects, changes in a domain controller database will become out of date after 10 seconds, but it makes no sense to replicate the changes until the database is stable (the bulk import is complete).

Intra-site replication avoids unnecessary network traffic by introducing a change notification mechanism that replaces the usual polling of replication partners for updates. When a change is performed in its database, a domain controller waits a configurable interval (default 5 minutes), accepts more changes during this time, then sends a notification to its replication partners, which pull the changes. If no changes are performed for a configurable period (default 6 hours) the domain controller initiates a replication sequence anyway, just to make sure that it did not miss anything.

Attribute changes considered security-sensitive are immediately replicated and intra-site partners are notified: lockout of user accounts, change of domain trust passwords, some changes in the roles of domain controllers.

Intra-site replication topology is a bi-directional ring built using domain controller GUIDs. If a ring contains seven or more DCs, bi-directional connections are added to keep the path between any pair to less than three hops. New DCs configured in the site are included in the ring. One bi-directional ring is built for each naming context available in a site. Schema and configuration information share the same topology and only one bi-directional ring is built for them, because they must be replicated to all domain controllers.

If all of a site's domain controllers are in the same domain, the two rings are the same—the ring that includes all site domain controllers is equivalent to the ring that includes all domain controllers in that domain. You have more than one distinct ring only when your site contains more than one domain: 2 domains = 3 rings, 3 domains = 4 rings, and so forth. To find out what rings exist in a site, use the Active Directory Sites and Services Manager snap-in to check the connection objects and see what incoming replication connections they represent.

Inter-Site Replication

Inter-site replication is based on the assumption that the WAN is connected by slower links, so it is designed to minimize traffic rather than CPU cycles. Before being sent out, data is compressed to about 10% to 15% of original volume.

Inter-site replication topology is a spanning tree. As long as a replication route can be constructed between all sites in the enterprise, the replication topology is functional. It is not necessary to create additional links. The administrator decides which sites are connected, and can create a site link that allows domain controllers from any site to talk to domain controllers in any other site. Site links are based on the cost of replication (which reflects the speed and reliability of the underlying network) and its schedule (which defines a window when replication is allowed over the link).

Unlike Intra-site replication, inter-site replication does not use a notification process. Inter-site replication can be fully scheduled by the administrator on a per site-link basis.

Since there is no notification between the replication partners, a domain controller does not know which naming context was updated on the sourced replication partner. Therefore, it has to check all existing naming contexts on the source machine. A normal domain controller (that is, one that uses a GC as replication partner) will check only the normal three naming contexts on the GC (schema, configuration, and its domain) but never the partial naming contexts of other domains. For that reason, the initial replication setup traffic is slightly higher in the inter-site case. But if many objects are replicated, compression kicks in and makes this kind of replication more efficient.

Replication Transports

While intra-site replication supports only replication based on remote procedure calls (RPCs), the initial release of Windows 2000 offers two transports for inter-site replication:

- Synchronous (scheduled) via RPC over TCP/IP
- Asynchronous via simple mail transfer protocol (SMTP) using the Collaborative Data Objects (CDO v2) interface and the SMTP component in IIS 5, that is included in Windows 2000.

The intra-site RPC transport does not support data compression; the inter-site transports, both RPC and SMTP, do. RPC-based replication can be used for any kind of replication—intra-domain, configuration information, or global catalog information.

The SMTP transport has some restrictions: It can be used to replicate configuration and global catalog information, but cannot be used for replication between domain controllers that belong to the same domain and therefore have to replicate the full domain-naming context. The reason for this restriction is that some domain operations (for example: global policy) require the support of the file replication service (FRS) that does not yet support an asynchronous transport like SMTP for replication.

How to Measure Replication Traffic

Windows 2000 gives you some tools for assessing network load:

- Performance Monitor
- Event Log
- Network Monitor

The Windows 2000 Performance Monitor looks slightly different than previous versions available in Windows NT. It is implemented as a Microsoft ActiveX control that can be used either as an Microsoft Management Console (MMC) snap-in, or as a control in a Web page. This allows you to monitor servers and network traffic from a browser.

The Performance Monitor counters most frequently used to measure replication traffic appear under the NTDS object. They are:

- **DRA Inbound Bytes Total**. Total number of bytes replicated in. Sum of the number of uncompressed bytes (never compressed) and the number of compressed bytes (after compression).
- **DRA Inbound Bytes Not Compressed**. Number of bytes replicated in, that were not compressed at the source (which typically implies they arrived from other DSAs in the same site).
- **DRA Inbound Bytes Compressed (Before Compression)**. Original size in bytes of inbound compressed replication data (size before compression).
- **DRA Inbound Bytes Compressed (After Compression)**. Compressed size in bytes of inbound compressed replication data (size after compression).

- **DRA Outbound Bytes Total**. Total number of bytes replicated out. Sum of the number of uncompressed bytes (never compressed) and the number of compressed bytes (after compression).
- **DRA Outbound Bytes Not Compressed**. Number of bytes replicated out that were not compressed (which typically implies they were sent to DSAs in the same site, or that less than 50,000 bytes of replicated data was sent).
- **DRA Outbound Bytes Compressed (Before Compression)**. Original size in bytes of outbound compressed replication data (size before compression).
- **DRA Outbound Bytes Compressed (After Compression)**. Compressed size in bytes of outbound compressed replication data (size after compression).

You can also retrieve a subset of this information from the Event Log. The Event Log for directory service logging is set to the lowest level by default. This reduces the size of the log files, and restricts logging to important events such as errors, lost connections to replication partners, etc. Activating higher levels of event logging consumes CPU time and can present you with the tedious task of finding the right information in huge log files.

The third tool is Network Monitor. Measuring replication traffic with a network "sniffer" helps you isolate network packets that belong to replication between domain controllers. These figures differ for the RPC transport and the SMTP transport.

Sniffing RPC Replication Traffic

An easy way to detect replication traffic is to start Network Monitor and then force replication, which you can do either by using the Sites and Services Administration snap-in in MMC, or REPADMIN.EXE, which allows you to specify the particular naming context that has to be replicated. Once REPADMIN.EXE returns and reports that replication was successful, you can stop Network Monitor.

At this point, however, you have measured *all* incoming and outgoing packets from the server machine. Some could have been sent by other services running on the machine, such as NetLogon or the file server.

It is not easy to determine which packets belong to replication. One way would be to use the IP port that is used by replication. In general, this is not possible because replication uses dynamic RPC port mapping (as a means of security). This process allows the replication server to request an available port from the RPC port mapper interface, which tells the requesting client the port used by the replication interface, which the client then uses to communicate with the replication server.

One way to get around this is to configure the IP port used on the replication server by adding this value in the registry:

HKEY_LOCAL_MACHINE\CurrentControlSet\Services\NTDS\Parameters\TCP/IP Port

You can set this to 1349 (decimal), for example, to make 1349 the IP port, then find all replication-related packets by filtering on that port with Network Monitor.

Sniffing SMTP Transport Replication Traffic

Finding packets that belong to SMTP replication is easier because the SMTP service always uses port number 25 (decimal). Filtering network traffic using this port number shows only the SMTP-related replication packets.

Traffic Scenarios

This section discusses the traffic caused in two scenarios: single attribute replication, then complete object replication (such as users, groups, etc). It examines replication between domain controllers in the same domain (intra-site and inter-site), and global catalog server replication (intra-site and inter-site). The inter-site GC replication examines the RPC and SMTP transports. In the other cases, only the RPC transport can be used.

This is the basic scenario:

Single Attribute Changes

The Windows 2000 Active Directory has a replication granularity of one attribute: if only a single attribute changes, only that one new value is sent over the network.

There are two areas to examine: how efficient single-property replication is when compared to whole-object replication, and how replication traffic grows with attribute size.

The tests use non-security attributes because replicating security-related attributes (attributes owned by the security accounts manager—SAM) involves a special domain controller, the PDC emulator, that adds non-replication traffic onto the wire. (Passwords are tested later, however.) Specifically, the tests use string-data attributes taken from the user object because these affect traffic growth clearly.

Replication of one attribute with string size 1 – 75 characters.

Character	Bytes	Diff	Character	Bytes	Diff	Character	Bytes	Diff
1	4396		26	4444	0	51	4492	0
2	4396	0	27	4444	0	52	4492	0
3	4396	0	28	4444	0	53	4492	0
4	4396	0	29	4444	0	54	4492	0
5	4396	0	30	4444	0	55	4492	0
6	4396	0	31	4444	0	56	4492	0
7	4396	0	32	4444	0	57	4508	16
8	4396	0	33	4460	16	58	4508	0
9	4412	16	34	4460	0	59	4508	0
10	4412	0	35	4460	0	60	4508	0

Replication of one attribute with string size 1 – 75 characters. *(continued)*

Character	Bytes	Diff	Character	Bytes	Diff	Character	Bytes	Diff
11	4412	0	36	4460	0	61	4508	0
12	4412	0	37	4460	0	62	4508	0
13	4412	0	38	4460	0	63	4508	0
14	4412	0	39	4460	0	64	4508	0
15	4412	0	40	4460	0	65	4524	16
16	4412	0	41	4476	16	66	4524	0
17	4428	16	42	4476	0	67	4524	0
18	4428	0	43	4476	0	68	4524	0
19	4428	0	44	4476	0	69	4524	0
20	4428	0	45	4476	0	70	4524	0
21	4428	0	46	4476	0	71	4524	0
22	4428	0	47	4476	0	72	4524	0
23	4428	0	48	4476	0	73	4688	164
24	4428	0	49	4492	16	74	4688	0
25	4444	16	50	4492	0	75	4688	0

The table shows that the replication of a 1-character string property causes 4396 bytes of traffic. Increasing the string size up to 8 characters does not change the value. From 9 to 16 characters the traffic increases by 16 bytes, an increment that recurs up to 72 characters. This result is not surprising because the Active Directory uses Unicode to store strings in the database. Each Unicode character is 2 bytes, so for every 8 characters a 16- byte buffer is created. From the 72nd to the 73rd character is a big jump. This was caused by network fragmentation; the packet that contained the changed value reached its maximum size of 1,500 bytes and a new packet had to be created (causing overhead for an empty packet). After this jump, the 8-character/16-byte pattern resumes.

The next table shows what happens when multiple attributes are changed at the same time. It begins with one attribute and increases to six. Two things are examined: how traffic grows as attributes grow from one to ten characters, and how replication traffic increases as attributes increase.

Changing multiple attributes simultaneously.

	One Attribute		Two Attributes		Three Attributes		Four Attributes		Five Attributes		Six Attributes	
Character	Bytes	Diff	Bytes	Diff	Bytes	Diff	Bytes	Diff	Bytes	Diff	Bytes	Diff
1	4396		4460		4524		4736		4800		4864	
2	4396	0	4460	0	4524	0	4736	0	4800	0	4864	0
3	4396	0	4460	0	4524	0	4752	16	4816	16	4880	16
4	4396	0	4460	0	4524	0	4752	0	4816	0	4880	0
5	4396	0	4476	16	4688	164	4768	16	4832	16	4912	32
6	4396	0	4476	0	4688	0	4768	0	4832	0	4912	0
7	4396	0	4476	0	4704	16	4784	16	4848	16	4928	16
8	4396	0	4476	0	4704	0	4784	0	4848	0	4928	0
9	4412	16	4492	16	4720	16	4800	16	4864	16	4960	32
10	4412	0	4492	0	4720	0	4800	0	4880	16	4960	0

Replicating one attribute with a one-character string size takes 4396 bytes. Two attributes with one-character strings each take 4460 bytes—a difference of 64 bytes. The growth from two attributes to three is again 64 bytes. From three attributes to four is a bigger jump, however, because the increases exceeds the maximum Ethernet packet size and an extra packet has to be created. From four to five and from five to six attributes, the pattern resumes the 64-byte jump.

It can be surmised, then, that it takes 64 bytes to replicate one attribute if it has a one-character string. Ten-character-string attributes show an increase of 80 bytes per attribute (except when a new packet has to be created).

These tests again show the 8-character/16-byte jump. For example, in the column for 4 attributes, there is a 16-byte jump after two characters are added to the string size. This is the same behavior seen during the single-attribute replication.

Since the replication of single attributes causes little network traffic, it is not useful to research the behavior in different domain/site scenarios.

Object Replication

For object replication, all domain, sites and GC scenarios are covered. Here is the scenario:

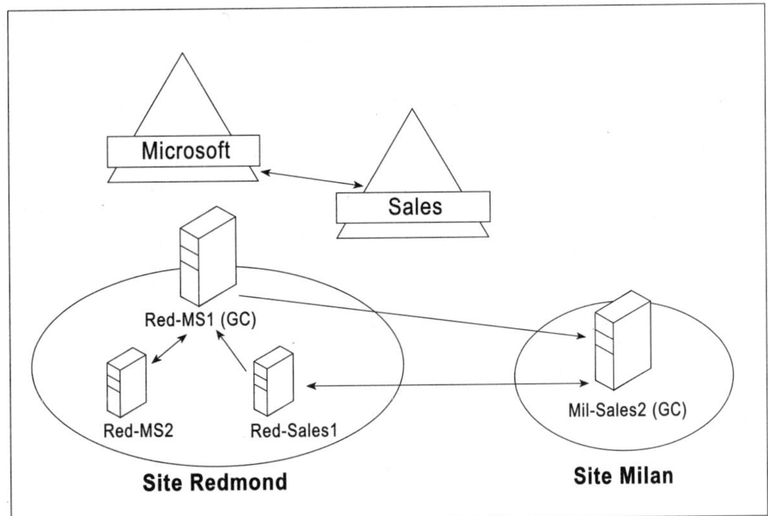

Figure 11.1 Replication scenario for object replication testing.

This small environment consists of two domains: *Microsoft.com* and *Sales.Microsoft.com*. Each has two domain controllers. Microsoft.com has Red-MS1 and Red-MS2: Sales.Microsoft.com has Red-Sales1 and Mil-Sales2.

The network is distributed over two sites: Redmond (headquarters) and Milan. Both sites have one global catalog: Red-MS1 for Redmond, Mil-Sales2 (the only domain in Milan) for Milan.

This small scenario covers all replication cases.

- Between two domain controllers that belong to the same domain, both intra-site (Red-MS1 and Red-MS2) and inter-site (Red-Sales1 and Mil-Sales2) replication occurs
- Partial global catalog server replication, both intra-site (Red-MS1 and Red-Sales1) and inter-site (Red-MS1 and Mil-Sales2). Replication between Red-MS1 and Mil-Sales2 can use either the RPC or the SMTP transport.

Intra-Site Domain Replication (Red-MS1 and Red-MS2)

Intra-Site replication assumes fast and reliable network connections. This should be a 10-Mbps Ethernet network or a comparable network topology. The emphasis on intra-site replication is on using the fewest possible CPU cycles at the domain controllers. This frees the domain controllers for other tasks, such as client logon, search operations etc. This is why data compression is not available within a site; it would cause additional CPU load.

In this sample case, both the global and the universal groups had no members. For all objects, only the mandatory attributes were set.

The following table shows how many bytes were created when objects were sent from one replication partner to another:

Intra-site domain replication.

#Objects	Users	Global groups	Universal groups	Volumes
1	13,019	11,309	11,145	10,277
10	47,037	26,902	26,823	22,848
100	386,148	187,754	185,606	149,736
500	1,914,087	905,015	906,079	715,577
1,000	3,818,256	1,815,170	1,803,090	1,436,085

This shows that the network traffic is absolutely predictable. Replicating 1,000 users, for example, causes twice as much traffic as replicating 500 users.

Replicating user objects causes more traffic than replicating objects that are not security principals. This is not surprising; the same effect was evident in the database sizing tests in Chapter 10.

The next test examines the replication of additional attributes. For the test, user objects were created, and filled with different sets of attributes. In the first test, only mandatory attributes were set. For the next test, one attribute was added to the mandatory attributes, then three added, then five added. All additional attributes were string attributes filled with 10 characters. The numbers in quotation marks show the overhead per attribute. For the replication of one user with five additional attributes, for example, this is (13,451 bytes – 13,019 bytes)/5 = 86 bytes.

Replication of additional attributes.

#Users	Mandatory attributes	Plus 1 attribute	Plus 3 attributes	Plus 5 attributes
1	13,019	13,233	13,439	13,451
		"214"	"80"	"86"
10	47,037	47,917	49,923	51,765
		"88"	"96"	"96"
100	386,148	396,308	416,107	435,496
		"102"	"99"	"96"

Replication of additional attributes. *(continued)*

#Users	Mandatory attributes	Plus 1 attribute	Plus 3 attributes	Plus 5 attributes
500	1,914,087	1,966,967	2,064,423	2,160,454
		"106"	"102"	'94"
1,000	3,818,256	3,919,177	4,123,535	4,328,794
		"101"	"103"	"107"
5,000	19,123,820	19,619,815	20,628,381	21,611,973
		"99"	"102"	"98"

Again, the traffic is very predictable. Adding one attribute to the object adds around 100 bytes of traffic. This makes it easy to compute additional traffic caused by replicating objects with a specific attribute set.

The next test concentrates on *group replication*. Group size depends on the number of members. This test shows how much overhead is created for a single group member (results are in bytes transferred). The numbers in quotation marks show the overhead per group member. To replicate 1 group with 100 members, this is: (29,212 bytes – 11,309 bytes) / 100 = 179 bytes.

Group replication test results.

#Groups	No members	10 members	20 members	100 members
1	11,309	13,023	15,028	29,212
		"171"	"186"	"179"
10	26,902	45,180	36,199	206,193
		"183"	"191"	"179
100	187,754	370,333	549,351	2,007,563
		"183"	"181"	"182"
500	905,015	1,822,257	2,745,787	9,956,677
		"183"	"184"	"181"
1,000	1,815,170	3,633,795	5,458,848	19,920,866
		"182"	"182"	"181"

The results again show a very predictable pattern. The overhead per group member is around 180 bytes.

The next test shows one of the most common operations: password changes. In this scenario, the PDC emulator was used for the password change, and only the replication traffic between this domain controller and a replication partner was captured. The numbers in the second column represent the bytes per operation. The third column shows the bytes per changed password.

Password change traffic.

#Users	Bytes	Bytes/user
1	10,805	1,842
10	12,811	385
100	59,856	509
500	275,422	533
1,000	444,085	425
5,000	3,014,610	601

Again the results are predictable: about 500 - 600 bytes/user. The test stops at 5,000 password changes, since more than that many per day would be rare; if users changed their passwords every 14 days, this would be the equivalent of 90,000 users in the same domain and in the same site. (Inter-site replication works differently, and is covered later.) Even if a company uses Windows 2000 or Windows NT workstations exclusively, with 45,000 users working on 45,000 workstations, the resulting 3 MB each day for password changes would be rare. And remember: intra-site traffic assumes a good network connection.

To summarize, intra-site domain replication is very predictable. Replicating more objects or attributes just increases network traffic following the same ratio. Intra-site replication assumes good network connection, so domain controllers don't waste expensive CPU cycles on compression.

Intra-Site GC Replication

Intra-site global catalog replication involves two domain controllers (one of which is a global catalog) that belong to different domains. The global catalog holds a partial replica of the domain-naming context of the other domain, and because only this subset of attributes has to be replicated, replication between these two domain controllers is also called *partial replication*.

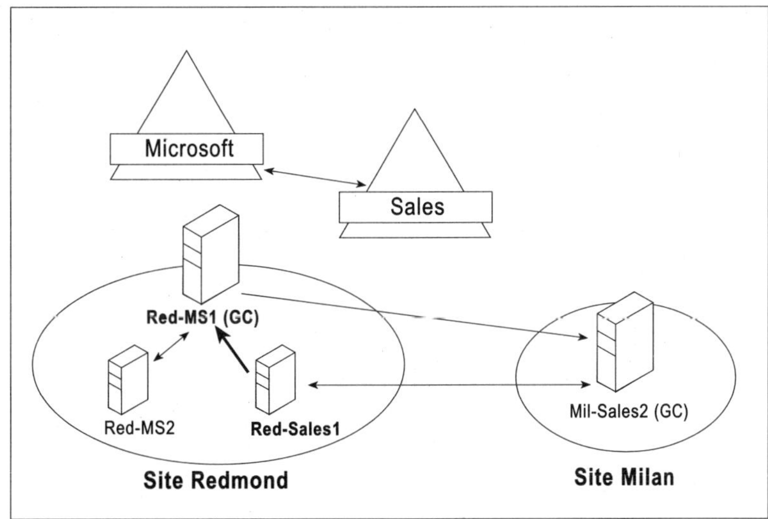

Figure 11.2 Intra-site global catalog replication.

This scenario examines the traffic between Red-Sales1 (domain controller in Sales.Microsoft.com) and Red-MS1 (domain controller in Microsoft.com), and a global catalog server.

The first test examines the traffic generated for objects. Except for domain replication, group type plays a role in global catalog server replication. Universal groups publish the group memberships in the GCs, but global groups do not, so more replication traffic is expected for universal groups than for global groups.

The table shows the bytes per object. The numbers in quotation marks are the domain replication numbers for comparison.

Intra-site replication traffic.

#Objects	Users	Global groups	Universal groups	Volumes
1	12,401	11,601	11,437	11,101
	"13,019"	"11,309"	"11,145"	"10,277"
10	35,595	26,783	26,862	23,011
	"47,037"	"26,902"	"26,823"	"22,848"
100	272,877	183,123	183,205	145,199
	"386,148"	"187,754"	"185,606"	"149,736"
500	1,323,177	879,823	879,990	690,042
	"1,914,087"	"905,015"	"906,079"	"715,577"
1,000	2,640,974	1,750,665	1,751,239	1,370,457
	"3,818,256"	"1,815,170"	"1,803,090"	"1,436,085"
5,000	13,189,354	8,735,103	8,745,150	6,860,815
	"19,123,820"	"8,985,915"		

The test shows that the replicated objects for GC replication are smaller than for domain replication. For user objects, the difference is not big. For smaller objects (non-security principals such as volume), the traffic is around 2/3 of what is replicated within a domain.

Universal and global groups are the same size because they were created with no members.

The next two tables compare global and universal groups.

Global groups.

#Groups	No members	10 members	20 members	100 members
1	11,601	11,519	11,437	11,437
10	26,783	26,783	26,783	26,783
100	183,123	183,369	183,369	183,041

The amount of data does not change if members are added to the group because Global Groups do not replicate members to the GC.

Universal groups.

#Groups	No members	10 members	20 members	100 members
1	11,437	13,491	17,149	31,731
10	26,862	46,816	67,256	245,908
100	183,205	388,725	593,623	2,207,641

Universal Group replication traffic depends heavily on the number of group members. To replicate 100 groups of 100 members each, the traffic is 12 times as big as for the comparable Global Group.

Intra-site GC replication is predictable. The objects replicated are smaller than within a domain—they can be as much as 1/3 smaller. However, this relates only to objects that were created with the minimum possible number of attributes set. If additional attributes are used, they won't be replicated to the global catalog, so the ratio goes down. However, if you change the schema so that attributes are added to partial replication, or if applications (such as messaging systems) add them, global catalog server replication traffic increases. Group type is also relevant for the traffic to the global catalog, because universal groups replicate their group members.

Inter-Site Domain Replication

The next scenario covers inter-site domain replication, which involves two domain controllers in different sites within the same domain. These serve as *bridgehead servers*, and are the only domain controllers of this particular domain that replicate over a WAN link. Once they receive updated information, they distribute it to the other domain controllers in their site.

This scenario examines replication between Red-Sales1 and Mil-Sales2. Both domain controllers are in the Sales.Microsoft.com domain, but are in different sites (Redmond and Milan).

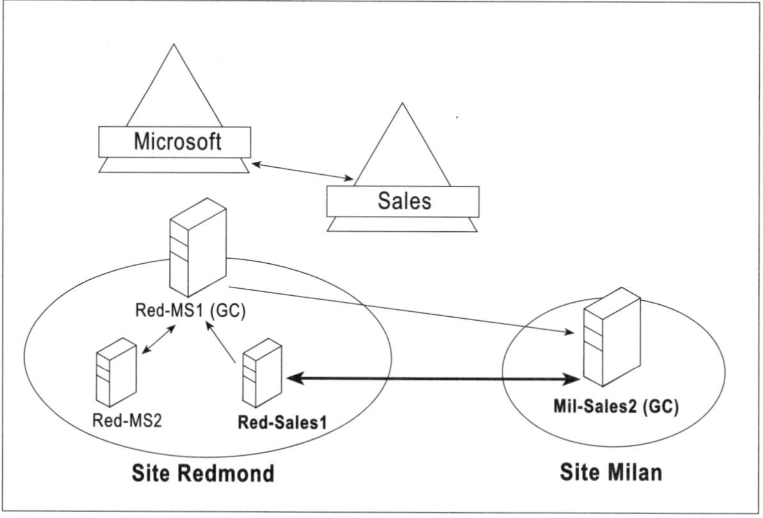

Figure 11.3 Inter-site domain replication.

Only object creation was tested. Changing the number of group members is not a factor because group members are *always* replicated between domain controllers of the same domain.

The table shows the traffic for object creation. The numbers in quotation marks are the intra-site results for the same operations for comparison:

Traffic generated by object creation.

#Objects	Users	Global groups	Universal groups	Volumes
1	14,108	10,437	11,227	9,667
	"13,019"	"11,309"	"11,145"	"10,277"
10	45,563	25,683	26,741	21,691
	"47,037"	"26,902"	"26,823"	"22,848"
100	39,583	28,743	29,675	22,602
	"386,148"	"187,754"	"185,606"	"149,736"
500	173,105	102,404	119,180	81,691
	"1,914,087"	"905,015"	"906,079"	"715,577"
1,000	291,041	194,926	199,054	151,989
	"3,818,256"	"1,815,170"	"1,803,090"	"1,436,085"

The results demonstrate how compression works. Up to a certain size, data is not compressed. In fact, for small replications (such as replicating one user) there is slightly *more* traffic than in the intra-site case. This is caused by the need to source more naming contexts (schema and configuration). Once the size of the data that has to be replicated exceeds 50,000 bytes, compression kicks in and reduces the amount of data considerably. A good example is the replication of 10 users and 100 users. Replicating 100 users causes much less network traffic (per user) than replicating 10 users. This is clearly the result of compression.

Inter-Site Global Catalog Replication—RPC-over-IP

The next scenario is inter-site GC replication, which involves two domain controllers (one a GC) that belong to different domains and are replicating schema, configuration, and the partial domain naming context. This type of replication can use RPC-over-IP or the SMTP transport. The first test uses RPCs.

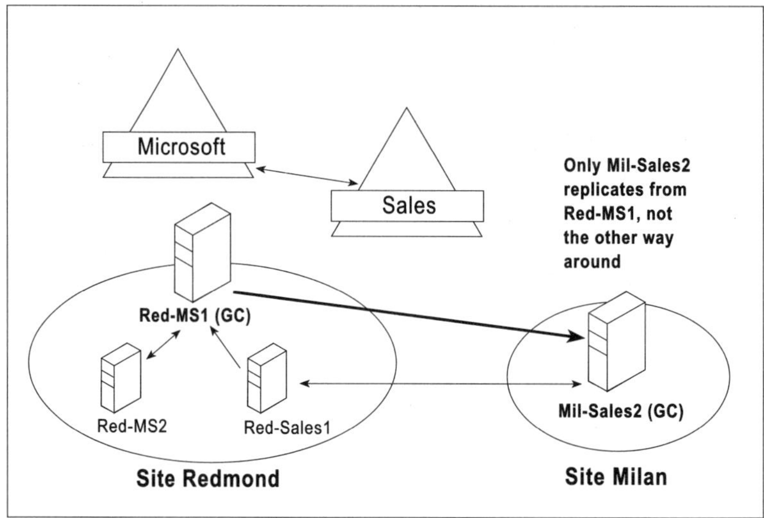

Figure 11.4 Inter-site global catalog replication.

In the example, Mil-Sales2 (a GC in Sales.Microsoft.com) replicates partial Microsoft.com information from Red-MS1. Note that Red-MS1, which is also a GC, would not use Mil-Sales2 as a source for the Sales.Microsoft.com naming context, because Red-MS1 can find a closer domain controller in Sales.Microsoft.com (in this case, Red-Sales1 is in the same site).

For this replication set, two factors are of interest: how does partial inter-site replication compare to partial intra-site replication, and how does group membership affect the overall picture?

The first table gives an overview of partial replication of objects. The numbers in quotation marks are the figures for intra-site GC replication, for comparison.

Partial inter-site replication.

#Objects	Users	Global groups	Universal groups	Volumes
1	12,565	11,471	11,389	11,183
	"12,401"	"11,601"	"11,437"	"10,277"
10	36,018	26,895	26,813	23,171
	"35,595"	"26,783"	"26,682"	"23,011"
100	32,391	28,600	28,379	24,598
	"272,877"	"183,123"	"183,205"	"145,199"
500	121,481	101,858	102,200	83,099
	"1,323,177"	"879,823"	"877,990"	"690,042"
1,000	233,503	194,047	194,357	170,918
	"2,640,974"	"1,750,665"	"1,751,239"	"1,370,457"

The table shows interesting differences between inter- and intra-site replication; again, replicating 100 users causes much less network traffic (per user) than replicating 10 users. In fact, inter-site replication of 1,000 users generates less traffic than intra-site replication of 100 users.

The next two tables show group memberships again, beginning with global groups. The numbers are much smaller again, compared to intra-site replication. The number of group members does not change the picture.

Global groups.

#Groups	No members	10 members	20 members	100 members
1	10,437 "11,601"	11,951 "11,519"	11,389 "11,437"	11,553 "11,437"
10	25,683 "26,783"	26,141 "26,783"	26,223 "26,783"	26,223 "26,783"
100	28,743 "183,123"	28,227 "183,369"	28,319 "183,369"	28,781 "183,041"

Universal groups.

#Groups	No members	10 members	20 members	100 members
1	11,227 "11,437"	17,010 "13,491"	15,786 "17,149"	32,270 "31,731"
10	26,741 "26,862"	46,898 "46,816"	12,999 "67,256"	17,902 "245,908"
100	29,675 "183,205"	39,120 "388,725"	46,912 "593,623"	107,551 "2,207,641"

Again, the numbers are much lower than for intra-site replication. However, this time traffic increases with the number of group members.

Inter-Site global catalog replication—SMTP Transport

This uses the same scenario, replicating between one global catalog and a domain controller that belongs to a different domain; the machines reside in different sites. This time, the SMTP transport is used.

The table shows the replication traffic. The RPC numbers are added in quotation marks.

Inter-site global catalog replication.

Object replication in bytes			Inter-site RPC replication	
No. Objects	**Users**	**Global Groups**	**Universal Groups**	**Volumes**
1	22,253 "12,565"	20,714 "11,471"	20,855 "11,389"	20,078 "11,183"
10	52,887 "36,018"	40,499 "26,895"	40,417 "26,813"	35,409 "23,171"
100	59,675 "32,391"	55,537 "28,600"	55,587 "28,379"	41,375 "24,598"
500	224,804 "121,481"	203,787 "101,858"	203,629 "102,200"	182,324 "83,099"
1,000	440,165 "233,503"	281,916 "194,047"	394,434 "194,357"	349,389 "170,918"

Again, compression helps to minimize the traffic. The threshold at which compression kicks in is higher when compared to the RPC transport; this threshold is around 65,000 bytes. Also, the SMTP transport creates more traffic overall than the RPC transport—about 80% to 100% more.

Summary of Network Traffic Analysis

To summarize, here are some replication recommendations:

- Intra-site replication assumes good network connectivity so domain controllers can save CPU cycles (for client logons, search operations etc.) by not compressing data for intra-site replication.
- Replication traffic is predictable. Use the tables in this chapter to find the data for your objects. If you set additional attributes on objects, add 100 bytes per attribute with a string size up to 10 characters.
- Partial replication (global catalog replication) is smaller than normal replication. The difference is bigger when more attributes are used on objects.
- Inter-site replication adds compression. If there is a slow link between domain controllers, create a new site.
- Inter-site replication is scheduled. This reduces communication between domain controllers.
- The SMTP transport creates more network traffic than the RPC Site connector. Use RPCs between sites whenever possible.

How can you choose between the two inter-site transports?

- If good network connectivity is available and fast client logon is desired—use one site.
- If reduced network traffic is desired, but the connection between domain controllers is fairly reliable—use multiple sites and the RPC-over-IP replication connector.
- If the network connection is unreliable, or domain controllers have no direct network connection (connected only through a messaging system)—use the SMTP replication connector. Remember that it can be used only for schema, configuration, and partial replication, not for replication between two domain controllers in the same domain.

Appendix

APPENDIX

References and Resources

This list contains references to Microsoft support offerings and other sources of information on Microsoft Windows NT Server and Microsoft Systems Management Server found through Microsoft Press, on the Microsoft Web site, or on TechNet.

Support and technical resources	Where found
Microsoft Support: Pointer to Support Online and support options	http://www.microsoft.com/support/
Microsoft Support Online: Access to Microsoft Technical Support's entire collection of problem-solving tools and technical information, including the Knowledge Base, troubleshooting wizards, service packs, and other downloads	http://support.microsoft.com/support /a.asp?M=F
Microsoft Enterprise Services: Worldwide services and support for large organizations	http://www.microsoft.com/Enterprise /support.htm
Premier Technical Support	http://www.microsoft.com/Enterprise /support/techsupport.htm
Premier Technical Account Management	http://www.microsoft.com/Enterprise /support/TAM.htm
Basic and Enhanced Supportability Review	Consult your Microsoft Consulting Services liaison or Technical Account Manager for additional information

Support and technical resources	Where found
Microsoft Support: Pointer to Support Online and support options	http://www.microsoft.com/support/
Microsoft Support Online: Access to Microsoft Technical Support's entire collection of problem-solving tools and technical information, including the Knowledge Base, troubleshooting wizards, service packs, and other downloads	http://support.microsoft.com/support/a.asp?M=F
Microsoft Enterprise Services: Worldwide services and support for large organizations	http://www.microsoft.com/Enterprise/support.htm
Premier Technical Support	http://www.microsoft.com/Enterprise/support/techsupport.htm
Premier Technical Account Management	http://www.microsoft.com/Enterprise/support/TAM.htm
Basic and Enhanced Supportability Review	Consult your Microsoft Consulting Services liaison or Technical Account Manager for additional information
Microsoft Certified Solution Providers	http://www.microsoft.com/mcsp/
Microsoft Certified Professional (MCP) training	http://www.microsoft.com/mcp/
Microsoft Training and Certification	http://www.microsoft.com/train_cert/

Support and technical resources	Where found
Microsoft Certified Technical Education Centers (CTECs)	http://www.microsoft.com/train_cert /train/ctec.htm
Microsoft Press: Look for the following titles: Networking Essentials, Second Edition Microsoft Windows NT Network Administration Training Microsoft TCP/IP Training Microsoft Windows NT Server 4.0 Enterprise Technologies Training BackOffice Resource Guide, Second Edition Microsoft Windows NT Server 4.0 Resource Kit Microsoft Windows NT Server Resource Kit Version 4.0, Supplement One Microsoft Windows NT Server Resource Kit Version 4.0, Supplement Two Microsoft Windows NT Workstation 4.0 Resource Kit ALS Microsoft Windows NT Technical Support	1-800-MSPRESS (677-7377) http://mspress.microsoft.com/ For a complete listing of available titles on Windows NT, go to: http://mspress.microsoft.com/ findabook/list/subject_5T.htm

Support and technical resources	Where found
Microsoft Windows NT Technical Support Training	
Microsoft Systems Management Server Training	
Microsoft Press ResourceLink: Provides direct access to complete resource kits, training kits, and other titles, as well as the latest technical updates and tools	http://mspress.microsoft.com/reslink/
Microsoft BackOffice Web site	http://www.backoffice.microsoft.com
Microsoft Windows NT Web site	http://www.microsoft.com/ntserver/
Microsoft Systems Management Server Web site	http://www.microsoft.com/smsmgmt/
Microsoft Security Advisor Web site	http://www.microsoft.com/security
Microsoft TechNet: The central information and community resource designed for IT professionals	http://www.microsoft.com/technet/
Microsoft Developer Network (MSDN)	http://msdn.microsoft.com/developer/
Microsoft Year 2000 Readiness Disclosure and Resource Center	http://www.microsoft.com/technet/topics/year2k/default.htm

General information	Where found
Microsoft Solutions Framework: *To help you plan an enterprise architecture that adapts to (or drives) industry change, consistently build business-driven applications, and manage your computing environment*	http://www.microsoft.com/msf/ You can also find an overview article on TechNet.
"Managing Infrastructure Deployment Projects"	Search TechNet
Internet Connection Services for Microsoft RAS, Standard Edition	Search TechNet, under Windows NT Server Manuals
Microsoft Cluster Server Administrator's Guide	Search TechNet, under Windows NT Server Manuals
"Automating Microsoft Windows NT Setup Deployment Guide"	http://www.microsoft.com/ntworkstation /info/Deployment-guide.htm
"Customizing the Windows NT 4.0 Upgrade Process"	http://www.microsoft.com/ntserver You can also search on TechNet
Overview of Windows NT registry and Registry Editor	See "Appendix A – Windows NT Registry" in Windows NT Server Concepts and Planning Manual (also on TechNet)

Windows NT Server-related tools (noted in this volume)	Where found
Network Monitor	See "Chapter 10 - Monitoring Your Network" in Windows NT Server *Concepts and Planning Manual* (also on TechNet) *Microsoft Windows NT Server 4.0 Resource Kit Supplement 1,* "Chapter 7: Monitoring Bandwidth and Network Capacity"
C2CONFIG.EXE	Found in the *Microsoft Windows NT 4.0 Resource Kit, Supplement Three*
NLTEST.EXE	Query TechNet using the "Q" number
Refer to Q158148, Title: Domain Secure Channel Utility – NLTEST.EXE	*For the most up-to-date collection of Knowledge Base articles, search Microsoft Technical Support online: http://support.microsoft.com/support /a.asp?M=F*
KIX32.EXE	Found in the *Microsoft Windows NT 4.0 Resource Kit, Supplement Three*
NETDOM.EXE	Found in the *Microsoft Windows NT 4.0 Resource Kit, Supplement Three*
REGBACK.EXE	Found in the *Microsoft Windows NT 4.0 Resource Kit, Supplement Three*
REGMON	http://www.sysinternals.com
ROBOCOPY.EXE	Found in the *Microsoft Windows NT 4.0 Resource Kit, Supplement Three*

Windows NT Server-related tools (noted in this volume)	Where found
SCRIPTIT.EXE	http://www.microsoft.com/ntserver
See also:	Query TechNet using the "Q" number
Q191605, Title: Incorporating ScriptIt with Unattended Installation Q191667, Title: How to Use ScriptIt to Install FPNW via Unattended Installation	*For the most up-to-date collection of Knowledge Base articles, search Microsoft Technical Support online: http://support.microsoft.com/support /a.asp?M=F*
SU.EXE (Switch User utility) and SUSS.EXE (SU Service)	*Microsoft Windows NT Server 4.0 Resource Kit—Supplement Two*
WINDIFF.EXE	Found in the *Microsoft Windows NT 4.0 Resource Kit, Supplement Three*

General Windows NT networking information	Where found
Microsoft Windows NT Server: Communication services technical details	http://www.microsoft.com/ntserver /commserv/techdetails/default.asp
Look for these whitepapers:	
"Virtual Private Networking Overview" "Internet Connection Service" "Routing and Remote Access" "Understanding Point-To-Point Tunneling Protocol (PPTP)" "Using Point-to-Point Tunneling Protocol" "Unicast Routing Principles" "TCP/IP Implementation Details"	You can also search TechNet.

General Windows NT networking information	Where found
"Guide To Microsoft Windows NT 4.0 Profiles and Policies"	http://microsoft.com/ntserver/management/deployment/planguide/prof_policies.asp
"Windows NT 4.0 Remote Troubleshooting and Diagnostics"	Search on TechNet
Windows NT Server: *Security services technical details*	http://microsoft.com/ntserver/security/default.asp
Windows NT Server downloads Web page	http://microsoft.com/NTServer/all/downloads.asp
Microsoft Windows Hardware Compatibility List (HCL)	http://www.microsoft.com/hwtest/hcl/
"Active Directory Service Interfaces—The Easy Way to Access and Manage LDAP-Based Directories (Windows NT 4.0)"	Search TechNet.
"Planning for Windows NT Server 5.0"(Windows 2000)	http://microsoft.com/ntserver/management/deployment/planguide/PlanForNT5.asp
Also listed as:	
"Planning Windows NT Server 4.0 Deployment with Windows NT Server 5.0 in Mind"	Search TechNet.

General Windows NT networking information	Where found
"Configuring DHCP"	*Microsoft Windows NT Sever 4.0 Resource Kit: Networking Guide*
"Browsing and Windows 95 Networking"	http://www.microsoft.com/win32dev/netwrk/browse1.htm http://www.microsoft.com/win32dev/netwrk/browse2.htm
"Performance Analysis and Optimization of MS Windows NT Server, Part 1"	Search on TechNet.
"Appendix A - RAS Registry Values"	
NetLogon: Q163204, Title: Increase Domain Logon Timeout over Network Q151259, Title: New Netlogon Registry Entry for Dialup Routers ***Pulse:*** Q150350, Title: NetLogon Maximum Value of Pulse Should Exceed 3600 Q102717, Title: Windows NT UAS Replication (Windows NT and LAN Manager) Q135360, Title: Periodic Re-Transmit Times for Packets	Query TechNet using the "Q" number, or search on the registry subkey. *For the most up-to-date collection of Knowledge Base articles, search Microsoft Technical Support online: http://support.microsoft.com/support/a.asp?M=F*

General Windows NT networking information	Where found
"DisablePasswordChange:	
Q154501, Title: How to Disable Automatic Machine Account Password Changes	
Q175468, Title: Effects of Machine Account Replication on a Domain	
ExpectedDialupDelay:	
Q152719, Title: WAN and Trust: Traffic on the Wire	
Q154355, Title: How to Tune Trusts for Dialup Routers in a WAN	
Q163204, Title: Increase Domain Logon Timeout over Network	
DisableServerThread:	
Q131902, Title: Printer Browse Thread May Cause Extensive Network Traffic	
BcastQueryTimeout & BcastNameQueryCount:	
"Windows NT 3.5, 3.51, 4.0 - TCP/IP Implementation Details"	
"Windows NT Server 4.0 - WINS Architecture and Capacity Planning"	
Q120642, Title: TCP/IP & NBT Configuration Parameters for Windows NT	

General Windows NT networking information	Where found
AutoDisconnect:	
Q97559, Title: How Remote Access Service Processes Datagram Traffic	
Q97599, Title: Windows NT RAS Registry Parameters	
Q181407, Title: Troubleshooting Proxy RAS Autodial and Autodisconnect	
Q134346, Title: Remoteboot Workstation Cannot Reconnect After Net 808 Errors	
Q103003, Title: REG: Network Services Entries, Part 7	
Q117304, Title: RAS Event ID (Error Code) Information	
Q138365, Title: How the Autodisconnect Works in Windows NT	
Q105134, Title: AutoDisconnect Default Incorrect in Online Help	
EnableRaw:	
Q127023, Title: Raw SMB Requests Across Router Results in Session Termination	

General Windows NT networking information	Where found
SizReqBuf:	
Q177266, Title: Remote Directory Lists Are Slower Than Local Directory Listings	
RPC_Binding_Order:	
Q174701, Title: XCLN: Troubleshooting RPC Problems for Exchange Clients	
NetServerEnum:	
Q131902, Title: Printer Browse Thread May Cause Extensive Network Traffic	
Q136712, Title: Common Questions About Browsing with Windows NT	
"Appendix F: Browser Traffic"	
MaintainServerList:	
Q136712, Title: Common Questions About Browsing with Windows NT	
MasterAnnounce:	
Q191611, Title: Symptoms of Multihomed Browsers	
ReplicationGovernor:	
Q140422, Title: Domain Synchronization Over a Slow WAN Link	

General Windows NT networking information	Where found
TCPWindowSize, TCPRecvSegmentSize, & TCPSendSegmentSize:	
Q102973, Title: REG: TCP/IP Transport Entries, Part 1	
Q140552, Title: How to Optimize Windows NT to Run Over Slow WAN Links w/TCP/IP	
Q120642, Title: TCP/IP & NBT Configuration Parameters for Windows NT	

WAN planning and design	Where found
Q120151, Title: Browsing a Wide Area Network with WINS	Query TechNet using the "Q" number. *For the most up-to-date collection of Knowledge Base articles, search Microsoft Technical Support online: http://support.microsoft.com/support/a.asp?M=F*
Q154355, Title: How to Tune Trusts for Dialup Routers in a WAN	
Q152719, Title: WAN and Trust: Traffic on the Wire	
Q134985, Title: Browsing & Other Traffic Incur High Costs over ISDN Routers	
Q140552, Title: How to Optimize Windows NT to Run Over Slow WAN Links w/TCP/IP	
Q159168, Title: Multiple Default Gateways Can Cause Connectivity Problems	

Tuning Windows NT Server for dial-on-demand & slow links	Where found
Enterprise Networking, by Daniel Minoli.	ISBN 0-89006-621-3
The Simple Book, by Marshall T. Rose.	ISBN 0-13-451659-1
DNS and Bind, by Paul Albitz and Cricket Liu.	ISBN 1-56592-236-0
How to Manage Your Network Using SNMP, by Marshall T. Rose and Keith McCloghrie.	
The Basics Book of Frame Relay, by Motorola Press University.	ISBN 0-201-56377-0
The Open Book, by Marshall T. Rose.	ISBN 0-13-643016-3
TCP/IP Explained, by Phillip Miller.	ISBN 1-55558-166-8
RFC 1001 and RFC 1002: Protocol Standard for a NetBIOS Service on a TCP/UDP Transport.	
RFC 1541: Dynamic Host Configuration Protocol.	

Tuning Windows NT Server for dial-on-demand & slow links	Where found
Q164308, Title: Windows NT 4.0 Clients May Refresh WINS Entries Frequently Q139270, Title: How to Change Name Resolution Order on Windows 95 and Windows NT Q120642, Title: TCP/IP & NBT Configuration Parameters for Windows NT Q102878, Title: Information on Browser Operation Q134985, Title: Browsing & Other Traffic Incur High Costs over ISDN Routers Q102981, Title: REG: Workstation Service Entries Q131902, Title: Printer Browse Thread May Cause Extensive Network Traffic Q124184, Title: Service Running as System Account Fails Accessing Network Q154501, Title: How to Disable Automatic Machine Account Password Changes	Query TechNet using the "Q" number. *For the most up-to-date collection of Knowledge Base articles, search Microsoft Technical Support online: http://support.microsoft.com/support/a.asp?M=F*

Directory replication & synchronization	**Where found**
"Synchronization over WAN and Remote Area Service"	"Chapter 2 – Network Security and Domain Planning" in *Microsoft Windows NT Server 4.0 Resource Kit, Networking Guide*
"Implementing Directory Services Using MS Windows NT Server - Part 2"	Search on TechNet.
Q140422, Title: Domain Synchronization Over a Slow WAN Link	Query TechNet using the "Q" number *For the most up-to-date collection of Knowledge Base articles, search Microsoft Technical Support online: http://support.microsoft.com/support /a.asp?M=F*

Systems Management Server—network traffic related information	**Where found**
"Deploying Applications and Content Using Systems Management Server 1.2"	Search TechNet
"Distributing Software over Slow Links"	http://www.microsoft.com/smsmgmt /support/out_of_band.asp?A=5&B=3
Q191317, Title: SMS: "Not Mandatory Over Slow Link" Check Box Has Been Removed Q185805, Title: SMS: Disabling the Mandatory Countdown Timer in PCM Q185346, Title: SMS: Logon Script Takes a Long Time over RAS or Slow Connection	Query TechNet using the "Q" number. *For the most up-to-date collection of Knowledge Base articles, search Microsoft Technical Support online: http://support.microsoft.com/support /a.asp?M=F*
"Remote Control Troubleshooting"	http://www.microsoft.com/smsmgmt /support/remotecontrol.asp?A=5&B=3

General Systems Management Server information	Where found
SMS Installer Download	http://backoffice.microsoft.com/downtrial/moreinfo/smsinst.asp
Q191441, Title: Systems Management Server 1.2 Service Pack 4 Fixlist	Query TechNet using the "Q" number. *For the most up-to-date collection of Knowledge Base articles, search Microsoft Technical Support online: http://support.microsoft.com/support/a.asp?M=F*
"Chapter 3—Understanding Sites" in the *Microsoft Systems Management Server Planning Guide*	Search on TechNet
"Chapter 3—Installing and Upgrading Sites, Servers, and Clients" in the *Microsoft Systems Management Server 1.2 Resource Guide* (of the *BackOffice Resource Kit, Second Edition*)	Search on TechNet
Q125487, Title: SMS Administrator Unable To Retrieve Machine List Q110352, Title: Optimizing Microsoft SQL Server Performance Q138347, Title: SMS: Procedure for Backing up and Restoring a Secondary site	Query TechNet using the "Q" number. *For the most up-to-date collection of Knowledge Base articles, search Microsoft Technical Support online: http://support.microsoft.com/support/a.asp?M=F*

General Systems Management Server information	Where found
"Automated Client Upgrade Process For Windows 95 and Windows NT Workstation 4.0 Through Systems Management Server"	Search on TechNet
"Remote Control Troubleshooting"	http://www.microsoft.com/smsmgmt /support/remotecontrol.asp?A=5&B=3
"Package Definition Files"	http://www.microsoft.com/smsmgmt /support/PDFs.asp?A=5&B=5
"Troubleshooting Remote Control" in the *Microsoft Systems Management Server 1.2 Resource Guide*	Search on TechNet
"Working with Remote Control" in the *Microsoft Systems Management Server 1.2 Resource Guide*	Search on TechNet
"Updated Tracer Utility - SMSTRACE.EXE"	Search on TechNet
Q161216, Title: SMS: Client Setup Fails to Update Sms.ini on Windows NT System. Q123317, Title: SMS: Enabling Help Desk Options from Logon Servers Unsupported. Q170440, Title: SMS: Remote Controlling a Multihomed Windows NT Client Computer	Query TechNet using the "Q" number. *For the most up-to-date collection of Knowledge Base articles, search Microsoft Technical Support online: http://support.microsoft.com/support /a.asp?M=F*

General Systems Management Server information	Where found
SMS and Novell NetWare and NDS related information	Where found
SKIPINV.EXE	*Microsoft BackOffice Resource Guide, Second Edition* (Utilities)
Configuring Systems Management Server and Novell's NDS	http://www.microsoft.com/smsmgmt /support/ndswp.asp?A=5&B=3
Q152469, Title: Hardware Inventory Hangs at 30% When Detecting the Game Port	Query TechNet using the "Q" number. *For the most up-to-date collection of Knowledge Base articles, search Microsoft Technical Support online: http://support.microsoft.com/support /a.asp?M=F*
Q157838, Title: SMS: NetWare Client32 for Windows 95 Stops Responding on Logon	
Q156402, Title: SMS: PCM Looks in Wrong Path for Default Distribution Server	
Q140802, Title: Package Command Manager (PCM) is Limited to 10 Servers	
Q154411, Title: SMS Err Msg: Unable to Initialize IPX Protocol	
Q159539, Title: SMS: File Transfer Fails with Client Running NetWare Client32	
Q159540, Title: SMS: HelpDesk Cannot Reconnect to Windows 95 with Client32	
Q182593, Title: SMS Err: "Unable to Initialize NetBIOS Protocol" on Win95 Client	

Windows NT security	Where found
"Microsoft Report on C2 Evaluation of Windows NT"	http://www.microsoft.com/security
C2CONFIG.EXE	Found in the *Microsoft Windows NT 4.0 Resource Kit, Supplement Three*
"Guide To Windows NT 4.0 Profiles and Policies"	http://www.microsoft.com/ntserver /management Search also on TechNet
Appendix D, "Security In a Software Development Environment," in the *Microsoft Windows NT Resource Kit Version 3.5 Update*	Search on TechNet
Internet Explorer Administration Kit Web site	http://ieak.microsoft.com
Q161990, Title: How to Enable Strong Password Functionality in Windows NT	Query TechNet using the "Q" number.
Q189746, Title: How to Use Proxy Server with Content Replication System.	*For the most up-to-date collection of Knowledge Base articles, search Microsoft Technical Support online: http://support.microsoft.com/support /a.asp?M=F*
Q143475, Title: Windows NT System Key Permits Strong Encryption of the SAM.	
Q189595, Title: PPTP Performance & Security Upgrade for WinNT 4.0 Release Notes	
Q167029, Title: Resource and Master Domain DCs Do Not Load-Balance Validation	
Q188855, Title: Security Privilege Must Be Enabled to View Security Event Log	

Windows NT security	Where found
Chapter 11, "Registry Editor and Registry Administration," in the *Microsoft Windows NT Version 3.5 Resource Guide*	Search on TechNet
"Creating Certificate Hierarchies with MS Certificate Server Version 1.0"	Search on TechNet
Chapter 6, "Backing Up and Restoring Network Files" in *Microsoft Windows NT Server Concepts and Planning* manual	Search on TechNet

Secure client logon	Where found
Q175025, Title: How to Build and Reset A Trust Relationship from a Command Line	Query TechNet using the "Q" number.
Q156684, Title: How to Use NLTEST to Force a New Secure Channel	*For the most up-to-date collection of Knowledge Base articles, search Microsoft Technical Support online: http://support.microsoft.com/support/a.asp?M=F*
Q158148, Title: Domain Secure Channel Utility—NLTEST.EXE	
Q181171, Title: Secure Channel Manipulation with TCP/IP	
Q165202, Title: WinNT Client Logon in Resource and Master Domain Environment	
"Systems Engineering—Under the Hood of Client Logon (Windows 95 and Windows NT 3.51 and 4.0)"	Search on TechNet

Microsoft Cluster Server-related information	Where found
"Setting Properties" in Chapter 4 of the *Microsoft Cluster Server Administrator's Guide*	Search on TechNet
Hardware Compatibility List (HCL)	http://www.microsoft.com/ntserver/info /hwcompatibility.htm
Chapter 6, "Backing Up and Restoring Network Files," in *Microsoft Windows NT Server Version 4.0 Concepts and Planning*	Search on TechNet
Chapter 5, "Preparing for and Performing Recovery" in the *Microsoft Windows NT Server Resource Kit Resource Guide*	Search on TechNet
Q112019, Title: Changing Primary Disk System After Installation	Query TechNet using the "Q" number
Q130928, Title: Restoring a Backup of Windows NT to Another Computer	*For the most up-to-date collection of Knowledge Base articles, search Microsoft Technical Support online: http://support.microsoft.com/support /a.asp?M=F*
Q139822, Title: How to Restore a Backup to Computer with Different Hardware	
Q139820, Title: Moving or Removing Disks & Fault Tolerant Drive Configurations	
Q113976, Title: Using Emergency Repair Disk With Fault Tolerant Partitions	
Internet Assigned Numbers Authority (IANA): RFC 1597 and RFC 1631.	http://www.safety.net/rfc.htm

Windows NT Server 4.0 Service Pack 4	Where found
"List of Bugs Fixed in Windows NT 4.0 Service Packs (Part 1)" also Microsoft Knowledge Base (KB) article Q150734	http://support.microsoft.com/support/kb/articles/q150/7/34.asp
	You can also search TechNet for this article and the following using the Qxxxxxx number. *For the most up-to-date collection of Knowledge Base articles, search Microsoft Technical Support online: http://support.microsoft.com/support/a.asp?M=F*
"List of Bugs Fixed in Windows NT 4.0 Service Packs (Part 2)" also KB article Q194834	http://support.microsoft.com/support/kb/articles/Q194/8/34.asp
"Windows NT 4.0 Service Pack 4 README.TXT File (40-bit)"	http://support.microsoft.com/support/ntserver/content/servicepacks/readme.asp?PR=NTS&T1=7d&FR=0&A=T&T=B&S=F&
"How do I install Service Pack 4?"	http://support.microsoft.com/support/ntserver/content/servicepacks/instalsp.asp?FR=0
"Before Installing a Windows NT Service Pack" also KB article Q165418	http://support.microsoft.com/support/kb/Articles/Q165/4/18.asp?PR=CHS&T1=7d&FR=0&A=T&T=B&S=F&

Windows NT Server 4.0 Service Pack 4	Where found
"Eight Steps to Take Before Installing Windows NT 4.0 Service Pack 4"	Search on TechNet.
"Year 2000 Information for Windows NT 4.0 Service Pack 4 Installation"	Search on TechNet.
"Common Service Pack Questions and Answers"	Search on TechNet.
Full download page for Windows NT Service Pack 4 (starts with license agreement)	http://support.microsoft.com/support/ntserver/content/servicepacks/sp4start.asp?PR=NTS&T1=7d&FR=0&A=T&T=B&S=F&
"Repairing Windows NT After the Application of Service Pack 3" also KB article	Search on TechNet
"Tips for Deploying MS Windows NT Server 4.0 Service Pack 3"	Search on TechNet.
"How to Search Windows NT Articles by Topic"	http://support.microsoft.com/support/kb/articles/q102/6/52.asp?FR=0

List of Knowledge Base article fixes in Service Pack 4	Where found
The titles below are separated by keyword topic.	http://support.microsoft.com/support /kb/articles/q150/7/34.asp *You can also search TechNet for this article and the following using the Qxxxxxx number.* *For the most up-to-date collection of Knowledge Base articles, search Microsoft Technical Support online: http://support.microsoft.com/support /a.asp?M=F*

16-Bit Windows Version 3.x-Based Applications

Q142026, Title: Err: "Hidden Console of WOW VDM" Running 16-bit or MS-DOS App

Q154791, Title: MS-DOS-based Applications May Not Find All Files

Q167969, Title: Under Windows NT, Win16 Applications Opening MS-DOS Devices Fail

Q169020, Title: 32-bit Help Fails to Start When 16-bit Help Is Running

Q170753, Title: Window Focus Set to Invoke Wrong 16-bit Application Through DDE

Q174233, Title: KeInitSystem Function Returns Uninitialized Stack on Alpha

Q174234, Title: Computer Hangs with Intensive 16-bit Code Running in a VDM

Q174266, Title: "Print Screen" from MS-DOS Application May Print Twice

List of Knowledge Base article fixes in Service Pack 4 *(continued)*

Q176211, Title: Console-mode Apps May Run Slowly on Multiprocessor Computers

Q177631, Title: Comdlg32 Fails to Display Drives Mapped by SUBST Command

32-Bit Windows-Based Applications

Q146965, Title: GetAdmin Utility Grants Users Administrative Rights

Q167871, Title: Error When Connecting to a Share on WinNT 4.0 NTFS Partition

Q170057, Title: Dr. Watson Dialog Box Stops Responding

Q170509, Title: Memory Leak in SERVICES.EXE Causes Performance Degradation

Q170510, Title: Double-Clicking the Mouse Button Acts as a Single Click

Q171996, Title: Winsock Function Calls Generate Non-Paged Pool Memory Leak

Q173993, Title: Dialog Message Not Sent Correctly from 32-bit to 16-bit App

Q173994, Title: GetTextExtentPoint32W May Fail with Unicode Characters > 0x

Q174531, Title: DirectDraw Fails Surface Creation with Large Dimensions

Q176319, Title: Docfile Standard Marshalling Returns 0x800706f4

Q177684, Title: Application Using SetOwner May Hang Windows NT User Interface

Backup Issues (NTBACKUP.EXE)

Q170566, Title: Ntbackup.exe Log Has Additional Space at Beginning of Each Line

Q170568, Title: Seagate Tape Drive Light Stays Lit After Exiting NTBACKUP

Boot Process and Startup

Q157913, Title: Services Set to Interact With Desktop May Fail to Start

Q163855, Title: STOP 0x0000001e May Occur in Srv.sys w/ Down Level Client

Q174932, Title: STOP 0x0000000A with Halmps.dll When Restarting

List of Knowledge Base article fixes in Service Pack 4 *(continued)*

Configuration and Tuning

Q174625, Title: Environment Variables May Prevent Logging On

Q175745, Title: Memory Leak When Using Win32 GetClipboardFormat API

Domain Administration

Q166822, Title: Remote Password Change Works Incorrectly to Down-Level Server

Q171308, Title: Explorer File Properties Dialog Version Tab Missing

Q172003, Title: Macintosh Change Password Fails on Down Trusted Domain PDC

Q173385, Title: System Policy Editor Will Not Allow More Than 255 Characters

Q174058, Title: Delayed Worker Threads Causes a STOP 7A

Q174076, Title: Invalid Password Message When Strong Passwords Are Required

Q174205, Title: LSASS May Use a Large Amount of Memory on a Domain Controller

Q174840, Title: Disabling Buttons in the Windows NT Security Dialog Box

Q175468, Title: Effects of Machine Account Replication on a Domain

Q175641, Title: LMCompatibilityLevel and Its Effects

Q178109, Title: Roving Profiles for Windows 95 Clients Stop Working

Q190928, Title: Poledit Spin Boxes Limit Max Value to 9999

MS-DOS-Based Applications

Q171940, Title: MS-DOS Application I/O Operations Cause Floppy Drive Access

Device Drivers

Q138791, Title: SCSI Printing Devices Requiring Wide SCSI May Fail

Q154094, Title: Using Iomega ATAPI Zip Drives with Windows NT

Q157032, Title: Services for Macintosh May Cause STOP 0x0A During High Load

Q167703, Title: Canon Bubble Jet BJC-4300 Does Not Support Ledger Paper

Q170572, Title: Unable to Format a 1.44-MB Disk on an LS-120 After SP3

Q174187, Title: WinNT Does Not Display IBM PS/2 TrackPoint as the Mouse Driver

Q174764, Title: Memory Leak in Ntfs.sys

Q175321, Title: SNA Client Sessions Hang Until SNA Server Is Restarted

Q177257, Title: STOP 0x0000000A or Difficulty Recognizing IDE CD-ROM Drives

File Systems

Q165387, Title: Sharing Violation When Deleting a Folder

Q169404, Title: NTFS Directory Corruption with Frequent File Creation

Q169608, Title: Occasional File Corruption When Using Unbuffered I/O

Q171213, Title: Copy to Removable Drive in Explorer May Fail After Media Swap

Q172930, Title: Removing Bypass Traverse Checking Causes Copy to Drop Streams

Q173322, Title: How to Disable Autochk During a Windows NT Reboot

Q174502, Title: Fault Tolerant Recovery Does Not Reoccur After Shut Down

Q171458, Title: Windows NT May Fail On Request to Open Large Files

Q172705, Title: Explorer Access Violates When Viewing a File's Properties

Q177591, Title: Service Pack Version Truncated in About Box

Q185727, Title: BUG: closesocket() Fails with 10038 After _open_osfhandle()

Interoperability

Q146095, Title: STOP: 0x0000000A or STOP: 0x0000001E in Tcpip.sys

Q147222, Title: Group of Hotfixes for Exchange 5.5 and IIS 4.0

Q150953, Title: Nwuser.exe Send Function Truncates Messages to 38 Characters

Q165404, Title: NTVDM AV on Servers with Exchange cc:Mail Connector

Q173526, Title: "Serious Disk Error" When Saving Word 6.0 Document on Windows NT

Q173533, Title: WinNT Radius Client Sends Incomplete Accounting Information

Q173998, Title: Middle East/Thai Windows NT May Print Incorrect Characters

Q174478, Title: Minimizing or Maximizing Does Not Redraw Window Properly

Q174541, Title: Publisher 3.0/4.0 Does Not Print Brick or Vertical Line Patterns

Q175877, Title: CSNW Connection Leak When Running 16-bit Applications

Q178202, Title: Fix for Loss of Data Records or Partial Records Written to Disk

Q180356, Title: NWConv Fails to Apply Correct Group Permissions

Macintosh Connectivity

Q171989, Title: Windows NT Services for Macintosh May Not Start in Desired Zone

Q177644, Title: Commenting Macintosh File Changes Date and Time Stamp

Q177660, Title: Access Violation Occurs in Sfmprint.exe on Busy Print Server

Q178364, Title: Macintosh Clients See Files on WinNT Server Constantly Moving

Q180716, Title: SFM Fails to Accept Associations with Two-Character Extensions

Q180717, Title: SFM: File Date and Time Stamp Change with Get Info

Q180718, Title: SFM: Disconnect Macintosh Clients before Dismounting Volume

Q185722, Title: SFM Rebuilds Indexes upon Restarting of Windows NT

Q188315, Title: Stop Error Message in Sfmsrv.sys

Network Issues (Services and Protocols)

Q109993, Title: Winsock Application Causes 0x0000000A Blue Screen STOP Message

Q125020, Title: NetBIOS SEND WAIT Call Returns Before RECEIVE is Sent

Q141496, Title: DHCP Client Comment Disappears When Obtaining IP Address

Q154990, Title: SETPASS May Change Password of Wrong User

Q155701, Title: Invalid UDP Frames May Cause WINS to Terminate

Q156655, Title: Memory Leak and STOP Screens Using Intermediate NDIS Drivers

Q157911, Title: Deadlock in Service Control Manager During System Shut Down

Q161968, Title: NetBT Tears Down TCP Session with Many Concurrent File Transfers

Q167110, Title: WinNT Err. Msg: Stop 0x1E in FPNWSRV.SYS

Q167395, Title: RIP Routes May Expire Early When Running Windows NT 4.0 RIP

Q168662, Title: DLC May Fail When Connecting Through an IBM 2210 Router

Q169847, Title: SNMP SysUpTime Counter Resets After 49.7 Days

Q171997, Title: WINS Replication Does Not Start As Scheduled

Q172030, Title: WinNT Err Msg: Stop 0xA in TCPIP.SYS

Q172290, Title: Routing and Remote Access "Out of Buffers" Event Logs

Q172512, Title: Routing and Remote Access Event ID 20100

Q172613, Title: Errors Connecting Through RAS When Password Expires

Q173525, Title: WINS Client May Switch Primary and Secondary WINS Servers

Q173676, Title: Client Cannot Resolve MX Record via Microsoft DNS Server

Q173753, Title: Duplicate IP Addresses After Upgrading DHCP Clients to SP2

Q173941, Title: Windows NT DNR Does Not Cache Short Names

Q174676, Title: NetWare Authentication Failure When Logging On to NetWare Server

Q174869, Title: WINS Client Sends Refresh Requests to Secondary WINS Server

Q175035, Title: Diskless Workstations Cannot Find BOOTP Server with DHCP

Q176082, Title: RRAS Server Updates Link State Database but Not Route Table

Q176209, Title: RAS or RRAS Server Fails to Answer Incoming Calls

Q176502, Title: RAS Authentication Rechallenge Resets Compression Flag

Q177125, Title: User Cannot Log On to LAN Because of RAS Logon Failures

Q177654, Title: Slow Network Performance Using NetBEUI Across Bridges

Q181120, Title: Manual Dial Dialog Fails to Appear when Logging On

Q184026, Title: NetDDE Causes Dr. Watson When Closing Incomplete Connections

Q151677, Title: NWLink SPX Ignores Allocation Number Sent By Peer

Q152079, Title: SNMP Traps Contain Invalid Agent ID Field

Q157123, Title: Communicating with SNA Hosts May Cause STOP 0x0A in DLC.SYS

Q163662, Title: Running Multiple Instances of an Application Causes STOP x50

Q166846, Title: Cannot Reconnect to TN3270 Server with Close Listen Sockets

Q170534, Title: Microsoft FTP Client Echoes Gateway Password on the Screen

Q174465, Title: Bad SAP Packet Causes 0x0000000A In Afd.sys

Q177113, Title: Incomplete Print Jobs Using JetDirect over SPX

Q177245, Title: Multiprocessor Computer May Hang Because of Tcpip.sys

Q177653, Title: CRT Conflict with Getservbyname

Q177680, Title: With GSNW, WinNT Client Cannot See All Files on NetWare Server

Q178381, Title: SNMP Leaks Memory If the OID Cannot Be Decoded

Q179092, Title: NWLNKIPX Sends Broadcast RIPX Packets Over the Network

Q181799, Title: RPC/TCP Connection Attempt Made Only to First Address

Q178110, Title: FPNW Does Not Allow OS/2 Clients to Open Files

Printing

Q141708, Title: Printing to LPD Printer Is Slow or Fails with Windows NT

Q143160, Title: Enterprise Server Stops During Print Spooling

Q149658, Title: TCP/IP Printing Causes File Cache to Grow

Q151778, Title: Huge Downlevel Print Job Causes File Cache to Grow

Q152764, Title: Garbled Characters Appear in Windows NT Print Queue

Q152993, Title: Raster Fonts Print Different on Windows NT 4.0 Than on 3.51

Q154475, Title: Add Printer Wizard Printer Browse List Not in Alphabetical Order

Q161969, Title: LPR Printing Device Reports an Error If Printer Not Available

Q164438, Title: FPNW Print Jobs Do Not Print or Errors Occur in FPNW Interface

Q169131, Title: Print Setup Dialog Box May Take a Long Time to Display

Q172147, Title: Add Printer Wizard Hangs When Searching for Remote Printers

Q174333, Title: Installing Win95 Print Drivers on WinNT 4.0 Asks for Wrong Disk

Q174510, Title: Print Job Corruption Printing on Fast Hardware Across Slow Link

Q174540, Title: Extra Page Printed on Epson Stylus Color Printers

Q174871, Title: Printer Shares Lost after Changing Server Name

Q175637, Title: Poor Print Quality with Epson Stylus Pro XL ESC/P 2

Q175643, Title: CR Interpreted As CR/LF When Text Job Is Converted to PCL or PS

Q176087, Title: LPRMON Status Strings Are No Longer Localized on German Version

Q177445, Title: Use LoadLibraryEx When Loading Printer Drivers

Q177471, Title: EBCDIC Characters not Properly Converted to ANSI Characters

Q179156, Title: Updated TCP/IP Printing Options for Windows NT 4.0 SP3 and Later

Q181022, Title: Err: Cannot Write to LPTx Printing to Parallel Port

Q183292, Title: Print Preview Frequently Causes Access Violation in Spooler

Remote Access Service

Q112547, Title: Dial-Up Networking Hangs After Failed Multilink Attempt

Q123597, Title: WinNT Err Msg: Error 614 Out of Buffers When Using RAS Script

Q160517, Title: RRAS May Decrement Local Static Route Metric

Q169822, Title: DSMN RAS Dial-in Properties Deletes NetWare Compatibility

Q177670, Title: RRAS Does Not Enforce Strong Encryption for DUN Clients

Q178205, Title: Connecting to a Server is Slow over RAS Using LMHOSTS File

Q186904, Title: MPROUTER Access Violation on Invalid Radius Response

Q186905, Title: Radius Client Uses 100 Percent CPU on Invalid Response

Q187940, Title: Input Filters over IPX WAN Routing May Fail to Filter Packets

Security

Q175020, Title: BUG: Remote COM Server Shuts Down After 6 Minutes

Q129457, Title: Anonymous Connections May Be Able to Obtain the Password Policy

Q147706, Title: How to Disable LM Authentication on Windows NT

Q154087, Title: Access Violation in LSASS.EXE Due to Incorrect Buffer Size

Q154174, Title: Invalid ICMP Datagram Fragments Hang Windows NT, Windows 95

Q154694, Title: New Policy Available to Hide Go To on Tools Menu

Q173817, Title: Savedump.exe Now Provides More Security to Memory.dmp

Q175048, Title: CACLS Quits on Access Denied Errors with /c

Q182918, Title: Account Lockout Event also Stored in Security Event Log on DC

Q183054, Title: Taking Ownership Remotely May Set Owner Incorrectly

Q184017, Title: Administrators Can Display Contents of Service Account Passwords

Setup

Q158548, Title: Sysdiff Changes Dates on Files It Applies to Windows NT

Q159839, Title: Sysdiff Does Not Add Empty Directories

Q174927, Title: Error Message During Setup of Noncritical Changes

Q175266, Title: Creating Many Partitions Causes Double Drive Letters

Server-Related Issues

Q154162, Title: Memory Leak in Perfmon.exe Occurs Monitoring WINS Counters

Q154398, Title: BDC Secure Channel May Fail if More Than 250 Computer Accounts

Q154984, Title: DNS Server May Not Recursively Resolve Some Names

Q154985, Title: DNS Registry Key Not Updated When Changing Zone Type

Q157182, Title: FPNW Causes STOP 0x50 When Connection Is Closed Twice

Q158706, Title: Netmon Performance Counters Support a Maximum of Eight Adapters

Q159599, Title: WINS Consistency Checking May Not Start at Scheduled Time

Q163055, Title: DHCP Client May Fail with WinNT 4.0 SP2 Multinetted DHCP Server

Q167038, Title: RAS Clients Run Winsock and RPC Applications Slowly

Q167629, Title: Predictable Query IDs Pose Security Risks for DNS Servers

Q167708, Title: BootP Client Names Disappear in DHCP Manager

Q168076, Title: WINS Fails to Converge

Q169274, Title: TCP/IP Causes Time Wait States to Exceed Four Minutes

Q169461, Title: Access Violation in DNS.EXE Caused by Malicious Telnet Attack

Q170518, Title: DNS Admin Fails When Managing Large Number of Zones

Q170965, Title: SFM Time and Date Stamp Change Copying Between Volumes Locally

Q171180, Title: Non-Paged Pool Memory Leak in IRP Pool Tag

Q174509, Title: Stop 0x0000000A in Ndiswan.sys with Digiboard ISDN Board

Q176973, Title: Stop 0x0000000A in Netbt.sys on BDC When WINS Server Shuts Down

Q178393, Title: SQL Server Hangs When Sending a Message Using SQLMail

Q178546, Title: CSNW Does Not Display Directory Name with Extended Characters

Q179995, Title: Memory Leak in FPNW Causes Windows NT Server to Hang

Q180532, Title: Xircom PC Card Fails to Function

Q180963, Title: Denial of Service Attack Causes Windows NT Systems to Restart

Q181311, Title: Data Corruption Occurs with Record Locking on FPNW Server

Q181928, Title: Using POLEDIT to Save Policy Files on NetWare Servers May Fail

Q182205, Title: Clients Cannot Send Mail Attachments Through Modem Sharing

Q182227, Title: DNS Server Does Not Check for Delegations Before Forwarding

Q182441, Title: Full Synchronization from WinNT PDC to LanMan Server May Fail

Q182816, Title: WINS PriorityClassHigh Parameter Does Not Work After Restarting

Q183677, Title: Client Authentication with Personal Certificates Fail

Q183718, Title: CACLS Not Resolving Principle Names Correctly

Q183832, Title: GetHostName() Must Support Alternate Computer Names

Q184219, Title: Access Violation in Microsoft TAPI Browser 2.0

Q184228, Title: Dr. Watson in Nwssvc.exe Deleting Queue and Printer from FPNW

Q184229, Title: Copying Files to a Macintosh Volume Changes Date and Time Stamp

Q184344, Title: Reconcile on DHCP Scope Does Not Work Correctly for BOOTP Client

Q184353, Title: DHCP ALT+H Shortcut Key for HELP Is Not Available

Q184414, Title: Access Violation When Printing PostScript to SFM Print Server

Q184744, Title: DHCP Server Leaks Registry Quota on Alpha Version of Windows NT

Q184754, Title: Several Threads Created in LRPC Running Stress Test in IIS

Q184832, Title: Intermittent Name Conflicts with WINS Server

Q185051, Title: Restarting Cluster Service Causes Services.exe to Crash

Server and Workstation-Related Issues

Q129047, Title: Synchronizing DNS Information in Registry with Boot Files

Q137565, Title: System Error 53 When Connecting to a FQDN

Q143478, Title: Stop 0A in Tcpip.sys When Receiving Out Of Band (OOB) Data

Q151860, Title: STOP 0x0A While Writing to the Middle of a Cached File

Q153161, Title: WinNT Systems Running RAS May Exhaust Available DHCP Leases

Q153296, Title: Write Cache on IDE/ATAPI Disks Is Not Flushed on Shut Down

Q154387, Title: TAPISRV.EXE Thread Uses Excessive CPU Time

Q154460, Title: Denial of Service Attack Against WinNT Simple TCP/IP Services

Q154552, Title: NETSTAT Causes Memory Leak

Q155495, Title: Reference Counter Overflow in Security Descriptor Causes STOP

Q158396, Title: Explorer Hangs When Creating a New Folder On a MAC Volume

Q158516, Title: Access Violation in RPCRT4.DLL When Pickling Buffered RPC Data

Q158581, Title: Icon Position Not Stored When Using Roaming Profiles

Q158682, Title: Shortcuts Created Under Windows NT 4.0 Resolve to UNC Paths

Q159595, Title: Missing Uppercase "A" Character in the 1257 Font

Q159909, Title: STOP 0x0000000A May Occur on Multiprocessor Systems

Q163251, Title: STOP 0xA Due to Buffer Overflow in NDISWAN.SYS

Q163852, Title: Invalid Operand with Locked CMPXCHG8B Instruction

Q164023, Title: Fix for Gethostbyname() IP Address Order on Local Multihomed Mac

Q164253, Title: WinNT Err. Msg: Event ID 2018 When Srv.sys Is out of Memory

Q164314, Title: WinNT Err Msg: STOP 0x0000001E in Win32k.sys When Moving Mouse

Q165005, Title: Windows NT Slows Down Because of Land Attack

Q165181, Title: EISA Configuration Boot Code Is Replaced on Mirror Drives

Q165439, Title: Parsing LMHOSTS with Invalid Entries Can Cause Stop 0x1E

Q165664, Title: RPC Encoding API "MesInqProcEncodingId" May Not Work

Q165989, Title: GetPeerName() Returns WSAENOTCONN After Select() Returns Success

Q166571, Title: Creating an SFM Volume on Large Partition Causes a Stop 0x24

Q169888, Title: User-Define Path Dropped When User and System Paths Too Large

Q170626, Title: DDEML: Memory Leak in Global Shared Memory

Q170817, Title: Windows NT Causes APC Smart UPS Battery to Discharge

Q170880, Title: Diskdump.sys Common Buffer Size Is Changed

Q171181, Title: Deadlock in TCP/IP on Multiprocessor Computers

Q171295, Title: Fault Tolerant Systems May Encounter Problems with WinNT SP3

Q171307, Title: How to Disable SAP Broadcast for RPC Service

Q171386, Title: Connectivity Delay with Multiple Redirectors Installed

Q171564, Title: TCP/IP Dead Gateway Detection Algorithm Updated for Windows NT

Q171790, Title: Time Incorrect After Restarting Multiprocessor System

Q172122, Title: Toshiba I586 Pro 230 MHz System and the National 307 Chip

Q172511, Title: Stop 0x0000000A w/ Services for Macintosh & McAfee Anti-Virus

Q172885, Title: NetWare Print Server Names With Periods Truncated in Explorer

Q172982, Title: 16-bit ShellExecute Fails if Application Exists in Long Path

Q173277, Title: No Memory.dmp File Created with RAM Above 1.7 GB

Q173881, Title: STOP 0x0000000A in Netbt.sys on a Multiprocessor Computer

Q173997, Title: Drive Letter Not Displayed in Error Message Box

Q174020, Title: STOP 0x0000001E During Forced Shutdown and Program Exit

Q174534, Title: BitBlt May Not Work When Raster Operation Mode Is NOTSRCCOPY

Q174535, Title: Access Violation When TCMAPP Exceeds 16 Users

Q174543, Title: Enabling the Shift Lock Feature on Windows NT 4.0

Q174830, Title: NMI Error Message on Blue Screen May Be Garbled

Q174844, Title: Spooler Service Causing Access Violation

Q174929, Title: No Response to ARP Causes Duplicate IP Addresses on Network

Q175225, Title: Disabling Context Menus Does Not Disable Key Combinations

Q175667, Title: Error Message: Copy Profile Error

Q175687, Title: Win32k.sys Causes STOP 0x0000001e and 0x0000000a On SMP

Q175738, Title: Collate Feature May Not Work with PostScript Printing

Q176081, Title: Access Violation in Explorer.exe Removing a Share

Q176322, Title: The Far East GetTextExtent API Fails with Null LPNFit

Q176976, Title: Wrong Return Value from MkParseDisplayName

Q176977, Title: STOP 0x00000023 FAT_FILE_SYSTEM with Corrupted Floppy Disk

Q177647, Title: Nonpaged Pool Size Incorrectly Displayed in Performance Monitor

Q177650, Title: Remote Shutdown Fails If User Is Logged On Without Rights

Q177651, Title: AT Command Handles Quotation Marks Differently

Q177655, Title: Negative Values in Performance Monitor Data

Q177668, Title: Calibration Does Not Change When You Calibrate Foot Pedals

Q177676, Title: Stop 0x00000024 May Occur When Bypass Traverse Checking Disabled

Q177757, Title: Dr. Watson Does Not Report Service Pack Number

Q177868, Title: SnmpMgrTrapListen API Returns ERROR_SERVICE_NOT_ACTIVE Error

Q178113, Title: Specifying a Group Name in LMHOSTS File May Cause STOP 0xA

Q178208, Title: CrashOnAuditFail with Logon/Logoff Auditing Causes Blue Screen

Q178413, Title: Windows NT System May Hang When Running a Filter Driver

Q178414, Title: Archive Bit Is Not Reset When a File Is Renamed

Q178550, Title: IP Address Conflict with Address 0.0.0.0

Q178557, Title: Dr. Watson May Display Message Box Even When Disabled

Q178636, Title: Directory Listing Not Correct When Using Russian Characters

Q178723, Title: Problems with "Run Only Allowed Windows Application"

Q178741, Title: Event Log Opening Problem Causes Services.exe Failure

Q179107, Title: STOP 0x0000000A in Raspptpe.sys on a Windows NT PPTP Server

Q179129, Title: STOP 0x0000000A or 0x00000019 Due to Modified Teardrop Attack

Q179147, Title: Access Denied Starting Program

Q179187, Title: Problems Using TAPI 2.1

Q179190, Title: NWRDR May Send Excessive GetNearestServer Requests

Q179433, Title: Cache Manager May Cause Data Corruption on SMB Servers on FAT

Q179553, Title: Access Violation in PolEdit When Defining Allowed Windows Apps

Q179741, Title: STOP 0x0A Due to Duplicate Free in Afd.sys

Q179827, Title: Registry Handle Leak Causes Random Blue Screens

Q179873, Title: Files Open with UNC Path May Be Closed Prematurely

Q179983, Title: RDR Sessions on UNC Name Images May Log Off Prematurely

Q180622, Title: STOP:0x0000001E with STATUS_INSUFFICIENT_RESOURCES in Sfmsrv.sys

Q180648, Title: Windows NT 4.0 Traps with a Stop 0x24 or Stop 0xA

Q180854, Title: Access Violation in Winlogon with Third-Party Gina.dll

Q180875, Title: Russian Clients May Have File I/O Problems on an FPNW Server

Q181859, Title: Stop 0x0000000A When Using UltraBac to Back Up a SQL Server

Q182005, Title: Euro Currency Not Available in Windows NT Character Sets

Q182047, Title: DHCP Server Performance Degraded by Large Number of Scopes

Q182288, Title: RPC May Cause System to Stop Responding during Shutdown

Q182322, Title: SNMP Appends Garbage to Data in Response to SNMP Get

Q182333, Title: Excessive Processor Usage on Print Servers

Q182444, Title: NBF MaxFrameSize Calculated Incorrectly on Token Ring

Q182781, Title: Client Connections to Multihomed Server Not Load Balanced

Q182817, Title: CSNW: Unable to Rename File on NetWare Server

Q182825, Title: NET USE Returns Error 53 When Host Has 3 or more NICs

Q183069, Title: Ensoniq PCI Sound Card Experiences Static When Disk Is Accessed

Q183335, Title: Calling Card and Area Code Not Dialed Using Both TAPI Options

Q183419, Title: Memory Leak in Spoolss.exe Causes Performance Degradation

Q183581, Title: Out of Virtual Memory Messages During Windows NT Installation

Q183651, Title: Default Memory Settings for Lexmark Optra S 1250 Incorrect

Q183652, Title: Access Violation When More Than 200 Adapters Are Installed

Q183653, Title: Client Authentication Fails Connecting to Netscape Server

Q183654, Title: IBM DTTA-351010 10.1 GB Drive Capacity Is Inaccurate

Q183656, Title: XCOPY Returns "Invalid Parameter" When Using Date Switch

Q183657, Title: Unable to Insert OLE Objects into Application Documents

Q183664, Title: NDS Logon Scripts Do Not Execute Correctly

Q183699, Title: Winsdmp.exe Inefficiently Dumps WINS Databases with Large ID

Q183704, Title: Hide Drives Policy in Common.adm Has No VALUEOFF Statement

Q183705, Title: RPC Mishandles Changes in the Number of IP Addresses

Q183709, Title: Printing from Xerox 3006 May Cause Paper Jams

Q183812, Title: Problems When a Connection over an ISDN Bridge Is Not Closed

Q183819, Title: DCOM over HTTP Method Calls May Hang for up to 15 Minutes

Q183840, Title: Stop 0xC000021A When Starting Task Manager with CTRL+ALT+DEL

Q183859, Title: Integrity Checking on Secure Channels with Domain Controllers

Q183930, Title: FIX: IP Is Mangled When Using UDP on Multihomed Computers

Q184072, Title: HasOverlappedIoCompleted, GetOverlappedResult Give Wrong Value

Q184101, Title: Small Single and Double-Precision Values Are Rounded to Zero

Q184132, Title: Err Msg: Value Entered Does Not Match with the Specified Type

Q184139, Title: Stopping RPC Locator Service Causes Error 2186

Q184213, Title: SystemFileCacheInformation Can Be Changed Without Privilege

Q184232, Title: DCOMCNFG Saves Incorrect Display Name in Services

Q184278, Title: Server in One Domain May Disconnect Client in Another Domain

Q184350, Title: WordPerfect Suite 6.0 Setup Fails with Multiple CD-ROMs

Q184537, Title: Very Large Files Cause Performance Problems

Q184538, Title: Error Message: A Controller for This Domain Could Not Be Found

Q184752, Title: Xerox PCL Does Not Print Landscape

Q184758, Title: STOP 0x78 When NonPagedPoolSize > 7/8 of Physical Memory

Q184794, Title: STOP 0x50 May Be Caused by PPTP Registry Entries

Q184954, Title: Computer Hangs While Booting with HP 6L Printer out of Paper

Q185203, Title: SPOOLSS Hangs When Printing a File With a Corrupted EMF Record

Q185668, Title: IntelliMouse TrackBall Wheel Does Not Work with Service Pack 3

Q187392, Title: PATCH: Stop 0x0000000A in Wind32k.sys xxxDDETrackWindowDying

Q192127, Title: BUG: RpcTestCancel() Always Returns Error Code 5

Stop Messages/Blue Screen

Q172762, Title: Continuous Bhnt.sys Load and Unload Causes STOP 0xA and 0x7F

Q174555, Title: STOP 0x0000001E When IIS Service Is Stopped

Q185300, Title: STOP 0x24 in Ntfs.sys Function NTFSMoveFile()

Q185624, Title: Calls to NtQueryVolumeInformationFile May Cause Stop 0x0000001E

Q193532, Title: Stop 0x0000000A When Running Executable from Floppy Disk

Q193548, Title: Stop 0x0000002E Using Qlogic Driver Version 2.29

TCP/IP

Q162230, Title: Fragmentation and Performance Issues with PPTP Connections

Workstation-Related Issue

Q183676, Title: Window Position of Windisk.exe Causes Access Violation

Internet Information Server 3.0 Related Issues

Q143484, Title: IIS Services Stop with Large Client Requests

Q185870, Title: IIS: SQL Server Insert Error Regarding Column Name Mismatch

Q189462, Title: Only Partial Pages Displayed or Error "The Connection Was Reset"

Internet Information Server 4.0 Related Issues

Q183283, Title: IE Through Proxy Server to IIS May Stop on Page with Scripts

Q184288, Title: GP Fault May Occur with IIS on Multi-processor System

Q184891, Title: Server.HTMLEncode Garbles Extended Characters

Q185219, Title: IIS 4.0 with Multiple Certificates May Return Error

Q185349, Title: Problems Remotely Accessing W3 or FTP Perfmon Counters

Q186929, Title: LowercaseFiles Registry Key Has Added Functionality

Q188806, Title: "::$DATA" Data Stream Name of a File May Return Source

Q189262, Title: FTP Passive Mode May Terminate Session

Q190009, Title: Client Cert. Mapping Only Works w/First Page on Proxy Connection

Q190010, Title: Logging Performs Unwanted Flushes of Log Data Buffer

Q190015, Title: Setting LogonMethod to Batch Causes "Parameter is Incorrect"

Q193525, Title: Access Violation Occurs When Viewing Web Sharing Tab

Q193526, Title: W3SVC Counters Fail after a Successful Install

Q193528, Title: Internet Service Manager Does Not Allow Wildcard Redirections

Q193613, Title: ADSI Paths Greater than 80 Characters Causes Access Violation

Q193614, Title: Viewing Computer from MMC Causes Access Violation to Occur

Q193688, Title: HTMLA: Object Already Exists When Creating New Web Sites

Q193689, Title: IIS Security: Mapping IDC Reveals Paths for Web Directories

Q193793, Title: ":$DATA" Data Stream Name Returns Source of a Remote File

Q193812, Title: Extended Characters in URL Translated into UTF-8 Characters

Q194393, Title: New Window From Here Option in MMC May Cause Fatal Error

Q194787, Title: XFOR: IIS 4.0 SMTP Does Not Retry Delivery on HELO/EHLO Failures

Microsoft Commercial Internet Server Issues

Q190785, Title: IMS Not Trying Next MX Record If Session to Port 25 Established

Q193686, Title: SMTP Services Do Not Start Automatically After One Is Stopped

Q193687, Title: Invalid Handle Exception Error During SMTP Server Maintenance

Q194785, Title: XFOR: Windows NT Option Pack Certificate Causes MCIS SSL to Fail

Q194786, Title: XFOR: MCIS SMTP Service Strands Messages

Proxy Server Issues

Q176922, Title: Multiple IP Addresses Cause Dynamic Packet Filter to Fail

Q189276, Title: ODBC Causes Access Violation in 16-Bit Winsock

Site Server 3.0 issue

Q187999, Title: "Access Denied" w/ Personalization & Membership Authentication

General Service Pack 4 Fix

Q192292, Title: Unpredictable TCP Sequence Numbers in SP4

Q142047, Title: Bad Network Packet May Cause Access Violation (AV) on DNS Server

Q142615, Title: Event Log Service Fails to Check Access to Security Log File

Q142635, Title: Cannot Change the Drive Letter of Removable Drives

Q159310, Title: Updated Version of Dns.exe Fixes Several Problems

Q167040, Title: PPTP Performance Update for Windows NT 4.0 Release Notes

Q168748, Title: Java Applets Cause IE 3.02 to Stop Responding w/ SP3

Q169291, Title: Using Scopes with Different Subnet Masks in a Superscope

Q169839, Title: XFOR: Cannot Enable (Appletalk) MTA Service NT SP3

Q170517, Title: Cannot Log on Using IPX After Installing SP3 on Windows NT 4.0

Q173059, Title: Security Events Are Not Logged During Audit

Q173523, Title: IIS 3.0 Can Fail in Low Memory Conditions

Q174748, Title: XADM: ESEUTIL /g Returns Error -1022

Q175093, Title: User Manager Does Not Recognize February 2000 As a Leap Year

Q177154, Title: Access Control Causes Reverse Proxy to Fail

Q177677, Title: TSR Applications Hang While Login.exe Is Running

Q177906, Title: Caching Does Not Work Under Reverse Proxying

Q177983, Title: Stop 0xA in Netbt.sys with Greater Than 64 Adapters

Q178302, Title: XADM: Upgrade to Exchange 5.5 Fails If Virus Software Is Enabled

Q178471, Title: STOP 0XA Caused by Race Condition in VDM and Process Delete

Q179157, Title: Stop 0xA in Tcpip.sys When Source Routing Data Exceeds 18 Bytes

Q180122, Title: After Changing the Time, Windows NT May Skip a Day

Q180168, Title: Novell Client 32 for Win95 Displays Duplicate Files on FPNW

Q182540, Title: WinNT x86 MPS HAL Can Fail To Map System Relative IRQs

Q182644, Title: DNR Sorts IP Address for Multihomed Hosts Before Returning List

Q183123, Title: Find Files Displays Garbled Date if Year is 2000 or Greater

Q183125, Title: Shell Doc Property Dialog Custom Date Incorrect after Year 2000

Q183749, Title: Access Violation in INETINFO:TerminateExtension

Q183755, Title: More Than One Internal IP with Socks Enabled Causes Dr. Watson

Q183875, Title: DHCP Server Leases Excluded Addresses if the Scope Is Expanded

Q183886, Title: Access Violation in LSASS When Logging on System

Q184835, Title: Explorer on Windows 95 DFS Client May Hang

Q184836, Title: Application Access Violates When Session Is Terminated

Q184875, Title: API Function BroadcastSystemMessage() Always Returns 1 (Success)

Q184879, Title: Windows NT Logon Dialog May Disappear

Q184881, Title: Reverse Lookups with BIND Earlier Than 4.8.3 Fail

Q184937, Title: Session Between Multihomed Computers May End Unexpectedly

Q184996, Title: Incomplete List of NetWare Server Volumes with CSNW/GSNW

Q184998, Title: RDR May Read or Write from Wrong File If File Is Memory Mapped

Q185081, Title: No Domain Controllers Found When Logging on Using RAS

Q185137, Title: Log Logical Record Request May Be Sent to Wrong Server

Q185142, Title: NetWare API Log Logical Record May Incorrectly Succeed

Q185212, Title: Cluster Server Does Not Support More than 900 Shares

Q185260, Title: User Accounts May Get Locked out After Entering Wrong Password

Q185323, Title: Pool NonPaged Bytes Not Accurately Calculated for User Mode

Q185355, Title: Printers Folder Displays Printer Error When Printer Is Busy

Q185559, Title: Negative Value in NtGdiFastPolyPolyline Causes Blue Screen

Q185568, Title: WlxCloseUserDesktop Function Unavailable for GINA Writers

Q185571, Title: Printing from Lotus Freelance 97 Produces Thin Horizontal Line

Q185605, Title: Stop Error Caused by Invalid Use of Private Video Driver Handle

Q185625, Title: Windows NT Client Logon Fails with EnableSecuritySignature Set

Q185682, Title: Bugcheck When IPX Is Bound to Only Ndiswan Adapter

Q185723, Title: Explorer File Copy from Windows 95 Share Fails

Q185729, Title: Computer Becomes Unresponsive During CGI Stress Test

Q185734, Title: DNS Server Access Violation in Dns!sendNbstatResponse Routine

Q185735, Title: Explorer Crashes When Dragging Lotus Notes Files over Toolbar

Q185736, Title: Applications May Appear Hung or Unresponsive on Windows NT 4.0

Q185765, Title: HP LaserJet 4Si Driver Unprintable Region is Incorrect

Q185773, Title: NTFS Corruption on Drives > 4 GB Using ExtendOEMPartition

Q185787, Title: STOP 0x0000002E on Alpha with ISA Sound Card

Q185788, Title: Windows NT Hangs on Boot on DEC Alpha Clustered Servers

Q185791, Title: STOP on DEC Miata and Rawhide Platforms Using Graphics Tablet

Q185867, Title: STOP 0x0000000A in Win32k.sys After Installing Korean Office 97

Q185892, Title: Unwanted Popup Message While Printing to an LPR Printer

Q185944, Title: Stop 0x7B After Installing Windows NT on an ALR Evolution-V ST

Q185945, Title: Access violation in win32k!HMMarkObjectDestroy in JPN and KOR NT

Q186051, Title: Archive Bit Is Not Set with File or Directory Rename

Q186078, Title: Name Resolution May Fail If NetBios Name Has ASCII Character

Q186081, Title: STOP 0x0000000A When Restoring Tape

Q186101, Title: FTP Client Does Not Show the Correct Transfer Size for Files

Q186150, Title: NetBEUI May Hang When Using Arcnet Under Heavy Network Traffic

Q186158, Title: Blue Screen When Shutting Down with RAS Connection Established

Q186217, Title: 3C509 Is Not Autodetected During Setup on ThinkPad 760EL & XL

Q186241, Title: Dr. Watson May Cause CPU Usage to Spike

Q186247, Title: Users Are Unable to Print to Server

Q186339, Title: Adobe ATM 4.1 OpenType Fonts Not Showing up in Font Menu

Q186357, Title: RPC UseWinsockForIP is Only Applicable to UDP and IPX

Q186416, Title: System Hang Results from Large Number of Notify Syncs

Q186434, Title: Slow Network Default Profile Operation

Q186439, Title: Removing Server Service Results in Memory Leak

Q186455, Title: Mgmtapi.dll Opens Trap Socket in Exclusive Mode

Q186463, Title: Windows NT Replies to Address Mask Requests

Q186473, Title: You Can Delete All Records on a WINS Server Using SNMP

Q186494, Title: Event ID 517 Not Created When Security Log Is Cleared

Q186495, Title: WOW Leak Launching Many Instances of a 16-Bit Application

Q186669, Title: FPNW Logout.exe Incorrectly Reports Year After Jan. 1, 2000

Q186743, Title: International Characters Print Incorrectly in Schedule Plus

Q186746, Title: International Calling Codes Updated in Service Pack 4

Q186770, Title: Windows NT Hangs Trying to Access SuperDisk SLS-120 Disk Drive

Q186805, Title: Intermittent Stop 0xA in Srv.sys on Shutdown

Q186820, Title: DNS Server Returns Wrong Response When WINS Lookup Is Enabled

Q186860, Title: Update Memory Settings and Add Exec Paper Size to Sharp Models

Q186873, Title: Netbios Delays Sending/Receiving Packets When Session Is Lost

Q186963, Title: Incorrect Dimensions in Executive Form with Mannesmann Driver

Q187277, Title: The FTP PORT Command Fails in IIS 3.0

Q187302, Title: Stop 0x00000040 in NetBT Protocol

Q187493, Title: Some Netscape Client Certificates Rejected by IIS

Q187508, Title: FTP Server Fails to Respond If First Binding Does Not Work

Q187518, Title: Apps Using Beep API on Multiprocessor Systems May Crash

Q187519, Title: NTBackup Will Not Run from Command Line with Blank Space

Q187520, Title: Tandberg SL5 Tape Device Not Auto-Detected in Window NT 4.0

Q187555, Title: WINS Incorrect Version ID Assigned During Scavenging

Q187576, Title: Stop 0x0000000A May Occur in TCP/IP

Q187577, Title: STOP 0xA Because of Spin Lock in Sfmatalk.sys on DEC Alpha

Q187615, Title: Setup Hangs When System Includes More Than Two RAW Drives

Q187669, Title: Unable to Use NetBIOS Resources over SLIP

Q187672, Title: Access Violation in RAS Using Multilink

Q187686, Title: LookupAccountSid Causes Access Violation on Multihomed System

Q187696, Title: Changes to Calculator in Service Pack 4

Q187705, Title: Application Error in CorelWEB.GALLERY

Q187708, Title: Cannot Connect to SQL Virtual Server via Sockets in Cluster

Q187709, Title: Domain Name Resolver Caches Responses

Q187769, Title: Application Error in NTVDM Running cc:Mail Utilities

Q187802, Title: DHCP Assigns "Bad_Address" to "Host Unreachable"

Q187830, Title: Performance Decrease Transmitting Data over the Network

Q187856, Title: IIS: Limit SSL Message Size to 16 KB for Netscape

Q187884, Title: CoCreateInstance on Multiple Threads Causes Hangs or Failures

Q187936, Title: Application May Hang Calling LogonUser() API

Q187939, Title: IPX May Not Work When Packet Size Is Larger Than Receive Buffer

Q187941, Title: An Explanation of the New CHKDSK /C and /I Switches

Q187947, Title: 100 Percent CPU System Handle Problem

Q187964, Title: MGI PhotoSuite May Paste Screenshots as Garbage or an AV Occurs

Q188000, Title: Cannot Enter Stand-Alone Dieresis Character on Swiss Keyboards

Q188027, Title: Performance, Audit Logging, and Fixes to the DHCP Service

Q188303, Title: Random Stop 0x50 Errors on Cirrus Video Adapters

Q188312, Title: Lexmark Optra E+ Unprintable Region Is Incorrect

Q188414, Title: Random Stop 0x0000000A When Running IPX over Token Ring

Q188424, Title: Multilayered Display Driver Produces Black Line in Word

Q188571, Title: STOP 0x0000000A in Netbt.sys Caused by Invalid DNS Record

Q188652, Title: Error Replicating Registry Keys

Q188700, Title: Screensaver Password Works Even if Account Is Locked Out

Q188838, Title: Task Manager CPU Usage Only Displays Eight Processors

Q188879, Title: RPC Endpoint Mapper Will Not Register All Interfaces

Q188896, Title: Access Violation in Explorer.exe Changing Share Permissions

Q189010, Title: SBS: RAS Leases Six Addresses from DHCP

Q189011, Title: Using Performance Monitor Remotely Causes Access Violation

Q189012, Title: Clicking Default Scope Does Not Open Active Lease Window

Q189013, Title: Atapi.sys Does Not Support Multiple Logical Devices

Q189032, Title: Floating Point Arguments Won't Pass Between NT RPC and IBM RPC

Q189061, Title: Repeated Regsavekey/Regrestorekey Actions Corrupt Registry Hive

Q189080, Title: TCP Connection May Drop When Transferring Large Amounts of Data

Q189114, Title: NetDDE Refuses Incoming WM_DDE_INITIATEs from Windows 95

Q189119, Title: UserEnv Returns Corrupted Profile for All Failures

Q189171, Title: WinSock Applications May Fail or Stop Responding

Q189225, Title: LMMIB2 Unable to "Walk" from .1.3.6.1.4.1.77.1.4.4

Q189245, Title: Lmmib2.dll Does Not Support All Objects

Q189283, Title: No More Than About 570 Reservations Visible in a DHCP Scope

Q189290, Title: Loss of Desktop After Logon When Using a Filter Gina.dll

Q189291, Title: Hang in Winlogon on Workstation Locked Dialog Box

Q189395, Title: Support for Canadian ACNOR Keyboard

Q189471, Title: WpuOpenCurrentThread Does Not Work

Q189522, Title: Network Drive Letters in PATH Statement Causes Excessive Traffic

Q189579, Title: F11 and F12 Keys Do Not Function in MS-DOS Applications

Q189606, Title: Browser Service Fails to Start or Stop Button Is Unavailable

Q189612, Title: Access Violation Occurs in Windows NT Explorer (Explorer.exe)

Q189756, Title: PerfMon Percentage of Registry Quota in Use Displayed Wrong

Q189988, Title: CMPXCHG8B CPUs in Non-Intel/AMD x86 Compatibles Not Supported

Q190011, Title: Perl Script Mappings Converted to Uppercase During Upgrade

Q190288, Title: SecHole Lets Non-administrative Users Gain Debug Level Access

Q190354, Title: Unattended Setup of MSCS with -JOIN Parameter Requires Input

Q190449, Title: Corrupted SAM Hangs Windows NT Server

Q190506, Title: WINS Replication Problem Events 4262, 4261, and 1c Replication

Q190552, Title: WinNT 4.0 DHCP Client Modified to meet RFC 2131

Q190791, Title: STATUS_CANT_WAIT Returned from an NTCreateFile Call

Q190834, Title: SCSI Adapter Is No Longer Visible from SCSI Adapters Utility

Q190931, Title: Snmptrap.exe Ignores SNMP Trap PDU Greater Than 4,096 Bytes

Q190932, Title: SNMP Service Ignores SNMP Trap PDU Greater Than 4,096 Bytes

Q191088, Title: Printer Prompts for Paper with Dutch Workstations

Q191098, Title: Large File Copy Operation Causes Available Bytes to Drop

Q191284, Title: STOP 0x0000001E in Netbt.sys

Q191285, Title: Services for Macintosh Index Corruption on Large Volumes

Q191309, Title: ALT+Numeric Keypad Problem When CHCP Command is Used

Q191362, Title: FPNW Pass-Through Authentication from Trusted Domain May Fail

Q191387, Title: Unable to Run 16-bit Apps If FILES= Is Greater Than 255

Q191418, Title: Arcs Print Incorrectly with EMF on PCL Printers

Q191419, Title: GP Fault or Access Violation When Buffer Too Small

Q191428, Title: WINS Replication Fails If More Than 30 Partners Are Configured

Q191614, Title: Able to Commit More Memory Than Is Available

Q191634, Title: Group Policies Cause Excessive \PIPE\samr Connections on PDC

Q191689, Title: Incorrect Font Characteristics May Be Used on Imported Graphics

Q191751, Title: Smoothing Fonts Disabled Using ETO_GLYPHINDEX

Q191756, Title: Stop 0x1E Switching Between System Menus in Application Window

Q191767, Title: LogicalDisk Partition Missing in Performance Monitor

Q191768, Title: Date of Print Job May Be Displayed Incorrectly in Print Queue

Q191775, Title: WINS Service Fails to Start With More Than 99 PNG Entries

Q191830, Title: Memory Leak Due to Repeated Logon/Logoff May Corrupt Profiles

Q191832, Title: Access Violation in Hangul Version of Lotus Organizer 97

Q191834, Title: Network Problems That Occur When Logging Off May Corrupt Profile

Q191850, Title: Convert Reports Cannot Create Elementary File System Structures

Q191852, Title: Bhnetb.dll Leaks Memory in Winlogon.exe Process with NetMon

Q191896, Title: Printing to NT LPD Server from SUN OS 4.1.4 May Not Process C/R

Q191915, Title: Screen Saver Time-out is Limited to 60 Minutes

Q191992, Title: NdrConvert Causes Access Violation in RPC Client on WinNT 4.0

Q192051, Title: LDAP Does Not Authenticate on French WinNT Due to Encryption

Q192056, Title: Point and Print Functionality with More Than 20 Driver Files

Q192104, Title: Windows NT Does Not Start If Primary Partition Is Above 2 GB

Q192126, Title: Add Workstation Fails with RestrictAnonymous

Q192132, Title: STA Threads Lose Thread Token

Q192229, Title: Login Script Group Membership Mapping on BDC Fail If PDC Is Down

Q192265, Title: Srvinfo.exe Does Not Close Registry Handles with SMTP Service

Q192266, Title: Sockets-based Child Processes Are Not Stopped

Q192267, Title: Various STOP Errors When Opening Files on Novell NetWare Servers

Q192293, Title: IIS Stops ODBC Logging after Failing to Communicate with SQL

Q192409, Title: Open Files Can Cause Kernel to Report INSUFFICIENT_RESOURCES

Q192453, Title: MoveFile API from Windows 95 with Invalid UNC Causes STOP 0xa

Q192457, Title: Downloaded File May Be Saved in Incorrect Folder with IE

Q192460, Title: Matrox Video Driver Causes STOP 0x00000050

Q192547, Title: WINSADMIN Writes Invalid SP Time to Registry

Q192690, Title: Search: Unable to Connect to Catalog Server via Search MMC

Q192736, Title: STOP 0x0000000A Blue Screen on Alpha AXP

Q192749, Title: Multiple SSL Connections May Cause Error Starting Security Sys

Q192773, Title: Cluster Server Memory Leak When MTS Explorer Is Running

Q192774, Title: Stop 0x0000000A in Tcpip.sys Processing an ICMP Packet

Q192786, Title: Event ID 11 Changed to an Informational Message

Q193056, Title: Problems in Date/Time after Choosing February 29 in a Leap Year

Q193064, Title: Pressing Cancel Button in Date/Time Utility Changes Date

Q193090, Title: Inetmib1.dll Causes Memory Leak in Winlogon.exe Process

Q193106, Title: Filesystem Filter Drivers may Unload Unexpectedly

Q193121, Title: Cannot Connect to DFS Leaf a Second Time if Server is NetWare

Q193157, Title: TCP/IP Does Not Allow MAC Addresses to Change Dynamically

Q193169, Title: Script Mappings Are Not Removed from the Registry after Migration

Q193206, Title: Acquiring SNMP Info For OSPF in RRAS Hangs

Q193209, Title: Gethostbyname Not Working Correctly with Only DUN Installed

Q193233, Title: Rpcss.exe Consumes 100% CPU Due to RPC Spoofing Attack

Q193271, Title: Cannot Create Virtual Directory in Administrator Program

Q193371, Title: WINS/DHCP Admin Show Expiration Dates 2000 - 2009 with One Digit

Q193436, Title: DHCP Client Shuts Down After Two Declines

Q193499, Title: Multiple RRAS Client Disconnects Cause Increased CPU Usage

Q193529, Title: Modem Sharing Clients Cause Stop 0x000001E on SBS

Q193530, Title: Access Violation in WINSCL When Using CR or SDB Parameter

Q193596, Title: RASMAN Registry Values Cannot Be Set Higher Than 0xFF

Q193646, Title: Event ID 10005 from DCOM After Installing IIS

Q193654, Title: Services Continue to Run After Shutdown Initiated

Q193655, Title: Multiple Entries for AUTOCHK Abort in System Log

Q193779, Title: Cluster Server Drive Letters Do Not Update Using Disk Admin

Q193781, Title: Cache Manager May Cause Data Corruption

Q193806, Title: CSNW Error 85, Local Device Already in Use

Q193891, Title: HTTP Through Firewall and "Bypass Proxy for Local Intranet"

Q193899, Title: Event ID 1008, 4005 with Missing TCP/IP Performance Counters

Q193921, Title: Virtual Server Is No Longer Viewable Through MMC

Q194130, Title: SNMP Edit Box Drops a Character When Writing to the Registry

Q194133, Title: Remote Shell (RSH) Commands Hang w/ Multiple Sessions Running

Q194168, Title: Dns.exe Dr. Watson When Changing the TTL of a Cached Record

Q194193, Title: STOP 0xA in Sfmatalk.sys When Copying Files on an SFM Volume

Q194194, Title: DNS Fails with Error 1201 If Secondary Zone File Not Specified

Q194200, Title: Cannot Change WinNT Passwords from Exchange and Outlook Clients

Q194228, Title: Rule Containing Multiple Clauses Only Functions Properly Once

Q194322, Title: T/R NIC May Fail Windows Hardware Quality Lab (WHQL) Test

Q194336, Title: ERROR: Destroyed NTFS Directory

Q194340, Title: Access Violation when Using Rcp.exe to Copy to Unix

Q194341, Title: Simple TCP/IP Services Can Be Driven to 100% CPU

Q194424, Title: DHCP Server May Fail to Record Lease

Q194429, Title: TCPIP Timewaitstate may not remain in 2*msl

Q194431, Title: Applications May be able to "Listen" on TCP or UDP Ports.

Q194465, Title: PPTP May Refuse Connections When VPNs Are Free

Q194726, Title: FPNW Client Does Not Get Correct Time or Date After Y2K

Q194850, Title: IMS: SMTPSVC May Display BCC Addresses on Outgoing Messages

Q194919, Title: Windows NT Boot Process Hangs Because of DST Manipulation

Q195083, Title: Access Violation Installing News Service on DEC Alpha Computer

Q195084, Title: Cannot Send SSL Messages after Installing New Certificate

Index

Numbers and Symbols

A

B

C

D

E

F

J

K

L

N

O

P

Q

R

S

U

V

W

X

Y

Z

MICROSOFT LICENSE AGREEMENT

Book Companion CD

IMPORTANT—READ CAREFULLY: This Microsoft End-User License Agreement ("EULA") is a legal agreement between you (either an individual or an entity) and Microsoft Corporation for the Microsoft product identified above, which includes computer software and may include associated media, printed materials, and "online" or electronic documentation ("SOFTWARE PRODUCT"). Any component included within the SOFTWARE PRODUCT that is accompanied by a separate End-User License Agreement shall be governed by such agreement and not thc terms set forth below. By installing, copying, or otherwise using the SOFTWARE PRODUCT, you agree to be bound by the terms of this EULA. If you do not agree to the terms of this EULA, you are not authorized to install, copy, or otherwise use the SOFTWARE PRODUCT; you may, however, return the SOFTWARE PRODUCT, along with all printed materials and other items that form a part of the Microsoft product that includes the SOFTWARE PRODUCT, to the place you obtained them for a full refund.

SOFTWARE PRODUCT LICENSE

The SOFTWARE PRODUCT is protected by United States copyright laws and international copyright treaties, as well as other intellectual property laws and treaties. The SOFTWARE PRODUCT is licensed, not sold.

1. **GRANT OF LICENSE.** This EULA grants you the following rights:

   a. **Software Product.** You may install and use one copy of the SOFTWARE PRODUCT on a single computer. The primary user of the computer on which the SOFTWARE PRODUCT is installed may make a second copy for his or her exclusive use on a portable computer.

   b. **Storage/Network Use.** You may also store or install a copy of the SOFTWARE PRODUCT on a storage device, such as a network server, used only to install or run the SOFTWARE PRODUCT on your other computers over an internal network; however, you must acquire and dedicate a license for each separate computer on which the SOFTWARE PRODUCT is installed or run from the storage device. A license for the SOFTWARE PRODUCT may not be shared or used concurrently on different computers.

   c. **License Pak.** If you have acquired this EULA in a Microsoft License Pak, you may make the number of additional copies of the computer software portion of the SOFTWARE PRODUCT authorized on the printed copy of this EULA, and you may use each copy in the manner specified above. You are also entitled to make a corresponding number of secondary copies for portable computer use as specified above.

   d. **Sample Code.** Solely with respect to portions, if any, of the SOFTWARE PRODUCT that are identified within the SOFTWARE PRODUCT as sample code (the "SAMPLE CODE"):

      i. **Use and Modification.** Microsoft grants you the right to use and modify the source code version of the SAMPLE CODE, *provided* you comply with subsection (d)(iii) below. You may not distribute the SAMPLE CODE, or any modified version of the SAMPLE CODE, in source code form.

      ii. **Redistributable Files.** Provided you comply with subsection (d)(iii) below, Microsoft grants you a nonexclusive, royalty-free right to reproduce and distribute the object code version of the SAMPLE CODE and of any modified SAMPLE CODE, other than SAMPLE CODE, or any modified version thereof, designated as not redistributable in the Readme file that forms a part of the SOFTWARE PRODUCT (the "Non-Redistributable Sample Code"). All SAMPLE CODE other than the Non-Redistributable Sample Code is collectively referred to as the "REDISTRIBUTABLES."

      iii. **Redistribution Requirements.** If you redistribute the REDISTRIBUTABLES, you agree to: (i) distribute the REDISTRIBUTABLES in object code form only in conjunction with and as a part of your software application product; (ii) not use Microsoft's name, logo, or trademarks to market your software application product; (iii) include a valid copyright notice on your software application product; (iv) indemnify, hold harmless, and defend Microsoft from and against any claims or lawsuits, including attorney's fees, that arise or result from the use or distribution of your software application product; and (v) not permit further distribution of the REDISTRIBUTABLES by your end user. Contact Microsoft for the applicable royalties due and other licensing terms for all other uses and/or distribution of the REDISTRIBUTABLES.

2. **DESCRIPTION OF OTHER RIGHTS AND LIMITATIONS.**

   - **Limitations on Reverse Engineering, Decompilation, and Disassembly.** You may not reverse engineer, decompile, or disassemble the SOFTWARE PRODUCT, except and only to the extent that such activity is expressly permitted by applicable law notwithstanding this limitation.
   - **Separation of Components.** The SOFTWARE PRODUCT is licensed as a single product. Its component parts may not be separated for use on more than one computer.
   - **Rental.** You may not rent, lease, or lend the SOFTWARE PRODUCT.
   - **Support Services.** Microsoft may, but is not obligated to, provide you with support services related to the SOFTWARE PRODUCT ("Support Services"). Use of Support Services is governed by the Microsoft policies and programs described in the

user manual, in "online" documentation, and/or other Microsoft-provided materials. Any supplemental software code provided to you as part of the Support Services shall be considered part of the SOFTWARE PRODUCT and subject to the terms and conditions of this EULA. With respect to technical information you provide to Microsoft as part of the Support Services, Microsoft may use such information for its business purposes, including for product support and development. Microsoft will not utilize such technical information in a form that personally identifies you.

- **Software Transfer.** You may permanently transfer all of your rights under this EULA, provided you retain no copies, you transfer all of the SOFTWARE PRODUCT (including all component parts, the media and printed materials, any upgrades, this EULA, and, if applicable, the Certificate of Authenticity), **and** the recipient agrees to the terms of this EULA.
- **Termination.** Without prejudice to any other rights, Microsoft may terminate this EULA if you fail to comply with the terms and conditions of this EULA. In such event, you must destroy all copies of the SOFTWARE PRODUCT and all of its component parts.

3. **COPYRIGHT.** All title and copyrights in and to the SOFTWARE PRODUCT (including but not limited to any images, photographs, animations, video, audio, music, text, SAMPLE CODE, REDISTRIBUTABLES, and "applets" incorporated into the SOFTWARE PRODUCT), and any copies of the SOFTWARE PRODUCT are owned by Microsoft or its suppliers. The SOFTWARE PRODUCT is protected by copyright laws and international treaty provisions. Therefore, you must treat the SOFTWARE PRODUCT like any other copyrighted material **except** that you may install the SOFTWARE PRODUCT on a single computer provided you keep the original solely for backup or archival purposes. You may not copy the printed materials accompanying the SOFTWARE PRODUCT.

4. **U.S. GOVERNMENT RESTRICTED RIGHTS.** The SOFTWARE PRODUCT and documentation are provided with RESTRICTED RIGHTS. Use, duplication, or disclosure by the Government is subject to restrictions as set forth in subparagraph (c)(1)(ii) of the Rights in Technical Data and Computer Software clause at DFARS 252.227-7013 or subparagraphs (c)(1) and (2) of the Commercial Computer Software—Restricted Rights at 48 CFR 52.227-19, as applicable. Manufacturer is Microsoft Corporation/One Microsoft Way/Redmond, WA 98052-6399.

5. **EXPORT RESTRICTIONS.** You agree that you will not export or re-export the SOFTWARE PRODUCT, any part thereof, or any process or service that is the direct product of the SOFTWARE PRODUCT (the foregoing collectively referred to as the "Restricted Components"), to any country, person, entity, or end user subject to U.S. export restrictions. You specifically agree not to export or re-export any of the Restricted Components (i) to any country to which the U.S. has embargoed or restricted the export of goods or services, which currently include, but are not necessarily limited to Cuba, Iran, Iraq, Libya, North Korea, Sudan, and Syria, or to any national of any such country, wherever located, who intends to transmit or transport the Restricted Components back to such country; (ii) to any end-user who you know or have reason to know will utilize the Restricted Components in the design, development, or production of nuclear, chemical, or biological weapons; or (iii) to any end-user who has been prohibited from participating in U.S. export transactions by any federal agency of the U.S. government. You warrant and represent that neither the BXA nor any other U.S. federal agency has suspended, revoked, or denied your export privileges.

DISCLAIMER OF WARRANTY

NO WARRANTIES OR CONDITIONS. MICROSOFT EXPRESSLY DISCLAIMS ANY WARRANTY OR CONDITION FOR THE SOFTWARE PRODUCT. THE SOFTWARE PRODUCT AND ANY RELATED DOCUMENTATION IS PROVIDED "AS IS" WITHOUT WARRANTY OR CONDITION OF ANY KIND, EITHER EXPRESS OR IMPLIED, INCLUDING, WITHOUT LIMITATION, THE IMPLIED WARRANTIES OF MERCHANTABILITY, FITNESS FOR A PARTICULAR PURPOSE, OR NONINFRINGEMENT. THE ENTIRE RISK ARISING OUT OF USE OR PERFORMANCE OF THE SOFTWARE PRODUCT REMAINS WITH YOU.

LIMITATION OF LIABILITY. TO THE MAXIMUM EXTENT PERMITTED BY APPLICABLE LAW, IN NO EVENT SHALL MICROSOFT OR ITS SUPPLIERS BE LIABLE FOR ANY SPECIAL, INCIDENTAL, INDIRECT, OR CONSEQUENTIAL DAMAGES WHATSOEVER (INCLUDING, WITHOUT LIMITATION, DAMAGES FOR LOSS OF BUSINESS PROFITS, BUSINESS INTERRUPTION, LOSS OF BUSINESS INFORMATION, OR ANY OTHER PECUNIARY LOSS) ARISING OUT OF THE USE OF OR INABILITY TO USE THE SOFTWARE PRODUCT OR THE PROVISION OF OR FAILURE TO PROVIDE SUPPORT SERVICES, EVEN IF MICROSOFT HAS BEEN ADVISED OF THE POSSIBILITY OF SUCH DAMAGES. IN ANY CASE, MICROSOFT'S ENTIRE LIABILITY UNDER ANY PROVISION OF THIS EULA SHALL BE LIMITED TO THE GREATER OF THE AMOUNT ACTUALLY PAID BY YOU FOR THE SOFTWARE PRODUCT OR US$5.00; PROVIDED HOWEVER, IF YOU HAVE ENTERED INTO A MICROSOFT SUPPORT SERVICES AGREEMENT, MICROSOFT'S ENTIRE LIABILITY REGARDING SUPPORT SERVICES SHALL BE GOVERNED BY THE TERMS OF THAT AGREEMENT. BECAUSE SOME STATES AND JURISDICTIONS DO NOT ALLOW THE EXCLUSION OR LIMITATION OF LIABILITY, THE ABOVE LIMITATION MAY NOT APPLY TO YOU.

MISCELLANEOUS

This EULA is governed by the laws of the State of Washington USA, except and only to the extent that applicable law mandates governing law of a different jurisdiction.

Should you have any questions concerning this EULA, or if you desire to contact Microsoft for any reason, please contact the Microsoft subsidiary serving your country, or write: Microsoft Sales Information Center/One Microsoft Way/Redmond, WA 98052-6399.

start
faster
go
farther

start
faster
go
farther